ISLINGTON

KU-288-622

Please return this item on or before the last date stamped below or you may be liable to overdue charges. To renew an item call the number below, or access the online catalogue at www.islington.gov.uk/libraries. You will need your library membership number and PIN number.

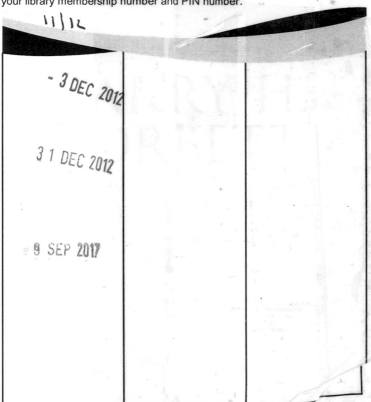

11/12

- 3 DEC 2012

3 1 DEC 2012

9 SEP 2017

Islington Libraries

020 7527 6900   www.islington.gov.uk/libraries

HARRY H. CORBETT

The Front Legs of the Cow

SUSANNAH CORBETT

For Maureen

First published 2012

The History Press
The Mill, Brimscombe Port
Stroud, Gloucestershire, GL5 2QG
www.thehistorypress.co.uk

British Library Cataloguing in Publication Data.
A catalogue record for this book is available from the British Library.

ISBN 978 0 7524 8787 8

Typesetting and origination by The History Press
Printed in Great Britain
Manufacturing managed by Jellyfish Print Solutions Ltd

Contents

Acknowledgements

I would like to thank all those whose contributions have made this possible …

Firstly, my interviewees, who so generously and willingly gave up their time – Nicolas Amer, Douglas Argent, Desmond Barrit, Lynda Baron, the staff of Benchill Primary School, Neil Benson OBE FCA, Major M. Bentinck (RM Ret.) the Royal Marines historian, Richard Briers CBE, Diane Cilento, Barry Clayton, George A. Cooper, Kenneth Cranham, Michael Crawford OBE, Tina Cross ONZM, Carmel Cryan, Barry Cryer OBE, Clive Dunn OBE, Shirley Dynevor, Glynn Edwards, Barry and Paul Elliot, Fenella Fielding, Sir Bruce Forsyth CBE, Terry Gilliam, PO Robin Guyatt (RN Ret.) Royal Navy Memories, Sheila Hancock CBE, Jim Hamman, Karen Harris, Ewan Hooper, Professor John Hill, Miriam Karlin OBE, Marjie Lawrence, Rosemary Leach, Joanna Lumley OBE FRGS, Ian McGarry, the staff of Manchester Central Library, The Rt Hon Lord Morris of Manchester AO QSO, Brian Murphy, Jean Newlove, Diana O'Connor, Michael Palin CBE FRGS, Freddie Ross Hancock MBE, Carolyn Seymour, Joseph Siddall, Peter Sloan, Victor Spinetti, Frank Thornton, June Whitfield CBE, Barbara Windsor MBE, Aubrey Woods, Henry Woolf, and Barbara Young. Going above and beyond the call were Mrs Stella Goorney, for giving me Howard Goorney's interview tapes; Harry Greene for more than he knows; Murray Melvin for always saying yes and, of course, the incomparable Ray Galton and Alan Simpson.

I would also like to thank my agent, Eve White, my editor, Mark Beynon, and the team at The History Press for their unfailing enthusiasm.

Special mention is due, as well, to my friends and family who were happily press-ganged into being sounding boards – Malcolm, Jennie and Simon Blott, Jonathan Corbett, Elizabeth Hall, Cynthia Whittaker and lastly Enyd Williams, for her tea, her sympathy and her precision.

Above all I am grateful to my husband Dan Hallam and my children, Lily and Elena, for their belief, their patience and their love.

Author's Note
Every effort has been made to secure permission from the copyright holders of all photographs in this book. I apologise for any omissions.

Foreword

We first met Harry on the morning of the read-through of the first ever *Steptoe and Son* in 1962. But of course we knew of him. Everybody in show business knew of him. He was an actor's actor. Whenever he was on television every actor in the country who was not working (which in a good year was about 80 per cent of them and still is, although these days with different actors) would find a TV set and closely study his technique. Methodish, Brandoish, Theatre Royal Stratfordish, Joan Littlewoodish, but above all very Harry H. Corbettish. Halfway through writing the first *Steptoe* script we knew exactly who we wanted for the son. We'd never met him but found out that he was playing two weeks of Shakespeare at Bristol Old Vic. Alan always said it was *Richard III*, Ray always said it was *Henry IV, Part 1* and when we read this book we found out it was *Macbeth*. Anyway it was some old king.

He loved the script and persuaded the Old Vic mob to give him a week off and thus began fourteen of the most enjoyable years of our career. The wisdom of our choice was confirmed on the first day in the studio. After five days of rehearsal we were enthusing at the wonderful seediness of the set but Harry said, 'Never mind the set, what are those seats doing there?'

They're for the audience,' we said. 'Audience?' he said. 'Nobody told me there was going to be an audience.' And then the clincher, 'I shall have to re-think my entire performance.'

We looked at each other. Fantastic. A proper actor at last. This was underlined in the last scene. Trying to leave home he has piled his belongings on the horse and cart but his father won't let him have the horse. So he decides to pull the cart himself. It won't budge.

He gradually breaks down until he is in tears. Normally the type of actor we were used to would have just shaken their shoulders with their backs to the audience. Not our method man. We looked at each other in amazement. They were real tears. Blimey we've got a right one here!

Present at the show was Tom Sloan the head of BBC light entertainment. 'You know what you've got here?' he said. 'A series.'

'No way,' we said. 'It's a one off.'

We knew he was probably right but after nine years of *Hancock's Half Hour* we weren't ready for another series. For the next six months he kept on at us and eventually we agreed, if the two of them wanted to do it. We were convinced that two classical actors wouldn't want to sully themselves with a commonplace sitcom. It would be like Laurence Olivier and John Gielgud in *Are You Being Served?* Mind you that's not a bad idea. Why didn't they think of that? And how wrong could we be. Harry and Wilfrid both jumped at the idea. We'd forgotten that time-honoured panacea that never fails to work on actors: money. Light entertainment fees were about five times more than the drama rates Harry and Wilfrid were used to. Of course they'd do it. There was no madness in their method. Incidentally we have it on good authority that had our two turned it down Olivier and Gielgud had been seen in the Goldhawk Road taking horse and cart driving lessons just in case.

And now years later comes this wonderful book by Harry's daughter, Susannah. Despite our many years of friendship with Harry much of this book was a revelation to us. Testimony to his inherent modesty and lack of self-aggrandisement. He was always happiest talking about the profession rather than himself. We don't know if Shakespeare missed Harry but we certainly do.

Ray Galton and Alan Simpson

Prologue

Any Chance?

'He should have been dead when you woke up,' so said the doctor with a well-practised knack of combining optimism with arse covering. 'If he can survive 48 hours he's got a good chance.'

Harry H. Corbett had suffered his second heart attack, so massive that doctors were astounded that his wife Maureen had not woken in their rural farmhouse to find him cold at her side. But Harry was made of strong stuff. He had managed to rouse her in the dead of the night. She in turn woke their children, Jonathan and me. Leaving me with instructions to warn the hospital that they were coming, Maureen helped Harry to the car and they disappeared into the night. She drove like Fangio though the dark, quiet, twisting lanes of East Sussex to get him there in time.

Well, this could be it; this could be the big one. He masked his fear by joking with the staff. He had them in stitches – he'd had a lifetime of practice. During a quiet moment, he had the foresight to apologise to Maureen in case he croaked. Raising their two young teenagers alone would be tough.

The minutes stretched into hours, creeping towards the magic forty-eight. Alerted family paced the corridors, teasing life back into legs numbed by hard chairs. The unnerving fluorescent lights creating a twilight zone where drawn faces betrayed inner thoughts. If he didn't make it, would they say the right thing? Would they be any use? They hoped they wouldn't have to find out.

Trapped in this half-life limbo world, Harry surveyed the view from the bed. The scuttling nurses, the steady drip, drip, drip in the tubes and the web of wires leading to the machines that reassuringly continued to go 'bing'. He turned his large, soulful blue eyes to Maureen and with a wistful smile softly curling around his mouth he asked, 'I suppose a shag's out of the question?' As ever his timing was superb.

Harry fought for forty-five hours. He died 21 March 1982. He was 57 years old.

On the Road to Mandalay

He is a dear little fellow, and so very clever and bright.

Beatrice Collins

Harry Corbett was the youngest of seven children, six boys and one girl. He was a late, and probably unexpected, addition to the family. His father George was in the regular army with the South Staffordshire Regiment, having joined up in 1904 at the age of 18. George married Caroline Barnsley at St Gabriel's church, Birmingham, on 31 October 1905. Their witnesses were George's sister, Annie, and her husband Albert Williams. Annie would later play a significant part in Harry's life. George and Caroline's first child, Albert Isaiah, was born in January 1907. He was followed fourteen months later by twins Carrie and Willie, but Willie died in infancy.

George and Caroline lived in Birmingham with Caroline's mother Emily, who looked after the children while Caroline worked in a screw-making factory. In May 1911 George was promoted to sergeant and two weeks later James was born.

Another son, William, came along in 1914 (Caroline's grandfather and George's eldest brother were both called William, which might explain why they just couldn't let the name go). Later that year Sgt George joined the British Expeditionary Force in France. He was with the 1st Battalion attached to the 22nd Brigade, 7th Division. He fought at the Battle of Loos, where the British first used poisoned gas, at Ypres and the Somme. He was sent home after being wounded in the ankle in 1916, and early in 1917 forfeited pay for being absent for thirteen days – exactly forty weeks before another son, Francis George, was born. However, by the time of the birth, Sgt George was at Passchendaele and, although he was wounded again (this time by shrapnel in the shoulder), he remained on duty. Two weeks after this Caroline registered the new baby back in Birmingham – but as Beaumont George, not Francis George. There was a fashion for naming children after battlegrounds you'd survived. He was most likely named for Beaumont-Hamel, a place made famous for being the scene of the Hawthorn Ridge mine explosion, captured on film on the first day of the Somme.

At 2.30 a.m. on 25 April 1918, during the Battle of Lys, the German army began their attack on the highly strategic hill, Mont Kemmel. They started shelling the Allied lines with explosives and gas, concentrating on the gun emplacements. At 5 a.m. they bombarded the French troops on the hill. Those French soldiers who had survived the 'wringer of Verdun' later described the shelling as the worst they had gone through. At 6 a.m. the Germans sent in the infantry and by mid-morning the hill was theirs. Today the remains of more than 5,000 soldiers who fell during Lys lie in the French Ossuary on the hill. On the night of the 25th a heavy rain fell. At 3 a.m. the next day the Allied counter-attack was launched, hampered by the flooding of the Kemmelbeek River. Sgt George was with the 25th Division as they fought to take the railway line. Under fierce fire, they couldn't hold it. The division fell back to the Kemmel Road and suffered heavy losses in the withdrawal. Sgt George was caught in the open by machine gunners; he saw them strafing down the line of men towards him. Just as the bullets reached him he jumped for his life and was wounded for a third time. But unlike those around him who were hit in the guts, he was shot in the thigh. He was one of 7,700 casualties during that battle; 270 were known to be dead, 3,400 were missing. He was sent home and two months later was posted to the Command Depot. From there he was sent to 3rd Battalion and was with them at Newcastle when the Armistice was signed. He was a lucky man.

A year later, Sgt George was posted to Singapore with the 1st Battalion. Life here was literally and figuratively as far away from the horrors of the Western Front as you could get. One of the highlights of the tour was the battalion winning the Singapore Amateur Football Association Challenge Cup in 1920.

In February 1922 Sgt George was posted to Burma and by September 1923 was in Maymyo, the upcountry summer home of the British in Burma, civilian as well as military. It was a one-time hill fort where they could escape the oppressive heat and humidity of Rangoon. *Maymyo* in Burmese meant May's Place, imaginatively named after the first commander of the post, Colonel May. It was originally, and is now again, called Pyin U Lwin. It was from here that Sgt George waited for the family to join him, according to some humourous fictitious letters he had published in the journal of the regiment, *The Staffordshire Knot*:

From: Chief of the General Staff,
Married Quarters,
Maymyo.

To: Sergt. Corbett,
O.B.E., O.B.Z., O Buz Off.
Maymyo,
September 29th 1923.

Sir,

I am directed to inform you that, in view of the fact that your old woman, with a certain number of followers, is expected to arrive at an early date, arrangements have been made for you to take over No. 24-6 Married Quarter.

I much regret that the electric lighting of the Quarter has not been completed as yet, but no doubt this will be done in the space of a few years.

The hot water apparatus is also suffering from frost-bite, but I take it neither you nor your family require a *bath* before next Pan-cake Day, by which time you may get caught in a shower, thereby doing away with the need for a bath.

The cookhouse is a torra musty, but as I believe you will have nothing to cook, there is no need to worry on that point.

In case you overlook it on your inspection, the piano is in the cellar, this will no doubt require a pull-through through it before being used; also a bit of whitewash on it to smarten it up; these can be obtained from this department on the usual indent forms.

Any further information on the subject of maternity benefits, charcoal issues, how to lose fowl, or a polite way to borrow things from your neighbours will be gladly supplied by this office.

I have the honour to be,
Sir,
Your obedient Servant,

From: Sergt. Corbett, X Y Z, MUG., ETC.

To: Whom This May Concern.
Maymyo,
October 9th 1923.

Sir,

Reference my application for Quarters.

The arrangements made by you regarding the arrival of my detachment are quite good, but I should like to draw your attention to the following points: –

You make no mention of a Tennis Court which is absolutely necessary, seeing that my old woman is always trying to catch someone on the bounce.

I quite expected to have a Skittle Alley for the use of the followers (when off duty). I should feel extremely grateful if you would make the necessary arrangements.

I should be thankful also if you would extend the electric light on to the lawn, as my wife is fond of watching the grass-hoppers make grass, also it would make things better if you could arrange for a small pool in the garden, for summer bathing.

The piano I found hanging on a nail in the cookhouse, I would esteem it a great favour if you could arrange for it to be taken to the coalyard for repairs.

You have overlooked the fact that my old dutch will require transport on arrival; the following will be quite sufficient: – A.T. carts, 30; Tongas, 10; motor-cars (not Fords), 5.

In case the monsoons are still in season I should be thankful if you would add a further 30 sampams.

If the above cannot be carried out within the next 24 hours please let me know so that I can make a complaint to the Vice Roy on his arrival at Rangoon.

It's easy to imagine that the men and women glimpsed in grainy footage of nearly a century ago are somehow different from their counterparts today, but if Sgt George were serving now he'd be posting mockumentaries on the internet. Caroline must have joined him by June of 1924, as this is when she fell pregnant for the last time. A convenient pay rise came along in the shape of George being promoted to staff sergeant in October.

Harry was born on Saturday 28 February 1925. Rangoon in those days, if you were British, must have been amazing – even for those born into the working class. It was a relatively minor corner of the Empire, under administration from India. In 1908 a traveller had written:

> As we drew near to Rangoon, the first object that lifted itself above the level land about us was the golden spire of Schwe' Dagon Pagoda, and the next distinctive feature were the elephants piling teak logs along the shore. The population is even more cosmopolitan than in Singapore and Klings, Tamils, Bengalis, Punjabis, Sikhs, Ghurkhas, Jews, Chinese, Arabs, Armenians, Malays, Shans, Karens, Persians and Singhalese jostle one another in the noisy streets, where barbers and cooks ply their trades on the curb, and every third shopkeeper is reading aloud out of the Koran. The strange fact is that one man in a hundred is a Burmese – south India has seized the town.

India may have seized the town but the British were ruling it. By the 1920s Rangoon had trams, theatres, sumptuous hotels, parks and every convenience. All this and an oppressed native people to make even the saltiest salt of the earth feel superior. At this time elite Burmese who had been educated in London were returning to effect reform. After all, there had to be some payback for the support given to Britain during the First World War. They achieved more autonomy from India and furthered the Burmese representation in the civil service. But this wasn't far enough or fast enough for most, so in 1920 the university students held a strike in protest. They were worried that a new University Act would ultimately perpetuate colonial elitism and rule. These were the first stirrings of nationalist feeling. They were followed by more strikes and tax protests through the 1920s and '30s. In the early 1930s a Buddhist monk, Saya San, led a rebellion against British rule. The rebellion was easily crushed and thousands of Burmese were killed. But back in the 1920s the well-heeled British still managed to enjoy themselves in their privileged whites-only world.

The Strand Hotel was part of this world. A sister hotel to Raffles in Singapore, its guests at the time included Somerset Maugham, who wrote in *A Gentleman in the Parlour* that Rangoon afforded him:

a cordial welcome; a drive in an American car through busy streets of business houses, concrete and iron like the streets, good heavens! of Honolulu, Shanghai, Singapore or Alexandria, and then a spacious shady house in a garden; an agreeable life, luncheon at this club or that, drives along trim, wide roads, bridge after dark at that club or this, gin pahits, a great many men in white drill or pongee silk, laughter, pleasant conversation; and then back through the night to dress for dinner and out again to dine with this hospitable host or the other, cocktails, a substantial meal, dancing to a gramophone or a game of billiards, and then back once more to the large, cool silent house. It was very attractive, easy, comfortable, and gay; but was this Rangoon? Down by the harbour and along the river were narrow streets, a rabbit warren of intersecting alleys; and here, multitudinous, lived the Chinese, and there the Burmans: I looked with curious eyes as I passed in my motor car and wondered what strange things I should discover and what secrets they had to tell me if I could plunge into that enigmatic life and lose myself in it as a cup of water thrown overboard is lost in the Irrawaddy.

I think it's fairly safe to presume that he never got out of the car. Another guest was Noel Coward, who drew inspiration for his later song *Mad Dogs and Englishmen*: 'The toughest Burmese bandit can never understand it. In Rangoon the heat of noon is just what the native shun, they put their Scotch and rye down and lie down, but mad dogs and Englishmen go out in the midday sun.'

Despite having been promoted to colour sergeant (Company Quartermaster Sergeant), the second most senior NCO in the company, I doubt George and Caroline would have been taking tiffin with Noel Coward or Somerset Maugham. But they would also not have been encouraged to fraternise with the natives. They lived in a cantonment, a permanent military base that covered a large swathe of the city, containing homes, shops, schools, hospitals, administration buildings and law courts. The stiff upper lip would find no excuse to wilt in the heat. The family, along with the rest of the white ruling classes, no doubt had access to the British Club and would have had Indian servants. From back-to-back houses in the industrial heartland of England to the twilight of the Empire must have been a surreal step. As a baby Harry would have seen more of local life than his parents when he was being taken out by his ayah, an Indian nanny.

George Orwell was a policeman in Burma in the 1920s; he described the Burmese market scene in *Burmese Days*:

> Vast pomelos hanging on strings like green moons, red bananas, baskets of heliotrope-colored prawns the size of lobsters, brittle dried fish tied in bundles, crimson chillies, ducks split open and cured like hams, green coconuts, the larvae of the rhinoceros beetle, sections of sugarcane, dahs, lacquered sandals, check silk longyis, aphrodisiacs in the form of large, soap-like pills.

Orwell also pointed out that: 'If a European woman went through the bazaars alone somebody would probably spit betel juice over her dress.' Millions in South-East Asia enjoy Betel chewing: the nut of the Areca palm, along with lime as a catalyst, is wrapped in a leaf of the Betel vine, and when this is sucked between cheek and gum the chemical reaction produces an invigorating pick-me-up that also stimulates the saliva glands. The overflowing juice causes heartburn so one must spit, not swallow. In Asia the streets are as covered in this spittle as Western pavements are covered in gum. The spittle, teeth, mouth, and any passing European dress, are stained a dark brick red.

I expect life for Caroline centred on the house and garden, with its neatly clipped suburban hedges in the cantonment, and the children who were with her. The two eldest children were back in Manchester under the eye of Sgt George's sister, Annie. Albert was by now 18 and Carrie 17; both would have long finished their schooling and be in the workplace. As was James, who in 1925 had travelled from Rangoon to Bombay to enlist in the South Staffordshire Regiment as a bandsman – he was 14 years old. But William at 11, George at 8 and Harry at only a year were too young to be separated from their mother. For the boys it would have been a paradise. George remembered their dad catching snakes in the house; you can imagine the fascinated revulsion shared by small boys worldwide as a snake's head was cut off.

It's hard to say how much the unrest in the country attached itself to them. It certainly attached itself to Orwell who wrote in his essay *Shooting an Elephant*:

> I had already made up my mind that imperialism was an evil thing and the sooner I chucked up my job and got out of it

the better. Theoretically—and secretly of course—I was all for the Burmese and all against their oppressors, the British. As for the job I was doing, I hated it more bitterly than I can perhaps make clear. In a job like that you see the dirty work of Empire at close quarters. The wretched prisoners huddling in the stinking cages of the lock-ups, the gray, cowed faces of the long-term convicts, the scarred buttocks of the men who had been flogged with bamboos—all these oppressed me with an intolerable sense of guilt.

Did the Corbett family have time for such musings? They were not as close as Orwell to the dirty underbelly of the setting Empire. They were probably too busy, in the way of most young families, getting through the days of work, play and school. But for Orwell and Harry one of the most dangerous aspects of life in the tropics was to send them both home, Orwell with the contracting of dengue fever, and Harry with the death of his mother.

Caroline died of dysentery on 4 August 1926. I doubt Harry knew much about it. He was, after all, barely 18 months old and Caroline would have been in hospital for weeks. It was not a pleasant way to go and at that time there was nothing to be done but wait and see if you survived it – antibiotics were not discovered until 1929. Dysentery is highly contagious. The rest of the family, especially Harry, were incredibly lucky not to catch it.

Apart from a photograph or two and a small mourning locket containing his mother's hair, the only thing Harry had from his time in Burma was a letter written to his Aunt Annie in Manchester following Caroline's death. It looks as if it has been read a thousand times.

39 B Budd Road

Cantonment

Rangoon

9 – 8 – 26

Dear Mrs Williams,

You will probably be surprised to hear from me, I am Mrs Collins and I live next door to your Brother. I feel I would like to tell you how <u>very</u> <u>deeply</u> I sympathise with you all in your very sad bereavement, but it is all God's divine will, and though it is a fearful blow, time will heal the wound, and I must tell you that I was numb with sorrow when Mr. Corbett brought us the news. Please tell Albert and Carrie not to grieve too much but they must bear up for their mother was a good woman, and her soul is happily released from its prison house. I say this, because to me she does not seem dead, for her soul still lives on, and I feel sure she is happy.

I am very glad you are taking little Harry Boy, he is a dear little fellow, and so very clever and bright, when his mother first went to hospital I took him, because he was so fretful, and now he is quite himself again and just worships his Daddy.

Mr. Corbett has been very brave and though of course he was <u>fearfully staggered</u> by the terrible loss; he has bucked up no end. Your cablegram arrived this morning and believe me Mrs. Williams you have cheered him no end by your goodness in saying you will have the children. Billy was completely done after the funeral, but Georgie has not seemed to realise, he just cried because he saw Billy cry. Sir Benjamin Heald, our C.O. has offered to do what he can for the children and we have all great hopes that Billy and Georgie will be able to go to the Duke of York's School, which will be the very finest thing possible for them, their future will be then assured, and you will find it very much easier if you have only little Harry Boy.

You know Mrs Williams, I have heard so very much about you, and Albert, & Carrie, that I feel I know you. Mrs. Corbett used to tell me so often how good you have always been to her and her children, and she was glad you had the two older ones.

You will like to know that she had a very peaceful end but she was unconscious for some time before she went, and she looked very nice, and <u>so</u> at rest.

Her funeral was a very nice one for she was carried to her last resting place by six fine soldiers and there were so many floral tributes, Mr. Delahay our Chaplain made an impressive service, and the hymn sung, was 'Jesu Lover of my Soul.'

I cannot tell you any more, and words cannot express my sympathy in your loss, but I know you will do all you can for those she loved so much. You and they were always in her thoughts, and when I used to visit her in the Hospital she always mentioned you. Mr. Corbett did all he possibly could for her, and she used to look forward to his visits each day, he was with her for over two hours at the end.

I'll close now with all my good wishes, and I'm sure Carrie will find a vast amount of comfort in her wee Brother for he is a pretty, and most lovable little Blossom; you cannot help but love him.

Mr. Corbett does not know just yet when he will be leaving for home, but you can be sure, it will be very soon.

My husband and myself and family are leaving Rangoon next month, had we been going straight on to England, I would have tried to take the baby with me, but we have to rejoin our regiment first, and are not sure when we will sail for home.

With all good wishes,
Yrs Sincerely

Beatrice Collins

(P.S) Mr. Corbett has asked me to send you the enclosed snap of Harry Boy taken with my small son; it is a very good one [see plate 1].

So they were set for England. Harry would leave the only home he had known and his mother's grave far behind. He always wanted to go back and find it but he never made it, and so far neither have I. I presume that she was buried in the Cantonment Cemetery. After the Second World War graves were moved to the mass war cemetery at Taukkyan, and many cemeteries have been moved or bulldozed as modern Yangon expands. I should think the chances of finding her are very slim.

So how much could Harry later remember of his birthplace, being so very young when he left? Nothing about his mother, nothing that he could ever latch onto. Just a ditty his ayah used to tell him: 'Pretty Polly, Polly dear, all the way from Kashmir. Did you walk it? No bloody fear!' This was later handed down to his children, along with his choice of lullaby, which I can still hear him singing – *On the Road to Mandalay*:

Come you back to Mandalay,
Where the old Flotilla Lay,
Can't you 'ear their paddles chunkin' from Rangoon to Mandalay?
On the road to Mandalay,
Where the flyin'-fishes play,
And the dawn comes up like thunder out of China 'crost the Bay!

It's the first song I can remember, and is now being inflicted on my own children.

Being born in Burma would later plague Harry, who wrote:

> My parents were British, which means I am British. But let me fill in a form saying I was born abroad but I'm really British and half bureaucracy is flung into confusion ...
>
> Me (answering questions while an official fills in a form): 'I'm British.'
>
> Him: 'I see, where were you born?'
>
> Me: 'Burma.'
>
> Him: 'How can you be British if you were born in Burma?'
>
> Me: 'Don't blame me. I wanted to be near my mother at the time. Wouldn't you?'
>
> Him: 'But that doesn't make you British.'
>
> Me: 'But Mum and Dad were British.'
>
> Him: 'Oh, I see. But how did you come to be born in Burma ...?'

But Burma did leave its mark on Harry in a lifelong love of exotic tropical climes, of feeling at home in foreign fields, of being comfortable with anyone from anywhere and of curries that could strip paint. Harry did remember the family's month-long journey back. 'The trip to England was the earliest part of my life I can remember. I lost an orange over the side of the ship and I complained to the captain for the rest of the voyage.'

Apparently he was a misery the whole long way home.

2

Welcome to Ardwick

I was a little sun-tanned bundle of joy when I first went to the Ardwick district … My father couldn't cope with the Corbett brood and defend the Empire at the same time. He sent [us] back to Ardwick. We joined [others] who were already being looked after by Aunt Annie. She had two girls and a boy of her own. I never really knew my uncle – it could have been he wanted some peace and quiet and joined my father in Burma.[1]

Harry H. Corbett

Young Harry Boy must have had many questions upon arriving in Manchester for the first time. 'Who are you people?' must have been right up there with 'Why is it so bleeding cold?' Annie Williams, his aunt, though forever after referred to as his mum, lived in a two-up two-down, red-brick terrace in Earl Street, Ardwick. Like the rest of the area the house had been built as part of the industrial explosion that had rocked the nineteenth century. Ardwick teemed with these jerry-built houses squeezed in amongst the factories and railway lines. By 1912 Longsight Railway Depot in Ardwick was home to over 200 steam engines. Endless plumes of steam and smoke from trains, factories and homes bled upwards, and toxic pollutants from factories were gaily pumped directly into the River Cornbrook, seeing it renamed locally as the Black Brook. All this made for a smothering fug that drew a veil over the occasionally glimpsed sun. Lowry didn't lie when he painted those washed-out skies.

Earl Street was not the worst in the area. Some of the houses had bay windows and a select few even afforded hankie-sized gardens. It was the very first in the district to have the cobblestones concreted

over – now there's posh! However, this did mean you had to watch
out for kids coming from all around to roller skate on the 'conky'.

In this desperately poor area Harry's family was one of the lucky
ones, thanks to Sgt George, who had soon returned to duty – this
time in the Sudan. Harry didn't have much time to 'worship his
Daddy' in person: 'My Father sent home a small allowance each
week, so, in comparison with the other families in the street, we had
it good. But so many youngsters in that district didn't know what a
square meal was. Unless a beef extract cube falls into that category.'[2]

The condition of these terraces was woeful. Poky, cold, leaking
and hopelessly overcrowded, one wonders what the then inhab-
itants would make of recent moves to turn the dwellings that
survived the slum clearances into a heritage site. Inside lavatories
were non-existent; in fact if you only shared the outhouse with
your nearest and dearest you were doing well. In some back alleys a
line of two or three privies served a whole terrace. Equipped with
newspaper on a string and a candle they must have taught generations of small children excellent nocturnal control. As for washing,
unless it was a tin bath dragged in front of the fire and shared with
your siblings on a Friday evening, there was the bath house, where
you had to be sure to ask the attendant to add some cold to the
scalding water that gushed into the huge slipper baths. The local
Victoria Baths not only afforded a luxurious weekly soak but also
provided a Turkish bath, swimming pools for males 1st class, males
2nd class and females, and since 1914 had controversially allowed
mixed bathing. If ever a finger needed to be pointed at the start
of social degeneration it was there. The Victoria Baths achieved
national fame in 2003 when the dilapidated building won the BBC
Restoration programme and was awarded £3.5 million for – you
guessed it – restoration. Work started in 2007. When it finally reo-
pens I wonder if males will be required to tax their soul with the
question of being 1st or 2nd class?

Although their surroundings were squalid, the tiny damp houses
themselves were kept scrupulously clean. There wasn't enough room
for dirt. Front steps were polished, windows gleamed and once a
week the women would pile washing into old prams or makeshift
trolleys and set out for the wash house. Three pence would buy you
an hour inside this steamy, noisy world. Wash times were allocated,
proof of which was your ticket. A conveniently timed ticket was
jealously guarded – if you missed your window twice it was up for

grabs. It was backbreaking work, scrubbing at the sinks, arranging the clothes over the drying racks – it was too damp at home to have a hope of drying anything. Conversations were limited to shouting over the deafening noise of the huge steam rollers pressing the sheets. All of it powered by boilers that were constantly fed coal by the boiler men.

For the women cleanliness may have just edged out godliness, and the men may have been sinking a quick sin or two in one of the many local pubs helping to blot out the reality of being one of the near 3 million out of work (one of Harry's brothers was unemployed for eight years), but every Sunday children were firmly marched to Sunday school, Harry's being the Earl Street Mission at the end of the road.

The churches, Sunday schools and Salvation Army did what they could to relieve the deprivation. Sunday schools would award regular attendees with a Christmas party. The weeks leading up to Christmas were rife with kids running to different Sunday schools and clocking up as many hours as possible so as to get into all the parties. The churches also arranged trips to green areas for the children, where it was not unknown to have to explain to the first timers that the 'funny smell' was in fact newly mown grass. I'm sure they were all very grateful, but charity could still leave an unpleasant taste, as Harry remembered: 'There was one day when they sent us to a poor children's party. People should never have to face that sort of humiliation. Anyway, I don't like talking about it. That's all so long ago. It's the future that counts.'[3]

The churches, Sunday schools and Boys' Brigade also arranged the biggest event of the year: the Whit Walk. This is making a comeback in Manchester. It is a procession of witness to faith, held during Whitsuntide, the week after Whit Sunday, which is the seventh Sunday after Easter. Early Christian converts were baptised on Pentecost Sunday, the fiftieth day after the Resurrection, when the disciples of Jesus had received the Holy Spirit, enabling them to carry on his law. The converts were dressed in white for their baptism, giving us White Sunday or Whitsun. In 1971 the Banking and Financial Dealings Act poetically renamed Whitsun as the Spring Bank Holiday, anchoring it to the last Monday in May. Whitsun was an extremely popular holiday, said to have been encouraged by Charles II, who was born at Whitsuntide, it was also the first time in the year that it was warm enough to have an al fresco knees-up.

On Whit Monday the Protestants would have their walk, followed throughout the week by the other denominations, ending with the Catholics on Whit Friday. Why not get it all over with on the Monday? Well, some say it was because Manchester had annual horse races on Wednesday to Saturday of that week. It was one way to stop them gambling.

In the procession of the walk, first would come the banner of the church or Sunday school, immediately followed by the May or 'Rose' Queen, with her attendants carrying flowers or scattering petals. Now, the May Queen might not have a lot to do with receiving the Holy Spirit, but she's fully part of the pagan rituals of the rebirth of the land in spring – as so often in our history we've dovetailed the old nicely with the new. The rest of the children, and a band, would then follow the May Queen, with the adults occasionally bringing up the rear but mostly lining the route. The day would culminate in the Whitsun Ale, 'ale' being the old word for a church fair – though there was plenty of quaffing of the other sort. Thousands took part. Yes, it was religious; yes, it was a proclamation of faith. However, it seems that the most important aspect of the Whit Walk was that new clothes were to be worn. For most, if not all, of the kids, these were the only new clothes of the year. A precious thing when you lived in a world of hand-me-downs. Harry was afflicted in later life with the most awful bunions – the blame for which he laid firmly at the door of never having had his own shoes until he could buy them himself. I remember him attacking most of his shoes with a Stanley knife (even those bought at vast expense from Dunn & Co.); cutting a spilt to give his bunions some much-needed room. Understandably, he was obsessive about his own children's feet; as such, my brother and I spent most of our childhood in the John Lewis shoe department – but I have to hand it to him, we don't have bunions.

For the Whit Walk, girls would have been bought a new crisp white dress and boys a new suit. Those families who could not save enough to buy these outright (practically all of them) pawned everything non-essential to raise the money, even if the new clothes were immediately pawned themselves after the walk. One enterprising outfitters, James Stewart and Sons, allowed you to spread the cost of the clothes over some weeks. The queues outside the shop on the Saturday mornings leading up to Whitsun were legendary.

On the big day kids would be able to run round the neighbourhood getting a penny from their neighbours for 'showing' their

new clothes – much like the Halloween tradition of trick or treating. They might not have had much, but they could still put on a
good show. What they lacked in funds they made up for in dignity.
No family would have been able to show its face if their children
were not decked out in 'new' for the walk. Harry remembered this
sense of pride when he used to tell of the etiquette involved in
simply going round to someone's house for tea. You did *not* clear
your plate – it would appear as if you weren't getting enough at
home. The other reason for not finishing was that the owners of
the house would need to eat your leftovers, though to acknowledge
this fact would have been the height of rudeness. You can just hear
the conversations:

'Eat up, there's plenty.'

'No, no, we had a big dinner.'

For years parents have used starving children in Africa as a stick
to encourage clean plates, but in the 1930s you didn't have so far
to look. Mind you, in Ardwick in the 1930s the kids wouldn't have
needed much encouragement to finish their food.

Relying on your neighbours was the norm. You had to look out
for one another – nobody else was going to. Living cheek by jowl,
being able to hear the minutiae of life next door, and whole families
lodging at addresses up and down the street, obviously led to a community spirit that has been lost today. If you could afford to help
next door this week, you did, and next week they would help you.
There was no alternative. Well there was, but that was the workhouse, or to be more precise, the 'institution', 'hospital' or 'Public
Assistance Infirmary' – the term 'workhouse' having been abolished
in 1930. To get Public Assistance the head of the household had the
demeaning task of going before a tribunal to plead their case for aid.
If you ended up there, you'd really hit bottom. However, the reforms
and change of name didn't seem to have had much effect on these
former workhouses, as witnessed by one M.B. of Northern Moor,
who wrote to a Manchester paper recalling the 1930s:

Those who had jobs worked long hours for low pay. There were
no school dinners or social service benefits as we know them.
There was only one week's paid holiday for those lucky enough
to be working.

Those who could not pay their rent, many unmarried mothers, and old people who could not look after themselves, were

put in the workhouse. Once there, old couples were separated, and parents only saw their children for an hour on Saturday afternoons. Epidemics of scarlet fever etc and TB were rife and Baguley Sanitorium[4] was always full.

Out of 30 teenage girls who were interested in the Girl Guides there, and whom I visited, only one survived after three years. Thank God those days will never return.[5]

Workhouses were still running into the 1940s. As Jim Hamman, a later school friend of Harry's remembers:

When I was a Telegraph Boy during the War, New Home in Nell Lane was a Workhouse and those that were able were allowed to walk out on Nell Lane and they all had the same suit on. The term New Home had been devised to lose its identity as a Workhouse but everyone referred to it as the workhouse on Nell Lane.[6]

Now when the old codger in the corner starts spouting about the welfare state and how 'You don't know you're born', I'll cut them some slack. I am, after all, only a generation away from the workhouse.

In 1890 the average life expectancy for a man living in a rural district of England was 51; in Manchester it was 28. Out of 100,000 children, 17,314 living in the countryside would die before their fifth birthday; in Manchester 37,674 would.[7]

Annie Williams was born in the 1880s; this might go some way to explaining why in photos of her with Harry in the late 1920s she already looks ancient.

Disease was still rampant in the 1920s. Damp, polluted, over-crowded and malnourished it was all too easy to succumb to one of many everyday conditions: bronchitis, TB, diphtheria, rickets and polio to name a few. All without the aid of antibiotics. Penicillin was still not available to the general public; the breakthrough in producing vast quantities occurred in 1944, to cope with the expected backlash of D-Day, and it was not generally prescribed until the 1950s. Nor was there a National Health Service, it being created in 1948. If you were ill and beyond the help of home remedies, and you had to be damn ill to be beyond that, the next step was to call in the doctor who was, at least, cheaper than the hospital. Though, of course, he would still have to be paid. He would employ the

'Doctor's Man', who would call every Friday to collect on the debt, when those fortunate enough to be in work got paid.

Harry remembered an occasion when even the local doctor wouldn't have helped:

> Times were hard, and in the area was a strange mixture of toughness and tenderness.
>
> The members of one family continually fought amongst themselves. The brothers would fight each other for the sheer joy of it – and in the next minute all was forgiven.
>
> One day a fight went a bit too far. An argument developed between two of the brothers. In a fit of anger one picked up a chopper and lashed out at the other. The chopper skimmed the top of his head and scraped the boy's skull. Blood poured from a nasty looking wound.
>
> But the lads were made of stern stuff. The brother who had used the axe picked up his father's carpet slipper and slapped it against the gash. He held it like that during the two-mile walk to the hospital. This action probably saved his brother's life.[8]

Every loving childhood is remembered with soft-focused affection, and Harry's was no different. As he said, he had a 'very poor childhood, but not an unhappy one.'[9] Kids of the 1930s, by standards today, had enormous freedom. They played their games in the streets as there was nowhere else to play them, and there were no parks in Ardwick for the smallest to walk to. At the top of Earl Street, opposite Yates' Shirt Factory, was an open patch of ground known as the Sand Park. It had once been the site of stables for the Manchester Carriage and Tramway Company. When these closed, an open shed was kept at one end and the area was covered in shale from which it got its name. A shale surface is enough to give modern health and safety officers palpitations; just think what they would have made of the more exciting games to be had amongst the railway lines, the reservoir and the clay pits.

The Sand Park was the home of the ever-present football game, with anywhere from five to fifty kids competing, dreaming of United or City. When the park was locked the match would continue in the street until broken up by parents sick of hearing the ball thump against the front wall. There were marbles, whip and tops, diabolos, trading of cigarette cards, tag, hopscotch, chalk drawing on the pavements and up the fronts of houses – I bet that went down well. An old sheet stretched from the front window to the pavement made a tent. The alleys behind the terraces linked up with the street to make a bike-racing circuit where you had to dodge the wheels of the horse-drawn carts belonging to the dustmen, coalman, milko and, yes, the rag-and-bone man. The fun didn't stop when the sun went down. The old gas lamps not only provided the closest thing to tree climbing but, with the aid of a rope swung over the arms, made a trapeze that would entertain for hours – swinging and spinning in the lamp's glow, islands of light hissing at the end of each street.

The lamp lighter would traipse from lamp to lamp at dusk, long pole over his shoulder; he'd reach into the glass with the end of the pole, turn on the gas supply with a hook and flip over to touch the wick to ignite. He'd be back at dawn to hook the gas off again. If he didn't also act as the 'Knocker-up Man' then he certainly would have passed him in the street. The 'Knocker-up' would, for a few pennies, rattle at your bedroom windows to get those on early shift up and out and rouse kids desperately hanging on to the comparative warmth of bed before setting out for school.

Harry's first school was Ross Place County Primary. Annie would meet him afterwards and together they would head south for the short walk to the Kings Opera House to catch a variety show or go to the pictures at the Shaftesbury nearby. If they were feeling upmarket they could head north to the Apollo cinema, which became a leading concert venue and is now home to the biggest live music and comedy acts. Generations of trendy young things strut their stuff where the ghosts of their grandparents lobbed sweets on a Saturday morning.

A special treat would have been a trip to the nearby Belle Vue Gardens. This fabulous pleasure park had a ballroom for 10,000, a zoo, lakes, Italianate gardens, a maze, a circus, fairground rides including a death-defying roller coaster, themed firework displays, a greyhound-racing track, horse shows, adult and school sports competitions, a miniature railway, a speedway track, concerts, boxing matches and an ice rink. These were just some of its wonders. In the 1980s they levelled it and built a housing estate, though the speedway survived.

Back in the early 1930s, parts of Ardwick were set for levelling too. Plans were afoot to begin the great slum clearances and deliver the long-awaited 'homes fit for heroes'. The 1930 Housing Act gave local authorities five years to clear out the worst slums and re-house those made homeless in new council estates. Some heroes would still be waiting into the 1970s. But for those who could afford the higher rents, housing was available in Wythenshawe – a new utopian council estate a few miles south of the city centre. Thanks to the money sent by Sgt George, Annie and Harry could afford to make the move.

And what of Harry's father and the rest of the family? Sgt George had come home from the Sudan in 1929. He must have seen Harry occasionally, though he was billeted at the Whittington Barracks near Lichfield, where he had requested to revert from CQMS to sergeant. There was never any question of Harry living with him, even less when Sgt George remarried in 1930; he finally left the army in 1935. He became a builder's handyman and settled in Whittington. In later life Harry rarely mentioned him; I guess there wasn't much to mention. Albert, Carrie and William, being so much older, were grown and gone to their own lives very soon, as were Annie's own children. James was still serving abroad with the South Staffs and George had been sent in 1930 not to the Duke of York's school but to the Army Technical School in Chepstow. George enlisted as soon as possible – Annie couldn't afford to keep him and it was the only job available – he became a senior tank instructor. Of course they would all see each other regularly; there are pictures of Albert playing with Harry in the Sand Park. Carrie especially tried to keep them all together, but she had married and had a son, James, in 1934 (James later joined the RAF and became a test pilot for Concorde). But for the most part it was just Annie and Harry who would settle into a new life in Wythenshawe.

I often wonder what he would have made of Manchester today. A few years ago I was mooching through the city centre when I saw two Premiership footballers returning to their matching his and his, top of the line, blinged BMWs, laden down with designer shopping bags. I'm sure Harry would have raised a wry smile, much like the one he would have worn when he returned to Ardwick some thirty-five years after he'd left.

Harry was working on a film nearby in 1969 and was invited by a paper to visit his old haunts. Much of the area was in the process of being knocked down. Earl Street had already gone. 'It's like a dream. I almost don't know where I am,' he said. 'Over there used to be a market, and there was a shop there where we used to scream for aniseed balls.' Along with the pubs, inviolate due to their licence, Ross Place school was still standing, alone in a sea of rubble. 'I'm glad that's survived,' he said. 'I remember marching in there one day with my father's medals pinned to my chest. But I'm not sorry to see the rest go. Everything looks so tiny. It makes me wonder how did they manage to pack us all in that small area.'[10]

Notes

1 *Manchester Weekly News*, 18/3/67.
2 *Ibid*.
3 *Western Eve Herald*, 19/1/67.
4 Now Wythenshawe Hospital, flagship of University Hospital of South Manchester NHS Foundation Trust.
5 Sutton, L., *Mainly About Ardwick*, vol. 2 (Les Sutton, 1975).
6 Now Withington Community Hospital, little sister to Wythenshawe Hospital.
7 Sutton, L., *Mainly About Ardwick*, vol. 2 (Les Sutton, 1975).
8 *Manchester Weekly News*, 18/3/67.
9 *Woman's Day*, 17/4/72.
10 *Daily Mirror*, 14/9/69.

3

Wythenshawe: The Garden City

All my childhood was spent in Ardwick, Manchester, where I lived a very happy slum life at the tail end of the glorious thirties ... From Ardwick we moved to Wythenshawe. This 'paradise' was pretty much like Ardwick only farther out in the country and picturesquely dotted with old brick and rubbish dumps.[1]

Harry H. Corbett

Aldermen William Jackson and Ernest Simon of Manchester City Council, together with City Planner Barry Parker, had a dream. They wanted to turn the countryside around Wythenshawe Hall into a garden city. There, slum dwellers would find a promised land.

The Tatton family had owned the land from the fourteenth century. When the last of the line, Robert Henry Grenville Tatton, inherited it in 1926, the council made him an offer he couldn't refuse. The estate of 2,569 acres was bought for £205,520. Alderman Simon sweetened the deal by privately purchasing Wythenshawe Hall and the surrounding 250 acres and immediately donating it to the city 'to be kept for ever as an open space for the people of Manchester'.[2]

Unfortunately, the land lay in the neighbouring county and would require that county's permission before building could begin. Yeah, like that would happen. They spent the next five years trying to reallocate the land to the control of Manchester City Council. Not easy when not only every adjoining council wanted a piece of the action, but members of Manchester City Council itself were objecting to the perceived inevitable rates increase. Jackson, Simon and Parker won the day however, and in 1931 control passed to Manchester and work could begin.

It was superbly timed. In 1919 the coalition government had brought in the Addison Housing and Town Planning Act, giving a subsidy to councils to provide better housing for the poor. In 1923 the Conservative government had reduced the subsidy with the Chamberlain Housing Act. Labour had another go in 1924 with the Financial Provisions Housing Act, which survived the next Conservative government. It was improved upon with the Greenwood Housing Act of 1930, which not only provided subsidies but *required* local authorities to re-house tenants. But it was all change again with the Conservative-led coalition's 1933 Financial Provisions Housing Act, which abolished the subsidy altogether. Councils were now directed to build cheaper blocks of flats.

While this tennis match of subsidies went on, Wythenshawe was born. The first houses were well built, with gable ends and mansard roofs. When the depression bit they tended to throw up box-like houses, cutting a few corners here and there. Jim Hamman, Harry's school friend, said: 'It was very much feeling as you go because they had this huge amount of people coming into Wythenshawe as they were building houses. People were moving into houses that still wanted painting and things like that.' Later on: 'When Hazel, my wife and I, moved into one of these houses we were amazed that they had left the bare bricks on the wall – everything to cut costs. They were painted a dull brown and green. They were very, very simple and the only heating for the water was from the fire. So in the summer, if you didn't want a fire you'd got to light one if you wanted a bath.'

But at least there were bathrooms and a patch of garden to call your own – luxury. Luxury for those that could afford it, and not many from the slums could. The average wage for a skilled factory worker was £2 15s (£2.75). The cost of the most meagre house for rent, rates, and electricity was 9s (45p), going up to 15s 9d (79p). In Ardwick a rent of over 9s would have been unheard of. A 1930s survey reported that out of 430 families only 155 had come from the slums. The new residents would have been most insulted at the notion that their estate was full of slum dwellers.

'Not anyone could get a house in Wythenshawe. Before we got one an official from the Town Hall wanted to know all about us … my husband had steady employment and a fair wage. We had to prove we would be good tenants. We also heard that some people were from slums but we never met any of them.'[3] So said an early resident.

The Corbetts made the grade (I'll have you know!) and moved into No. 48 Moat Road. As new residents they were instructed by the council to protect the wildlife, the grass verges, trees, hedges and flowering shrubs, and to *not* dry their washing outside on a Sunday. Good job they couldn't afford a car. There were no garages, for cars would: '1. Detract from the appearance of the estate, 2. Necessitate the widening of gateways, and 3. Lead to the formation of tracks across the greensward.'[4]

Joseph Siddall, a former resident, recounts how: 'Cook's Farm was at the top of Moat Road. My mother used to talk about how one of Cook's cows got jammed in the backdoor. We had a toilet on one side of this little passageway and a coalhole on the other. The cow had gone up the step and it was butting its head – we had to pull it out by the tail.' There appear to have been no restrictions on cows buggering up the greensward.

The problem with transplanting people into a new town is that it inevitably leads to zero community spirit. Given the fact that there were as yet few shops, local employers, post offices, pubs and all the other places that glue a community together, it would take a while to get that spirit soaring. One place to start would be the schools, though given the dispute over which local authority was to be eventually in charge of the area, the schools weren't quite up to speed when the first pupils arrived.

Benchill School was the first to open in 1934, and Harry part of the very first class. In January it opened to all ages, in April it opened again having separated the seniors from the juniors, then in August it was three times lucky when it got rid of the seniors altogether and settled down to life as Benchill Primary, though it took a while to iron out the wrinkles, as Harry remembered: 'We once got a lot of new equipment. But nobody ever let us use it. We never seemed to do anything but cut up daffodils.'[5] But this didn't stop him enjoying his time there:

> School was a great experience. I never really knew what it was all about. I was so terrible it was ridiculous. But one thing was important. I was good at looking as though I was good! I said: 'Aah, I see-e-e…' better than any other kid and the teachers thought I understood what they were saying. I can't even remember when I did understand. I always gave the impression that I was a late developer. It's fair to say I'm still developing … Sometimes,

when I look back, I probably worked far harder pretending I was busy than if I'd actually been busy. That's a confessed dedication to loafing if you like ... Do you remember the elaborate lengths you used to go to at school just to 'skive' – the comics tucked behind the textbooks and all the other little tricks.[6]

Despite the skiving off Harry was a clever boy, clever but still poor:

The humiliation I had when the school was very bold and experimental in wanting to take a class to London. The thing was, three quarters of the school couldn't afford it in any circumstances – more than 4 pounds it was – my aunt couldn't pay it. But I do remember my headmaster called me into his study because he thought I was such a bright boy and could benefit from the trip. He told me 'Every day you will come to my study and receive two and sixpence from me and take it to your teacher.' I know they didn't mean it, but that feeling of charity really hit home – there were so many of those little pinpricks.[7]

One charitable body was the Rosemary Fund, set up the same year as the school and opened by well-meaning villagers, businessmen and the Rotary Club. They delivered coal and food to old folks in the winter, and made sure that each child in need had decent warm clothing and a summer holiday. Eight hundred of them were sent on such holidays in three years. Along with the schools, churches and Sunday schools they filled up the calendar with fairs, dances and sporting events. The biggest 'do' of the year was still the Whit Walk, though the old guard at the established churches had noticed the new residents were rather missing the point:

The object of this combined procession to church is not a 'walk' in the sense in which 'a walk' is regarded in Manchester, but rather as a witness of the unity of Christian children, and of their desire to worship together at least once a year in their own parish church. Of course, it is pleasing to see children, especially the little girls, prettily dressed, and provided this can be done inexpensively there can be no objection to it but it is not right to spend money which is needed for more necessary things simply to make a pretty show, for our Procession is not a show but a witness.[8]

So did the newcomers heed this warning of *omnia vanitas*? Of course not:

> The new outfit was kept a closely guarded secret until the great day. Mothers must have scrimped and saved for weeks to ensure that their children were as well dressed as their neighbours … Whit Sunday arrived at last, and, in the morning the children called on their neighbours and relations to parade their finery.[9]

Competitive mummy had transplanted well. Bragging rights reached a zenith with the dreaded grammar school entrance exam. This exam sorted the wheat, who would get a coveted place at a grammar school, from the chaff, sent to the local comprehensive. A local girl recalled:

> Scholarship exam was taken at 10+ years. Some of us likely ones were pushed a bit; everyone took it but few thought seriously about it. I suppose most people were too poor to consider taking up further education. Most children treated it as a day out from school routine. The year I took it 2 of us girls 'passed' and 4–5 boys.[10]

The year was 1935, and Harry was one of those select few. Speaking in the early 1970s he said:

> I passed to go to grammar school, my aunt had to find the five pounds for books – she didn't have it. I realise that I accepted the economic limitations of a parent, but that did hurt, that really hurt. I wasn't madly grasping to go to a grammar school, but some of my friends were going, and obviously I felt something was wrong. I mean this terrible business now, which our government has introduced – no free school meals. In my day it was shameful to have a free meal and have to put your hand up in class for it. The Labour Government brought in free school meals for everybody. The present government goes back to knocking off the milk and going back to a system of children having fights over the fact that one has to take free meals and the other doesn't, goes back to that awful period 35 years ago when I faced the same thing.[11]

So the place at the elite Chorlton Grammar School for Boys fell by the wayside. 'Being poor can retard you' as he used to say. Still, not taking the bus in and out every day freed up time he put to good use. 'Soon to help Mum out, I got two paper rounds – one in the evening – the other in the morning. At the same time I got a Saturday bakery round. I brought home the princely sum, for those days, of 10s a week.'[12] No doubt some of it was spent at the pictures where Harry found his calling:

> Now, I wanted to be an actor because Auntie and I used to spend many a glorious hour in the dear old lovable Coronation Cinema in dear old lovable Wythenshawe outside dear old lovable Manchester. It's a bingo hall now but it was a dream palace of a different kind in those palmy days of childhood. I was reared on those marvellous films of the thirties. I idolised all and everything and that's where the spark first flew off the forge, I suppose.[13]

This spark was fanned at Sharston Secondary School, where he had ended up. Although Harry was good at English, his 'Mum' wasn't:

> My favourite was my English teacher. She once wrote on my school report, 'An asset in the class.' I took this home to Mum, feeling very proud of myself. This would show her the years of work on my behalf were worth it! Clump! My head reeled from a blow delivered with years of practice behind it.
>
> 'What do you mean coming home with a report like this?' she bellowed. 'An ass, indeed.' She'd only noticed the first three letters of 'asset'.

This favourite teacher was Miss White. If you enjoyed Harry's work tip a nod to her. If you didn't - it's her fault. Jim Hamman, also at Sharston, tells:

> Sharston was the only senior school. I think Harry was part of the very first year. I was a year behind Harry and when I went to junior school the senior school hadn't been completed because a lot of it was still being built. When I went to Sharston he would have just about been finishing, but we were both in Miss White's Amateur Dramatics class. He was very impressive.

As was Miss White, and she was most definitely a Miss. According to Jim: 'At that time you couldn't teach if you got married. That's why they were all "Miss". You had to leave school if you got married – you might have given the children bad thoughts!' Miss White did make boys tremble, though with decent, proper shame and not despicable lust, as Jim continues:

> Miss White had a very strong belief that Gentlemen had to be Gentleman even if they'd got patched trousers and darned socks and cardboard stuck in shoes with no bottoms in. She encouraged any of the girls from the class that if they met a boy or passed a classmate in the street, that if they didn't touch their forelock and say 'Good Afternoon' they'd have to report it to her, and she'd say 'Hamman! Aren't you ashamed? You passed Mary Dunn in Northenden on Saturday and never acknowledged her. What do you say? … Don't say it to me. You didn't offend me. Go and tell her how sorry you are.'

Jim had another, personal, reason to remember Miss White:

> My father was terribly crippled in the 14–18 war. He was at the Somme, both of his arms were crippled and he carried a machine gun bullet in his leg 'til he died. He spent most of his time in hospital. My Mother had to work in service, so when my Dad was in hospital, which was frequent … my brother and I were running wild at night. There were no parents in the house at all. Mum had to live in when she was working away, so we had to get ourselves off to school. I presume it must have been a neighbour who reported us to the authorities and we were wheeled in; and my brother went in the care of my Auntie but they wouldn't take me as well. They wouldn't take two. So Miss White, when I was in Court for this unruly behaviour, Miss White came – on her bike I hasten to add – to the Court in Manchester and said that she would look after me over the weekend. She was my teacher as well as the Drama teacher. She looked after me at the weekend and the Salvation Army looked after me during the week.

She was a class act. She was still teaching at Sharston in the 1960s and must have smiled when she caught Harry on TV, as Jim says: 'Miss White would have been proud of him.' I hope she knew it was, in good part, due to her. Harry certainly did. He said that Miss White once: 'took her best boys to see "1066 And All That" at the Opera House in Manchester. The show was a real eye-opener. It was wonderful to forget the poverty and harshness of life in two hours of gaiety and laughter. After that experience, I was determined to get in on every school play.'

> Teachers encouraged me to write scripts. I was proud of one play. A character had to ask another 'What is the time?' The reply was, 'One o'clock,' and the questioner should have been lightly tapped on the head. On the big night the play went well until it came to the question of the time.
> 'One o'clock,' said the boy. With that he crowned the other character with a mallet. The boy went out like a light.
> That's what I call enthusiasm and putting everything into a part.
> It was with similar enthusiasm I left school and went out to earn my keep. A career as an actor was now only in the back of my mind. What 14-year-old from Manchester could expect to take the profession by storm?[14]

Certainly not him. For a shy kid, as Harry was, the drama class had shown him the delights and freedom of taking on another character, the respect and adrenaline to be found in front of an audience. Like a lot of actors in waiting, it was a lesson he never forgot. As a breed, actors keep most of the world at bay with the razzle-dazzle; they're the jokers of the class with a secret, serious soul.

Although Miss White had opened Harry's eyes to the possibility of life as an actor, it would have to remain a childhood dream. Not only was Harry 'conditioned to a life where the father figure image was one of a man in big blue overalls with a two foot rule sticking out of a narrow pocket in his trousers'[15] but in the summer of 1939, when he left school, there were bigger fish to fry. All the talk would have been of the prospect of war, and how long it might last. The older Corbett boys were all of fighting age: Albert was invalided, stuck in a TB sanatorium; James and George were already career army. Acting was out, earning a wage was in:

> I worked three weeks for a grocer, but it wasn't the kind of job for Harry H. I rather fancied myself as a fitter. I started as an apprentice

at a machine tool factory – but as I wasn't 16 I couldn't work on the benches.

I became tea boy to about 50 workers. They gave me 3*d* a week for making their tea. I made quite a profit by keeping their brew 50 per cent under strength. I was able to give Mum something like eleven shillings a week. She was proud of her 'baby'.

When I started working in a biscuit factory, I kept an eye on the rows of biscuits as they travelled down the production belt. As each biscuit passed along, two tubes gave a squirt of chocolate and marshmallow. The Corbett mind pondered on the problem. 'What would happen if I put a finger against one of the tubes?' There was only one way to find out.

There was no one about – I carefully blocked the marshmallow nozzle. Hundreds of biscuits belted by with only a layer of chocolate on them.

There was consternation in the factory. The incident was passed off as something not likely to happen again.

I did it again. The engineers tore the machinery to pieces in an effort to find the fault. They couldn't.

But nasty looks were turned in the direction of young Corbett.

The management checked with the records and discovered the trouble had only started with the employment of Harry H. I was warned – but never got the sack because the start of the 1939–45 war was creating a manpower shortage.[16]

Harry had money coming in but it sounds like he didn't hang onto it for long. James, Carrie's son, remembers going round to the house in Moat Road during the war:

I remember at the age of about eight when I was there, they all had theatrical tendencies, quite eccentric. Even at that age I could work out it was no way to run the family budget. You got paid on a Thursday, they all went out to the chippy and had a blast, and by the following Wednesday there was no food, I mean there was bread. The other side of the family were all very practical so I thought 'this is no way to …' and come Thursday again, of course, they all went out again. None of them were any good with money.

In 1942 Harry left the biscuit factory, Wythenshawe and Manchester far behind. Annie's 'baby' joined the marines.

Notes

1   *TV Times*, 29/12/66.

2   Deakin, D., *Wythenshawe: The Story of a Garden City* (Phillimore, 1989).

3   *Ibid.*

4   *Ibid.*

5   *Sunday Citizen*, 7/8/66.

6   *TV Times*, 29/12/66.

7   *The Herald*, 20/4/72.

8   Deakin, *Wythenshawe*.

9   *Ibid.*

10 *Ibid.*

11 *The Herald*, 20/4/72.

12 *Manchester Weekly News*, 25/3/67.

13 *TV Times*, 29/12/66.

14 *Manchester Weekly News*, 25/3/67.

15 *Weekend News*, 12/8/72.

16 *Manchester Weekly News*, 25/3/67.

4

Per Mare Per Terram

When I was 17½ I applied to join the Marines, and they let me in.
It was a decision they were to regret until the last shot of the war.
I just couldn't keep out of trouble.[1]

Harry H. Corbett

Harry passed his medical in Manchester on 2 July 1942. Class 'A',
5ft 8in, complexion 'fresh', Corbett, Harry, officially enlisted as a
Royal Marine at Plymouth on 1 December 1942. When required
to fill in the 'next of kin' he naturally put down Annie's name, not
his dad's. He was billeted at RM Stonehouse Barracks and, along
with the rest of 242 Squad, commenced training on 14 December.
Months of drill, square bashing and indoctrination followed.

The Royal Marines were founded in 1664 when the Admiralty
raised a permanent regiment of soldiers to serve on Royal Navy
ships, replacing an ad hoc arrangement. The corps emblem is the
Globe and Laurel, the Globe granted by George IV in 1827 to
reflect the then over 100 battle honours won. Once a marine, always
a marine and Harry was always very proud of the corps. They had
made a man of him, but one who still knew how to take the piss:

There were times in the Royal Marines during the war when
I had to con myself to keep sane. I thought the entire set up was
absolutely wonderful.

But it was just that I was completely miscast. I couldn't really
believe it was all happening. Now I ask you, how can you take all
that old lark seriously? For instance, I could march perfectly well
with a rifle and all that but when a band started to play it was all

so idiotic I'd curl up with laughter and this did not seem to be appreciated.[2]

Harry went through months of basic training. He was efficient and of very good character as of 27 February 1943, the day before his eighteenth birthday. Usually character assessments were made on 31 December but Harry had been under age then and, as such, did not exist. As soon as he was old enough to be shot at, they started filling in the forms. Alongside the marching up and down, small arms and basic seamanship, they were even shown the correct way to wash. This is your flannel, this is water, this is soap, this is the wringer – it has an 'andle, this is how you turn the 'andle to h'operate. All of it, however, stayed with him. I remember him telling me that if ever I was on a sinking ship, to swim away from it as fast as possible otherwise it would suck you down with it – that gave me the willies for years. He also could always manage to get out *Reveille* on the bugle, one of his duties. He slept in and missed it one morning and spent the day in the stockade.

Squad 242 passed for duty on 22 July 1943. Proud, nervous and trying to look older than their tender years, they posed for the squad photo resplendent in their 'blues'. Harry was paid 16s, no doubt most of it going back to Annie. There wasn't a lot to spend it on and little time to spend it; they were all so busy with the unending training. Though perhaps he got a little time off in the autumn of 1943, not for good behaviour – there was never any of that – but for his dad's funeral.

Sgt George died of a heart attack in Whittington, Lichfield, a stone's throw from his old barracks. He was 57. He and Harry had had so little shared past, and now there could be no shared future. Of course there would have been regret and grief, though it must have been tempered by unfamiliarity. In his later years Sgt George's involvement in his children's lives had been so slight that when James had married, in 1937, Sgt George did not attend the wedding and Harry's eldest brother, Albert, would always tell his young children that their Grandfather George had died in India. But Harry had been proud of his father, wearing his medals into school, and his lifelong pride in king and country no doubt stemmed from that. Perhaps that had something to do with Harry's underage enlistment – I'm sure it wasn't Annie's idea.

Harry didn't have much time to dwell on his father's death. He was too busy developing into a lean mean fighting machine. Well that was the idea; in practice he developed a keen laconic sarcasm, a comprehensive vocabulary of international swearwords and a pre-dilection for Player's Navy Cut Cigarettes. 'Player's Please': the lung buster, high tar for Jack Tar. Meantime there was still the bloody training. He did well in gunnery training, scoring high in ammuni-tion. This led to more training with ship's heavy artillery while the Admiralty figured out what to do with him, and thousands like him, leading to the big push of 1944.

Harry joined HMS *Devonshire*, a county-class heavy cruiser, with forty-eight other marines on 11 March 1944. His prowess with ammunition saw him stationed in No. 1 Left Shell Room. His job was to feed shells to one of the 8in Mark 1 guns. This was the worst place to have your action station. Once inside the shell room an armour-plated hatch was battened down. It could only be opened from the other side with a chain hoist; once you were in you didn't know if you would come out. The ship could be hit and going down, with those above you, your mates who were supposed to let you out after the action, already dead. Imagine sinking lower and lower, the ship creaking as the lights went out, wondering how long the air would last. Far better to hope for a direct hit – standing next to the shells was a good spot for a quick death. When I was a child, Harry used to take us to HMS *Belfast*, a museum ship on the River Thames in London, similar to *Devonshire* (it's still there, have a day out, take the kiddies). When I heard these stories I looked at him in a whole new light.

Devonshire was working out of Scapa Flow, part of the Home Fleet in the far North Atlantic. In May the fleet were preparing for Operation Neptune, the Channel-crossing phase of D-Day. Come the landings, she provided distant cover from the north. The Home Fleet had quite a few ships up there. Partly they helped to fool the enemy into thinking that the invasion might be in Norway, but mainly they had to keep an eye on the 'Lonely Queen of the North', the German battleship *Tirpitz*.

Tirpitz was one of the most powerful warships in the world; she lay in a Norwegian fjord, threatening the Atlantic convoys and tying up ships that were badly needed in the Pacific. Throughout that summer, *Devonshire* acted as escort on operations to rid the Allies of that threat. On one of these operations she found herself within sight of this fjord. She was heading the fleet that awaited the return of 200-odd dive bombers, torpedo and fighter bombers.

Bob Maxwell, a young 'bunting tosser' (signalman), who was on board recalled:

> Our Captain, sitting in his chair gazing ahead at the Norwegian Mountains, shouted for my boss, the Chief Yeoman of Signals. Make a signal to Commander in Chief he said, 'Request permission to enter Alten Fjord and engage the Tirpitz' ... As I tapped out the Morse call sign on the lamp I said to the Chief 'He doesn't really mean it does he?' 'Course he does', he replied, 'That D.S.O. he's got isn't enough for him he wants a Victoria Cross to keep it company.' I transmitted the signal and waited for a reply.
>
> By now my earlier feeling of bravado was decreasing. The thought of our old under gunned ship entering Alten Fjord to face the juggernaut, five times our weight, that lurked inside plus the shore gun installations and a flotilla of German Elbing class destroyers. The patriotic vision of the bands playing and flags waving was receding into the far corners of my mind and reality loomed up as I thought of our immediate, possibly short-lived future.
>
> Our call sign flashed from the Duke of York. I read the signal while the Chief Yeoman wrote it down. 'From Commander in Chief to Devonshire, reference your last signal, not approved'. The Chief Yeoman went and stood behind the Captain and read out the reply. There was silence for a few moments only broken by the sound of a few dry throats swallowing, mine included. The Captain turned round and my heart missed several beats as I saw tears running down his cheeks. 'I wanted to show the Commander in Chief what my ship and my crew could do,' he said in a broken voice. The silence was only broken by the hiss of the bow wave. I walked back to my station at the after end of the bridge and it was then that I fully understood how and why the history of the Royal Navy had been formed. This was how men had acted to establish the tradition and verve that had kept our island home secure for so many centuries. This was Grenville fighting the Revenge against all odds; this was Drake fighting and dying in Nombre Dios Bay with the scuppers running blood; this was the Nelson dash that broke the line at Trafalgar flying his last signal 'Engage the Enemy more closely.' This had frightened the life out of me. I grew up then.[3]

There were many raids against *Tirpitz*. After coming back to Scapa Flow from yet another unsuccessful one, *Devonshire* was celebrating shooting down an enemy plane. But pride comes before a fall. As the ship approached the harbour's entrance she went off course and smacked straight into the boom net, wrapping hundreds of buoys around her sides. While she was untangled, a destroyer and frigate were dispatched to patrol the now gaping wound in the Scapa defences. For weeks afterwards, every time the lighter bearing the placard *Devonshire* came to shore to transport crew back to the ship there were cries of 'Look out, it's the Boom Boys boat.'

Tirpitz was finally put out of action in November 1944. By then Harry's ship had returned from escorting RMS *Queen Mary* on an Atlantic crossing, taking Churchill for a meeting with Roosevelt. *Devonshire* remained with the Home Fleet throughout the winter and served in the far north acting as escort for mine laying and shipping attacks, Operations Hardy and Lacerate. In February of 1945 she was off Scapa Flow when Harry had his first close call:

> It was while I was in the cooler for 14 days that I had my narrowest escape. I had not returned to my ship after a spot of leave. It was the first in 14 months – after spending most of the time in the waters around Iceland.
>
> The commanding officer didn't take too kindly to the fact that I had been AWOL. The excuse that I had been delayed by fog in travelling to Plymouth to catch the ship didn't go down too well. That's how I came to be in the cells when the ship was attacked by German aircraft off Scapa Flow.
>
> The first I knew of it was the vibration of exploding bombs. I had visions of going down with the ship. The door of the cell was kept ajar while at sea – it was held by a chain to prevent escapes. The gap was just three inches.
>
> The guard raced to his action station, but I beat him to the top of the gangway. Don't ask me how I got through that door. It's a mystery. I don't think the guard released the chain before leaving me. I am convinced I got through that three-inch gap.
>
> Impossible, I know – but when Corbett is in danger, then it is the time for miracles.
>
> Of course, I made no mention of my escapades to my mum. She thought I had won the war for Britain.[4]

On one occasion, a mine was spotted floating freely in the waters ahead. The captain ordered the ship to open fire. The 25mm Oerlikons were trained on the offending mine with no result. Right lads, let's bring out the 40mm anti-aircraft auto cannons (known as pom-poms for their distinctive sound), nope, nothing. Soon every man who could pull a trigger, from officers to cooks, was leaning over the rail armed with Brens, rifles and side arms trying to blow the damn thing up. None succeeded. As the mine bobbed serenely past without a scratch, you could have hit it with a lobbed boot.

Ah, a well-oiled machine at work. Harry would tell of another time when a friend was attending to the barrel of one of the main guns. The chap was sitting astride the end when action stations rang out. An enemy plane was buzzing them and the captain ordered the men to fire vertically at the plane – what goes up … The 8in guns were raised to their highest elevation. As the barrels went up Harry's mate clung on for dear life. He was thrown off as the guns recoiled, ears and nose streaming with blood from the force of the shockwave.

AfterVE Day the ship escorted the Norwegian royal family home. In 1940 *Devonshire* had evacuated them, allowing King Haakon to set up his exiled government in London. Now he requested she be the one to return them to Oslo.

To prepare for his arrival, members of his exiled government and the Norwegian heir to the throne, Crown Prince Olav, went on ahead – Operation Kingdom. *Devonshire* arrived in Oslo on 13 May to a rapturous welcome, enhanced by a party for 2,800 local children on board. This is what the local paper had to say:

> Norway's largest children's party on board the cruiser Devonshire yesterday. Huge crowds of boys and girls took the Devonshire by storm. They ate ice cream, chocolate, white bread and cakes. The warship was laid out as a children's paradise.

> Devonshire yesterday threw a children's party, an event which was greatly enjoyed and will never be forgotten by the young-sters of Oslo. The ship (Captain G.M.B Langley, OBE, RN) had invited the Oslo school children to a party on board.

> Devonshire, anchored in the main harbour, was besieged by the children. They arrived on board, a unique experience for them during the war, with the greatest expectancy. They were

living proofs of the friendship existing between Norway and Great Britain.

At 1400 the stream flowed up the ladder. Many of them had waited patiently at Honorbrygge for several hours. Their hopes were fully realised. It is not an exaggeration to say that the Devonshire was set out purely as a children's amusement park. Everything that could possibly gladden their little hearts was to be found on the upper deck.

There were seesaws and slides. At a 'Hoop-la' stall it was possible to win a bar of chocolate. Another popular feature was a real live Aunt Sally. Here a sailor, complete in clown's dress, poked his head from a series of holes, as balls were thrown at him. Everything possible in the way of games and amusements was to be found.

The whole ship's company made absolutely certain that this occasion would be as happy and enjoyable as possible. Officers and men took great care of the youngsters, particularly on the various slides. A small aircraft had been improvised and it was possible to fly from the highest point of the bridge along a wire to the forecastle. The youngsters under six years of age were not allowed to fly but they stood longingly and cast many admiring glances at the older children who enjoyed to the full this excellent air service.

The eldest guests were 12 years old, and as youngsters of a seafaring nation like the Norwegians they will never forget this occasion. Very soon after the first contingent had arrived on board, they were observed clambering high in the superstructure, a pastime which was universally enjoyed.

The ship's Royal Marine Band played on the quarterdeck. Many of the visiting 'young musicians' were eager to try the instruments and on one occasion a little girl actually conducted the band, most professionally, whilst seated on the shoulders of the Bandmaster. Of the other attractions, swinging round on the Oerlikon guns was very popular. Naval apparatus added a pleasing variety, such as the diving gear, where it was possible to talk to one another by telephone.

Everything was accessible because pleasing the children was the order and object of the day.

One of the members of the reception committee was the ship's padre, Reverend F.E.P.S. Langton, RNV. He had brought to Oslo a message from the Archbishop of Canterbury for Bishop Berggrav. This was handed personally to the Bishop of Oslo on the 17th and Bishop Berggrav had made a reply which was immediately sent back to England by radio.

It was long after tea before the children could tear themselves away from the cruiser. At teatime they had ice cream, tea and several large slices of bread and jam; and each was given a bar of chocolate before leaving. They were all overwhelmed. The scheme was a success from start to finish and it was a great joy for the older people to see the children happier than ever before in wartime.

Our sincerest thanks seem very small for this great festive occasion.[5]

A note on the chocolate bars -- it was the only way to get the kids off the ship. Party time was up and *Devonshire* was due to sail for Copenhagen in a couple of hours but no one was going. So the NAAFI manager announced that they would each get a bar of chocolate as they left. Apparently the *Devonshire* listed to port as the kids rushed to the gangplank to claim their prize.

It was all too much for one guest. After steaming away from Oslo, some way down the fjord, a small stowaway was discovered sleeping in a mess deck. After radio messages, a motor launch returned him, and no doubt his chocolate, to shore.

Captain Langley of the *Devonshire* relayed this message:

31st May 1945
From: HMS Devonshire
To: HM ships Apollo, Ariadne, Savage, Campbell, 40th M.S.F. and HMCS Iroquois, HMNS Arendal.

His Royal Highness Prince Olav has addressed me the following message:

'I should be grateful if you would be kind enough to convey to the Officers and Ships Company of all those of His Majesty's ships who took part in Operation Kingdom my warmest and most sincere thanks.
Our return to Norway was an occasion to which we had all looked forward for a long time, and of which we shall now

treasure the happiest memories of the efficient and successful
way in which it was carried out.

I am proud that a ship of the Royal Norwegian Navy was
selected to take part in the Operation and am most aware of the
close and friendly co-operation that has always existed with the
Royal Navy and which I am confident will long continue.

My best wishes to the future for you all,

Prince Olav'

In Oslo, the crew had been directed not to eat at cafes ashore – the
Norwegians didn't have enough to feed themselves – and definitely
not to sample the local drink Akevitt. Two crew members who didn't
heed the warning went on a bender with the locals, went blind and
were sent home. When *Devonshire* reached Copenhagen, guided in
by German minesweepers, she was the first Allied warship to berth
in the harbour since 1939. Grudging collaboration had ensured farm-
ing in Denmark had suffered little during the occupation: you could
order a full fry up not seen in the UK since before the war.

After leaving the city, the ship steamed to Rosyth to escort King
Haakon home – Operation Indestructible. It was escort and not
carry, despite His Majesty's request, as Vice Admiral Sir Rhoderick
McGrigor, KCB, DSC, Second in Command Home Fleet, insisted
the royal party should be aboard his flagship, HMS *Norfolk*. The king
returned to Oslo and the ecstatic crowds on 7 June, five years to the
day after he had left. This time *Devonshire* held a dance for teenagers
with the strict instructions that no young ladies were to be 'taken
below the Upper Deck'. Whether they were taken anywhere else ...

In 1947, the people of Oslo sent a Christmas tree to the people
of London as a token of friendship and gratitude. They have been
sending one annually ever since. The 70ft, 50-year-old Norwegian
spruce is placed in Trafalgar Square and is selected months, or even
years, in advance. The Norwegian foresters who care for the tree
call it 'the Queen of the forest'.

Returning the royal family had been a welcome interlude but
then it was back to business. Harry was set for the Pacific.

Bless 'em All, Bless 'em All, the long and the short and the tall
Bless all the sergeants and W. O. ones,
Bless all the corp'rals and their blinkin' sons,

'Cos we're saying goodbye to them all, as back to their billets
they crawl
You'll get no promotion this side of the ocean
So cheer up my lads, Bless 'em All.

Though I remember him teaching us a much 'bluer' version.

On the way out there was still time for silly buggers. While painting the ship, they would suspend a crewman over the side using a
boatswain's chair – a plank of wood with a rope round it. Instead of
securing the rope, the team of men slowly lowering the man down
would charge headlong at the gunwales, plummeting the luckless
rating and his paintbrush towards the foam below – the length of
the paint stripe dripping down the ship measuring the drop.

Devonshire had another chance to show her targeting skill
while racing to the Far East. Twenty-four hours after leaving Port
Tewfik, they discovered a small boat, as Bob Maxwell the 'bunting
tosser' recalls:

When we closed it turned out to be a dismasted dhow. Her crew,
5 men and a boy, were lined up on deck waving their gowns.

After stopping and lowering our sea boat to bring her alongside we learnt, by a dint, of Pidgin English, sign language and
the odd word of Arabic that the dhow had been sailing for Port
Sudan. Seven nights before she had been flung on her beam ends
in a sudden storm. The only way the crew had got her upright
was to sacrifice the mast. If there had been any cargo it had been
ditched. The dhow captain refused food and water and a spar
to replace her mast. The hull timbers were rotten he said and
they would be happy to take passage to Aden, our next port of
call, thank you very much. Our captain gave them permission
to come aboard and ordered our Executive Officer to sink the
dhow, as she would be a danger to navigation if left floating.

A burly leading seaman was lowered into the dhow and had a
large, sharp, damage control axe swung down to him. From the
after end of the bridge I watched him spit on his hands, grasp
the axe, swing it above his head and bring it down with all his
strength into the bottom timbers. A sound like a cathedral bell
rang out, the axe shot into the air as it jumped out of his paralysed fingers he crossed his arms put a hand under each armpit
and squeezed till his face went red.

The Executive officer leant over the guardrail demanding to know what was happening and was told in no uncertain terms that the timbers were not rotten but were made of tempered steel, or words to that effect.

By this time our Captain was getting fidgety because of his ship getting held up and ordered that the leading seaman be retrieved, the dhow cast off and the close range anti aircraft armament crews closed up so as to sink the dhow by gunfire. Getting underway we circled the dhow at slow speed and at a range of a thousand yards opened fire.

The air was filled with the solid thump, thump of the pom poms intermingled with the more staccato sound of the Oerlikons. The smell of cordite drifted across the bridge and our view of the dhow was obscured by the smoke of the guns and the curtain of water thrown up by the bullets and shells. When the smoke cleared away and the water subsided the dhow came into view, sitting there bobbing gently in the swell. Apart from a few sooty black marks on her side she appeared to be unscathed. The Gunnery Officer looking slightly askance and a bit down-cast before he ordered the guns to fire again. The guns opened up as before and after ceasing fire the dhow was still curtseying in the swell without any obvious signs of damage.

To say that our Captain was getting rather exasperated was putting it mildly. There was a war waiting for him a few thousand miles away and here he was getting held up with a stupid boat, which refused to sink. With a withering look and a rather sarcastic tone he ordered Gunnery Officer to secure the close range weapons and man the four inch guns while he opened the range to 3000 yards. Some minutes later with the ship stopped we fired off some twenty shells from the four starboard side four inch guns in the general direction of the dhow. As the fountains of water subsided it was obvious that the dhow had suffered some damage with holes in her side but she was still well afloat. By this time our Captain appeared to be doing an impersonation of Fred Astaire tap dancing on the bridge. The last straw was when the Major of Marines asked permission to engage the dhow with X turret's twin 8 inch guns.

'Secure all guns,' the Captain shouted, 'I'll ram her and be done with it.' The dhow had nearly disappeared over the horizon by the time we made a wide turn and headed back towards her. The

Devonshire started juddering, the boiler intake fans screaming at high pitch as the four propellers driven by 80,000-horse power built up speed to 25 knots. Our stem cut through the water like a sharp knife the bow waves curling over in white tipped crests before joining our broad frenzied foaming wake. I watched our Captain bending over the binnacle giving minute alterations of course as we rushed towards the dhow. She loomed up, growing rapidly larger and larger our jack staff centred dead amidships on her hull.

There was no sound as we struck. For a moment the dhow disappeared below our bows before reappearing, split in two, each half flung upwards, outwards and then astern by our bow wave.

From the after end of the bridge the two pieces remained in view in my binoculars as we sped on our way. The increasing distance tended to foreshorten my view of them and as they started to fade over the horizon it appeared visually as if they were joining together again.

As I strained my eyes for a last sighting it seemed strangely stirring that a centuries old design of boat, crafted by hand in wood with primitive tools had stood up to a steel riveted warship designed and built for death and destruction and, although broken, the dhow had certainly remained unbowed. I felt someone near me and looked up. It was my boss the Chief Yeoman of Signals. He lowered his telescope. 'I hope the Japs haven't got a lot of them,' he said, 'Or it's going to be a long bloody war.'[6]

Luckily for the ship, enemy planes were as good a shot. Harry remembered a time when a sea mist covered *Devonshire*. Only the top of the mast was visible, poking out of the fog. This meant that the enemy could see them, but they couldn't see the enemy. They could hear the droning of an enemy plane circling above, ears straining to catch first sound of the bombs as they screamed towards them. The plane didn't hit her once and they managed to arrive unscathed in the Far East.

'After jungle training in the UK, "I ask you, the UK for jungle training."' Harry remembered, 'I was due for demob, but they still sent me out here. I thought it was a bit of a liberty. By the time we got here the Pacific war was over and I saw what I'd fallen into.'[7]

Harry arrived in the Pacific just after VJ Day. But that didn't mean the fighting was over. It just meant you didn't get a medal for it. He was one of the many Allied troops involved in local fracas that mushroomed up all over the Far East in the autumn of 1945. The various empires were back to take control of their dominions, and after years of hard occupation the locals weren't having it. An example was that the British armed the former French POWs in Vietnam who were trying to regain control over Ho Chi Minh revolutionaries. When the French went on the rampage the Brits then rearmed the surrendered Japanese to help maintain order. It was much the same story in the Dutch East Indies, now Indonesia. It was a mess. Only a few weeks before, the Allies had been racing to free these people from the Japanese occupation. And there were still Japanese forces that hadn't heard of, or refused to believe, their surrender. During one of the many skirmishes that dotted the area – I believe it was New Guinea – Harry was fighting in the jungle. After trying to pick off the enemy with rifles it turned into hand-to-hand combat. He had to take care of two of them up close and personal – one with a bayonet and one with a commando knife – looking the guy in the eyes as they glazed over, knowing he was the last thing that poor little bastard saw.

He never told me about this; it's not the kind of thing to tell your little girl. He told my brother, once, and only after much prodding. He never spoke of it again.

That dreadful memory wasn't the only thing he got from the jungle. Due to personal experience he developed an admiration for the Ghurkhas that bordered on the religious. Many was the time, growing up, I heard their band music blaring out from the stereo, the LP fabulously entitled *Here Come The Ghurkhas*. The treatment of the Ghurkhas in recent years by the UK government would have seen him foaming at the mouth and camping out in Downing Street.

He also caught a large thorn in his eye, the red scar of which could easily be seen on screen in later years. He eventually had the scar removed. We all, kids included, went into his room after the op wearing eye patches shouting, 'Yar'. It didn't go down well. The last thing he got from the jungle was a horrendous infection, which meant that for the rest of his life he couldn't go for very long without a pee. Every time we went to the cinema he'd be off at least three times and would never take the star dressing room but the one closest to the loo. He used to say he gave his bladder for England.

At the end of 1945 Harry reached Sydney:

You see, I was from Manchester. I'd never seen a city with lights, a city lit up, until I hit Sydney. And shops with food in them. And an aeroplane over Bondi towing a sign that said 'I Like Aeroplane Jelly.'[8]

Navy men would stay at 'Johnny's', the Royal Naval House in Sydney:

They used to charge you a bob a bed, Double bunkers they were. You used to put a leg of the bed in each of your boots so some rotten cow couldn't nick them.[9]

It was a paradise and Harry loved it:

Luna Park, prawns out of a bag in the pubs, the lot. I remember the pubs in Australia, white tiles on the walls and a big bar in the middle. I got stoned on South African brandy. It was all we could get there during the war. They put ice in it because the weather was so hot. I stood up there drinking away, not feeling a thing, very bright – then I walked outside into that sunshine and pow! I've never drunk South African brandy since.[10]

He remembered the pies to be had at Harry's Café de Wheels on Woolloomooloo Docks. It is not only still there but is now on the Register of the National Trust of Australia and is quite the tourist attraction.

It couldn't last and it didn't. Harry was assigned to HMS *Euryalus* but:

the ship had orders to steam 2000 miles to Tonga. The idea was to install two saluting guns in a concrete base as a present to Queen Salote. It was the Navy's intention that Marine Corbett should be in the working party. I had visions of being left there and never heard of again. I knew my demob was near, but once on the ship, I'd be an old man before I saw Manchester again.[11]

Harry had had enough. It was months past VJ Day, hostilities were meant to be over, yet he had just returned from the horrors of the jungle. Then he received word that Annie, back in Manchester, was ill:

I could see myself faced with about two years in the Pacific. So
I went adrift and stood in the Domain waving as the ship left port.
You should have seen it – the troops dressing ship and the band
playing, and it was so close I could just see the Sergeant Major's
face. I don't know whether he could see me waving, but his face
was bright red. I don't suppose my old sergeant major has ever
forgiven me. If he reads this article I hereby apologise. Come to
think of it, he might still be on Tonga.[12]

Harry wasn't far wrong with his estimate. HMS *Euryalus* left
Sydney on 16 November 1945. She finally docked in the UK on
17 February 1947.

So Harry was on the run. He spent twenty exciting days fleec-
ing servicemen with 'find the lady' on Woolloomooloo Docks,
spending his nights in King's Cross, the red light district of Sydney.
I don't quite know what he got up to there, but I can guess. There
weren't many kids in 1980 who, when asking the question, 'What
did you do in the War, Daddy?' could have got such interesting
answers. But why exactly twenty days? Well …

Corbett knew his King's Regulations. If I was on the run for
21 days, I would be classed as a deserter. This offence carried a
punishment of six months or more. Up to the 21st day it was
simply a matter of being absent without leave, with a maximum
of ninety days detention. On the 20th day I gave myself up. (At
Darlinghurst Police station.) 'Here I am Sarge, lock me up. Royal
Marine deserter Corbett H.' 'Here we go,' said the sergeant,
'another bloody Pommy comedian.'[13]

Harry was sent to Warwick Farm detention camp:

It used to be a racecourse before it was a boob. They marched
us round with empty rifles, doing squats and they made us
splice lashings for hammocks. But they didn't know we loved it,
because the sun was great and we were Poms.

Mum was glad I was in no further danger and in the excitement of the moment showed the milkman a letter I had recently
sent her. The writing paper was headed 'Warwick Farm.' The
milkman read the letter and handed it back to Mum. He said, 'If
I were you, Ma, I'd send him a nice food parcel.' It was my luck

that he was an ex-serviceman and had heard of Warwick Farm. He knew I was not enjoying myself down on the farm – lapping up butter and eggs. I was up to my neck in trouble again.

I didn't bank on being in Warwick Farm for eight weeks while awaiting sentence. We lived practically on bread and water. So I mentally thanked the milkman when I received the food parcel from Mum. I eventually received 28 days' detention for jumping ship.[14]

When he got out of the 'boob' he was sent to Hong Kong where he joined HMS *Duke of York*. The ship steamed to Japan calling at Nagasaki, Kagoshima and Kure. When she arrived at Hiroshima, Harry and the rest of the crew were shown the devastation caused by the atom bomb. One can only imagine what effect this had on him.

When the ship docked again at Sydney:

There were quite a few servicemen hanging around Australia while waiting for their demob papers. Some of us joined forces to make a little pin money. We had a nice little racket, selling Japanese ceremonial swords to the Americans.

In the organisation there was a blacksmith – I never met him – who beat these swords out of the road springs of a jeep. I wonder how many Americans have, over their mantelpieces, 'genuine' Japanese swords made out of jeep springs.

It was my last adventure of the war. At 21 I was demobbed.[15]

It was possible to take your demob in Australia and settle there. Harry was sorely tempted. A Digger friend, whose family had a farm, offered him a job fruit picking in Griffith, 380 miles west of Sydney in the Riverina region, a great wine-growing district. But Annie needed him at home.

Harry finally made it back to Plymouth on 7 May 1946 (he had beaten the *Euryalus* by nine months). On 30 August he said good-bye to the marines:

I was as keen as most to get out of the old uniform after the war. Me as an Armed Force was a bit comical anyway. I think this was mutually appreciated and eventually the day dawned when it was all over. They pressed 60 'nicker' into my grubby hand and pushed me gently out into the real world again.[16]

Notes

1 *Ibid.*
2 *TV Times*, 29/12/66.
3 With kind permission of http://www.royalnavymemories.co.uk.
4 *Manchester Weekly News*, 25/3/67.
5 *Aftenpost*, 19/5/45.
6 With kind permission of http://www.royalnavymemories.co.uk.
7 Source unknown 13/9/72.
8 *Daily Mirror*, 8/9/72.
9 *Ibid.*
10 *Woman's Day*, 17/4/72.
11 *Manchester Weekly News*, 25/3/67.
12 *Manchester Weekly News*, 25/3/67.
13 *Ibid.*, and *Daily Mirror*, 8/9/72.
14 *Manchester Weekly News*, 25/3/67.
15 *Ibid.*
16 *TV Times*, 29/12/66.

I was given the job of drilling holes of about an inch in diameter in the pre-cast walls of new prefabs. The plumbing was then fed through to a tight fit.

I slogged away for hours. Surely there was a quicker way?

I found the answer. A few quick blows with a 14lb hammer did the trick. Wham! And a hole was made.

I felt very pleased with myself, but the foreman didn't share my sentiments. He howled with rage when he saw the jagged holes. I admit they weren't pretty – they were nearly four inches in diameter. I saw his point. The pipes would sag badly. I was given my marching orders.[6]

It's a shame the next foreman he worked for wasn't pre-warned of Harry's expertise. He was tasked with affixing drainpipes and guttering to the new houses. But screwing them all in individually was, yet again, far too slow a process. So he nailed them up. When the apoplectic foreman saw the now-useless guttering he screamed at him 'I'll see you never work in the building trade again!' Harry always said it was the emptiest threat he had ever heard. He never did get any better. After learning her lesson a couple of times, my mother later banned him from all forms of DIY. Harry subsequently wished that my brother, Jonathan, would grow up to be a plumber because he could 'never bloody get one'.

Back in 1947 Harry was looking for work again. He found it, and a home, at 47 Highfield Road (now Kingshill Road), Chorlton-cum-Hardy. Karen Harris remembers Harry's stay there. Her family had moved into the house in 1944. The building was originally a coach house, and at the side a drive led to a large yard with stables. These had been converted to garages and let out to various small car businesses by the owner, Eric Josephs. One of these was a car-spraying business – Harry was the junior partner and Karen's Uncle Sid the senior. They are still garages. In researching the building I contacted Joseph Siddal and Company, who had taken over from Eric Josephs. Joe told me: 'They look like the original building. They're not stables now but they look original – it's a bit like Steptoe's yard.' He said that before I mentioned Harry – you'd be amazed how often this happens.

In Harry's day, the house was converted into two flats. Karen's family lived downstairs and Uncle Sid and his wife Eileen lived upstairs, where Harry rented a room and had a brush with the occult as Karen describes:

Downstairs was a passage leading from the sitting room to the bedrooms and a walk in cupboard with a frosted glass window. I used to hate walking past the cupboard and that part of the passage – I always wanted to run past it because it scared me so much … [Harry] slept in the bedroom upstairs which was kind of directly over the scary place and the atmosphere up there was just as scary. Anyway [he] saw a figure/ghost in his bedroom and it really frightened him. My Mum once saw a woman in that bedroom too and I think that is why he didn't stay there too long. Mum and Eileen mentioned to Aunt Deborah (who grew up in that house) about the figure and she said she saw it all the time when she lived there and used to call it 'her white lady'.

This experience fostered in Harry a wary respect for all things occult. Even to the extent that while on a trip to the London Dungeon tourist attraction years later he patiently explained that my brother, Jon, and I should avoid walking over the witches' pentacle drawn on the floor. This, of course, is exactly what Jon immediately did. Fellow tourists were treated to the sight of a famous actor chasing his son as screams of 'Get off it, get off it!' echoed round the dungeon.

In 1947 events at the garage were to set Harry on that road to fame:

Eventually I became a partner in a two-man car-spraying business. I worked very hard at this, because I was the half-boss. There was only me and this other fellow and there was money in it. I sprayed and sprayed and sprayed. I sprayed when the dawn came up, when night fell – and when there wasn't a single car around – I still sprayed.[7]

I had to start at the bottom, and got the worst job of the lot – rubbing down paintwork with 'wet and dry' paper. In the winter it was murder. My fingers were blood red with the cold as I rubbed away at the old paint. I put my hands in so much water my thumbs must have swollen into the biggest in show business. I put them to good use in repertory – I could pencil more dialogue on my thumbnails than any other actor! I couldn't wait for lunch break to warm those mitts of mine. At the same time I'd entertain the other workers with imitations of Danny Kaye and Mickey Rooney, going into a routine that would have my audience in fits of laughter. 'You ought to take it up, Harry,' they chorused, showing their appreciation of the performance by slinging the odd nut and bolt at me.[8]

People kept telling me the Stage was all I was good for.[9]

The decision was made for me when the car business failed.[10]

From this developed my colourful language. Or at least my colourful language suddenly developed when the lease ran out. Like I said we were making a lot of money at the time.[11]

I was at a loose end again, and, at the age of 23, was nowhere near my childhood ambition of becoming an actor. The senior partner said, 'Why not try the local repertory company? They might have something for you.'

I went to the Chorlton Repertory, Manchester, and asked James Lovell, who was in charge of the company, whether he had a small part. I was staggered when he replied, 'Sure, we'll give you the leading part in our pantomime.' He wasn't kidding. It was the lead all right – the front legs of a cow. But who was I to turn down my first professional engagement at £2 a week? I was as nervous as a kitten when I arrived at the theatre on the first night. But as soon as I put the front legs on, I was a different man. I played the part of the cow like it had never been played before. I 'mooed' with a deep and rich voice, I rolled the eyes like a Don Juan, and waggled the ears in a most engaging manner. It was a command performance. Some actors might have been embarrassed by this part. I revelled in it. Others might have taken off the head of the cow in the seclusion of the dressing-room. Not I. I took the head off in full view of the audience. I wanted everyone to see who had given this marvellous performance. It paid off. I stayed with the Chorlton Repertory, and played all manner of parts.[12]

In Harry's not unconsidered opinion, this was to remain the finest portrayal of the character ever given … sadly, tipped for stardom as he was, he never appeared in the companion role of 'arse'. 'Oh, this was big time! Chorlton-cum-Hardy Repertory Theatre! Actors training ground extraordinaire.' he later said, 'This isn't meant to be a knock. It was really something for me.'[13]

After all, this was his big chance to follow his childhood dream. As he said 'the war did a hell of a lot for my generation. It threw us wide open and nothing was too good for us. We realised we didn't need a lot of the education and advantages which were taken for granted to get into the theatre.'[14] Besides, it was indoor work with no heavy lifting.

The Chorlton Repertory Theatre Club had been launched in 1946. According to the 'CRTC Souvenir 200th Production Volume':

> It all began when Arthur Spreckley and James Lovell decided to form a Repertory Company and chose Manchester as the venue. Much tramping of roads and expenditure of patience was experienced by the two determined pioneers before a hall was discovered. Weary, and possibly a little discouraged, after one of their many disappointing excursions, these two tired men halted for rest and refreshment at the Lloyd Hotel and on their emergence were confronted by the Public Hall! Their quest for a building was ended.

The building still stands opposite the Lloyds Hotel on Wilbraham Road. At the time it was home to the local Conservative Club. The theatre was upstairs; in recent years you could still see the stage, though it had been converted to table seating. The present ceiling hides the original vaulted one, the hidden apex of the wall still showing paint from productions long gone. I was told that: 'Behind the wallpaper on the back wall there's actually the original background. It's painted on. You can probably see it if you get up into the roof.' Today the building is a popular members social club; nice to know it's still packing 'em in.

Harry's first speaking role was as a Cockney detective in a play called *Black Limelight*. 'I couldn't manage the accent at all, I couldn't walk and speak at the same time. So I walked first and talked afterwards. The lines were written down in my policeman's notebook. Every theatrical copper does that.'[15]

He rapidly progressed to bigger and better parts, proving himself a popular and versatile member of the company, despite the fact that due to his car spraying days he was 'the only juvenile lead with arthritis'.[16]

Perhaps this helps to account for a review of George Bernard Shaw's *Arms and the Man* given by the company in 1949. According to the critic the character 'Saranoff should look like a dashing cavalry officer and behave like an adolescent' but 'Mr. Harry Corbett gives us a rather grubby Major Saranoff.'[17] Alas, it could have been a crushing moment for the young thespian. However, it started Harry on his path to enlightenment over reviews, good and bad – he didn't give a toss either way, it was bums on seats that counted.

It appears that the critic was a lone voice. J. Graven Hughes reported that: 'I was stage designer there when Harry began his acting career and what a marvellous asset he was to the company. He has the greatest and most natural sense of humour of any "pro" I have met and so often on dull rehearsal mornings he kept the cast in stitches with his stories.'[18]

Harry loved it, and why not, he was living his dream, even with, as it turns out, a lot of heavy lifting:

I became everything. I was a stage manager, I painted the scenery, I lit the stage and dressed the set. I also acted. Now it was a Conservative Club and we had the top floor. I had to carry huge flats, sofas and settees on my back up the fire escape, which gave me a constitution for life in the theatre. We would open with a new play every Monday, dress-rehearse it all day; then we'd do the show at night and so on every week. I would then start on Saturday night breaking the play up by eleven o'clock, work all through the night, putting the new set up for the next week's show; I then got about three hours' sleep. I turned in Sunday morning to light and dress the sets for the dress rehearsal, the following day carrying the things backward and forward. I ended up playing the lead, big huge fantastic leads, while doing all these things; it wasn't until some old actor stumbled over to me and said, 'Harry, you know you're a bit of a fool; when you are starring here you shouldn't be doing this, you know.' I hadn't thought about it. I just went to Jimmy [Lovell] and I said, 'Jimmy, he says I shouldn't be doing this.' He said, 'He's dead right.' So I stopped and just played lead parts from then on.[19]

But not all would remember Chorlton Rep so fondly. A young and green actress, whom Harry was to run into again down the road and come to adore, also got her first break at Chorlton. That bright and lovely star of the *Carry On* team, Joan Sims:

The rep routine went something like this. Wake up in the morning at about eight, swallow a quick breakfast, go off to the theatre,
spend the morning rehearsing the following week's play, short
break for lunch, then continue rehearsing, knock off at about four
or five, back to the digs for a quick meal, back to the theatre, into
costume and make-up, do the performance, finish at about half
past ten, out of costume, take off make-up, back into civvy clothes,
get back to digs and start learning more lines from the play you
were rehearsing that week. The rest of the day was your own.

    In theory you had Sunday off, but the great majority of actors
I knew in rep were so anxious at the thought of opening on
the Monday in the play they'd started rehearsing only the previous Monday that they'd spend all day Sunday swotting up their
part; for me, straight from RADA and its comparatively leisurely
schedules, this anxiety was compounded by the dreadful shock to
the system of the weekly treadmill.

    After a month in small roles with the Chorlton-cum-Hardy
players I was selected for my first leading part: the title role in a
play called 'Sarah Simple' … The cast of 'Sarah Simple' included
a young actor who would make it very big and whom I was to
encounter again in 'Carry on Screaming!' as well as in television
comedy. Like me, Harry H. Corbett was starting at the bottom
but fired with dreams of the top. I didn't get to know him very
well at Chorlton-cum-Hardy rep, not least because all the boys
had one dressing room and all the girls another, and there was
not the free-and-easy atmosphere which pervaded some theatrical companies.[20]

Joan didn't stay very long at Chorlton. After good notices and landing a lead part she felt that the other girls in the company, fuelled
by jealousy, were giving her the cold shoulder – moreover she was
homesick. Consumed by nerves of remembering the lines of *Sarah
Simple*, she turned to the wife of Arthur Spreckley, who ran the
company. Mrs Spreckley worked with her and Joan turned in a
word- perfect performance – it had, however, been all far too much:
'Five weeks after that I put the fleshpots of Chorlton-cum-Hardy
behind me. It took a little white lie to get me released – I told them
my mother was ill and needed me back home – but I knew that
I had to get back to Station House for some home comforts, and so
that's where I headed.'[21]

One girl in the company who did get to know Harry very
well was Avis Bunnage. Avis was born in Ardwick in 1923. Her
father was a dentist, though his passion was music and he would
travel far afield to play in bands. Her mother, a former Tiller girl
called Evaline Ward, who had appeared on the Variety circuit as
The Dainty Soubrette. Obviously it was in the blood and Avis had
joined Chorlton Rep in 1947. When Harry came along they hit
it off. They eventually started dating and Avis was a great success
when Harry took her home to meet the family. Cynthia, Harry's
niece, adored her: 'When they came round to the house, they
were always trying to get me dancing and singing with them in
the kitchen. They were always dancing and singing. She was lovely,
Avis … They borrowed Dad's tent once and went on holiday to
France. She bought an engagement ring; she kept trying to get him
to marry her. I thought she was wonderful but it mustn't have been
there, there must have been something missing.'

In May of 1950 Chorlton Theatre Club spread its wings and
staged *The Glass Menagerie* at the Library Theatre in Manchester
city centre. This was the big time. By March the following year
that elusive 'something missing' between Avis and Harry must have
finally been found, for in Chorlton Rep's weekly programme they
announced their engagement. Either that or, like the engagement
ring, Avis had taken matters into her own hands again. Can you
blame her? She was a nice girl, from a nice family, in the nice 1950s.

Whether Harry was settling down with Avis remained to be seen;
he was certainly getting restless at Chorlton Rep:

When you first become an actor you're thrilled that you're
on that stage, you're having a go at all the things you wanted
to have a go at, you're all the dreams you wanted to be, you're
really enjoying it. Then you suddenly discover that the audience
believes you. They believe you really feel the thing you're playing. You represent it. For example, I found myself at one period
in repertory playing a working-class man with red spotted hand-
kerchiefs, big old Bill moustaches, and all the maids had adenoids.
This was in that sophisticated kind of play with French windows, you know, and the fish tank down left, the tea and drinks
trolley over on the right. Then suddenly I realised that I was playing to people who were of the same origin as myself and that
they firmly believed that this was the way working-class people

should be portrayed on the stage, even though they themselves could see the evidence all around them that it was wrong and a lie. I wanted to get out of this completely.[22]

So did Jimmy Lovell, as Harry recalled:

the highlight of the year was doing two weeks in Platt Fields Park doing 'Arms and the Man' in the bloody blazing sun with the candles melting. Then we realised, James and I, that we wanted to do more. He had a mad idea, which at the time in my naïveté I thought might work, of going round the Music Halls doing excerpts from 'Shakespeare'. I wanted to do 'Shakespeare'; I'd never done it. You notice that even I, back in the old days, put 'Shakespeare' in inverted commas – in my life it always did and will always have inverted commas round it – We will do *'Shakespeare'* and he wanted to go round the Music Halls – and thank God we didn't![23]

In July 1951 a small innovative touring theatre company appeared at the Library Theatre with their production of *Uranium 235* by Ewan MacColl. The very next play at the Library was Chorlton Theatre Club's *The Rose Without a Thorn*, with Harry as Henry VIII. A letter in the Theatre Club's next programme, thanking club members for their support, crowed, 'We have, I feel sure, added to the company's prestige and judging by the many letters of appreciation, some from as far away as London, the fame of our little Company has crossed the borders of Chorlton.'

It had certainly crossed the borders of the *Uranium 235* company. One of their members, David Scase, appeared three weeks later as a guest artist at Chorlton. He and Harry got talking, and conversations on politics, the state of British theatre and its representation of the working classes followed. By now Harry was getting very tired of selling himself, and his audience, short:

I started to get nibbles from the West End. But this coincided with the beginnings of me saying: 'I'm sorry, I disagree with the load of rubbish I'm performing on this stage.' You begin to get a bit of a – not social conscience – a sense of power. Not that you influence people's lives or whatever – but you do to a certain extent make their thinking concrete. Our job is to get under the concrete, under the things that all people would like to agree on. Whereas the kind of plays I was doing were just confirming, confirming, confirming.[24]

Harry was persuaded by Scase to go and see the director of his touring company. This Harry duly did, and he followed directions to their mission control, 177a, Oxford Road, Manchester. This turned out to be rooms above a dubious second-hand car dealer, in a cheerless building off the main road.

Harry had found his way to the office, or rather digs, of Theatre Workshop.

Notes

1   *Ibid.*
2   *Television Today*, 5/1/66.
3   Burton, H., *Acting in the Sixties* (BBC, 1970).
4   *TV Times*, 29/12/66.
5   Harry, in conversation with Howard Goorney.
6   *Manchester Weekly News*, 25/3/67.
7   *TV Times*, 29/12/66.
8   *Manchester Weekly News*, 25/3/67.
9   *Manchester Evening News*, 25/9/65.
10 *Manchester Weekly News*, 25/3/67.
11 *TV Times*, 29/12/66.
12 *Manchester Weekly News*, 25/3/67.
13 *TV Times*, 29/12/66.
14 *The Age*, 4/7/72.
15 *Weekend News*, 12/8/72.
16 *Listener in TV*, 5/5/72.
17 *Manchester Guardian*, 19/7/49.
18 *TV Times*, 19/1/67.
19 Burton, *Acting in the Sixties*.
20 Sims, J., *High Spirits* (Partridge Press, 2000).
21 *Ibid.*
22 Burton, *Acting in the Sixties*.
23 Harry, in conversation with Howard Goorney.
24 Burton, *Acting in the Sixties*.

6

Come the Revolution

Then I joined Theatre Workshop – a group of actors who wanted to put on plays with a deeper meaning.

In joining, I took a pay cut. We could only afford to pay ourselves half a crown a day. But the experience was invaluable.

We toured the country, playing wherever was suitable, in an old barn, theatre or hall. Sometimes the stage was simply a few planks of wood.[1]

Harry H. Corbett

Theatre Workshop had started as a twinkle in the eye of Jimmy Miller. Born in Salford in 1915, he joined the Young Communists when he left school in 1929. He also joined the Clarion Players, one of the many socialist theatre groups springing up under the umbrella of the Workers' Theatre Movement, a cousin to all the national agit-prop theatrical movements worldwide.

But the Clarions were just preaching to the converted as far as Jimmy was concerned, so in order to take it to the people he set up the Red Megaphones in 1931, their slogan being 'A Propertyless Theatre for the Propertyless Class'.

They played open air to the striking cotton workers on the picket lines, Jimmy writing the scripts and songs. The shows were a touch amateur in comparison with European left-wing theatre groups. It was all content and no style, and Jimmy knew it.

To supplement his work with the Red Megaphones, Jimmy worked as an actor and folk singer on radio, and it was here he met a politically sympathetic young actress, Joan Littlewood. Joan had been born in London in 1914. She went to RADA at 16 but, despite winning awards, left early in reaction to the guff she felt was being fed to her. Planning to take a boat to America, so legend has it, she started hitch-hiking to Liverpool, made it as far as Manchester, where she joined a repertory theatre and started working on radio. Joan and Jimmy married, it appears mainly to keep Jimmy's mother happy, and together they reformed the group as the Theatre of Action in 1934. Its manifesto read:

> The commercial theatre is limited by its dependence upon a small section of society which neither desires, nor dares to face the urgent and vital problems of today. The theatre, if it is to live, must of necessity reflect the spirit of the age. This spirit is found in the social conflicts which dominate world history today – in the ranks of 3,000,000 unemployed, starving for bread, while wheat is burned for fuel.[2]

The goal was to create a theatre that reflected social issues and could translate those issues with poetic accessibility, using actors trained in movement, speech and song, enhanced by experimental techniques in stage design, lighting and sound. Despite fellow socialist activists telling them that they were wasting their time as 'art and politics don't mix' and that all that was important was the 'message', they concentrated on developing a better theatre.

This they did, achieving attention and good notices. Which got right up the nose of those members of the Communist Party who had looked down said nose on their efforts. With a well-deserved air of 'sod you then' the pair left Manchester, bound for Moscow to enrol at the Soviet Academy of Theatre and Cinema. Perhaps unsurprisingly, MI5 started to keep a file on the pair. They got as far as London where, whilst waiting for visas, they gave classes to would-be actors and added to their encyclopaedic knowledge of the history of theatre. Whilst still waiting they were asked to come back to Manchester and direct a play for the Peace Pledge Union, for a fee no less, and having met some of the others who were Moscow-bound decided to cancel the trip and head back north.

With new recruits that included Rosalie Williams, a university student interested in the theatre; Howard Goorney, a left-wing 17-year-old clerk, and his school friend Gerry Raffles, who came from a wealthy garment factory-owning family, they formed the company Theatre Union. They had successful tours of the north-east until war made continuing untenable. They agreed to meet up and carry on when the fighting was over.

By the time those that had survived the war met up again in 1945, Jimmy Miller had gone on the run from the army, evaded the police and MI5, grown a beard and changed his name to Ewan MacColl. Although his and Joan's romance had cooled, professionally they were as close as ever. They decided to call the reformed company Theatre Workshop and, joined a few weeks later by David Scase, who knew Joan from BBC radio, they picked up where they had left off. Over the next few years they grew in confidence, expertise and reputation, performing MacColl's startling plays for and to the working class. But as the working class don't pay very well they lived a hand to mouth existence, begging and blagging their way around the country. Interested by the work of Rudolf Laban, 'the father of modern dance', Joan wrote to him asking for a tutor. Laban's protégée, Jean Newlove, came to teach the company and stayed; in 1949 she married MacColl and soon gave birth to their son Hamish. Joan, by now, was with Gerry Raffles. John 'Camel' Bury and his wife Margaret joined, as did George Cooper and other actors tired of saying 'Anyone for Tennis?' or 'Lawks, Sir, 'ow you do carry on, an' no mistake.'

(If you would like further reading from this glib romp of the history of Theatre Workshop then see Howard Goorney's *The Theatre Workshop Story*, Ewan MacColl's *Journeyman* and Joan Littlewood's *Joan's Book*. These are personal recollections, making slight errors or omissions for the sake of tact – in Joan's case, her contemporaries tell me that she could never be accused of letting the truth get in the way of a good story. For the most widely held, accurate account see Robert Leach's excellent *Theatre Workshop: Joan Littlewood and the Making of Modern British Theatre*. Although written 'with the needs of theatre studies students in mind' don't let that put you off.)

On a tour of Wales, in 1951, Harry Greene found their performance so life changing that after a post-show conversation with Joan and Ewan, he chucked in his secure job as an art and drama teacher and followed the company to their base in Manchester where Harry arrived that winter day in 1951 fresh from Chorlton Rep.

Harry remembered:

We were doing a show that needed an outside artist, the outside artist was David Scase … and he said, at the end of this period,

'Well, I've seen you work, listened to you chat, you should work with Joan Littlewood.' And I said 'Oh yes, who the hell's Joan Littlewood?' He said, 'She's at Theatre Workshop. Why don't you go down and see her?'

At the time I did have a few testing enquiries from Tennent's, of all people, from London [H.M. Tennent's successful West End theatrical production company, headed by Hugh 'Binkie' Beaumont – said to have the power to make or break careers]. I'd got about a bit and you must realise the awful shock this was – a woman – unknown in the profession. To work with a woman was unbelievable. This was in the day when men spat when women drove past in sports cars, it was extremely rare, but men spat in the street and said it was all wrong, going against the ways of nature and things like that. To work with a woman was inconceivable. Anyway I went along to this place in Oxford Road, a very curious house; scrupulously clean in a dirty sort of way. A dirt that you cannot see, but aeons of dirt of people living there, of atmosphere, had left it looking superficially a slum – but it wasn't and all the people in it were scrupulously clean and they were actors and actresses.

It was very unfortunate, the meeting, in a sense, because I had just played the repertory actor in 'Monday Next' so I'd got a very cheap imitation camel hair coat for it. It was all I had in the world, this bloody camel hair coat. I had it belted and slung carelessly round my shoulders. I met Joan and burst out 'Are you a Communist?' And she said, 'Why, are you a fascist?' And I said, 'Not at the moment.' Anyway I stayed, got chatting, and she offered me Hal in 'Henry IV' – Prince Hal straight away, just like that. I mean no one in their right mind had ever offered me anything like that. I thought 'Well, yes!' Little did I realise that – and this was to last a whole lifetime – that there was also the gall to go with it which was Gogol's 'The Overcoat' [Harry later used to joke that he got Hal because Joan needed 'this bloody camel-hair coat' for the Gogol]. Life always seemed to be composed of that in the early days of Theatre Workshop. There was the nut and the sour outer kernel that had to be tackled first, which you usually agreed with and got on with and learnt a lot from.[3]

Harry Greene remembers that first meeting:

He had such a Manchester twang it was difficult for me as a
Welshman to understand him. The day that he came he enam-
oured himself to everybody, because he sat down cross legged
on the floor and told stories, stories about his travels, his time at
Chorlton cum Hardy. He could mimic, he had this brilliant gift,
like George Cooper, he could take a pencil or a walking stick
or a hat, using it as a prop and improvising. He sold himself to
us all, not least Joan, who invited him immediately to join and
he got up from sitting on the floor cross legged and said 'Oh,
I dunno about this,' he said something like 'you're a bunch of
scallywags, I don't know that I want to join you lot' and he
walked away and Joan was, of course, bemused and a bit angry
but he came next day, unannounced, he said 'All right, I'll give
it a try.'

Chorlton Rep's programme of 14 January 1952 broke the news of
his departure:

> I know you will be interested to hear that Harry Corbett has
> accepted an engagement with Theatre Workshops and will
> be touring the country playing in their productions of 'The
> Overcoat,' by Gogol and Shakespeare's 'Henry the Fourth.' He
> is just as sorry to leave us as we are to see him go but I know
> you will join with us in wishing him the best of luck. A warm
> welcome awaits him about the end of February when he hopes
> he will be joining us again.

Harry had given his last performance with Chorlton Rep on
11 January 1952, but he was already having second thoughts: 'Then
I found out we were going to tour all over the North East in
the middle of February – I suddenly started getting not terribly
thrilled about it. I'd hear tales like any recruit joining an army, tales
of what had happened in the past and what had not happened in
the past.'[4]

One of these tales was when the company had been playing in
Poole at Christmas, as Jean Newlove remembered:

> We were playing at some little theatre, or some place on the sea-
> front, which was wooden. And we noticed a few of the audience
> in the afternoon coming with blankets and hot water bottles.

And it didn't dawn on us 'til we got in there and had to change that it was absolutely freezing. There was a roaring sea outside you know, and oh gosh! And then in the evening there was just this one man who came. And Joan said 'Everybody's got to do their very best. He's come to see our show.' So we gave it our very best. And at the end, as the curtains went up he was so shy he ran out the theatre.[5]

When Harry joined them, they were as poor as ever. 'I had managed to save about £4.10s for a pair of snow boots, but we ate that in the first two days because all the actors were broke and I was the only one with money. I was God for two days; it was a splendid feeling. My first grasp of riches.'[6]

Which was as unfamiliar as his first grasp of the Gogol:

Well, the Gogol was the weirdest thing I'd ever done in my life, quite fascinating. The interesting thing for me was that I came to all this entirely as a virgin. I'd never even heard of Gogol and a thousand other things. One was continually having one's mind blasted wide open by these things without any preconception whatsoever.

Anyway, I did the Gogol – very beautiful music, atrocious dialogue – and I sprained my foot dancing about because there were huge cracks in the floor and I thought 'well, that's a perfect excuse to get out'. We were departing about half past seven one morning and I spent all night racked in pain thinking 'I've got to get out. I can't be doing with this Theatre Workshop'. I thought this is madness, it's not good at all, it's not funny at all because of things like – 'Well, we get half a crown a day for meals', all these horror stories, 'And we get hospitality.' 'Oh yes, what's that then?' 'Well we knock on doors and say will you take some actors in?' I thought 'Gawd Almighty, what are we in for?'

Anyway, a sort of inbred thing of 'the show must go on' prevailed and off I went with them.[7]

Avis came to see him off. As they left on the lorry, bound for a tour of the north east, Harry, nodding at her receding figure, turned to Joan and said, 'Bloody good artist, better than me.' Joan later wrote: 'Harry couldn't sit still on the journey. He was up and down like a jack in the box, abusing the driver, Gerry, issuing naval commands, singing:

Eileen – Oh me heart is growing grey
Ever since the day you wandered far away…
He kept us lively all the way to Eaglescliffe.[8]

They opened the tour at Loftus on 14 January. Harry was christened Harry C. to distinguish him from Harry G., Harry Greene.
They played the Gogol and *Henry IV*, where Harry had an opportunity to show he could already think on his feet, as remembered
by Harry G.:

> In the wings we were hard pressed to stifle our laughter as Harry
> C uttered the famous line 'and here draw I a sword' – sadly it
> remained wedged in it's damn scabbard! Then came a momen-
> tous and epic moment for us all, learning stagecraft from a gifted
> improviser. Harry C paused, looked around threateningly, as if to
> say 'make a move and I really will draw this sword'. Then, turning
> to Frank Elliott and holding out his hand, he said, 'Sire, nobody
> dares threaten me; your excellent sword', to which Frank drew
> his sword and tossed it to Harry who caught it proclaiming, 'two
> swords to defend myself'. Brilliant.

Harry G. also learnt early on that, for an inveterate scruff bag, Harry
could be, and always was, surprisingly squeamish:

> In January 1952 playing at Durham, George and I were staying in
> the house of a Mr Delicate, an undertaker. Harry C joined us for
> supper after the show. Left on the hob was a bowl of soup, bread
> on the scrubbed kitchen table with a jug of warm beer. Harry
> offered to ladle out the soup, shock horror; he almost screamed,
> 'It's bloody dog-hair soup'. Sure enough there floating in the
> grease, dog hairs. And there slumped and smelling, under the
> table, to add to the indignity, the farting, old, matt-haired overfed
> sheepdog. Harry C's last words as he raced out of the kitchen,
> 'never again and I hope the chippy is still open.' George and
> I didn't know that worse was to come – we actually slept in our
> macks in a damp bed next door to a rest-parlour with a full coffin.

They were playing the Gogol and *Henry IV* to miners, in miners'
welfare homes. They also took a group-devised piece, based on an
idea by Gerry Raffles, as Harry remembered:

We played this mining play 'The Long Shift'. John Bury had painted the set with real coal dust and it kept coming off. We had genuine miners' shorts, donated by the miners, and we took that all round the mining villages, on trestle tables mainly and it literally was 'If you don't help us shift the trestle tables – we can't do the next bit.' All the miners would immediately get up and oblige.

This went on, roaming around through three foot of snow, digging our way out of this, that and the other. There was a curious atmosphere all day, a monastic atmosphere. Joan was an abbess and ran her nunnery or convent on very strict lines, not lines of screaming or shouting, but lines of intellectual preciseness that defeated you – 'One should not waste one's energy chasing fripperies and get down to work, work, work, work, work.'[9]

They would arrive at the venue tired, numb from the cold and uncomfortable from the journey in the lorry. After cleaning the hall and stage if it had one (if not they would lash together the trestle tables) they would set up. The scenery, curtains, lighting rig, costumes: all of it was unloaded piece by piece from the lorry and carried in, often up and down flights of stairs. There were sound checks, lighting checks (the lights had apparently been pilfered from a crashed airplane full of stage equipment, discovered while walking on the Derbyshire Moors – it wasn't full for long). There were costumes to be ironed and props to lay out. After all this, they would sometimes rehearse if Joan felt it necessary, and she invariably did, but they would always have warm-up exercises. Then they would change into costume, their dressing rooms the freezing toilets of the hall. They were ready for their audience. As Harry said:

If it walked and talked, and would sit still for ten minutes we'd play to it[10] ... [We were playing] a mining documentary, of all things, to miners. This was a splendid thing to do, when we actually got there, because it was really testing to play a piece of what you thought was truth to people who experience it everyday. Now we didn't go in for the dramas, the huge coal fall and the hero hacking his way through for hours. We simply took a normal everyday fall in which two men were trapped for no more than two hours. But it contained the essence of the possibility of being trapped for longer. Marvellous things came out of it, like the release of their everyday tensions. Men started to behave like the human beings they are, in spite of the slavery of the coal-mine. Everything came out, the things they should have done, and if they had a chance would do. It wasn't as dramatic a set-up as if they were going to die; but they felt that when once they got out never again would they get stuck in that situation.[11]

After the performance and after the de-rig, carrying each piece back to the lorry after the notes from Joan, they would get their heads down. Often sleeping in their clothes on the freezing floor of the hall or on the trestle tables that had served as a stage, unless they were lucky enough to have been put up for the night. As Harry explained:

One of us, Margaret Bury or somebody like that, would forward the week before – everybody took it in turns – and would con people into putting us up for the week. The people were waiting, loving to have us there on this kind of hospitality basis. We were actually living with the audience who had seen our play. It was extraordinary the amount of desire they themselves had to write, perform, and be part of this drama. It shook me rigid at the time; of course, it was all the anger of the thirties coming out, I suppose. They were marvellous experiences – marvellous people. And my God, honest isn't the word … In one village we stopped the tram. They had one tram coming up the hill – and somehow or other there was confusion at the time, and someone, who shall be nameless, plugged into the main power source through the window and the tram came to a grinding halt. So they had to make up their minds whether they had light in our show or a tram service going up and down the hill.[12]

Although Harry didn't name the culprit, my money's on George Cooper who by his own admission acted as John Bury's lighting assistant and 'was like the kiss of death to anything electrical or mechanical!'[13]

Why did they put up with it all? Harry remembered why he was originally attracted to the group:

The fire was in the pure socialist attitude of everybody concerned. Now the euphoria that came from the ending of the war, combined with the returning soldiers; which must have been similar to the 1918 thing of 'a world fit for heroes to live in'; was very great with everybody in every walk of life – it didn't matter what political persuasion you were, basically they still subscribed to this feeling, things must be better.[14]

Harry Greene felt:

we were truly a group theatre. Every one helped each other. You know, if you were down you were helped to raise your spirits. And then of course in every town we were acclaimed, so that lifted our spirits as well. And we truly believed that one day we'd live and work together, without all this suffering and struggling. So on we went despite my misgivings.[15]

And they truly believed in their manifesto, which read:

What we are living and going through hell for is great theatre, and such things are never, ever borne easily. Compromise is no way out. We must do great plays, even though people would say it's impossible to exist in this society without compromise. Now at the moment they appear to be right. But we, as a team, shall become stronger. The great theatres have always been popular theatres, which reflect the dreams and struggles of the people. Theatre Workshop is an organisation of artists, technicians, and actors who are experimenting in stagecraft. Its purpose is to create a flexible theatre art, as swift moving, and as plastic as the cinema.

And they were young – and as such had all the ideals, ambitions and convictions that are natural to the young. Yes, they could have been better off financially elsewhere with a potentially more promising future. Jean Newlove tells:

I had dance scholarships that would have taken me elsewhere. Joan had the RADA scholarship, which she dropped out of. Ewan was offered a scholarship to go to Milan, or somewhere, to learn opera. And I refused mine, he refused his, Joan dropped out of hers and we all came together. It was almost as though it was meant to be, it seemed very extraordinary.

Harry had already turned down offers from the West End – for him and the others it was worth it. He had found what he was looking for and joined in with gusto, as told by Jean:

> Howard [Goorney] was a stalwart of Theatre Workshop and Harry, although he joined late, was also a stalwart. Both of them I admired tremendously for their talent and for their … one can't say common sense, I don't think either of them had common sense cause otherwise they wouldn't have been there. But they followed the manifesto and the ideals that we had.

They ended the tour mid-February, and then it was back to Manchester and a reunion with Avis, who was persuaded to join the merry band.

Harry returned to Wythenshawe and Annie, and he took with him fellow actress Barbara Young. Barbara was very young indeed when she joined Theatre Workshop. At 16 she had been recommended to Joan by one of her theatre school teachers, Rudolph Laban.

Barbara had been lodging with a male company member who was Russian and apparently quite barking. Joan and Gerry had decided that due to her tender years, she needed to be under the wing of someone more suitable and Harry got the job. She moved into Annie and Harry's house in Moat Road, as she recalls:

> I stayed there for about three or four months, because I didn't have anywhere to live. I was only about 17. The thing I remember most about Harry, apart from the fact he was a wonderful actor and made me laugh a lot, was that he used to love Wild West stories. And he used to come and sit on the end of my bed and read me a chapter or two every night. I mean, it was extraordinary and I knew Zane Grey, all those people that I'd only ever heard of – he used to read them all. And he was very entertaining. There was nothing more untoward in it than that.
>
> At that time he and Avis came in as a sort of engaged couple but Harry was always a very good actor, you know. He came in with that, he brought it with him and I remember we did 'The Overcoat', the Gogol, and I played his wife and, although I say it myself, I brought my own thing with me as well, and I think we recognised it in each other and I always used to feel at home with him – because he could act like I could.

The only thing Barbara remembered about Annie was 'the fact that she always wore a pinny'. Barbara had quite a steep learning curve with Joan and the company; she recounts her reception:

> I remember arriving in a rather nice coat that my mother had bought me and I remember the first thing Joan said was 'Well, you won't need that – that'll go into the wardrobe.' And she took my coat and the last time I saw it, it was on her back when she went off to do an interview in Edinburgh about something. And I remember thinking at the time, that's not right. 'That's very bourgeois, that coat', she said, and I thought it's only a coat but it's not bourgeois on her back.

The incident led to a questioning spirit that was not very well received, as Barbara tells, 'I remember her marching me up and down some street and saying "You're not fit to belong to a Workers' Theatre" and I was saying, "I don't want to belong to a Workers' Theatre, I just want to belong to a theatre" and I got a terrible telling off for that.'

Back in Manchester, the company had hired a basement in Lower Mosely Street to rehearse for their next booking at St Andrew's Halls, Glasgow. The play they would be taking was MacColl's *Uranium 235*.

Harry described the play as:

> a terribly serious piece of work, beautifully done by Joan, about the atom bomb. It was interesting because we researched it. Now there's two ways of doing this. Firstly there would be the normal, shall we say West End way, as it was then, the scientist living in a nice bungalow with stained glass, a wife or daughter problem possibly, and he's trying to resolve all the way through the play, should he work on the atom bomb or should he not work on the atom bomb. Our point was that science was there to be used; this was in the terribly early days, remember, it came as such a shock that science suddenly flung itself into the forefront of everybody's thinking, but it was not going to be resolved theatrically or dramatically in the way I've described. The way to get through was that science was our servant, so we decided to do, for want of a better term, a montage of the history of the atom right up from the early days of the Greeks.

It was a documentary play:

> Which necessitated the play being split up into little sequences, using song, dance, any technique we could possibly lay our hands on. We opened at a miner's gala somewhere, and it was rather curious because we kept getting terrific rounds of applause and laughs at the end of every terrible scene, although they were beautifully quiet during the playing of it. I understood afterwards that for the first half they were under the impression that this was the latest sophisticated review, from the West End. It was actually billed as such: we had to use all this kind of con.[16]

> We were always up against this. We were never received everywhere with open thirsting artistic souls who were being denied what they wanted. We were more or less thrusting it at them and 'it was good for them.' I don't want to undermine the miners because they're an intelligent group of people, fabulous group of people. I remember when a chap died in the pit, and they closed it and cancelled the show. We got our £25 guarantee, and that was desperately necessary for us to function, even for petrol – they paid us.[17]

If, in the beginning, Harry had been dubious about his future with Theatre Workshop, *Uranium 235* changed his mind. 'For the first time, without knowing it, I began to realise what "epic theatre" meant. I'd heard the phrase bandied about all over the place. It was the first time I realised what it meant to be in "epic theatre" and I realised that was *my* kind of theatre. I loved the big sweep.'[18]

This was the play that had made Harry Greene give up the day job. He tells of seeing it for the first time:

> It was all played in black drapes – velvets – so that the light was absorbed. And John Bury, an extremely clever lighting technician – even then in those days; the late forties, early fifties – he would create a scene, not with props, not with staging of furniture and so on, but with lighting. There was no furniture, only props that … each of the actors brought on. And this … all of this, of course, thrilled me. I'd been brought up with a straight set, painted or wallpapered. And we the audience were the fourth wall of the room – dull. When I saw that first of all, I said to myself 'what I've been looking at is dull and boring. This company has got

something, and the first thing they've got is a method, a technique of holding an audience immediately that the curtain went up'. Because this was different, totally different, and for me as a designer, illustrator, painter, what I saw then was something that excited me beyond measure. And then the actors. They came on, they were living, breathing [people]. You saw actors playing different parts … they would dash off and change a costume. But each part, each character, was a living person. George Cooper became the businessman. And George is a working class lad, was then. And yet here was a Manchester businessman. Everything from the tilt of the head, to the doff of the top hat, to the spats and the flick of the tailcoat. I'd not seen [anything like] this.[19]

The lighting made it a technically difficult piece; you had to hit the spot where the pre-arranged lights would come up. Not easy when the actors were scrabbling in the wings during the dozens of costume changes the play required. There was no time for mistakes, as George Cooper had learnt on a previous tour of Sweden:

We were doing the Scandinavian tour in 1951 of 'Uranium 235'. We were all playing between 10 and 12 parts so very quick changes, so you always had your costume all laid out ready for getting into it and we came up to the last scene where we were all scientists by that time and we just had long white coats on and trousers. The previous scene finished, we all shot off and a character we had with us at that time, Johnny Armitage, dashed off to where his trousers were and a large Swedish stagehand had decided to have a nap on top of his trousers, which were on top of the piano. We whipped back onto the stage and suddenly realised that four of us had trousers underneath our white coats but Johnny had not. The thing that really tickles me is that I bet there were Swedes there who said, 'I bet there's something very symbolic about that.'

A past performance had also nudged Barbara Young further along her learning curve, though not quite for the reasons Joan intended, as Barbara tells:

I can remember when we were in Tonypandy, or somewhere round the Welsh valleys, touring and I'd broken my ankle and

I was on a plaster cast and a stick and I couldn't do any of my parts in 'Johnny Noble' or 'Uranium' and I had to sit at the back and take the tickets and I had the extraordinary experience at the age of 17 or 18 of watching Joan do my part, and she was diabolical. And it was a wonderful experience for me, cause it suddenly made me realise that you can talk all you like and you can be perfectly good at directing but you needn't necessarily be able to do it. But she always thought you could, you see, she always wanted the last word on stage. It was her thumb that she wanted on it, naturally, but people like Harry, and hopefully me, didn't quite let her get her thumb there.

Whatever was going on onstage, for the audience the play was ahead of its time. The bomb had only been dropped a few years before and the world was still trying to wake up to the idea of what it meant to be living in the nuclear age. Harry, having seen first hand the effects of the bomb on Hiroshima, would have been better informed than most, but even he admitted:

I was in complete ignorance of the Atom Bomb until I joined Theatre Workshop. Then one realised what the future actually held. Very few people, I think, were conscious of what horrors could be unleashed. Now, unfortunately, we've got used to it but then it was really a shock. The newspapers used to draw concentric circles around various bits of Manchester saying, 'Wythenshawe's gone – watch out for Blakely! If you're living near Hyde, you might just miss it.'[20]

Back in the dingy basement in Manchester rehearsals were underway when the company had a visitor. Sam Wanamaker was an American actor working successfully in Britain, having been blacklisted by the House Committee on Un-American Activities (often referred to as the 'McCarthy witch hunts'). He was touring in a play and asked to return the next day with his leading man, Michael Redgrave, as Ewan MacColl remembered:

The rehearsal was in progress when they arrived, and they sat huddled in their overcoats for the next two hours trying to ignore the cold and the damp running down the walls. Like almost all our rehearsal rooms, it was a cheerless, miserable place with the kind of lighting that gave you the feeling that fog had crept under the door and was slowly filling the room. A stage area had been chalked out on the floor and we were wearing our ordinary working clothes (our only clothes, for most of us). None of these things appeared to worry our visitors. They sat for the entire rehearsal without once uttering a word, their whole attention centred on that chalked-out space.[21]

Captivated, Wanamaker and Redgrave declared they must have a showing in London; as they left, with their praise still ringing in the company's ears, they promised to see to it personally. The possibilities of 'big breaks' had been offered before: only time would tell. They could do with a break. The only way they had managed to eke it out this long, according to Barbara Young, was by the good graces of Gerry's family:

The Raffles had a garment factory. They made raincoats and things like that, and in fact we used to say that Joan was the only one who'd had a bath because she could go to the Raffles' house in Manchester and have wonderful hot water. It was because of Gerry that Theatre Workshop ever kept going in the beginning. I think he bought all the black curtains that we used to unpack every night when we were doing one night stands.

In the meantime it was off to tour Scotland and do the gig at St Andrew's Halls. Chorlton Rep diligently reporting in their programme of 10 March that 'Miss Avis Bunnage has joined Theatre Workshops for their Scottish tour of "Uranium 235." We shall miss her but our loss is only temporary, as she will be returning to us in about seven weeks time. Good luck Avis – we shall be pleased to have you back again.' As Avis climbed aboard their clapped-out vehicle for the first time she must have known they would need luck just to get north of the border.

Oh yes, the lorry – this pantechnicon, unholy offspring of furniture van and ex-GPO lorry, has remained vivid in the memories of all who sailed in her. This was a second home to the actors that travelled so many miles in the back, singing as they went. Of course, Ewan MacColl 'with his right hand cupped round his ear, head tilted'[22] led them in song. When it came to music Ewan always ran a tight ship, as Barbara Young had learnt, 'I think I very nearly got expelled from the back of the lorry for doing a jazzed up version of Frankie and Johnny, which I didn't realise you weren't quite allowed to do – it had to be pure folk music.'[23]

Jean Newlove remembers an occasion when she was on board:

> this bloody awful lorry. I was at the back with Hamish. Harry was leaning over the back and there was a young couple in a very posh sports car behind us trying to pass us and Gerry – whether he was being bloody minded or not – wouldn't let it pass. They were dodgy roads and this young man was getting very cross and Harry was looking over at him and I remember him saying something like 'Did you get that with Typhoo?' In those days Typhoo tea had coupons and you could get all sorts of things – but you couldn't get a sports car.

It wasn't all jolly jokes and singalongs, as Harry remembered:

> Belting along the road in this thing, squashed in amongst bits of scenery, Joan was striking matches and reading, giving notes at 12 o'clock in the bloody morning. This was a regular occurrence. One still felt the same guilt, if not more so, if one wasn't passionate about being given these notes. The standard answer was 'Yes, Joan, definitely'. I don't think this ever registered, because she never paused while going through the notes, which were copious and good and to the point.[24]

On the occasion of the lorry's most famous incident Joan wasn't with the company. According to her book, she had travelled up to Scotland, surprised that Harry Greene was at the wheel. Before they left, Gerry had sought a replacement driver in Harry G. (he went on a crash course in the lorry with Gerry round the twisting back streets of Manchester for two days before taking, and passing, the test – what a guy).

On arrival in Glasgow, Joan wrote that she was handed a telegram, 'Gerry was in hospital. I took the first train south, leaving Jimmie [Ewan MacColl] and Howard in command. Gerry had been operated on for a torn bowel. How long had he been in pain, without saying a word to anyone?'[25]

Harry G., however, remembers:

She and Gerry were the only members not on that tour. We were led to believe that Gerry was ill and in need of an operation, but doubts were cast when Frank [Elliot] in his inimitable Yorkshire comic voice said, 'Ee, they're off on bloody holiday leaving us to carry t'can up north'. Then after a week of phone calls trying to make contact, Frank again 'Try t'best hotel in Cannes, bet they're sunning themselves in the south of France.' Funny that because later on it transpired that they had the use of a boat in Cannes. And nobody was ever given information about a hospital, his professed operation or recovery. We were almost made to feel that it was intrusive to ask questions!

So the company set out for Glasgow with Harry G. at the wheel:

I knew then what I was in for when we started the tour. But on arrival at Glasgow I got a bit of a shock. George and I were going to be staying with Norman Buchan, the MP, and he had a message from Gerry. Gerry had forgotten to tell me that the push-and-pull rod – that's the column, the driving column, with a ball and socket joint at the end that moves the front wheel, to guide the lorry, or any vehicle – he told Norman to tell me that I ought to get the push-and-pull rod repaired. He also told Norman that it wasn't serious. But that damned rod held the steering together.

What with giving driving lessons while dealing with a 'torn bowel' or arranging travel plans, Gerry hadn't had time to fix the steering and unfortunately he had underestimated the problem:

It was deadly serious. So after unloading at the miner's hall in Stoneyburn, I was driving everybody, everybody in the back of an empty lorry, I was driving them down for fish and chips down to Bathgate. And this Bathgate was on the main Edinburgh–Glasgow highway. On that road, it failed. So I lost control of the lorry. I had no power over the steering.[26]

With the steering wheel spinning uselessly in Harry G.'s hands he turned to Frank Elliot, who was in the front with him, gestured at the wheel and said to him:

'Do you want this?' He took one look and shouted at the top of his voice 'My God, what's happening?'

Well it was terrifying, but it's strange how calmness takes over one … in an instant I saw these great iron railings and the embankment. Forty feet down was the main Glasgow–Edinburgh railway. I put my foot onto the brake, I eased down and drew the lorry very, very gently over on to the pavement. Now, those said iron railings, to my left, separated us from the embankment and the main line. From forty miles an hour, to the front wheels hanging over the railway line took seconds. Those railings certainly prevented the demise of the Theatre Workshop Company.[27]

If we'd had all our stuff on the back, six or seven tons of it, and those railings had not been quite so strong, we would have been right over the edge.[28]

Harry had grazes and bruises, Howard had, I think it was a broken wrist or a broken finger, something like that. Barbara Young had bad grazing to her forehead, and so on. Oh yes, everybody was hurt except Frank Elliot, who was sitting beside me, and I who was driving.

They all sat near the tail of the lorry when travelling and sang, Ewan MacColl was singing, he was badly bruised. Of course, stopping abruptly, they were all thrown to the front of the truck.

The lorry was beached on the railings, front wheels spinning uselessly over the drop. After having raced round to the back to help the others out, Frank Elliot leaned on the railings and screamed out: '"There's the train we would have been under" as an express thundered by a minute and a half later.'[29]

'Crash course' had proved prophetic. Thankfully Jean Newlove and her baby, Hamish, were not on board. Though they had their own close call, as Jean explains:

I had another experience in the lorry, I had come back home to Manchester and Hamish was in a pram and I couldn't get to Ewan's mother, who lived up a hill in Hyde in Cheshire. Gerry gave me a lift, but he didn't put the pram in the back and Hamish and me in the front – he puts us all in the back amongst the props, boxes and a huge wardrobe. Of course, going up the bloody hills the stuff starts to move towards me. I had to fix the pram so it didn't move and then hang onto the wardrobe to stop it crashing down on Hamish. Gerry couldn't hear me shouting or anything – he was a bit daft.

Back at the railway line, after nearly plunging to their doom, the company dusted themselves down, and in a few moments had gone from berating Joan and Gerry for sending them out in such a death trap to joking that it had all been a plot to drum up publicity – well maybe – no, I'm sure they were joking.

As Harry G. says:

> Well it was a company built on enterprise everyone was stoic. You know all behaved stoically. We got the lorry repaired and then we continued on the tour. But then the most dire thing of course, we got snow. Yes, black ice on the roads, cold digs, freezing church halls and as all miners' smoked, so we got smoky miners' institutes.[30]

The company were well received at St Andrew's Hall in March and continued to have a successful tour, as is borne out by good old Chorlton Rep who printed in their programme of 21 April:

> In response to the many enquiries as to the welfare of Harry Corbett and Avis Bunnage, I am pleased to say that I had a letter from them about a week ago and all seems to be going well. The Scottish tour of 'Uranium 235,' in which Harry is playing the lead, is gaining a great reception wherever it goes. Avis and Harry have asked me to give their kind regards and best wishes to their many friends in Chorlton and are looking forward to meeting us again about the middle of May.

That letter must have had Avis' fingerprints all over it.

She hadn't mentioned the time Harry got some rather exciting 'hospitality' digs, as he later recalled, 'I remember being put in some Glasgow tenement slum and we all had some tea. The lady was there with all her children. Then the husband came in and said, "Who the fucking hell's this? What the fuck are you doing?" – Hours and hours it took to convince him, I had to sit in fear all bloody night.'[31]

She also hadn't mentioned the lorry. It managed to limp through the rest of the tour, but only just. As they were finishing, a passing policewoman condemned the crumpled beast. She agreed the troupe could take it back to Manchester and repair it there. They got as far as Shap Fell, a high, exposed and treacherous stretch on the main road, as it was then, in and out of Scotland.

Avis remembered:

> a lorry driver behind us kept flashing his lights. We were all sitting in the back with the props, and waved cheerfully at him. He finally got through that something was wrong, but it took ages before Harry [Greene], in the cabin, heard us shouting. Finally, he stopped, and we found the wheel was coming off.[32]

The rest of the journey stayed with Harry for a long time:

> Fortunately, four of us got a lift to Manchester on the back of another lorry. The leading lady rode in the cabin – but three of us were stretched out flat on top of the lorry's cargo. It was hair-raising. We lay face down on the tarpaulin – our hands aching with the strain of hanging on to the ropes. Our pantechnicon eventually caught up with us in Manchester. A mechanic from a garage had put the wheel back on. I heard he was shocked by the bad state of repair. He would only accept responsibility for the rear wheel – not for any other part of the van.[33]

Welcome news awaited them in Manchester: Wanamaker and Redgrave had come through. The London run was on.

The company opened *Uranium 235* at the Embassy Theatre in Swiss Cottage on 12 May 1952. Michael Redgrave had written in a publicity leaflet:

> Several weeks ago I saw Theatre Workshop actors rehearsing in a cold, bare basement in Manchester. There were no lights, no costumes, none of the trappings of a complete performance. But those of us who saw that rehearsal were spellbound, and are still under that spell. Others had attempted to compound drama and ballet, verse and mime, burlesque, revue, satire and song, but this seems to me to achieve a synthesis, and one that is moving and exciting. The organisers and actors of the Theatre Workshop are not offering some high flown idea which has been cooked up overnight. They attempt to rediscover what is the essence of drama and theatre, and have rigorously trained themselves for over seven years, to express it. In any case the result is unique in

this country, and I think without parallel elsewhere. There is no knowing what they may not achieve in years to come.

Let us support them now.[34]

Critical reviews ranged from *The Times* – 'A model of what a theatre group should be' – to the distinguished critic Kenneth Tynan writing that the actors were 'in chains'. On the Saturday they gave a special performance for the profession: actors, directors, etc. They went down a storm. On the strength of this warm reception and hoping this would be the big break they had dreamed of, the applause and flowers to be followed by funding at long last, Gerry Raffles got them a transfer to the Comedy Theatre in the West End – where they died on their arse. It was June, not the best time to attract an audience, especially to something regarded as 'avant-garde'.

The support naturally dwindled. Well, they had tried. So the company found itself on its uppers again. They were due to go to the Edinburgh Festival in August and needed cash to get there.

They would have to get money any way they could. As George Cooper tells: 'I know Harry and George Luscombe were very good workers in doing various jobs – they went to France and were putting corks in bottles and all sorts of things and they actually both of them started eating raw garlic.' Substantial help came from a great supporter of Theatre Workshop for many years, the MP and future Chairman of the Labour Party, Tom Driberg, of whom Churchill had said: 'Tom Driberg was the sort of man who gives sodomy a bad name.'[35] Driberg allowed them to pitch tents in the grounds of his house in Essex, using the barn for rehearsals of *The Travellers*, the play they were taking north. Harry went ahead of the rest to try and find the company work:

> I turned up at Tom Driberg's place in the country, we were all supposed to rendezvous there with tents. Hadn't got any money, and the rest of them would be drifting in. In the meantime I got a job on a farm for a pound a week. It was the most astonishing experience of my life. I went into the Labour Exchange and there was one long counter separated by a door. I went to the man and he said, 'Where's your cards?' – 'I haven't got cards.' – 'Ah, haven't got cards. I haven't got anything for you.' – 'Oh well, that's that then.'

But then he said, 'Hang on a minute, I can get you Public Assistance. You have to go through that door there into the other room.' I walked into the other room and he walks round the counter and says, 'Now, what's the problem?' That's the God's honest truth. He says, 'Now then, have you applied for work?' – 'Yes, I've just seen you next door.' – 'I see, you've applied for work. Yes, yes, I see. Well, I can give you a Pound. Now, if you'll come through there.' So I follow him back through and he says, 'Are you interested in any kind of farm work?' and I say 'Yes, Anything!' So they put me down on the farm and my first job was cutting. I learnt to scythe nettles, to start, for silage. Then they put me in a field stooking. They'd get lots of corn together and bash it into little heaps. You learnt something all the time. There was a marvellous old fellow who used to say, 'Look out for the farmer coming!' They never used to work unless they got forced into it. Not really 'sons of the toil', it was just the same as working in a factory.

I started contracting fields from farmers for stooking. I'd all the cheap labour in the world. I got a thirty-acre field, a twenty-acre field and everybody was down stooking for hours. I had vicious God damn arguments with Joan – 'You can't have him for rehearsals, I need him for stooking.' So all those years of 'forward with the new society where we all share' disappeared into immediate private enterprise, which was always the nut of the problem. How do we get to Edinburgh? How do we get the fare? How do we get the money? We have to get it from some other way than a sort of communal effort. It doesn't work this community brotherly love. Money will get us from here to bloody Edinburgh, and it literally got to that state where I had terrible arguments with her.[36]

From the West End to farm labouring overnight. There's no business like show business.

Thoughts of all those beautiful young actors camping like fairies at the bottom of his garden was too much for Tom Driberg, as Harry G. recalls:

He was our great benefactor, we lived in tents on his lawns, were fed in the great barn by his cook and his delectable wife (of convenience) dear Ena. We had known Tom from the early

50's. We had really got on well whilst receiving Tom's hospitality at his home. He was a lovable rogue, a roué and a lecherous dandy given to slyly trying it on with every male in the company. However, he was a gentleman as far as the pursuit was concerned and smiled at every rejection. Often there was a caressing hand on my neck as I worked on a design on my drawing board. A sharp 'sod off' had him recoiling. But he only sidled up to Harry C once, just once, which was more than enough! Harry C rose from bending over a sack of potatoes in the barn and for a moment became a betrayed Richard. Tom was physically shaken by Harry C's remarkable performance. Controlled and well aimed staccato, bullet-like anger-laden words, lasting only 30 seconds but shook poor Tom's confidence, which was noteworthy! With Tom disappearing through the massive barn doors, he looked shrunken. Harry C smiled, then openly laughed, saying 'poor sod can't help himself'.

Money for petrol and food raised, they now needed a set, as Harry C. recalled:

We needed to get Harry Greene up there – this is a miracle. Harry Greene was worth I can't tell you how much in whatever terms of credit you give, financial terms and whatever terms you're allowed, to Theatre Workshop. Harry; who was by nature an honest man, by inclination a con man and the honesty always seemed to win over his being a con man; was sent up with a hammer, literally, and a bag of nails to Glasgow, walked into some furniture factory and conned them into letting him build a whole bloody set out of off-cuts with a bag of nails and a hammer. And he built the whole of 'The Travellers' set, which is quite incredible. 1st Class compartment, which we were still using years later, the 2nd Class compartment … My admiration for him – which I daren't let him know, because one thing you dare not be in Theatre Workshop was one down, cause everybody else was always more brilliant. Joan would swoop in and say 'Brilliant, brilliant Darling, brilliant. Now, all watch so-and-so!' and the utter hatred within five seconds for the poor sod. So I never let him know but I always thought that was the most marvellous thing I'd ever seen in my life.[37]

The carriages of the train stretched through the auditorium from the stage, which served as the platform; the audience were arranged 'catwalk' style, known as a traverse stage. This, added to the lighting and sound effects and actors' movement, gave the audience the feeling that they were on the train as it sped across Europe. It was the story of passengers from different countries sharing a train journey as war approached. 'The BBC Festival Round-up programme hailed it as the most exciting production of the entire festival.'[38]

After the festival closed they hung on at Oddfellows for another two weeks, quickly getting together performances of *The Flying Doctor*, a play based on Molière's *Le Medecin malagre lui*, and *Johnny Noble* by Ewan MacColl, a ballad opera telling the story of a young merchant seaman set against the build-up to the war.

Now, up until this time, when you went to the theatre, the curtain went up, there was a set that left little to the imagination, and there were the actors – they were in the 'library with the revolver' or on the 'battlefield rousing the troops' or whatever on stage and you were looking at them through the 'fourth wall'. But with Theatre Workshop you couldn't help but be sucked into that world. David Scase illustrated this very well, when talking about how Joan had staged a scene from *Johnny Noble* set at sea:

> I was sitting on the deck and another man was standing. I was taking the pitch and toss of the boat, the forward and aft movement, whereas the man who was standing was taking the roll of the boat, starboard to port. So in fact, we were side by side, moving in slightly different directions. On the side of the stage, to emphasise that, she had the green and port light going up and down with the ship moving at sea. This was all there was on the stage, two actors, two lights and the sound of the engine going 'debum … debum … debum …' People have told me they were literally feeling seasick at the end of the scene. Now this was genius.[39]

It's now old hat, but then: people had never seen anything like it. The message of a lot of Theatre Workshop's early pieces may have been a little too 'rise up, brothers' for the establishment's tastes – but how they put the message across was awe-inspiring.

After enjoying the stability of the runs in London and Edinburgh, the company were jobless and homeless again. It was now September of 1952 and they were facing another cold winter touring in the bloody lorry. Feelers were put out to find a permanent home, a theatre they could call their own. Scotland or Manchester seemed a logical choice; they had been most popular there. In the meantime Gerry blagged the company's way into a house in Belmont Street, Glasgow. It was a place Harry remembered well:

> We were all duty cooks for a week and we did the best we could out of what we'd got. I'll never forget George Cooper's first meal. It was water and three dumplings. It was unbelievable and at the end of the week he had about ten pounds left out of twelve and we chased him up the road pretending to kill him! Then Gerry got a wine importer's licence and we all sat around drinking, it was 3*d* a glass, you kept putting your hand up and a mark went into his little book but as we never got any money out of him anyway and some of us hadn't got any, we wondered how we were going to get round to paying this off. The place was littered artistically with all kinds of empty wine bottles, Chianti bottles hung from the ceiling, and we were having one of our big, end of the week type meals when a load of 'Friends of Theatre Workshop' came to see the starving actors, and there we were half drunk, raucously shouting out those terrible songs which were always traditionally sung on these occasions – revolutionary German songs of the 1920s.[40]

It was all one hell of an education, so long denied to him, more fulsome and varied than could have been found at any university. Harry drank it in, trying to slake a thirst that had never been sated, and never would be:

> We gained a lot, not just the ability to play plays, the ability to listen to Joan, the ability to read books, the smashing cultures that I never knew anything about, Zionism or Judaism. But I learnt, through the songs, of the East German situation. One learnt our political situation in a very curious kind of osmosis of meeting people. You were educated in food that you couldn't afford, don't ask me why but there were discussions on food. For example of a marvellous piece of education – I was working class and I'd never really made a fire, my mother had always done it for me I suppose. Well I cleaned the fire out and Camel Bury, who was middle class – very middle class, he was an ex-officer – he went

berserk. I'd never seen anyone go as berserk in my life over the fact that I'd not put the cinders back on to burn the fire again. I got a look into the middle class way of life, cause I'd always been rather envious of him, that he came from a middle class kind of background and could talk posh and there he was berating me. So one learnt the different ways of life. There was every kind of person, so you learnt to suffer people too.[41]

As Jean Newlove learnt to suffer Harry in her early morning classes, she remembers him 'coming down into this gloomy cellar that we had, a sort of part cellar, in those awful coloured tights that he got from the costume room, yawning his head off and exercising with the rest of us – but he came down.' He never was a morning person.

Belmont Street was also the place that Harry and Avis came closest to tying the knot. A licence had been obtained, Harry went off to meet Avis and do the deed and the rest of the company tried to clean his room up ready for the expected nuptials. George Cooper remembers fishing one of Harry's socks out of the hearth (he never was a tidy person). Well, nothing happened – in the words of Harry G.:

> It fizzled out and we were not privy to the intimate details! But they were very close and had a very good relationship. However, Avis was always feisty, which Harry sometimes couldn't handle and acted being sulky and moody. He was good at fooling people and enjoyed people's reactions to his pretend moods.

Although Joan later wrote that 'this time he was determined to be married' and that Avis 'didn't come', Marjie Lawrence doubts that it was Avis who backed out, as she remembered Avis as never being one to back out of anything: 'She was too much a feminist always making sure that the girls enjoyed equality with the boys. She'd be the first to dispute best seats for the lads on the lorry, the cooking roster written fairly and distribution of the occasional goodie bag from a well-wisher properly and evenly shared.' Barbara Young agrees with her: 'I expect it was Harry. I think he wanted something different.'

It just wasn't meant to be. Despite deciding against marriage, Harry and Avis remained intimate for some years, and later Harry always spoke of Avis very fondly. Even today I can't think of her without Harry's prefix; in our house she was and will always be 'Lovely' Avis.

Back in Belmont Street the company decided to put on a tour of *Twelfth Night* for local schools; it would keep the wolf from the door. Harry was playing Sir Andrew Aguecheek. During rehearsals Joan, according to her book, had discouraged him from playing for laughs and directed him to remain true to the character. But on opening night, hearing the schoolboys baying for blood, Joan became worried that he would regress. A minute before curtain up, while he was preparing to go on, she told him to 'stand his ground'. Although being given notes as you're about to make your entrance is bloody irritating, in this instance it proved fruitful, as Joan later wrote:

> I went round to the circle to watch. Sir Andrew's entrance … catcalls, wolf-whistles. He just stood there, lost – roars of laughter. He didn't react, he held on to the character so painstakingly evolved and at each simple, true reaction the boys yelled with delight. Not once did he fall back on an easy laugh. He looked vulnerable and the sadder he looked the more those kids roared.
>
> I was thrilled. This was the performer I'd been waiting for. Afterwards we met in the passage. 'Don't ever tell me what to do again. Come to that, don't speak to me again.' 'Harry. Listen …' 'No! Never again.' The kids were stamping and clapping. 'Can't you hear them? They're calling for Sir Andrew.' We went back to Belmont Street in the Alvis and he never looked at me.
>
> I waited anxiously for the next performance. Again, it was miraculous. Harry never went back. He couldn't. Once you have experienced the thrill of risk, the elation which often comes with fear, the beaten track is no longer inviting.[42]

Searches for a permanent home had yielded no results and the company were starting to get fractious. They had come from playing for two months in the summer in the same town and here they were back touring one-night stands. Never mind not knowing where the next venue would come from, they didn't know their next meal. There was never enough time to fit in all the training and rehearsing of new pieces; they had to be off for the next school performance. There was definitely no time to enjoy themselves, as Harry learnt the hard way:

> It all passed in a daze of work, work, work. Interspersed with the occasional fight, like the time George Cooper and I went to

the pictures one afternoon. We came back and, honest to God, it was as if we'd played the worst possible West End farce in our entire lives – just because we'd gone to the pictures, that was how sort of monastic Joan wanted the way of life. The life was monastic and damn hard, *Hard*. I don't mean physically hard, that was nothing – cold hands, cold feet, not having enough food or whatever – hard in the sense of the regime you were expected to subscribe to. Let me get the record straight, Joan is not a hard domineering woman, on the contrary, this is a very feminine, beautiful, wily woman, who led you ever so gently with, like any messiah, with a kind of simplicity that outweighed any possible convoluted argument *you* might have.[43]

But arguments were becoming more frequent and the cracks were beginning to show. One crack came as a result of a fundamental requirement of any theatre company – publicity. Going around telling people you were a political workers' theatre group wouldn't have them queuing round the block. What they needed was an original hook to drum up media interest. So how could they stand out from the crowd? They were a theatre group – in the 1950s – directed by a woman … Bingo. How could pushing Joan be a problem? Harry explains:

It suddenly became 'Theatre Workshop, directed by Joan Littlewood', and all the notices started off 'Joan Littlewood this, that and the other'; and only because we were so inculcated with the non-personality cult that Joan went in for, and we all agreed with was absolutely right for this group, this kind of work – this is beginning to sound petty, but it wasn't petty – I mean the gall was there because one felt, as one felt in a lot of things, that Joan was being forced into a situation that she didn't really want to – but for publicity purposes she was being put through the screws. So one inevitably sided with Joan, possibly wrongly for all I know, against other people who were forcing the issue for her.[44]

They were so tired and worn out from the road it was easy for debate to slip into debacle at the slightest provocation. But none of these things would matter with a little security. If they had their own place, where they could build up a local audience, they would have time to train and learn and, maybe one day, rest. Most still favoured the north, but a few were looking towards the very heart of the enemy theatre – London.

The company had always had disagreements, tensions sometimes leading to physical blows. Barbara Young remembers one incident with Joan:

> I had a very bad tooth and I had to go to a dentist. We were somewhere on tour, somewhere in Edinburgh, and she didn't accept the fact that I'd been to this dentist and I had a really sore mouth and she actually pushed me, and it hurt and I just lashed out and clouted her one, and I remember Ewan having to separate us. But oddly enough it never seemed to make any difference, that sort of thing didn't bother her, really. What bothered her was when you didn't work properly or you didn't do it right, you know.[45]

And of course there would be the fallout from romantic entanglements. When George Cooper joined, Joan had told him that they all had a fairly fluid and adult attitude to company dalliances. And yet, as George remembers, when Gerry, who was Joan's:

> 'boyfriend', which always seemed to me to be a little bit out of joint with the time, but anyway her boyfriend, took a fancy to one of the actresses in the company called ##### [if you must know, look it up] – who's still around, I think her daughter's acting as well. There came a moment with this place in Manchester … Joan went into the wardrobe room to get something and discovered Gerry with #####, in what we might call a compromising position. And all this business about, 'you know, we're very free and adult about our relationships with each other etc'; it suddenly got all very monogamous! And she called her a trollop and a whatsit and all the rest of it, and she got her kicked out of the company. The fact that Gerry had strayed to this little actress was not acceptable to Joan and yet she was very insistent as I say on, 'It's very adult the way we have a relationship with each other' etc, etc. So that was a little example of how the theory got a little bent when it came to, you know, an actual crisis![46]

Coming to Joan's defence is the 'trollop' herself, 'She tried to get rid of me but Ewan wouldn't let her. I had to sit in a room for about two days waiting for the axe to drop and Ewan saved my bacon. He said, "You're going to get rid of the only person who can act, the only girl you've got." And so she didn't, to do her justice, she didn't.'

If Gerry had a roving eye, it appears Ewan was no better; George Cooper describes him as having:

> in his opinion, some God-given right to get any young actress in the company into bed as soon as possible. [Ewan also] seemed to have, in his opinion, some God-given right that he could still have influence over Joan, and ignore Gerry altogether sort of thing. So there were quite a few hot exchanges between Ewan and Gerry from time to time. I always thought Gerry – who was a very, very strong powerful man – could have picked up Ewan and flung him across the room, but he was always very calm and cool about various things. So there was always that in the background, it wasn't a sort of, 'Oh isn't everything wonderful in Theatre Workshop' or lovey-dovey by any means, there was always this undercurrent: Ewan MacColl wanting to be top dog. Ewan could never accept the fact that we should have a permanent home, he wanted to keep perpetually touring ... [but] tours weren't paying, and Joan's objective of taking the theatre to the people of the country who'd been 'robbed' of their theatre so to speak, didn't really apply because there was so few people interested in coming to see us that they obviously couldn't care less.[47]

There were extremely heated discussions on whether to try London or not. Jean Newlove remembers that:

> very few of us wanted to go to London. The thing was we were so anti the West End. Ewan said, 'We're going to give up our sovereignty if we go down there,' because people were going to compare us to the West End, which from the artistic point of view we didn't mind – but we were very left wing and that wouldn't have gone down well because the audience in the West End were all middle class.

She believed that Harry, along with Howard Goorney, was a pragmatist: 'I think he probably would have been a lot like Howard in a way, "We can't go on living like this, but what are we going to do about it?"'

Gerry and Harry Greene left for the south as they had heard that there might be a theatre going, not in the West End but in the East End of London. 'We drove through the night, shared the driving, and we got to this place, Stratford East, in the early hours. A mad driver was Gerry – he was a mad driver. I remember coming down on the A1, pouring with rain, and I looked at the speedometer and it was over 90.'

When they arrived, Gerry went for sandwiches. The agent arrived, handed over the keys and Harry G. had a first look round the place. It was a pit. Urine and beer-soaked carpets, holes in the roof, dilapidated equipment. It was falling apart. Gerry, when he saw it, was ready to write it off, but Harry G. convinced him that they should try. They were desperate.

By now the school term, and with it the school tour, had ended. It was December. The company had put on a new translation of Molière's *Le Malade Imaginaire* to keep them going, but what next? A message was received from Gerry and a meeting was called, as Harry remembered while talking over the old days with Howard Goorney:

> I remember a telegram 'Can get theatre in Stratford. London.' And we had a big Company meeting to discuss whether we should go to London or not. And you were at that meeting, I distinctly remember you and me arguing on the same vote at the same time. 'What is the point? How can we fight the West End type of theatre from the middles of Auchtermuchty? We don't stand much bloody chance – Nobody's taking any notice of us.' That was our theory and our cry then. Both you and I knew that we should leave the wilds of touring and establish a base and the chance to go to London and establish that base and fight that type of theatre was fantastic.

The theatre may have been a shithole but it was a cheap shithole. They decided to take it for a six-week run. They borrowed £200 for the deposit of ten weeks' rent and made their way to the Theatre Royal, Stratford East.

Notes

1 *Manchester Weekly News*, 25/3/67.
2 Goorney, H., *The Theatre Workshop Story* (Methuen, 2008).

3 Harry, in conversation with Howard Goorney.

4 *Ibid.*

5 Theatre Archive Project, British Library.

6 Burton, *Acting in the Sixties*.

7 Harry, in conversation with Howard Goorney.

8 Littlewood, J., *Joan's Book: The Autobiography of Joan Littlewood* (Methuen, 2003).

9 Harry, in conversation with Howard Goorney.

10 Burton, *Acting in the Sixties*.

11 *Ibid.*

12 *Ibid.*

13 Theatre Archive Project, British Library.

14 Harry, in conversation with Howard Goorney.

15 Theatre Archive Project, British Library.

16 Burton, *Acting in the Sixties*.

17 Harry, in conversation with Howard Goorney.

18 *Ibid.*

19 Theatre Archive Project, British Library.

20 Harry, in conversation with Howard Goorney.

21 MacColl, E., *Journeyman* (Sidgwick & Jackson Ltd, 1990).

22 Goorney, *The Theatre Workshop Story*.

23 Theatre Archive Project, British Library.

24 Harry, in conversation with Howard Goorney.

25 Littlewood, *Joan's Book*.

26 Theatre Archive Project, British Library.

27 *Ibid.*

28 Goorney, *The Theatre Workshop Story*.

29 *Ibid.*

30 Theatre Archive Project, British Library.

31 Harry, in conversation with Howard Goorney.

32 Goorney, *The Theatre Workshop Story*.

33 *Manchester Weekly News*, 25/3/67.

34 Goorney, *The Theatre Workshop Story*.

35 Wilson, A.N., in the *Evening Standard*, 11/6/01.

36 Harry, in conversation with Howard Goorney.

37 *Ibid.*

38 MacColl, *Journeyman*.

39 Goorney, *The Theatre Workshop Story*.

40 *Ibid.*

41 Harry, in conversation with Howard Goorney.

42 Littlewood, *Joan's Book*.

43 Harry, in conversation with Howard Goorney.

44 *Ibid.*

45 Theatre Archive Project, British Library.

46 *Ibid.*

47 *Ibid.*

7

Calling Walter Plinge

> So we took it and we were grateful. Grateful is not the word;
> I mean, we played to twelve people in the middle of winter. I fol-
> lowed The Lady Stripped by Bullets, it said in my dressing room.[1]
>
> Harry H. Corbett

The Theatre Royal had been closed since the ecdysiasts of *The Lady Stripped by Bullets* had packed up their easily shed costumes and it was not a pretty sight. Years of neglect had produced peeling paint, broken chairs, dubious cracks in the walls and even more dubious rigging: ropes that should have been as fat as your wrist worn down to as thin as your thumb. The stairs from the dressing rooms to the stage trod as smooth as glass. It was dank, dilapidated and dangerous. And everywhere was the God-awful stench, compounded by the stink of the soap factory down the road.

Not all had made the move. Avis would join later, she had returned to Chorlton Rep and in the future would often nip back north when her parents were ill. But the company lost David Scase and Rosalie Williams, who had started a family and already put down roots in Manchester. David went on to become artistic director at the Library Theatre there and nurtured the early careers of Anthony Hopkins, Alan Rickman and Patrick Stewart amongst others.

Some that had come were not as grateful as Harry. Foremost of these was Ewan, who felt that they would start pandering to the critics, lose their working- class audience and ultimately their ideals. He was also of the view that:

A situation had arisen in the Company by this time where the management could more or less impose a policy, because they were holding the purse strings … a feeling of them and us was developing which was disastrous. There was also a lack of political training inside the group – a tendency, once we were function- ing, to believe that politics would take care of itself.[2]

Understandably Ewan's interest in the company dwindled with his influence. Though for a few years he would act as musical director when required, also coming in when they staged revivals of his own plays, later on he helped with fundraising by holding folk evenings at the theatre. He left to pursue his love of music. Joan took it well:

Where was he going? To join the 'Hootenannys', one of the many groups of folk artists who'd become fashionable. Folk-songs and singers were in demand at this time and the Hootenannys offered real money. He'd never earned money with his plays in England and all the hopes and dreams of his youth had faded, but abandon- ing Theatre Workshop to sing in London pubs – what a waste![3]

Jean Newlove, Ewan's wife, while firmly laying the blame for Joan and Ewan's split at the door of them both being 'bloody minded', agreed:

I thought it was a waste too, because he could have done what he was doing. I mean, he did do most wonderful radio ballads, and he got the Prix d'Italia for them, on two of them I think. And it was a new art form, it was fantastic. But I think he could have done all that by taking time out from the theatre but still work- ing in the theatre as a playwright. Hugh McDiarmid was very upset that he was wasting his time singing when he should have been writing plays.

The Scottish poet was not the only voice to praise MacColl: 'George Bernard Shaw said there were only two playwrights of genius in the country today, one was Ewan MacColl and the other was himself.'[4] Or as Barbara Young put it: 'In my book Ewan was the real talent – he was a bloody good writer.'

Ewan went on to have a hugely successful career, his many songs included *Dirty Old Town* and *The First Time Ever I Saw Your Face*, the latter written for the singer Peggy Seeger, his second wife, with whom he had three children. They followed him into the business, as did his children by Jean Newlove, Hamish and Kirsty MacColl.

Ewan's departure had long-ranging detrimental effects on the company, as Jean Newlove explains:

> The thing was that Joan and Ewan started everything out, and there was a balance there, and when Joan got flights of fancy Ewan could always bring her back – cause she did, she often went over the top – but Ewan could always bring her back a bit more down to earth. But he, in his own way, had flights of fancy but he was much better at getting, of being very logical about the theatre and when he left that collapsed, and I think Joan missed him terribly – but would never admit it, of course, and neither would he – and I thought it was absolutely tragic that they split up as a team.

In January of 1953 work started on getting the theatre into shape, and the people that had come south bonded even more closely during the long hard hours that it took to get the shoddy building in Angel Lane into a working order, using the tools and materials donated by Harry Greene's Uncle Bill, who ran a DIY shop.

Gerry's family no doubt sent money to help him out in his new post of company manager. The role of manager was influential, and gave an opportunity to steer company policy, which on the road had been the preserve of a small caucus made up of Joan, Ewan, Camel Bury, and contributions from favourite talents such as Howard Goorney, George Cooper and Harry, alongside whoever was company manager at the time. As Harry recalled:

> The Company Manager was elected. Now it was a job that was not sought after, it contained a lot of work and it needed a lot of application. Howard Goorney's mind was brilliant at it, so was Margaret Bury's – mine certainly wasn't and I dodged it on every possible occasion … Gerry was never really, in the early days, looked upon as a successful Company Manager, he was not *unsuccessful*, he was as good as anybody else in the job but he was never permanently at it in any way. Ewan's influence was still very strong in those days, cause he was inevitably called in to help with crises after crises.

When we got to Stratford we required, by law, a Manager and I remember saying at this meeting 'What's all this, with this big notice outside on the window? "*Gerry Raffles is now Manager of this Theatre.*"' – The answer – 'Well, we have to have one by law, we can't keep changing it every other week, so it must be somebody, so we're giving it to Gerry to do.' So that was it.[5]

Gerry, perhaps never quite as at home as the others on stage, had found a calling off it. He dedicated himself to Joan and to Theatre Royal. He organised the administration, box office, publicity, council contacts, and all the boring thankless tasks that make a theatre run. This he was to always do, leaving Joan to just concentrate on the art. Literally, when she needed a packet of cigarettes she would shout up to Gerry from the stage and the fags would appear. He even, on occasion, bought Joan sanitary towels – something that shocked the hell out of the company secretary who had seen him return from the chemist; we are talking the 1950s here. If Joan was the serene swan, Gerry was the feet going like the clappers, pushing through the waters of high expectation and no money. As the actors scrubbed, painted, built and renovated their new home, Gerry would hand out vitamin pills and steaming mugs of tea, deviously laced with Benzedrine to keep them all going.

This wasn't the only time Gerry would be so devious. Coming from a well-off family went slightly against the grain of Theatre Workshop – so any donations had to be kept under the radar. It is obviously harder to be taken for a staunch socialist by your slum-reared peers if you have had the misfortune to be born to capitalist pigs. Jean Newlove recounts an example of how Gerry tried to hide this fortune:

He did have a family that was pretty wealthy. Now I look back we didn't seem to be helped out very much but I think Gerry and Joan were helped out from time to time when we were desperate. They had a home in Blackheath. On one side it has a golf course and on the other side two flats, it's gorgeous. They got it shortly after moving to London. Joan thought they'd got it for a song, she said Gerry had told her 'Oh, it's only £3 or £4 a week.' Which was absolute nonsense. We all of us knew that, including Harry. But that's what Gerry had to tell Joan, you see, because otherwise she would never have accepted it.

He didn't always get away with it, as George Cooper tells: 'I do remember one incident ... Because Gerry came from a very wealthy Jewish family, he'd stolen his mother's earrings to sell for money to help the Theatre, and Joan made him take them back.'[6]

This feeling of guilt over being, or appearing to be, well off, permeated the whole company, as Jean remembers:

> We felt so privileged, and I'm sure Harry felt this too, to be part of this group. We felt so incredibly privileged to be so poor. I mean I remember going home and I didn't have a decent overcoat and my mother went out and bought me one. I went back to the theatre and I was so embarrassed because I'd got a new overcoat and I saw the girls looking at me, and nothing was said, but I'd got a new coat and I felt guilty.

For most people who were with Theatre Workshop, especially those who joined for only a production or two or who worked with the company in the later years, this guilt wasn't too hard to shake, but for some of the early members it took years to relinquish, and for a few, including Harry, it never left them.

When they first arrived, there was plenty of opportunity to feel the privilege of poverty, Avis remembered:

> I'd managed to get digs with Harry Corbett in West Ham for twenty-six shillings a week bed and breakfast, but before very long we were just too broke to afford it. Some of the group had already moved straight into the theatre, they were sleeping in the dressing rooms and either having their meals there or at a local café where the owners were immensely sympathetic. I followed them. It wasn't for any idea of romanticism or togetherness, we were simply without any money at all. In a small room overlooking the railway station I cooked chips on a small ring in the corner, slept there and lived there.[7]

Sleeping in the dressing rooms very nearly got them into trouble, as George Cooper relates:

> We eventually found that the lady we'd taken on, in the box office, was 'dusting the till', as I think they say, you know having a bit of quiet help yourself money. So we gave her the

sack of course. She immediately went to the Local Authorities in Stratford and said you know, 'You've got a bunch of gypsies in that theatre.' – and we were all sleeping in the dressing rooms, which of course is illegal. The sanitary inspector turned up.

Gerry convinced the inspector that the beds were merely to rest on before the performance; quite how he explained the gas cooker that Harry had hooked up to the mains in his dressing room we'll never know. From then on the company had to be ready for spot checks, though they had a cunning plan, as told by Harry:

> We had this password 'Will Walter Plinge come down for rehearsal please' whenever the fireman came in to inspect. You rushed into whichever room you were nearest to and tidied things away. My bed used to go up against the wall, like in a Marx Brothers film, the ropes fastening it went round coat hooks and underneath a notice said 'Props. Do not touch.'[8]

Years later this was used in our own house. 'Calling Walter Plinge' was the signal to clear toys and crap away when a visitor was expected; it still is.

One time Jean Newlove was chatting to Harry in his dressing room and they didn't hear the call:

> We missed the tannoy, and the word had gone round that 'Mr. Plinge was wanted on stage', and that meant the fireman … and the fireman walked in and the bed was down of course and I think I said something like, 'You better get your bed up, and I'll leave you now … as you've *had a nice rest*.' I don't know what it was Harry said, 'Oh, yeah.' I don't know whether Harry was taking the lead and we had said that 'The lead had to have a break – because it was such an exhausting time, you know, he had to have a break between the two shows …' And Harry started to lift his bed up, and that chap didn't say too much, but he knew – he was smiling.

They all pitched in to get the theatre up and running, Harry remembered: 'The ghastly job of going down and taking your turn to get that anthracite boiler going – Oh Jesus Christ – That was absolute murder, because we never had enough coal and we could only burn it when the audience came in.'[9] Then they could only afford to heat the auditorium. The wave of cold air that rolled over the audience from the stage whenever the curtain went up was enough to take the breath away.

They opened with *Twelfth Night*; given the theatre's recent burlesque history the locals were expecting something rather different. '*Twelfth Night*? Just foreplay on the first eleven then, eh, eh?'

'You can imagine the fun we had; it was hysterical,' Harry remembered. 'Malvolio kept getting sweets thrown at him, which was a mark of favour from the audience who were used to going there.'[10] He also remembered:

> a funny story of George [Cooper] going in 'Twelfth Night', and George is playing the Captain, and it was freezing, it was awfully freezing cold and he had a blanket round him which he was supposed to tenderly put round 'Viola'. Well, there was a fight over this blanket going on. It was the funniest thing I'd seen, all through the opening scene he would not give up the blanket. You know George – he would just giggle.[11]

It might not have been what they were expecting but the audience liked it and all twelve of them came back, bringing their friends and insulation, as Harry said: 'I've seen them bring hot water bottles and blankets.'

Harry summed up their start:

> We had a splendid beginning, far better than walking into a sophisticated repertory-run theatre … But rather than walk into that, we went into this free wheeling atmosphere of the East End theatre, run down and disreputable.
>
> It suited our sort of atmosphere perfectly, because we wanted to work in the run-down, the disrespectful, the cocking the snook. So it was absolutely splendid for us. The audience were really disrespectful themselves; they cocked a snook at the world. They didn't give a damn. It was far better than playing to a regulated set of penguins who were used to hearing a certain thing each week. That is why we had so much success. A splendid area to work in. Not only that; we had to work hard. I think we got £2 10s a week. Of course we all shared.[12]

We had a deal that the non-smokers could have the chocolates that were left in boxes in the auditorium. I had the stalls for cigarettes. George Luscombe had the circle. Joby Blanchard had the gallery for chocolates – poor sod, they ate more chocolates down below. The hard centres with teeth marks in Carol, the box-office girl, had. We drew very little money but you could buy off-cut ends of bacon for sixpence a plate in Angel Lane. We couldn't have survived without Angel Lane and its cheap food.[13]

Believe me it wasn't an enjoyable experience. We were semi-starving half the time. And thank God again for Angel Lane. You see this is the interesting point; I don't think it could be done nowadays; economically it wouldn't be possible. Where can you get bacon at 6d. a pound? … a plate of ham ends for 3d. Now Angel Lane was full of this kind of thing, up and down; we lived like the old-age pensioners had to live – it was practical, splendid experience.[14]

Practical, splendid and in the beginning, as Jean Newlove tells, disgusting:

The Upper Bar, the upper kitchen near the 'Gods' – it was dire, dire! The gas ovens were thick with grease and Gerry, because there was no money, said we were going to have our lunch there, somebody had made something. And I looked at the gas stove and I thought 'I'm not having anything from there at all.' And I thought we looked like the poor from some dreadful Dickensian novel as we chewed up. And somebody had made some disgusting soup and I wouldn't touch it. I would much rather have gone hungry – well I did go hungry.

No wonder Harry hooked up an alternative cooker.

Not surprisingly the local café, mentioned by Avis – Café L'Ange – became an unofficial green room for the actors. Run by Bert and May Scagnelli it offered cheap food in large amounts and, crucially, on credit. Most importantly, Bert and May offered warmth, love and support – for years. They were the unsung heroes of Theatre Workshop.

By and large Angel Lane welcomed these new weirdos at the theatre. Many businesses sponsored the company: free equipment and props for free advertising. 'Virginia Cigarettes by Abdullah' appeared in all the programmes, even Shakespeare – 'Prithee, Sirrah, give us a light.'

'The cigarettes by Abdullah were cut up every week; I remember we got five and a half each. There were even razor blades wielded by Gerry, who was manager, to give us our share.'[15] Harry recalled. He also recalled Gerry's conviction that disinfectant would prevail over the state of the toilets – 'He always wanted more Jeyes' Fluid' – 'In the interest of Public Health this Theatre is disinfected throughout with Jeyes' Fluid' similarly made it into the programmes.

Germ free, they were ready for the critics. From the beginning they caused a stir with one from *The Stage*:

> Theatre Workshop, which recently opened a season at Stratford Royal, is unlike any other repertory company in the country. It bears a closer resemblance to some of the experimental groups that have been formed in America to provide a workshop for all kinds of theatre artists, and has evolved methods of acting and production that are largely a revolt against the narrow conventions of the present day commercial theatre.[16]

Let us pause for a moment and examine those methods of acting. No really, it's interesting.

At the time, drama schools on the whole were teaching actors to not bump into the furniture, to never turn their back on the audience, to always lead off with the upstage foot when crossing the stage, to never 'scissor' cross another actor, to feel the chair with the backs of the legs before sitting down so elegance was achieved and to speak the Queen's English with precision etc., etc. Yes, it does sound like a finishing school.

This, Theatre Workshop believed, was bollocks. How can every character walk and talk in exactly the same way? Although they agreed with precision they didn't find it shocking to have regional accents. Yes they could speak Queen's English when needed, but more important was the quality and control of the voice. They would listen to their vocal deficiencies on tape, then work to eradicate sloppy diction with tongue-twisting exercises. Singing classes improved resonance and extended vocal range into the upper and lower registers, and breathing exercises trained lung capacity and stamina. By using a partner's hand pushing into the diaphragm and working that muscle, the voice was re-educated to come from the guts and not the head. Supported by the diaphragm it had a much greater power. Next time you come across a bawling baby and wonder how something so small can make so much noise, check where it's breathing from. It won't be the chest, shallowly, which only comes as we grow up, it will be from the belly. Even your average toddler can raise enough noise to melt earwax quite naturally and without any training. It's only after years of being told to 'be quiet and stop making that racket' that one learns to inhibit the voice.

Right, let's turn you into a Theatre Workshop actor. Go on, give it a go – first try resonance, start humming. Can you feel the vibrations either side of your throat just under the jawbone? Of course you can. Now feel either side of your nose – you're resonating into your sinuses, which, as we know from decongestant adverts, extend under the cheeks and above the eyebrows – can you make it vibrate there? Try the lips. Try and make the vibrations stronger in the mouth. What about the chest? Put your hand flat on your chest below the collarbone – anything? With practice you can resonate strongly in all these areas. Where you resonate will colour your voice. If you ever have a chance to feel up an opera singer – try it out on them.

Let's try another. Say 'a'. Now did you have a glottal stop? That mini explosion of the vocal chords, heard in 'Uh, oh'. Not every dialect has a glottal stop so let's get rid of that. Say 'hay', now say it without the 'h'. Ok, when you say 'a' you might be able to get your little finger between your teeth, but put two fingers in, really open up you mouth. Breathing. Breathe into your belly, now put your hands round your ribs, breathe in pushing your hands outwards – see, you've got a good lungful and you haven't even used your chest yet. Place your fist into your solar plexus (bread basket). Breathe in, say 'a' and while sustaining the 'a' push your fist away by tensing the diaphragm.

Can you hear the difference? If not there's no hope for you, but if you can, with a little work you too can sound great, even out of the shower.

Right, you have a marvellously flexible voice, but what about your body?

Start in a neutral, completely relaxed state. Are you relaxed, or are your shoulders round your ears? I suspect the latter. To be utterly relaxed is one of the hardest things you can do, even when asleep. Think of the phrase 'dead weight' – a dead body is so hard to shift because it has finally given up all muscle control. Relaxation exercises will go some way to achieving a neutral state upon which you can build movement. However, if you can't touch your toes then you can only play characters who also can't touch their toes. Ballet and dance classes will improve flexibility, strength and control of your body. Offhand I can't think of any classic role that specifically calls for the touching of toes, but if one comes up – you'll be ready.

So you've got a strong, agile voice and body that will do what you want, but what do you want them to do?

What's your character, who the hell are you?

Enter the world of Constantin Stanislavsky. Director of the Moscow Arts Theatre, Stanislavsky developed his own system for acting.

Firstly what's your motivation? There are the apocryphal stories of actors when asking 'What's my motivation?', being answered with – 'the cheque.'

But what's your motivation, what's your objective?

This can be applied to a huge ultimate objective – 'I want to climb Everest' – or a very small one – 'I want to get out of this chair and find a map of Nepal.' You can chart your character's path along the objectives that take you from opening the atlas to planting your flag on the summit.

Obstacles in your way – you don't have an atlas.

Overcoming your obstacle – the library has an atlas.

Method you use to overcome your obstacle – 'Dear, sweet librarian, I can't find an atlas of Nepal, could you please help poor silly old me.' Or 'Look, book-worming bitch, I'm not moving 'til you get me the atlas.'

Use your imagination – right, so you're on the summit, you've just planted your flag. Is it the most joyous moment of your life – if so what are the moments in your own life that you can draw on to relive that joy? Perhaps you are in despair that your life's work is achieved and there is nothing left but the slow crawl to old age and the grave. Remember a moment from your life when you were most in despair. Now to be utterly in despair for eight performances a week is a one-way ticket to the hospital, so remember what it felt like so you can recreate it while remaining emotionally detached.

Improvise – now use your imagination along with the rest of the cast. Imagine the summit – what does it feel like up there, imagine the cold. Is it clear weather, will you get back down, do you like the people you're with? Are you leading the climb, an experienced mountaineer, young and fit? Or are you 45, wheezing, a bit flabby and ready to take orders? Are you longing to get back home, or enjoying the break from your divorce proceedings?

Research – when are you? Are you climbing with bits of string and hobnail boots or with oxygen and the latest gear?

Why are you? – Are you a businessman paying to join the climb, putting others at risk while you live out a middle-aged fantasy, or are you part of a national team, determined to put your piss ant country on the map?

And so on, by researching the world your character inhabits and using your imagination you can create a detailed life history based on a few scripted directions. By improvising situations with other members of the cast you start to inhabit the character's world and play from truth.

Ever seen a little girl playing dress up, being a princess or a fairy? She invents an entire world full of complex imaginary friends or foes, and she truly believes that world – she is living in the moment. Well you're doing the same thing, only without so many sequins.

Right, you've got the character. What you need now is a method of translating that character into the physical – how they walk and talk – using your wonderful new voice and body.

Rudolf Laban was a dancer and choreographer who developed a system that analysed human movement. Known as 'the father of modern dance', he opened institutes all over Europe, and was eventually appointed as director of the Deutsche Tanzbühne, the German stage dance, in 1934. By 1938 he wasn't Nazi enough for the Nazis, so he fled to England where he opened the Art of Movement Studios in Oxford Road, Manchester, in 1946, where Joan's letter found him the following year. Jean Newlove, who was teaching at the studios at the time, remembers:

> It was Joan that wrote. She had been introduced to 'Laban' by Annie Fleig at RADA, but Annie's English was not good – so she couldn't fully explain Laban's work. Joan found out that Laban was in Manchester and wrote to him. I was there when the letter arrived. Laban came into the room and said, 'You can do zis with zis woman?' Of course we had no idea who 'zis woman' was, so I said, 'I think I've got time.' You know, it was just another job really.

Jean came to work with the company and stayed, applying Laban's technique to the actors. As she explains:

> All living matter conforms to certain basic principles. They have always existed, but Laban was the first to tabulate them. He discovered there was a certain crystal shape from which all living matter developed, called the Icosohedron [a twenty-sided crystal]. He was able to give us exercises to make us aware of the space in which we move, based on this Icosohedron and the three dimensions in which all life moves. Now all this was totally different from any series of gymnastic exercises, or even meditation exercises. So far we've got the structure of movement and we know where we are moving in space. How do we move? How can we analyse? We are now concerned with observation and analysis of movement, and this is where my training came in. Laban divided all movement into eight basic efforts. When you move, you use not only three dimensions, but also three elements. Space, Time and Energy; and a variation in one of the elements will change the effort. For instance, if you say, 'I am Direct in Space, Quick in Time and Strong in Energy, that is a punch or a thrust. If I change the time to Slow, we have a press. So one works on these efforts, not just punching with one's fist, but with every part of the body – and not just in front of you. Actors work creatively and their working area is all around them, unlike most people whose working area is just in front of them, in the kitchen, at a desk, in a car. [17]

The Laban Efforts Table:

Effort	Space	Time	Energy
Thrust	Direct	Quick	Strong
Slash	Indirect	Quick	Strong
Wring	Indirect	Slow	Strong
Flick	Indirect	Quick	Weak
Press	Direct	Slow	Strong
Float	Indirect	Slow	Weak
Dab	Direct	Quick	Weak
Glide	Direct	Slow	Weak

Right, got that? So James Bond is a **Thruster**, Darth Vader is a **Presser**, and Mr Bean is a **Flicker**. All of these efforts can be combined to create the movement of the character at any point in the play, and can similarly be applied to how one delivers each individual line. One cannot **Thrust** all the time, one would be knackered.

Now the movement will dictate the voice, if you are a **Pressing** Darth Vader will you have a **Flicking** Mr Bean voice? Maybe, if you want to have the effect of playing against preconceived perceptions.

Think of examples you may have come across: a **Slashing** yoof, bursting with energy as he aimlessly ricochets down the streets, leading from the groin, will have the voice of a geyser, an inarticulate bubbling interspersed with random explosions; the **Gliding** curator of an art museum, greying, neat, bespectacled and tweeded will have a cushion of a voice, one that wouldn't dream of disturbing the acoustics echoing around his marbled halls.

So now you have spent years training your voice, body, and imagination. You've studied world, social, and theatre history; you've studied people around you and discovered why they react to given situations in a certain way. You can give a 'real' performance, only limited by the fact you are 'on stage' with a hopefully large audience and, as such, need to make that performance 'big' enough to be seen. Add all of that to your 'it' factor, the charisma that makes people want to watch you. Congratulations, you are a Theatre Workshop actor. You are not 'acting' you are 'being'. This is the modern theatrical ideal. Although revolutionary in the 1950s, these methods are now routinely taught to trainee actors and give us the naturalistic realism we have, as an audience, come to expect and demand. It can of course go too far: directors are now occasionally prone when casting, say, an East End chav, to employ an actual East End chav with the ability to emote their way out of a paper bag coming in second to authenticity. That is if they have not been cast for winning Strictly Ice Pop Factor.

Clive Barker, the actor, director and theatre lecturer, wrote:

> The late Harry H. Corbett, who could stand as the epitome of the Theatre Workshop actor, said to me once that his ambition was to give one performance in which he had only one motivation, the one which took him out of the wings and on to the stage. From that point, he wanted to play only off his reaction to the other actors. In a theatrical world where so many stages are

littered with actions and questions to which no one responds, Theatre Workshop approached that ideal.[18]

That first Theatre Workshop season at Stratford East that had so arrested *The Stage* critic continued with *Le Malade Imaginaire* followed by Ewan's *Paradise Street*, which gives a good example of the 'method of production'. Sets, lighting and costumes all grew out of rehearsal and, of course, financial constraint. Theatre Royal had one of the deepest stages in London; the back wall was brick, perfect for the street setting the play required and Harry Greene took advantage:

> So for this particular play, all I did was one flat, as we call it, in perspective. From the proscenium arch, you had this one flat at an angle from the proscenium arch, at about 30 degrees back to the back wall. So you saw part of the back wall, but this flat was probably about 15 feet high at the proscenium arch end, and going back to about 10 feet. Built, as it were in perspective, which gave the effect from the stalls, or from the auditorium, that you were looking at a long street. And then I cut into the flat doorways – all in perspective – and one window each. And then we laid the flat on stage, painted it with what was then called Unibond, which is a very strong adhesive, and then sprinkled sand on it, and then aggregate – like pebbles. So we created what looked like a real wall.[19]

It must have been a bugger to shift, but it was designed with Camel Bury's lighting in mind. 'The setting had to be a sounding board, as it were, to the light. You couldn't do the sort of lighting we wanted to do inside a box set, so our early settings became an extension of our lighting technique. You needed clear angles, you needed textured rather than painted surfaces.'[20]

For a while keen, young set designers came with models of their keen, young finished sets, which Joan and the company treated merely as works in progress. 'Yes, it's a nice start, lad, but the final set will grow out of rehearsals.' This obviously came as a rude awakening to the designers; they would be fully awake and properly indignant when they heard they would personally, with the help of the cast, have to build the set for a fiver. It was mutually agreed that they should stop coming.

Costuming budgets were also tight. The amount given for plays needing lavish period costumes – well, period costumes – was £10. Costume designers Josephine Smith and Shirley Jones would work miracles from a small room at the top of the theatre – always a popular spot, it being one of the few places that was heated – as sewing, irritatingly, is a job for which you need to be able to feel your fingers. Costumes would be recycled, unpicked carefully ready to be put back together again or made with rags and hope. Flea markets were regularly raided and if an actor joined the company with a nice article of clothing it would soon be swallowed by the wardrobe. Very, very rarely could they afford to hire anything in, including wigs, which meant kings and beggars had the same dreadful haircut. Costumes also developed from rehearsal, they would be a work in progress, altered along the way as problems with movement or actions arose. By the time the play opened they would be a familiar second skin.

Combining all of this with the performance of the actors, the result was stunning. Sitting in the audience local resident Peggy Soundy certainly thought so, 'You could forget the theatre was cold and none too clean, that the seats weren't comfy and there were only twenty people in the audience. I felt I'd got to do something to help keep this going.'[21] Peggy founded the Supporters Club, which, at its height, boasted 2,000 members.

They needed all the support they could get. No one really wanted to go back to the dreadful touring. At least they now they knew where they were sleeping each night, even if it was in the dressing rooms. But they had swapped that life of having enough time to work on plays for the unrelenting pressure of fortnightly rep. Two weeks was the maximum that the small local audience would sustain a production. For those who had never done rep, unlike Harry, it came as something of a shock. The task now was to try and build up the local working-class audience.

Many local people helped spread the word, and helped in more personal ways, with one of the theatre secretaries even letting Harry and Avis sleep on their floor occasionally to have a break from the dressing room. Harry and George Luscombe started painting houses, including the secretary's parents' house, in order to make much-needed funds. Ewan would come back and organise folk evenings. There would be open days for the locals when kids were encouraged to come in. The councils were also encouraged to get involved and to give some funding – although no real funding was forthcoming while Harry was with them. This explains why, to supplement the theatre, he moonlighted as an occasional bouncer in Soho.

Audiences became even more unsustainable during the summer months, so the theatre was kept dark during this time. The company played the Edinburgh Festival and then returned to the theatre that autumn. They continued with *Uncle Vanya*, *The Alchemist* and *The Government Inspector*. Adaptations of *Treasure Island* and *A Christmas Carol* proved especially popular. As Harry Greene remembers:

> takings were pretty high, and we did three shows a day, for £7 a week! We all thought though that perhaps soon we wouldn't have to paint shop fronts, or labour on building sites – because that's what we did to supplement our wages. At the time, thinking back, we talked about it in fact, and we sensed the revolution that was coming. And each successive production brought more acclaim, the critics came, bigger audiences. That was when it became quite exciting.[22]

The 'especially popular' *A Christmas Carol* cast included new member Shirley Dynevor, recently graduated from drama school in South Wales. She remembers:

> Harry was playing Bob Cratchit and I played his daughter Martha, and it was a wonderful start. I loved it. I think we all played about six parts. I remember meeting Harry then, of course, for the first time and it was just an absolute delight – in spite of Joan … it would be probably on the stage, straight into rehearsals and he was superbly kind. It was a bit scary for me coming into the company and I just remember his enormous kindness, which was a delight.

With the success Joan decided to extend the company and auditions were held to find two new members on New Year's Day 1954. Over 100 turned up. Most of them were under the impression that Theatre Workshop would be a good career move and a one-way ticket to the West End – they didn't make it. Gerard Dynevor did.

Shirley Dynevor had missed the auditions. She had been away on a pre-arranged tour for an outside company. She returned to meet her future husband, Gerard, who became, as she says 'a great friend of Harry's. I always felt those two were very close and Gerard appreciated Harry's brains, his work and his approach. He really was wonderful over detail and thought and so they got on tremendously well.'

The other successful auditionee was Marjie Lawrence, who remembered: 'In 1953, fresh from Drama School in Birmingham, I was doing the rounds of auditions in London. I attended a very crowded audition on New Year's Day 1954. I was told 112 people were being auditioned in two days. Gerard Dynevor and I were the only two people offered a contract – at £3/10/- per week.'[23]

If Marjie was pleased at her success, then Harry Greene was ecstatic. He had noticed Marjie at the audition. Noticed? She had struck him like a thunderbolt. They very quickly fell for each other. Marjie moved into Harry Greene's dressing room and he tells what happened next:

> I have a good story regarding our first night in our own shared dressing room, just after Marjie joined the company. Not previously told because of the embarrassment it caused the company. A plot was hatched by the jealous John Bury, to invade our boudoir by breaking a door panel and spraying the room and us with a fire extinguisher. He had been bothering Marjie every day with sexual innuendo, but getting nowhere. She was offended by his constant attention and said so to me and to Joan. A tap on our door at midnight was followed by Harry C's low voice 'be prepared for an invasion by the infidels, take care Harry boy'. Apparently Harry C had been against the drunken plot and was unceremoniously bundled out of the green room, so slipped quietly to warn us his pals.
>
> Soon after, the door panel was crashed through and a huge red extinguisher poked into the hole. But the beer soaked mob were not prepared for what happened next. I was ready waiting at the side of the locked door, wrenched the thing out of Camel's hands, turned it around and gave the lot a good old dousing as they slipped and staggered, falling over each other on the wet corridor floor. It quickly sobered the sods up. Gerry arrived worried by the shouting and gave them a stern warning to get back to their rooms or else. He gave us a thumbs up and returned to Joan's room!

High jinx apart, the company still hadn't attracted the local working class to the kind of plays they felt the local working class should be seeing. They put on a production of *Van Call* by local playwright Anthony Nicholson. It was set in Stratford, and had been worked on by the company along with locals whom they invited to rehearsals. It went down like a lead balloon. Peggy Sounder said: 'In Van Call you were trying to put across a line and you could feel it. If it doesn't come from somebody's gut, in a real sort of way, it shows, and I think the locals saw this.'[24] The audiences that did turn up showed no interest in seeing themselves on stage, 'they could get all that at home'. It was hard enough dragging them away from televisions bought at huge expense for the Coronation eighteen months earlier.

They did all they could to drum up publicity. According to Harry Greene, this went a little too far during a production of *Red Roses for Me*. He and Karl Woods were asked:

> to go into Epping Forest for trees. And Karl and I, guess what, spent a night in the local jail after being prevailed upon by that devious so-and-so, Joan Littlewood, to go at night with tiny torches and hand saws, and an axe, to Epping Forest to nick those trees. Of course cops came, bells rang, clanked, we were surrounded, and in no time at all we were in clink. It was awful. Of course, once you're there you don't know what's happening. You're not told anything. But then Gerry came next morning and got us out, and once again the story went round that she'd tipped off the police to get publicity. Oh yes! The company, they were also, I recall, furious, especially George, my pal. And George demanded a company meeting: 'Why should we be, you know in clink, in jail because of this?' But the company meeting got nowhere. But I suppose I can be thankful that Joan praised my initiative. Nothing more – just praised my initiative.[25]

Harry Greene certainly did use his initiative – in the end the forestry men 'actually delivered the stuff to us, and then the front row of the stalls on the first night was full of policemen and their wives.'

Ah, company meetings. When touring, Theatre Workshop had truly been operated on a democratic basis, the whole company taking decisions on policy and productions to be staged. While the company still held to basic principles of that equality, with work, pay and credit all being shared – Theatre Workshop, for instance, was the first to print the names of the theatre cleaners in its programmes – by this time deciding policy wasn't such a free-for-all, as Howard Goorney pointed out:

> We continued to function as a co-operative in the sense that we all received the same money. We didn't have Equity contracts because, strictly speaking, we didn't have a management and couldn't afford the Equity minimum anyway. In theory, all members of the Company continued to have a right to participate in policy-making, but after our move to Stratford, Company meetings became more and more a formality, and only decisions on minor issues could be influenced. Gerry's phrase 'If you've got a dog, why do the barking yourself' rather summed up the situation. He would sit calmly smoking his pipe, listening to the argument and discussion, knowing that, in the final analysis, Joan, John Bury and himself would make the decisions. In that particular situation, perhaps it was the only way we could function efficiently. What is arguable, and it was certainly argued by Ewan, was that whether it was the right sort of situation for our sort of company to be in. However, most of the Company were happy enough to get on with their acting. Harry Corbett put it this way:

> 'We never really argued about the policy in Company meetings, looking back, because everything that was presented to us was wilder than our wildest dreams. I mean, who's going to argue with *Volpone* or *Richard II*? Or *Arden of Faversham* and *The Dutch Courtesan*? Or *Hobson's Choice* and *Schweik*? Who's going to argue?'[26]

Although the company remained fairly invisible as far as the critics were concerned, this did have its advantages, as Harry remembered:

> You see we had this fantastic freedom, we weren't under great critical approbation, we could get away with murder then … we were ignored. But this was splendid for us because that meant we could do anything we liked. When we played 'The Enemy of the People', well, the second act was set inside the huge big room in the house; so we said, to hell with that if it's supposed to be a meeting, we will put it in the theatre itself. So we had the

entrances through the auditorium, the fumbling with the curtain and the whole meeting; we literally had half of Angel Lane
working there, May who ran the café, and thousands of others
all screaming and shouting. This was the first sort of living-
incident-type theatre that we'd ever experimented with. Once
it got us into trouble, I must admit, because of some Indian
students. It was a fabulous week, and at one point the play was
interrupted by somebody shouting 'Rubbish … I think this is a
load of nonsense.' It's always a marvellous opportunity, you pray
for this, because then you say, 'How do you mean rubbish?' and
get your point over beautifully. Unfortunately one of the Indian
students who was the comedian of the camp had volunteered to
do this. Well he got as far as 'Rubbish' and he was set upon by
twenty other people: 'How dare you say that?' Then a huge fight
broke out. They were splendid days.[27]

Splendid but still not paying. In that spring Harry and George
Cooper had gone off for two weeks' intensive Laban training
under Lisa Ullmann. George and Harry telephoned to say that they
were not only crippled but broke. As Jean Newlove remembers:
'They rang and said they were stiff and whatever, and Harry said
that he needed to smoke – and they couldn't afford cigarettes and
I had absolutely very little money and I sent five cigarettes and
a bit of cardboard through to him.' When Harry returned he was
incommunicado for days, having buried his head in a book of crys-
tallography given to him at 'Laban Camp'.

By the summer things were no better, as Joan wrote:

We had a pile of debts and an income which would hardly sustain a flea circus. In June 1954, we split. Gerry couldn't feed us
through the summer months when theatres are always empty,
separately we might survive. We went camping in France and
took Harry and Avis with us. It never stopped raining and Harry
got more and more miserable. He'd taken his teapot with him
but even that didn't help. He longed to be in one of those warm
restaurants eating a posh French meal. He and Gerry tried to
find work in Les Halles and failed. So Avis went to the British
Consul and borrowed the fare home. If we didn't reassemble
soon we'd be finished, for ever.[28]

Tom Driberg allowed the company to camp out at his house again for the rest of that summer where they rehearsed the new season. The actor Barry Clayton joined at this time, as he recounts:

> The summer of '54 we all went down and lived under canvas at Tom Driberg's house in Bradwell. Gerry took us all in his big car to register for dole money each week and at the weekends we were all taken back to Stratford because we were redecorating the theatre, which was pretty shabby. That was throughout the six or eight weeks we spent at Bradwell and then we came back and we opened in the O'Neill sea plays[29] 'Bound East For Cardiff' and one or two of the other ones in the Caribbean and that was when I worked with Harry for the first time, playing Yank in 'Bound East For Cardiff' and he was an actor who wasn't acting. I always say acting is doing nothing, but with precision, and he was that kind of actor. And in that I was playing the American sailor who was dying because he'd been in an accident on board and for me it was not a moving play, it was a desperate play. But on the other hand Harry's – the way Harry worked and the generosity of the way he worked, no matter what he thought of you he was a very generous actor. And he would come off stage sometimes and say, 'What the fuck does he think he's doing?' but nevertheless he was ... I found him a very isolated man, I never found out much about him.

Not many did, as Harry always played it close to his chest, only letting a very select few in behinds the walls. Most were kept at bay with jokes and stories and, if all else failed, by agreeing with them 'til they went away. He also possessed a sense of humour that was dry to the point of brittle. Some just didn't get the joke, some like it damp, but then, you can't please everyone, you'd go nuts trying. Someone who did get the joke was Barbara Young: 'Harry always had, I can just see his face now, he had a really laconic, laid back sense of humour. Which was very funny and was kind of out of the side of his mouth – so he would get away with murder very often, because he would smile sweetly and then it would come out of the side of his mouth.'

He certainly did get away with murder, as witnessed by Barry Clayton:

Harry was a great, wonderful moaner. I mean he'd always say, 'What the fuck is she on about now? I'll do it my way, anyway.' And he'd wring his hands – he was always cold. He was always in his overcoat – a shabby old overcoat. I don't know how many years he'd had it and then he was always wringing his hands and leaning in places and getting out of everybody's way until they absolutely insisted on him turning up.

But when he did turn up he delivered, which is why Joan adored him.

After O'Neill's sea plays they staged the production that finally put them firmly on all of the critics' radars, *Arden of Faversham*. Published in 1592 the title page reads:

The Lamentable and True Tradegie of M. Arden of Feuersham in Kent. Who was most wicekdlye mvrdered, by the meanes of his disloyall and wanton wyfe, who for the love she bear to one Mosbie, hyred two desperate ruffins Blackwill and Shakbag, to kill him.

Wherin is shewed the great mallice and discimulation of a wicked woman, the unsatiable desire of filthie lvst and the shamefvll end of all murderers.

If that didn't get bums on seats, nothing would.

Barry Clayton remembers the play:

What was so wonderful, it was an unknown anonymous murder mystery and we actually went down to Faversham to look at the house where the murder took place, and that was another thing that Joan would always do, you know, if there was something that was connected with a play that we were doing say, 'Right, well we're going off to see that.' So you would get the feeling of the place.

Arden created a stir of publicity. Not only was Theatre Workshop's the first modern production, but by being anonymous it afforded theatre critics, profs and buffs a chance to postulate on whether its author was Shakespeare or one of his contemporaries.

But this new attention had a detrimental effect on the company, as described by Harry: 'Then came massive Sunday coverage. They tried to single out the actors, and eventually they got to know them and that, quite rightly, caused a certain amount of dissention.'[30] Harry was one of the few actors singled out: 'Mr Harry Corbett's Mosbie is good enough to make us wonder what he would do with Shakespeare's Crookback.'[31]

He was noticed again along with George Cooper in the subsequent production of Jaroslav Hašek's *The Good Soldier Schweik*. *Schweik* became one of Theatre Workshop's landmark productions, due, in no small way, to the utter brilliance of George in the title role. When Hašek wrote the original novel, it must have been George he saw dancing before him. 'In Mr George Cooper, the Theatre Royal, Stratford, have found a remarkable clown, who convinces us that he may well have been Schweik himself' and 'There has not been a much funnier performance in London this year.'[32]

Kenneth Tynan, the legendary theatre critic, wrote:

> With half a dozen replacements, Theatre Workshop might take London by storm. Already they have an actor of genius in Mr. Harry Corbett, who should impinge on the West End before he loses his finesse. Whether scratching and mumbling as a punch-drunk malingerer or cavorting, bewhiskered and brandy-sodden, as a romantic policeman, Mr Corbett shows greater command and composure than any young character-actor in my memory.[33]

Shirley Dynevor remembers one review in particular:

> There was one that sticks out in my mind and that was a Ken Tynan one, I'm pretty sure it was Ken Tynan, about Harry's work – how he should be picked up and garlanded and just paraded around the theatre as a tremendous triumph. It was the thought of him being carried head high that sticks in my mind … I think that is the best appreciation of an actor I ever read.

If you plug it they will come. So many came to see 'Schweik' that a transfer to the West End was mooted. Pleasing the critics and West End transfers, just what Ewan had been afraid of.

Success continued in January of 1955 when they staged a production that was to have far-reaching effects on Harry, the company and the evolution of British theatre: *Richard II*.

Notes

1 Burton, *Acting in the Sixties*.
2 Goorney, *The Theatre Workshop Story*.
3 Littlewood, *Joan's Book*.
4 Theatre Archive Project, British Library.
5 Harry, in conversation with Howard Goorney.
6 Theatre Archive Project, British Library.
7 Coren, M., *Theatre Royal: 100 years of Stratford East* (Quartet Books, 1984).
8 Goorney, *The Theatre Workshop Story*.
9 Harry, in conversation with Howard Goorney.
10 Burton, *Acting in the Sixties*.
11 Harry, in conversation with Howard Goorney.
12 Burton, *Acting in the Sixties*.
13 Goorney, *The Theatre Workshop Story*.
14 Burton, *Acting in the Sixties*.
15 *Ibid.*
16 *The Stage*, 19/2/53.
17 Leach, R., *Theatre Workshop: Joan Littlewood and the Making of Modern British Theatre* (University of Exeter Press, 2006).
18 Hodge, A., *Twentieth Century Actor Training* (ed.) (Routledge, 1999).
19 Theatre Archive Project, British Library.
20 Goorney, *The Theatre Workshop Story*.
21 *Ibid.*
22 Theatre Archive Project, British Library.
23 Goorney, *The Theatre Workshop Story*.
24 *Ibid.*
25 Theatre Archive Project, British Library.
26 Goorney, *The Theatre Workshop Story*.
27 Burton, *Acting in the Sixties*.
28 Littlewood, *Joan's Book*.
29 *Bound East for Cardiff*, *In the Zone*, *The Long Voyage Home*, and *The Moon of the Caribbees* – sometimes referred to as the SS *Glencairn* plays, after the fictitious ship in all of the plays.
30 Goorney, *The Theatre Workshop Story*.
31 *The Times*, 29/9/54.
32 *Evening Standard*, 10/11/54.
33 *Observer*, 14/11/54.

8

Dick 2

'Richard II' was one of the happiest plays I've ever been in –
a silly thing to say, I don't mean it in that twee way, we were
all lovely with each other. I mean purely and simply that the
greatest joy for me and a lot of the other actors was working at
rehearsals. Ah, that's when it's fantastic. It begins. You create. You
create in rehearsal, then you spend ages and ages through the run
of the play trying to recreate that first beautiful, savage getting
of the idea. I'd envisaged it in silks and gowns and everybody
looking lovely; it's all the verse, it's so beautifully done. Then you
get down to the horrifying reality of the grey stone wall, that a
man is saying, 'If only my fingernails could rip through the cages
of these walls'; we tried to create the walls – it was a fantastic
experience, the happiest. [1]

Harry H. Corbett

The company had originally staged *Richard II* a year earlier. Harry
Greene said, 'Joan confided in us at a company meeting that she
thought Harry C. would make a brilliant Richard II, which was
prophetic of course. It was one good reason to choose the play, she
said. And this from one of the most exceptionally gifted theatre
directors in the UK.'

Barry Clayton recalls the rehearsals:

It was one of the most grilling, on one level, periods. The way
Joan worked, the way rehearsals were planned minutely for three
or four weeks in advance. She would have each scene written
out and what we were doing on that day. And working with

the Company physically, you know, when we did things like 'Richard II' in which Harry gave an extraordinary performance as Richard and Joan had us play the opening scenes of 'Richard II' at a football match – and you know it's a battle between Bolingbroke and Mowbray and they were kicking a ball at each other and getting the effect as Joan and Laban would always talk about, the effort of energy, not to waste energy and how we had to observe the economy of the energy we get.

Then it would be on to that night's performance, as Barry continues:

Joan would always start the evening, we had an hour call not a half hour call, and we would go in and do movement exercises, Laban stuff or vocal things and sometimes improvisations which were based on the theme of the play in order to revise our memory of the training we'd discovered through the rehearsal period.

For those who have never caught the play or studied it at school, Shakespeare's *Richard II* tells the story of a young king who has not furnished the throne with an heir and is more interested in the latest Italian fashions and in his divine right to rule than actually getting on with doing a good job of ruling. He also overly relies on the advice and 'company' of a few favourites – never a good idea. Instead of letting a duel sort out an argument between his cousin Bolingbroke and another nobleman, Thomas Mowbray, he banishes them both. Bolingbroke's father, John of Gaunt, staunchly believing in the divine right of kings over 'This blessed plot, this earth, this realm, this England' tries to get Richard to pull his socks up. Gaunt then dies and Richard nicks his vast wealth and lands, and thus Bolingbroke's inheritance, to pay for a war in Ireland. He also funds this war with taxes on the poor and by fining the nobles for 'ancient quarrels'. While Richard is away in Ireland, Bolingbroke returns and reclaims his inheritance. When the king returns, Bolingbroke seizes the throne and is crowned as Henry IV. Richard is sent to Pontefract Castle, where he ruminates on his downfall while losing his grip on reality, and is then murdered.

This is the first of the Wars of the Roses cycle of plays that continues with *Henry IV Part I* and *Part II*, *Henry V*, *Henry VI Part I*, *Part II* and *Part III*, and only resolves at the end of *Richard III* when Henry Tudor wins Bosworth and is crowned

Henry VII. And there was much rejoicing. Now Shakespeare's *Richard II* is a tad dubious as far as historical fact is concerned, in reality parliament was so worried about John of Gaunt seizing the throne for himself that they banned him from being sole regent when Richard II inherited the throne at age ten (very divine right of kings). Gaunt's son, Bolingbroke, not only usurped Richard but also the rightful heir to the throne, the Earl of March, another cousin ahead of Bolingbroke in the line of succession. But the play was written in the 1590s when the then monarch, Elizabeth I, was old and had no heir, had a penchant for favourites and was not as popular as she once was; to point out those similarities to *Richard II* was bad enough (as was well known to the Earl of Essex who, on the eve of his rebellion against Elizabeth, paid to have the play performed to rouse the rabble of London – well the rabble weren't roused and Essex lost his head) but only the most suicidal of playwrights would have also pointed out that John of Gaunt's descendants through his third marriage, Henry Tudor and his granddaughter Queen Elizabeth, were specifically banned from the line of succession by Richard II due to illegitimacy. History is written by the winners, and to be on their team meant playing up *Richard II*'s faults and John of Gaunt's glories.

Theatre Workshop decided to revive the production at the beginning of 1955 to deliberately coincide with a much more lavish production, as Harry explained:

> The Old Vic was doing 'Richard II', so we thought what a splen-
> did idea; we'll do 'Richard II' right? We'll have two 'Richard II's',
> then you can have a classical mean. People can visit the Old Vic's
> 'Richard II', discuss it, and they can have a real go. Because every
> Sunday we used to throw the place open and have general criti-
> cism, people coming in and shouting and screaming what they
> felt and what they thought should be and should not be.[2]

The Old Vic production had a cast of forty-five and cost thou-sands, Theatre Workshop's had a cast of fourteen and cost fifty quid. Howard Goorney wrote:

> At the Old Vic all was pomp and ceremony. On a stage full of
> light, coloured pennants flew, fanfares played, and the atten-
> dant Lords and spear-carriers manoeuvred into position, while

everyone waited for the scenes to begin. The actors were elegantly dressed and beautifully spoken. John Neville's Richard, as befitted an actor who had been compared to the young Gielgud, was a truly regal figure, always aware of his bearing and the poetry of the lines, even when chained to the floor of his cell. While not pretending to be objective in our judgement, we didn't feel that anyone on the stage was really involved in the events taking place. In John Bury's stark setting, conceived to emphasise fear and oppression, we aimed to bring out the hatred and cruelty of the period. Light was used to break up the stage, scenes were able to merge swiftly one into another and there was no pause for spectacle. Our concern always was for the inner action behind the lines – what they meant, rather than the poetry of the words.[3]

The chance for direct comparison obviously caused quite a commotion with the critics, just as it was meant to. *The Guardian* had the honours even – agreeing with Howard on the poetry of Neville and the gritty realism of Theatre Workshop's production. *The Times* critic found Joan's production so startling he was 'asking if this can possibly be Shakespeare's play at all. Is it not that lost play about Richard which some editors have postulated, and on which they suppose that Shakespeare based his own pathetic symphony?' He added: 'Mr Harry Corbett's King is not merely effeminate and cruelly capricious, his sudden fluctuations from arrogant self-assertion to cringing submissiveness are from the outset the symptoms of insanity.'[4]

The Stage recommended the production at Stratford to those who 'like their Shakespeare straight, that is, with the beauty of the verse undimmed, but with a complete absence of the customary trappings of a West End staging.' It continued: 'As Richard, Harry Corbett gives a powerful and touching performance, bringing out the weakness in the King, yet giving the touch of nobility that the part demands.'[5]

Kenneth Tynan in his review – which is now studied at universities my dear – said: 'Truly, an embarrassment of Richards. On my right, the Old Vic's Richard II, a well scrubbed fighter of spare physique; very much on my left, Theatre Workshop's production at Stratford E., a crowding south-paw. The Old Vic wins, as it was bound to do, on points.' Tynan, who had called Harry an actor of genius, was seemingly livid with the performance:

I guessed beforehand that Mr. Harry Corbett, a natural choice
for the third Richard, might make heavy going of the second:
I could never have guessed to what extremes his temperamen-
tal wrongness would lead him. The part is played in a frenzy
of effeminacy ... I take Mr. Corbett's to be a highly effective
rendering of a totally false idea. The inference that Richard was
a pervert rests on a few ambiguous lines wherein Bolingbroke
condemns the caterpillars for having

> Made a divorce betwixt his queen and him,
> Broke the possession of a royal bed

Which might mean no more than Richard took concubines.[6]

It might indeed, but Joan thought otherwise as George Cooper,
who played Bolingbroke, remembered:

> Joan would say, 'Look, you are wanting the throne aren't you? You've
> got to get rid of this homosexual freak, this Richard II, so what are
> you going to do to achieve that end?' ... I enjoyed Bolingbroke as
> well, come to think of it really and truly. Because he's a real, you
> know, he's a real bastard, out for power etc. How Harry survived
> that I just do not know, because Joan decided to accentuate the
> homosexual thing. And so Harry obligingly ... because you always
> did what Joan told you to do, played it you know a little bit sort of
> like this. And we had a school audience on one occasion, and they
> of course took the mickey. As soon as they realised how Harry was
> playing the part they went, 'Ooh, hello' and all this business was
> going on. How Harry survived that I do not know because ...
> He did, he played it, but it nearly finished him, I'm sure, because
> I mean, Joan had to sympathise with him afterwards, and saying you
> know, 'Little sods, they were just sort of being you know, crummy,
> as far as I'm concerned. You know, just ignore them.'[7]

Though it would never have happened I can't shake the image
of the fearsome critic Kenneth Tynan surrounded by school kids
shouting 'Hello sailor.' Oh, if only.

Barry Clayton tells of a compliment paid to the company from
perhaps a surprising source:

> I ṭḥink Harry in 'Richard II', his voice changed, the way he com-
> manded being a king and yet being aware of his own weakness

as a king and as a man was something which he conveyed which could be quite chilling.

John Gielgud used to come, I'll never forget after a performance I saw him standing in the wings and he sort of said, 'I don't know what it is you people are doing here but it's absolutely wonderful and I could never do it myself.' It might even have been 'Richard II'. He was one of our regulars. He was a man who was a certain kind of actor out of a certain sort of period but he had a love of theatre and a love of people who were kicking a few arses, artistically speaking.

He wasn't the only Old Vic actor who saw the production, as Barbara Young tells:

People still talk, I've got old friends, old actors now, Nicky [Nicholas] Amer, for example, who was at the Old Vic doing 'Richard' when Harry did 'Richard' and he talks about how they were all given free seats to go and see the Theatre Workshop production because they'd been in one that John Neville was in and none of them could believe how much better was the one at Theatre Workshop with Harry playing 'Richard'. But he always remembers going to see, the whole Company went, that they were doing at the Old Vic, and they all sort of sat there and their jaws dropped and thought 'Oh my God, this is how it should be done.'

Nicholas Amer remembers that night:

Our production was very Hollywood. John Neville looked very dishy in gorgeous costumes and Virginia McKenna was just beautiful. We were invited by Joan Littlewood to see their production and I can remember being on the tube and being in a very happy mood because we were getting the chance to see it and we were all struck dumb – because it was a totally different play. It seemed, in a way, a much better play because it doesn't really work doing it à la Hollywood.

You couldn't get in at the Old Vic because everyone flocked to see their matinee idol. John was a lovely guy; he was the successor to Gielgud.

Here was a totally different Richard. I thought it was totally mesmerising and really excellent. Some of the members of our

company were a bit miffed 'Oh, ours is so much prettier and nicer'
but I thought no, this had got real life about it. We came back on
the tube really quite chastened. We met all the cast afterwards but
we were a bit monosyllabic – we didn't know what to say and
they didn't know what to say. It was a bit before its time in a way.
We did miss the lovely verse speaking and the music but I though
Harry was superb. I thought he was destined for great things.

For a couple of youngsters who saw that production it was a
life-changing experience. The actors Murray Melvin and Brian
Murphy have a strikingly similar story. Murray Melvin was a
teenager taken to Stratford by his youth club drama teacher, Jess
Harrison, as he recalled:

> One week she announced that we would not rehearse the fol-
> lowing week as she was going to take us all to the theatre. She
> had read that there was a company that she had seen when
> she lived in Glasgow, they were called the Theatre Workshop,
> and this company had taken over a theatre at Stratford in East
> London. Now, she considered them to be the finest theatrical
> company in the country. So the following week we all met after
> work and took a long – for those days – long journey to the
> Theatre Royal in the East End of London. The play we saw
> was *Richard II* ... Now, Stratford was run on a shoestring, so
> there were no long golden cloaks, no long fanfares, no great
> long processionals coming on stage – just raw Elizabethan lan-
> guage. And you were on the edge of the seat the whole evening.
> Elizabethan language spoken on the moment, rather than on
> the breath. I considered that to be the first time I had seen real
> theatre. It was gob smacking.[8]

> It made sense, every second of it. It was accessible – Miss
> Littlewood's mantra – it's got to be accessible, everything you're
> doing, Ben Johnson or a contemporary piece, it has to be acces-
> sible – you don't put on a mystery tour.[9]

Murray later joined the company, was in the original stage and film
versions of *A Taste of Honey* and, in addition to his career, is now the
Archivist of Theatre Royal, Stratford East. He works tirelessly to
keep the Workshop's spirit alive and is a veritable dynamo.

Brian Murphy was at Borough Polytechnic and was persuaded by his mentor, who ran evening drama classes there, to come along and see the company he would join years before his rampant success on television:

The first time I'd ever seen Workshop in all its glory was when Harry was playing Richard II. Most of my ambition was to join the Old Vic and there was John Neville playing at the same time but I had a wonderful mentor – Tom Vaughan – who said 'There's this wonderful company out at Stratford East,' hardly celebrated at that time at Stratford because it was derelict, it was run down. Only one oxy acetylene lamp hanging from the ceiling for lighting and warmth and I said 'Oh really, I haven't heard of them before, I'll go with you.' The seats were held together, many of them, with nails.

Now the first innovation was that when we went into the theatre the curtain was up. And I had never been into a theatre where the curtain was up. And I could see the set. And my first reaction was can't they afford a curtain. But soon my attention was grabbed, because I was now looking at the set, and I was scanning it and thinking 'oh that's interesting, I wonder what they're going to use that for', and things. And suddenly you realise of course that's quite a cunning move, because instead of when the curtain goes up, now you've got all the actors exploding on the stage, and you've got to take in who's who, what's what, and the set – you've got the set out of the way.[10]
Suddenly you heard a row and it sounded like a row that was being held in the wings, you know, and you thought 'this is a bit noisy, isn't it?' but it was a row that got closer and closer and you suddenly distinguished words and onto the stage burst Harry and George Cooper as Bolingbroke and literally, for that first ten minutes in particular myself and my friends, we fell out of our seats – it was easy, of course, because they were only held together by hope – but the excitement, our jaws were open throughout the whole evening. I'd never seen theatre at that level, that was literally in your face in the best sense of the word. There was no poncing around in wonderful costumes. They wore what it looked like were their outfits, what they would normally be wearing. The king's were a bit more 'royal' than the people – but they looked as if they weren't wearing costumes,

they were wearing their clothes, it was remarkable. That was the first time I'd seen him – I mean I'd heard about Harry, cause the jungle drums had reached the other side of London about the good stuff that was going on at Stratford – but seeing him there in the flesh, I thought he was totally remarkable.

None of the Shakespeare was beautifully spoken in the sense of the 'Old Vic' which was delivered in rotund terms, there was a driving force – it was a language used, and Harry seemed to me, as I found later, was one of the best exponents of making it his own. But it wasn't like they do today; they sometimes play down to the Shakespeare, don't they. They try and make it commonplace, as you would exchange in the street with pauses. No, this was a driving language, you felt it to be of another period, but it made absolute sense. Harry was one of the finest exponents of that.[11]

It was a whole new approach, and it left a legacy. In his book on Theatre Workshop, Robert Leach, the theatre scholar and director, wrote that *Richard II* was:

a production that examined the play anew, and sought to find how its ideas might resonate with the times. It is difficult today to believe how original this was in 1954. The climax came on John Bury's gloomy, dimly-lit prison set, when the king was seen sackcloth and tethered to a stake, limping in a slow circle round it, and startling the spectators with 'I wasted time and now doth time waste me'.

For Tom Milne:

Joan Littlewood's production had rough edges in the minor roles and costumes, but the core of the play was thrust forward with passionate conviction, and it was impossible to fail to be excited, to think about the play and what it meant. By contrast [the Old Vic] production, elegantly dressed and spoken, remained quite dead.

Another critic captured the brilliance of the performer's ability to relate the internal truth to the external, while simultaneously making Elizabethan history relevant to 1950s Britain:

Harry Corbett in the part of Richard displayed deep understanding of the character and with great artistic ability interpreted it
with a variety which never ran counter to the inner consistency
of the part of a ruler mentally unbalanced from the beginning
of the play. Mr Corbett was properly theatrical in externalis-
ing the mind of a real man and it was noteworthy how exactly
Shakespeare's words express a condition of mind which is
so grave a problem with us today. The actor interpreted the
character through the malady, making it sadly familiar to our
understanding whilst keeping it in period.

This was a performance that gave back to the age both its own
pretensions and its own pitifulness. Corbett's achievement, which is
more broadly true of the Theatre Workshop company of actors as
a whole, was to set British acting on a new, more truthful, course.[12]

As a particularly pertinent example of Harry and Theatre
Workshop's legacy one could look to the Royal Shakespeare
Company's production of *Richard II* in 2000, with Sam West playing Richard. Maxwell Cooter wrote of the production in 2001:
'Sam West's flighty, duplicitous, arrogant and overly-gay Richard is
almost unable to comprehend the extent of Bolingbroke's revolt
until the last possible moment. In this production, Aumerle is
fashioned as his lover, an interesting twist, which makes Aumerle's
participation in the anti-Henry plot more credible.' 'Overly-gay' –
I wonder what Tynan would have made of it?

Robert Hole went on to comment:

This is a wonderful production, but it will not be to everyone's
taste. If you like your theatre to be a charming box of delights
with beautiful period costumes and elaborate sets, then forget it.
But if you enjoy demanding drama which is powerful, intense
and challenging, then Steven Pimlott's studio version of Richard
II is for you.' 'If anyone is so naive and foolish to believe that
politics is an honourable profession for decent men and women,
they should see this play. They'll soon be disillusioned. This is a
Richard II for the year 2000, Shakespeare at the cutting edge.

After forty-five years that cutting edge must have been getting pretty sharp. By a remarkable twist of fate, history repeated
itself even more. Sam West opened as Richard II at Stratford on

20 March, and ten days later Ralph Fiennes opened as Richard II at the Gainsborough Studios – the critics salivated at the prospect of a direct comparison between the two. Ah, how the wheel turns ...

In 1955 the company were not aware this was one of their many landmark productions, to be later dissected by then embryonic theatre professors – turning a play around every three weeks does not give much time to keep an eye on posterity or inspect the fluff of the artistic navel. *Richard II*'s success saw it extended to a fourth week, while the company rehearsed *The Other Animals* by Ewan MacColl, with Ewan – taking a break from 'wasting' his time with folk music – as a political prisoner undergoing interrogation and Harry as the prisoner's 'other self'. They were also rehearsing a modern dress production of Ben Jonson's *Volpone*. Howard Goorney later wrote of the production:

> Without needing to alter or cut, it transposed to modern day Italy, as a satire on spivs and hangers-on; Mosca rode a bicycle laden with pineapples and champagne, Corbaccio wheeled himself around in an invalid chair and Sir Politic Would-Be, the Englishman abroad, wore swimming trunks and carried a snorkel.[13]

Harry remembered:

> I was told to play Politic Would-be and I sort of did a pretty moo at this cause I wanted to play Mosca or one of the other parts and Joan said, 'This part's been un-actable for years, you're doing it', and I thought – Hello, there goes the butter again. So I just took it, slung it around and did a comedy review job on it, and low and behold people said it had been un-actable. All I'm trying to say is, one did not have a preconception going into a part – 'My God, this part's been un-actable for years. Will Macbeth ever work on the stage?'[14]

According to *The Stage* it was 'one of the most excitingly alive productions that London has seen for many months ... The part of Sir Politic has always been a challenge to the actor but Harry Corbett, presenting him as an inane Tory back-bencher with deer-stalker hat and binoculars, gives him unusual vitality.'[15]

Despite all this critical success they were still operating on a shoestring. Howard Goorney wrote: 'I had to make an appeal for money from the stage after each show with the cast lined up behind me shuffling their feet and cringing with embarrassment. There was a white box in the foyer to receive donations.'[16]

Given how charity had stuck in Harry's craw as a boy, you can guess who was the most embarrassed. This appeal fund was for the direct benefit of the starving actors. Shirley Dynevor, who after meeting Gerard immediately fell pregnant with their son Josh, remembers: 'If you had a baby you'd get a bit extra. It came out of the till at the door. Quite often Howard Goorney used to stand at the door when people came out of the Theatre with a little tin and people used to put in and it would be divided and if you had a baby then you'd get an extra quid.'

Even if actors had a good fighting weight when they arrived, they soon lost it. Josephine Smith, the costume designer, recalled, 'One actor was so thin I had to build him padded tights, to wear under the other ones, he was so skinny! That was Maxwell Shaw. Ooh, he was thin. Poor chap. When he was wearing black he nearly disappeared, so I had to build him padded tights.'[17]

Gerry had contacted all the local authorities for help but none was forthcoming until 1957. The Arts Council itself gave Theatre Workshop £150 for the financial year 1954/55, the next year this jumped to the princely sum of £500. As a comparison, at the end of 1954 the English Opera Group received £4,000, with a supplementary £2,000 to cover any deficit. 'Ah yes, but that's opera,' I hear you cry. Well in 1956 the embryonic English Stage Company at The Royal Court 'was offered £2500 start up money and £7000 for its first year. Yes these were meagre by Continental standards; nonetheless during 1956–1957 the ESC was already the fifth largest recipient of money from the drama panel. By the end of the second year only the Old Vic theatre and company got more.'[18]

At the risk of adding to the one-upmanship later contrived between Theatre Workshop and the Royal Court, the latter says of itself (in a statement that would have early members of Theatre Workshop frothing at the mouth): 'On 8 May 1956, John Osborne's *Look Back in Anger* opened at the Royal Court on Sloane Square. It was the third production of the new English Stage Company, under Artistic Director George Devine, and is now considered the play that marks the beginning of modern British drama.'

This was the play that gave the world 'The Angry Young Man'. Some would argue that Osborne's angry young man was middle class enough for the Arts Council to smile upon it, and smile they did: 'In Autumn 1957, the Arts Council itself managed a tour of *Look Back in Anger* to Wales and the North East.'[19] Bill Ormond, who had joined Theatre Workshop for *Richard II*, commented that *Look Back in Anger*: 'looked a bit left wingish, protesting and revolutionary at the time in the West End. But you put it in a mining village it would be reactionary, I mean it would entertain the miners, yeah ok, but they would get bored – they wouldn't see anything about it that would reflect their lives.'

For the Arts Council, the problem wasn't so much Theatre Workshop's politics but their professionalism and personality, as explained by John Bury:

> In the early days, we were regarded as a bunch of Reds. Moscow Gold and all that stuff. At Stratford East, I think it was the lack of accountability that worried them. There was a lot of fuss about the books and keeping it together, programming and playing. Joan would always be rude to them. We didn't play their game and they weren't going to play ours.[20]

In their defence Anthony Field CBE, the former finance director of the Arts Council, when asked why Theatre Workshop lost out on funding had this to say:

> There was always a slight problem. The Drama Panel and we in the Finance Department would say, 'OK, whether it's Sheffield or Birmingham Rep or Bristol Old Vic, they are servicing an area', and there was always a worry ... although the English Stage Company got itself well established from the early years as a sort of purveyor of new plays, there was always a slight worry with Guildford, Leatherhead, Hornchurch, Theatre Royal Stratford, that they were so near the London conurbation they weren't necessarily servicing a region in the way that, say, Birmingham Rep was or Bristol Old Vic. And I think in a way they lost out by being on the fringe of the whole of the West End, in a way, and there was always this worry about 'Are we in fact subsidising a theatre company servicing a region or in those days of course we were also subsidising Hazel Vincent Wallace at Leatherhead, David Poulson at Bromley, but should we be subsidising Joan Littlewood or the Theatre Royal Stratford Company?' And there

was always this worry as to whether we were subsidising a char-ismatic person or a theatre.[21]

In 1957, the year Anthony Field took over as its finance director, the Arts Council awarded Theatre Workshop a whole £1,000, and it's hard to say whether Field's appointment helped or hindered the company, what with him being Gerry Raffles' cousin.

Two years earlier this was all still to come, and our merry band at Stratford were eking out the 150 quid. Harry was to comment:

> And so Joan had a lifetime of patching and stitching together bits and pieces and making do, and inside I always felt that her heart yearned for something better. We had to do the Moliere without ballet shoes, without proper costumes, so all we had were tights with bits of ribbons tied round, and the critics made such a song and dance about how brilliant this was. This must have galled her – she must have wanted to say 'I would have put bloody costumes on if we could have afforded the sodding things'.[22]

How was it possible that this little company should be staging such remarkable work with no backing and no financial reward? Most of the business thought of them as a bunch of barking zealots. The actor and writer Clive Goodwin put it to Harry that sections of the establishment thought of Theatre Workshop as a cross between a trade union meeting and a concentration camp:

> Concentration camps! Certainly not concentration camps. You know the most precious thing we have is time, we have so little. There's no time for champagne. There's very little time for night-clubs, even when you're a so-called success. The kind of thing we were doing was a twenty-four-hour day. I would rehearse four hours in the morning on Volpone, and four hours in the after-noon on Volpone, and I'd go on and play three hours of Richard II: pretty tough. As soon as the curtain dropped at eleven o'clock, I would be starting the first fencing lesson.
>
> Now this produced an atmosphere of its own. There was liter-ally no time to do anything else but concentrate; people lived, breathed, and fed on it: you had hardly any time for food.[23]

Yes, pretty tough. So why do it? Was it for Joan? Was she some kind of grubby Gloriana with her court of kinder, her clowns, at her feet, idolising her every word? Not in Harry's view:

> Well one thing we really must get away from is the idea of a personality cult about Joan. Joan was nothing apart from the material she worked with, and if ever Joan had bad material, actors, etc., there was very little she could do with them. Joan was the beginner, the suggester, the bringer of ideas, but they all found an echo within the people she was working with, and they were loyal to her ideal. We had company meetings in which she was really ripped apart at times, believe you me; there certainly was no iron hand about it whatsoever.[24]

The 'Cult of Joan' started in the 1960s, when Theatre Workshop had become dependent on critical approval, regularly transferred plays to the West End and had been going so long that it was becoming the establishment, which, as Ewan had predicted, would mean its doom. Joan's reclusive later life only enhanced her mystique.

Harry Greene, when asked what he thought of this view of Joan as a director of genius, had this to say:

> Yes, she has been called a genius, she's been called a director of distinction. We've read that in books, magazines, articles and over the last twenty years we've read even more about her genius.
>
> But I think that sometimes these writers' works on Joan are glorifying her. Sometimes the works of idolatrous writers represent her productions in their sort of ideal forms, rather than as they were, as we knew them. I think that they miss one essential, they were not there at the beginning, and let me explain about that.
>
> In those formative years Joan's experimentation and the shaping of her, and of our ideas as well, began to determine the future style of the company's productions. You see, only we had full knowledge of what went on during the always closed rehearsals, and always secret company meetings. But at those meetings she encouraged us to join her sometimes in seeing current West End plays.
>
> We saw all the big stars you know. We saw Gielgud at the Queen's, declaiming, you know – not real theatre, as we knew

it. Michael Redgrave, always camping it up, and always Michael Redgrave, and then John Neville – always strident, we always thought. And all being stars, with no rapport with fellow actors. We used to talk about that, and we all knew that Joan had more creative ideas in her little finger than all those West End producers put together.

Joan went to the Old Vic at times and she loved the Palladium, she loved some of those big, larger than life people. But I think she went in order to give us notes – she always gave us notes. Yes, it was wonderful. It was wonderful living and breathing the air of Theatre Royal, Stratford. Still poor though.

Joan always said, 'Have a pride in belonging to an ensemble, a group. Everybody equal, no hierarchy.' Except of course, I always believed, Joan really enjoyed her dictatorship – oops, I'd better reword that! – a benign dictatorship.

But what you've got to remember is a boss is a boss in any group or organization. And sometimes that boss has to be devious or a bit of hypocrite to get results. She dictated, certainly. She got her way, fair enough. But Joan was interested in what happened to people when they worked together with as much security as they can get. She wrote, 'The notion that drew us together was the exploration of a method of work. It was not in the presentation of ideas in dramatic form that an aesthetic developed. It was in analysis, research and a study of human expression. If we only touched on these things we sharpened our sensibility.'

Think about it … we were doing actually everything that she preached. So, dictator, yes. Group theatre, sure. She had the ability and the knowledge to tower over all of us. Nevertheless, each one of us enjoyed an experience that comes once in a lifetime.[25]

Harry would remember well the methods that Joan would employ to make sure that 'she got her way':

She would use tears, if it would get her point. She'd cry, weep bitter tears, and always when you didn't expect it. You were all primed to have a go at Joan, a real go, then would come the tears; or you were primed to be lovely and you'd get the screams. I mean, she would come on with that walk, off would go the hat on to the floor. 'Now listen, Kids …' We knew what we were in for. It was splendid.[26]

Tears, naturally, wouldn't have worked quite as well on the female members of the cast – so they usually only got the screams. As George Cooper said: 'I've always thought that any girl who joined the company was in for a rough time because Joan had such a hell of a time as a young kid and all the rest of it, she thought "Well. I went through it, let's see if they can go through it."'

Marjie Lawrence remembered that Joan would:

> sit up in the balcony every night, the front row balcony, taking copious notes about the performances. She would then pin them up on the board, just inside the stage door, for everybody to read. Sometimes they could be quite insulting, like saying 'oh, you came on stage like a sack of flour' – really hard, she was quite hard on women, on younger women in a way, I felt. I suppose that was quite natural in a sense … I don't know whether I should put this in really, I sometimes felt she was a little bit off if you were attractive and so on. But that was a sort of natural thing.[27]

According to Barbara Young it was the other way around: 'Actually she was always much more lethal with the men than she was with the women. It was easier for her, I expect, to crush the chaps than the girls, or maybe she wasn't as interested in the girls.' Or maybe Barbara knew Joan well enough to ignore her.

Avis remarked:

> Of the women, I think I survived longer than any of them because I wouldn't always give in to Joan. There was always a girl in tears somewhere because Joan was very hard on women. The men she got on with fabulously. She used to upset me in the first year, but I tried not to show it. She used to hate people saying 'Oh yes, Joan, you're right Joan.' I was the one that used to say 'No, that's stupid, I'm not doing that.' I didn't actually argue with her but I wouldn't do everything she said and I think she liked that. If you had ideas of your own she'd use them and build up on them.[28]

The inevitable high turnover of actresses benefited Avis: 'There weren't so many girls in the company and they were all inexperienced, so, having had so many years in repertory, I got all the best parts. I was playing dumb blondes and all sorts of parts I would never normally play.'[29]

Harry and George Cooper were also cast into a myriad variety of roles – for which, at first glance, they would appear unsuited – often with wonderful results. Though this was, perhaps, truly a case of necessity being the mother of invention. Peter Rankin, a friend and confidant of Joan's, said:

> Of course the place was always evolving, because to start with you had a team of people who were politically aligned and aligned with the whole idea of Theatre Workshop, but you get a feel from Gerry's diaries, notes and letters that he thought they were very keen but not very talented. That sounds a bit blasphemous, but as I said, I am reading between the lines. When two actors, Avis Bunnage and Harry Corbett came along, now they were not so politically aligned by any manner of means, and Joan used to be quite scornful about their politics, but they could do it. They could do what she wanted, and so could an actor called George A. Cooper, and they became her principal actors. Gerry would have been very appreciative of that, because he did like solid, strong performers. He likes clear voices and this whole idea about Performance with a capital P.[30]

Barbara Young agreed with Gerry: 'There were quite a lot of people in the company, although they were lovely and good company members, they weren't necessarily proper actors in a way, and Harry always was. He was a proper actor.'

Joan always wanted the very best that you could be and would use any means to get it out of you. She was cruel to be kind – well, perhaps not kind – she was cruel to be effective. Only very rarely did that cruelty spill over into the real world and only at moments of high drama. Jean Gaffin, a secretary at the theatre remembered:

> I forgot a crucial appointment that Gerry had. I just forgot to remind him to go to see someone … I can't remember where it was, maybe it was Newham, maybe it was the Arts Council, but it was very important and I … it was in the diary and I just forgot to tell him. And so I was really upset … she was very angry. He was very angry with me. And Gerry developed diabetes around that time, and she once came into the office and harangued me, and said it was all my fault and it was because I was so incompetent that Gerry had got diabetes. And I was just

absolutely flattened by it, you know in a way that … You know, at 70 I wouldn't be, but at 16, 17 I was absolutely … So, you know, she could be very nice and warm and friendly, but somehow or other I'd … you know, I worked for Gerry, and I worked for the company but somehow or other I didn't have a relationship with Joan that was anything but scary for me.[31]

Murray Melvin said of Joan that:

She could see the potential. That's why it was so difficult. She was always demanding from you more than you knew was there. She always wanted that next step – that's why she battered you. She railed at you. You had to be strong. Oh, I've seen so many come and go. I can remember she got somebody doing a show – we'd been at it a couple of days and she started tearing into us and after about a week she tore into this chap and he suddenly flipped and said 'I don't understand, I can't seem to do anything good for you.' And she went 'Oh love, I'm sorry. Oh, I don't do praise love – none of my kinder get praise. I haven't got time to tell you when you're good. You have to accept that if you're in my company – you're good. All I've got time for is to try and get you better.' If you wanted praise – off! And it was wearing, it was, that continual charging at you verbally, screaming at you.

For some her approach had no end game. Barbara Young thought that:

Joan had an amazing ability to get you to a certain point when she was directing you, then systematically she would proceed to knock you down bit, by bit, by bit in order to get you back to exactly the same place she had you before she started knocking you down. So you never really got any further, because she couldn't take you further.

The playwright Henry Livings had a brief stint with the company and recounted that a Workshop production of 'Edward II was to put the lead actor [Peter Smallwood] in a psychiatric hospital for a time and out of the theatre permanently.' While after Joan had:

demolished a scene in performance by changing all the lines round, in the cause of spontaneity, she offered 'Better wasn't it?'

I rejoined that it was the worst fucking seven minutes I'd ever spent onstage. Her eyes softened to clear entrancing blue pools of love, and she murmured 'There has to be a destructive as well as a creative art, you know, they go together.'[32]

Obviously not many could cope with this. George Cooper said: 'She always tried to destroy people when they joined the company. In my case it was a good idea because I always have been a real old ham. If you've got the humility to take it all, it's the best thing really.'

Destroying without rebuilding can be a dangerous business and one that needs careful handling. Barbara Young remembered an occasion involving Harry Greene's Epping Forrest accomplice:

> There was a chap called Karl Woods, a beautiful lion headed boy from Northumberland. He was going to play Prince Hal. I don't think he ever got around to playing it. She decided he could play Henry – of course he couldn't. What she did to him was indescribable. She made him sweep the stage. I discussed it with Harry, how she destroyed him. You do not put a boy like that on the stage.

Karl's closest friend in the company, Harry G., remembers him as a decent, sensitive man and honest citizen. But Karl could also be overly introverted. When Joan decided he would make a tough Prince Hal, she said, according to Harry G.:

> 'He'd have too much to do in his examination of the life of Henry's son in the external world, rather than directing his mind to his own inner problems.' She was wrong and he became more obsessed with not being able to sort out minor problems of daily existence. She failed to see that he was a man with a mind in turmoil. So she gave him hard physical tasks to do but he said that he felt himself a failure. At Stratford he became boilerman and played odd and sods as well as doing the tough tasks like lowering and raising the iron curtain nightly. [And, of course, nicking trees.] Anyway, not unexpectedly he left one day soon after and I heard that he lived rough for some time up north, apparently living in a back garden sleeping in a barrel. We lost touch with him in the early 60's and he died over twenty years ago. Lots of people blamed Joan for not caring more and I have mixed feelings.

Another who couldn't cope was Harry's friend Gerard Dynevor, not from want of humility but for need of a gentler touch. Gerard suffered from occasional black depressions and his wife Shirley said of Joan: 'I think she damaged Gerard, I think she took his actor's life away from him.'

Harry wouldn't have enjoyed witnessing any of that. He always had a very nurturing attitude to his fellow actors, especially the young. I would imagine Theatre Workshop was where he formed his life-long habit of always leaving the dressing room door open, at the ready for a chat, or a quiet word if needed. However, when asked directly by Howard about Joan's approach he succinctly said: 'You can't destroy confidence that's not begging to be destroyed.'[33]

So to get through it you did have to possess a certain toughness and humility. Given Harry's experiences up to this point, he had already lived through far worse than what show business would ever throw at him. Josephine Smith, the costume designer, guessed at this when she noted that: 'Harry Corbett was awful on firework night. He had quite a bad war, I think. And pops and bangs and things used to give him the jitters. So he used to have to be … used to stay in out the way of fireworks.' I would like to point out that he did get better, and during our childhood would take on boxes of fireworks in the back garden – though his enjoyment of firework night was probably always once removed. Harry never discussed with the company what he'd gone through in the war. One didn't. In conversation with Jean Newlove I mentioned his experiences and she had this to say: 'If Harry had had to do hand to hand combat and bump people off – I can't imagine him ever wanting to do that, him being in that position – it would be almost like therapy being in Theatre Workshop.'

For those actors who could stay the course the rewards were immense, as Harry explained:

> Consequently the actor found a freedom he'd never had before. If he said he couldn't do a thing, he was allowed to say why he couldn't do it. Some actors had cried out for freedom for ages, and Joan gave them that freedom. Then for the first time they were face to face with their deficiencies, their lack of knowledge; they were at the lowest point of creative endeavours in their lives. After they'd dressed themselves up in a world which relied on 75 per cent bull and 25 per cent knowledge – that was the

commercial world – they used to scream and say the commercial theatre is terrible, it's this, that, and the other. When they were given their chance to have a real go, it hurt them to find out how much they had relied on tricks, on make-up, on lighting. At Stratford East we used little make-up, if any at all, it was completely verboten; we had three-dimensional side lighting, or the House lights up: anything that made the point. This was no help to the actors who came with their tricks. [Joan wouldn't allow them.] No. Not in the actors she was working with. I wouldn't allow it when I was on stage. And they could see that. They had to work; to fight. You see, what was most important was the fact that you had to fight for your character. It's not all beautifully drilled: your character now. No, after you, partner!

It was get straight in there. Believe in the man. If for instance you played Hitler, not that I'd ever want to play the man, but the first premise is that you must love the character. You've got to learn to love him or you can't play him, or any other character. You can't play him with tricks. You can, but it's terribly unsatisfactory. You've got to get that audience transfixed with the ideas you're putting over. They had to find out what the character was and get on to that stage and fight for their character, because if they didn't they would get trampled under the rush of everybody else fighting for theirs, believe me.[34]

One of the irritations for Harry was that with critical success many actors who joined the company saw it merely as a good thing to have on the CV. 'The tragedy was that actors were inevitably seduced away from us by the commercial managements when they were only half-way through Theatre Workshop's programme. This meant sometimes a complete recouping of cast for a new season.' Success had also attracted the 'wrong' kind of audience. Howard Goorney wrote:

The extent to which Theatre Workshop succeeded in building up a local audience was always a matter for conjecture, but it was certainly never sufficient to keep the theatre going without support from other parts of London. As costs increased and no subsidy was forthcoming, even that wasn't enough and we had to look for transfers to the West End. Harry Corbett had no illusions about the audience:

'We never appealed to the working class. All I could ever see were beards and duffle coats every time I peered into the audience. It was the day of the angry young whatever. No way was there a local following, only in the sense of a few eccentrics – Johnny Speight[35] was one – and they were leaving their working class environment. Never a solid working-class audience in any way.'[36]

Jean Newlove agreed with him: 'I used to laugh, because we used to say "We're going to take our theatre to the man in the street, to the working class." But the working class weren't bothered about it – if they were that bothered we wouldn't have had to go to London.'

George Cooper also agreed:

Joan of course kept talking about it – about bringing theatre to people who've been dispossessed. And I have to say I never accepted it. You know, it just wasn't working. We were getting all sorts of posh, you know, theatre intellectuals and all the rest of … And the real people that we were supposed to be attracting into the theatre couldn't care less.[37]

It appears that, by and large, the only poor downtrodden masses at Theatre Royal were the ones on stage.

The original ideals of the company were being stretched as thin as the budget. This lack of subsidy was most ludicrously highlighted when representatives of the International Theatre Festival in Paris came to see a performance of *Volpone* and out of all the companies in the country the director general of the festival invited Theatre Workshop to represent Great Britain. You can imagine how well that went down with the establishment: cries of 'Those dreadful, pinko commie bastards are going to carry the flag' must have echoed backstage up and down the land. So how much was given to the company to help them carry that flag? Not a sausage. Murray Melvin said of Joan's detesting of the established commercial world: 'That's why she got bitter against the establishment because she couldn't believe they weren't going to support her – but they couldn't, cause they couldn't keep up with her brain.'

The knock-on effects of this can been seen in the minutes of a company meeting held on 31 March 1955 while they were in rehearsal for a production of *The Midwife* (or *Haben*, to give its original German title) by Hungarian playwright Julius Hay. Gerry reported that: 'There is a fairly constant debt of £400.' And that 'There are more people in the theatre for the *Midwife* than can be paid a living wage.' Harry had commented that he: 'Thought £3 minimum wage inadequate. Suggested £4 would be more realistic.'[38]

To put that into context, £4 equalled 960 pence. Beer was 9½ pence, milk 3*d* a pint. In 1955 the Deptartment of Employment and Productivity put the average minimum wage paid to ordinary agricultural labourers for a basic forty-seven hours' work at £6 4*s* 10*d* or 1,498 pence. The actors were routinely still getting only £2 or 480 pence. One wonders how many other theatre companies invited to the festival would have been financially better off threshing?

In the minutes there followed a discussion on the widening gap between the actors and the company. Gerry, who had the worst job in the theatre, said:

> It had been suggested to him that he had a 'boss' complex and asked the Company to voice its opinions'. Gerard [Dynevor] said he felt uninformed about Company affairs – perhaps because the previous Company meeting had been held so long before. Joan considered that there was disunity in the Company. She said that there seemed to be two, often antagonistic, blocs – the Management and the Company and that we must find a democratic way of working. Howard [Goorney] considered that a vital subject was being discussed flippantly and the important issue obscured.[39]

It was decided that for the Paris Festival: 'The Company will be asked to sign a document saying that they have been paid in advance to avoid having to place a deposit with Equity.'[40]

Things were still tetchy three weeks later during the run of *Haben*. To make ends meet:

> Gerry thought Appeal Fund would have to be used to subsidise wage. There would only be 30/ – to £2 per person this week. Howard [Goorney] and Joby [Blanshard, who had joined in the mid-1940s and left three months after this meeting] were violently opposed to this proposition and said that Gerry had been opposed to the appeal from the start and seemed to do everything in his power to oppose it. Howard submitted that the fund was administered by a committee subject to the Company

and completely independent of the Management of the Theatre. There was a fracas over putting out the collecting boxes on the first night of *Haben*. Gerry said that it was tactless to ask our first night audience containing so many Press to contribute to the appeal fund. Howard maintained that he was attempting to carry out a Company decision. Gerry said that he was reconciled to the appeal continuing for the remainder of the season.[41]

The meeting went on to discuss topics as diverse as whether they should or should not take part in any political demonstrations on May Day to John Bury requesting 'that the pigeon that had built a nest in a fire bucket should be respected.'[42]

It is typical of the man that in all this argy bargy, Harry's contribution to the meeting (aside from being appointed costume liaison for the trip to Paris) was that he 'suggested Company give J Spinner present at end of season as some return for his free work.'[43] John Spinner took the most beautiful photographs of company productions for the cost of materials only, and in Murray Melvin's words became a real member of the company. When he died he bequeathed his collection of photographs to the Theatre Royal Archive. They now form an integral part of Murray's book, *The Art of Theatre Workshop*, and he chose a select few to hang on the walls of the Theatre Workshop Bar at Stratford East. During renovations Murray himself painted the bar a deep, rich red to show off Spinner's black-and-white images to full advantage. If you can, go and see them. Have a meal. Then why not take in a show – they've fixed the seats.

While Gerry wrestled with the problems of getting the company to Paris, there was one long-time member who didn't need to worry about it – he wouldn't be going, he'd been sacked.

Harry Greene had already had a minor run-in with Joan when he married Marjie Lawrence in March of 1955:

> God, we decided to get married! Now, I was now – to Joan – the villain and I'll tell you why. She actually cursed me – she said, 'You're ensnaring one of my best actresses.' She was actually bitterly abusive to me – can you believe it? And when I went back one day, she caught me off balance and well, we were on top of the stairs, so you can imagine what happened.[44]

Joan also had words with Marjie:

> She wasn't too well pleased when I said I was going to leave the
> company and get married. She said, 'oh you don't want to be just
> some provincial, suburban housewife, you've got the makings of
> a great actress, this is a waste of talent', all that sort of thing. She
> was a bit cross with Harry about that. I said I had no intention of
> becoming a provincial or suburban housewife, I intended to go
> on being an actress, which I did.[45]

Things had come to a head over an incident involving of one of
the company actors, Stephen Dartnell, who happened to be gay.
This incident, according to George Cooper, 'kicked off a whole
chain reaction,' and 'It was all further signs of what was happening
to the company.'

Stephen Dartnell and Harry Greene were busy at work outside
the theatre when a passing homophobic local youth began to tor-
ment Stephen, as Harry G. explains:

> Stephen was a close friend of mine and the time that this boy
> was harassing Stephen, he and I were on the pavement painting
> flats, because the loading bay had doors 15ft high at the side of
> the theatre and we had these open and the trestles out, and the
> flats on the trestles, and we were painting and he came and threw
> paint over Stephen and mimicked him and called him a 'queer'
> and all sorts of things. The second time he came I told him in no
> uncertain terms to 'bugger off and leave us alone,' and he went
> home and told his father that Stephen had propositioned him
> and interfered with him and of course the father thought that
> he'd make money out of this by us paying for it to be kept quiet.
> But we refused this and then he said that we'd offered *him* money
> for *him* to be quiet.

The youth's father went to the police and surprisingly Joan was of
no help:

> She hoped it wasn't going to be a court case. She hoped that
> she or Gerry could talk to the man who lived in the same street,
> in Salway Road, just down the road from the theatre. Anyway,
> Harry C stood up for us and so did Marjie, but Joan wanted us

out of the way because she didn't want any adverse publicity for the company and she felt that there was some truth in what the guy was saying – that Stephen had propositioned him, this young man, and interfered with him – and it was totally, totally untrue because I was there throughout.

And what happened when it came to court?

It was thrown out by the judge as indefensible and the local thug and his father were fined for wasting police time and lying in court and Joan kicked me out of the Company, and Stephen Dartnell, because I stood up for him; and after we were kicked out Marjie was still there.

Harry was always a defender of injustice – that's one of the great things about him. Marjie and Harry were the two who literally told Joan, in no uncertain terms, that she was a hypocrite.

Harry had called Joan a hypocrite in a private company meeting, and that's how he kept it – private. He never mentioned the incident, he was never one to wipe his feet on the reputations of those he respected and loved. It's hard to find him saying a bad word about anyone. It wasn't his style. But given how injustice and hypocrisy were to always be such anathemas to him it must have opened his eyes to a side of Joan that I don't think he was expecting.

And what happened to Harry Greene? David Scase recommended him as stage director for the Arena Theatre. Fabulously they toured Wales where Harry was able to go up to his old headmaster at Tredegar Grammar School and say, 'I did make it, Sir.' Marjie left the company after Paris and she and Harry went for jobs on the very first ITV soap. At the audition they had to improvise being a married couple who owned a DIY store. Given that Harry G. had helped out at his uncle's DIY store as a boy, had been cobbling sets together for years and the pair of them had just left the UK's home of improvisation, it was rather a doddle. At five o'clock on ITV's launch day Marjie opened the new soap *Round at the Redways* with the line, 'Darling, summat's up with the telly.'

There was some redemption in 1959 when Joan invited them back:

to join the cast of 'Make Me an Offer', because it was destined for the West End and she wanted a nucleus of old members in the cast. She had productions in the West End and we felt that she was changing. We felt that she liked the success but we also found, Marjie and I, that going into a company where there were, in inverted commas, 'stars' made rehearsals very difficult for her – in fact we know, we experienced it. None of the 'stars' – Dan Massey, Dilys Laye, Diana Coupland, Meir [sic] Tzelniker, all big names – were used to her approach. And like most West End actors, they all came line perfect, as the saying goes. They were not going to be influenced. There was no improvisation that they wanted to do. No development of their character – they knew what the characters were; they were going to play them night after night after night. And the writer, Wolf Mankowitz, and Joan had quite embarrassing arguments in front us all. But there were two lovely people, Sheila Hancock and Roy Kinnear, who fitted in more easily. They had similar backgrounds and training to us and Joan. And not only that, they went into theatre with similar thoughts – realism, reality. Joan was very, very impressed with them, and she said so, oh yes.[46]

Back in 1955 Harry G. and Marjie were doing DIY for real at home, as their salary had jumped from £3 with the Workshop to £30 on TV, they could afford to buy a flat and do it up. They did such a good job that *Ideal Home* magazine wrote a feature on them. This led to Harry G. coming up with the concept of putting a DIY show on TV. In January 1957 this first DIY show aired with *Harry Greene being Handy round the Home*. He has since written over twenty books on DIY and presented many shows; he also came up with the original concept for *Changing Rooms*. If you've seen a DIY show, Harry G. probably had a hand in it – so we can blame him then. He also kept up his acting career, appearing in over thirty-five films. Marjie herself had a very successful career, working non-stop on screen with many 'big names' for nearly fifty years.

Harry and Marjie had three successful children – Sarah and Laura are well -known TV presenters and Robin runs a business in Switzerland – and they were married for over half a century until Marjie's death in 2010, still as in love as the first day they met. Please form an orderly queue behind me to be suitably jealous of them.

One person you wouldn't have been jealous of was Gerry, who had to find a way of getting the company, the sets and costumes to Paris for the International Theatre Festival without any money for the fares. They would be presenting *Volpone* and *Arden of Faversham*, the set for which included life-size tree trunks.

Gerry came up with a cunning wheeze, as Barry Clayton remembers:

> there was a Friends of Theatre Workshop who were regular supporters. And he found that if you had a certain number of people travelling, you could have a luggage van to yourself. And so he got all the Friends and said, 'Right, we're all going to Paris.' And he booked … And we took the scenery … we loaded it at Stratford into a van, Railway Union wouldn't let us load it on to the train, nor would the Seaman's Union – quite rightly – at Dover, or wherever it was.[47]

So how did they get the set onto the boat? Harry explains :

> It was quite hysterical. We had no money to pay freight charges, and we had to take all the set over as personal hand luggage. Gerry held the ferry up for two hours while he argued with the crew and the customs. We had masses of stuff including cheese-shaped rostra and two pillars, about twelve feet high and three feet wide. I carried one of these up the gangplank as personal luggage! We all carried a piece of the bloody set.[48]

Notes

1 Burton, *Acting in the Sixties*.
2 *Ibid*., (they had an 'open house' policy with all productions).
3 Goorney, *The Theatre Workshop Story*.
4 *The Times*, 18/1/55.
5 *The Stage*, 20/1/55.
6 *The Observer*, 23/1/55.
7 Theatre Archive Project, British Library.
8 *Ibid*.
9 In conversation with Murray Melvin.
10 Theatre Archive Project, British Library.
11 In conversation with Brian Murphy.
12 Leach, *Theatre Workshop: Joan Littlewood and the Making of Modern British Theatre*.
13 Goorney, *The Theatre Workshop Story*.
14 Harry, in conversation with Howard Goorney.
15 *The Stage*, 10/3/55.
16 Goorney, *The Theatre Workshop Story*.

17 Theatre Archive Project, British Library.

18 Rebellato, D., *1956 And All That: The Making of Modern British Drama* (Routledge, 1999).

19 *Ibid.*

20 Goorney, *The Theatre Workshop Story*.

21 Theatre Archive Project, British Library.

22 Goorney, *The Theatre Workshop Story*.

23 Burton, *Acting in the Sixties*.

24 *Ibid.*

25 Theatre Archive Project, British Library.

26 Burton, *Acting in the Sixties*.

27 Theatre Archive Project, British Library.

28 Goorney, *The Theatre Workshop Story*.

29 *Ibid.*

30 Theatre Archive Project, British Library.

31 *Ibid.*

32 Goorney, Howard, *The Theatre Workshop Story*.

33 *Ibid.*

34 Burton, *Acting in the Sixties*.

35 Prolific television writer and creator of the character Alf Garnett.

36 Goorney, *The Theatre Workshop Story*.

37 Theatre Archive Project, British Library.

38 Goorney, *The Theatre Workshop Story*.

39 *Ibid.*

40 *Ibid.*

41 Goorney, *The Theatre Workshop Story*.

42 *Ibid.*

43 *Ibid.*

44 Theatre Archive Project, British Library.

45 *Ibid.*

46 *Ibid.*

47 *Ibid.*

48 Goorney, *The Theatre Workshop Story*.

Sous le ciel de Paris

Somehow, we got there and took Paris by storm.[1]

Harry H. Corbett

On arrival at customs, Shirley Dynevor remembers that fellow company member, 'George Luscombe had 1/ 8½d when coming into France. I think you were limited on the amount of money, I think you could only take £20 or something – but George Luscombe had under 2 shillings.' That's 20½d or about 9p.

Barry Clayton tells that after the company had unloaded the set from the train at the Gare du Nord in Paris, they made their way across town to the Hébertot Theatre, 'and it was all very funny because we were all in our overalls and one of the stage hands said to me, "Ou sont les comédiens?" And I said, "Nous sommes les comédiens". You know they couldn't believe that not only were we lumping the scenery about but we were also doing the play.'

Marjie Lawrence was amazed by their welcome:

We were met at the station with bouquets of roses for the girls. Such a difference to what [it was like at home]. Oh extraordinary! I mean the other end of the scale really. I mean, as I say, we were fêted like great stars, because they read about this play, and they'd sent somebody over to see it. And we were invited to the town hall to meet the equivalent of whoever the mayor, or whatever he was, of Paris, and they gave us a special dinner for that, and champagne. And we had our photograph taken with the owner of the Hébertot Theatre where we played. He had his photo taken with us all around him you know. And yes, it was … well it was wonderful really and getting to know Paris.[2]

As they rehearsed at the Hébertot the company contacted the British Embassy to see how many would be coming, after all, as Howard Goorney later wrote:

> The theatrical establishment was quite outraged that this invitation should have been extended to an 'unknown' company, and after a great deal of hesitation, 'Under the patronage of the British Ambassador' was reluctantly allowed to be printed on the programmes. This was the total extent of official support for our visit. No message of greetings from the Ambassador appeared in the Festival brochure, though there were messages from the mayors of some of the East End boroughs.

So how many tickets did the embassy want? None thanks.

Though this lack of support no doubt incensed Joan, that wasn't really what she was worrying about, as told by George Cooper:

> Something else was happening at about that time. We were very aware that whatever we did, Joan would flog us again and again to say 'No, you must be better than that' and 'You must improve this' and 'Forget that' and all the rest of it; and I think Tom Driberg was absolutely on the spot when he said that when we first went to Paris that she was getting really frightened that the company were going to be recognised and have a swelling of the head and all that. And so she still kept yakking on about how we needed to improve ourselves.

Joan was not only 'yakking' but schmoozing, as Harry remembered: 'She was forever being feted, which in a sense didn't bother us at all because we got to run around Paris, which was quite pleasant.'[3]

Some bright spark at the embassy must have remembered that the company were actually under the boss's patronage for, as Barry Clayton recalls:

> as it got nearer to the opening performance, they told us at the box office that the British Embassy has asked for tickets and so-and-so … First of all curtain up at nine o'clock. You looked through the hole, and I said, 'It's just like bloody Stratford, there's about 35 people there.' And then half past nine it was perhaps half full. Quarter to ten, three quart … ten o'clock they decided it

was full enough, up would go the curtain. Well I mean, we were not used to that … And the atmosphere was electric. I mean, there was Harry Corbett giving an amazing performance, and a wonderful actress called Barbara Brown, who was really a nice dumpy little English lass who suddenly became this electrifying, sexually avaricious woman … and then at the end, the curtain went down and there was silence. And you could hear a pin drop. You stand on the stage and you think they're all dead. They must be dead, why aren't they clapping? And then the curtain went up, and it was … literally there were 25 curtain calls. And the theatre cheered to the echo you know.

And then afterwards, two wonderful things which I'll never forget, it was … Gladwyn Jebb was the British Ambassador, and he had a wife with a hat like a galleon. And they said, 'Oh darlings, that was wonderful. We had Michael Redgrave and Peggy Ashcroft last year doing *Antony and Cleopatra*. It was … we couldn't hold our heads up, but this is really wonderful!' They invited us to the British Embassy even.[4]

Barbara Brown, the leading lady and coincidentally an assistant stage manager (or, as they are often called, 'Oi you'), was, according to Barry:

> devoted to picking forks and other goblets out of the floats at any spare moment she had and yet she would come onto that stage – and the costume girls did a marvellous job with her costume – and the relationship which she and Harry developed was really passionate … it was lovely when we went to play in Paris. All the critics came round and said 'Ou est Barbara Brown?' and by this time she'd changed out of her costume and she was picking forks out of the floats and you could see their faces dropped.

They weren't the only ones left open mouthed that night, for, as Barry continues, 'at the end of that electrifying opening night at the Hébertot Joan came round and said "I have some notes for you." And Harry and George Cooper said "Look, if you didn't like it tonight – they did – so bugger off!"'

Joan was right to be worried – the worms were turning. Shirley Dynevor remembered the morning after the night before:

We woke up the morning after our opening performance to find that the whole Company was being celebrated and applauded. Suddenly, Theatre Workshop was famous, and I remember Joan coming into the auditorium, where we were all gathered, with her hat squashed down on her head, and she looked so miserable, so fed up about the whole thing. And I remember her saying 'Ah well, now that we're a success, the whole thing will fall apart.' One felt that success was the last thing she wanted and that we could only really survive with struggle, there had to be something to fight against.[5]

But even Joan's mood couldn't have rained on the company's parade, as Shirley remembers, her excitement still bubbling after more than fifty years:

Ah Paris! They were the greatest moments in my life because I was desperate to go to Paris and to go with Theatre Workshop. It was just amazing because we were treated in this country as sort of scruffs and in Paris as something terribly special and when the newspapers with all the reviews after the first night – we were so astounded. I think they more or less exclaimed us as the best company in the whole set up and it was glorious, and it put everything into perspective.

The French journalist Morvan Lebesque wrote in *Carrefour*:

The Miracle of the Workshop,
     This story resembles a fairy tale: once upon a time there was in London a company of actors who ran a people's theatre. I repeat, a people's theatre, the like of which no one has done in this country as yet, in a small theatre in a working-class quarter of East London [translated that meant playing not in Chaillot but in Belleville].
     Then see what happens: one day the organisers of the Festival of Paris hear news of Theatre Workshop and decide to invite it. They asked the officials who immediately cried out loudly 'You want an English company? Very well. Take X. or Y., famous companies, of noted worth, the glories of our national stage, but, by God, not this Workshop. They have no renown and no splendour, and their productions are not fit to represent the British theatre abroad.' Fortunately the French organisers held firm. Against

wind and tide, against the indignant cultural attaches, against the British Council which refused a subsidy, against Her Majesty's Government which would not deign to write a word of introduction in the programme, against the Ambassador himself who, right up to the last moment, could not make up his mind to be present at the opening night, Theatre Workshop came, installed themselves in the Herbetot Theatre, and carried off the biggest, the most unexpected, the most extraordinary success that a British company has known in France: in that same Paris where, not long ago, a very official British company bored us so implacably during a whole evening.

My admiration for Theatre Workshop can be expressed in a few words: we do not possess a single company in France comparable to this one. Nothing which resembles its ardour, its generosity, and, to say all, its youth.

There were incomparable moments. And what diction: what spirit: what discoveries. Dear friends of the Workshop, I will not take up space to list your names which would not mean anything yet to French readers. Besides, do you really care? You form a company which is very obviously the pride of the contemporary English theatre. You have set the Festival of Paris alight in its first week. We salute you with joy as being the purest, the simplest, and the greatest artists. We hope to see you again and to applaud you once more.

Perhaps thoughts of this ebullient press that had so depressed Joan continued to affect her during one of her rare stage appearances in their alternate offering in Paris, as remembered by Barry Clayton:

Joan played a part in 'Volpone' as well and we would always say 'If any of us acted the way she is, we'd be out tomorrow' because she did all this, it was 'tirribly middle claws Inglish Laydee,' she would do all that and lay it all on with a trowel and it was a lovely irony, in fact it was quite endearing because you thought, 'Well, what is it she thinks she's doing?' Nobody dared to tell her. I'm sure it was Harry who said, 'If I did any acting like that, she'd tell me to piss off tomorrow.'

Success abroad was reported in the British press. *The Times'* Paris correspondent said:

Theatre Workshop, with its playing of 'Arden of Faversham' and 'Volpone' has had a success at the Paris Drama Festival far exceeding that accorded to any other British company in France since the war. Apart from the intrinsic merit of the Company's performances and choice of plays, French audiences and critics seem to derive much satisfaction from the fact that Theatre Workshop is a popular theatre, which they compare with the Theatre National Populaire – not, alas, a fair comparison, for the T.N.P. is heavily subsidised by the State. There is also something attractive about the idea of a theatre group, in which individual performances count for less than does the joint effort ... As those connected with the Company themselves observe, this is a triumph that they never knew in their own country – but none the less pleasant for that.[6]

Whereas *The Guardian*, with an intrinsically British reaction to success and rather smug air of 'told you so', seemed to attribute the fortunes of the company to incomprehension on the part of Johnny Foreigner:

Recently in Paris the group known as Theatre Workshop, which has had many an honourable mention for its work in such places as Stratford, East London, scored a success in the Parisian press which must have made the average Briton stretch his eyes. 'The English discover in Paris their best company of actors.' 'Staggering performance by Le Workshop.' were sample headlines, and there was hardly the faintest disagreement on the fundamental fact 'that the excellent company, headed by Joan Littlewood, set a standard of acting unapproached hitherto in the United Kingdom.' This is gratifying but puzzling to some of us not necessarily blind to the merits of the Workshop's original acting abilities. The point raised seems to be: Can one judge a performance in a language not one's own? 'If one can understand an actor without understanding the language he speaks, then he is a good actor,' a distinguished player said to me the other day. I begged to differ. I do not believe that an Englishman, even speaking good French, can, for example, truly assess the points which make, say, one interpreter of Phedre superior to another.[7]

Perhaps Joan was grateful for anything that could bring the company down to earth. George Cooper tells:

Even after we'd sort of had the initial recognition and been to the British Embassy – we all had lots of drinks and came back and did the show in slow motion according to Joan – but she, rather than let us have a, say, couple of days off, she started rehearsals for the play for when we came back to Stratford, E15. But I'd just married Shirley [Shirley Jones, who was costume designer at Theatre Workshop] just before that and I thought, 'Oh, sod it. I'm going to have a honeymoon in Paris.' We tried to get married in Paris but we couldn't do it because they had to have a residential qualification, which of course we didn't have, and I'm quite sure there were signs then that what I always call the old Theatre Workshop were breaking up. We were physically exhausted and financially approaching bankruptcy, or whatever, and that's why it all broke up.

Marjie Lawrence left Theatre Workshop after the festival and decided to stay on in Paris: 'Friends, actor Zach Matalon and Barbara Young, an actress, who were working on the Left Bank, you know in sort of the nightclub scene, said "Well, why don't you stay on?" – which we did just for a while.'8

Barbara Young had already sought pastures new. The story of her split from Joan sounds familiar, as she laughingly recounted:

I'd left her and I don't think my name was spoken for several years. I was going off with some chap I'd met. He had been trained at the Actors Studio in New York and it was very interesting, all this stuff he was telling me. And she said 'Well, you may find happiness as a woman – but you'll never find it as an artist.' And in fact, she couldn't have been more wrong because I learnt an enormous amount from him about acting but I wasn't terribly happy personally.

The rest of the company packed their laurels, bid *adieu* to the adoring French press and begged the money for the fare home.

Back in Blighty it was down to earth with a bump and bankruptcy.

At a company meeting on 31 May it was divulged that 'Theatre Workshop Ltd. Now wound up. At the moment Company technically employed by a committee of the four directors. Future Company will be called Theatre Workshop Drama Group Ltd. Made bankrupt by Mavis Clavering – ex member of Group. Present trading debt about £1,000.' The meeting went on to note that 'Date for next season's opening vague. Possibly early September. Whole of future season depends on many possible happenings.'

Howard Goorney later wrote of this time:

> Despite these successes abroad no subsidy was forthcoming and we were still wholly dependent on the Box Office for our wages which, if receipts permitted, were now £4 a week. A substantial nucleus had now been working together for some time, Harry Corbett, Joby Blanshard, George Cooper, Gerard Dynevor, Marjorie Lawrence, George Luscombe, Maxwell Shaw and myself. The measure of understanding between the actors and the complete trust in each other was reflected in the productions of this period. It was a group theatre in its truest sense and, with Joan as its catalyst, was at the peak of its achievement.

Which unfortunately supposes that the only way was down.

But Howard was right. For a while they had bloomed, until the white heat of critical success burned them. Before the Sunday coverage Joan had been alone in the limelight. Now she had company. Whether she was annoyed at having to share because, as Murray Melvin put it, 'She was the biggest star of them all underneath' or whether she was frightened of her favourites leaving, is open to debate. As Murray also pointed out:

> everybody forgets that underneath Joan there was that incredible sentimentality ... Because they were together that length of time in the old days, Joan's sentimentality was that they were going to stay that way forever – 'Oh, now come on, Joan. It doesn't work like that.' But she was a sentimental Victorian Lady.

To survive without funding the company had to stop trying to beat the West End theatres – they had to join them. Commercialism was the only way. Harry remembered:

> The beginning of the end, in the sense of relationships changing, came in a long Company meeting when we all argued about various things we would like to do. What the aims of this theatre were, because we did have one very Christian lady, we had one Polish lady who was very down with the Communists and it had

gone on for hours, and Gerry very calmly puffed on his pipe and said, 'Well, quite frankly, the aim of this theatre is to keep it in with the Co-op once a month.' I just felt, 'Well, that's it – let's all not waste any more time.'[9]

Time that might be better employed elsewhere, for a few members of the company there were outside temptations. These were becoming more frequent as Murray remembers: 'In those early days, nobody was getting a job out of here – they were frightened of them – but then they realised they were bloody good actors.'

The West End production company H.M. Tennent's had been stalking Harry for years. Head of Tennent's, Binkie Beaumont, had spies out in every theatre in the land to keep his company at the top. Their latest offer to Harry was a season with Paul Scofield, directed by Peter Brook. The writing was definitely on the wall, and outsiders were writing it. Harry remembered the:

> visiting dignitaries of the theatrical world who started to flock. One's dressing room was full, stars of the theatre, directors, people like that. There were visiting people from all over. From the Cameroon's to the macaroons, from all over the world – which started to take Joan's time, but she still kept going.[10]

She was still going but on a new course, as Harry goes on:

> She had changed round to say she was only really interested in people in doing Cabaret and Musical, those were the real actors, you know, she'd had a falling in love with the people from Cabaret.'

Yes, the times they were a changing, but as Harry said, Joan had a gift for change; she was a genius in her ability to 'absolutely change and completely reject all that she'd lived and sworn by before'.[11]

While the company reeled from the changes, Joan decided to follow their success in Paris with *The Legend of Pepito* by Ted Allan. This would prove the end for Harry. Not just because of what was happening onstage, though that didn't help, but what was to happen off it.

Onstage, Harry wasn't happy with Joan:

She ditched me and Barbara [Brown] with this 'Legend of Pepito'. Well it wasn't quite the thing I'd hoped to do. It was a pastiche, an American kind of pastiche, very light, not quite what I was desperately interested in. I wanted to continue the marvellous fare of Classicism we were on, and by Classicism I definitely mean 'Hobson's Choice' to 'Enemy of the People' and so on. Classicism is not just an ancient Classicism, it was a modern Classicism – and then, to be faced with this pastiche about a Mexican making baskets with pretty trousers on and an American gently trying to persuade him to go mass produced, it seemed a long and far cry from what we were doing at the time – 'Volpone' and 'Arden of Faversham'. She said, 'Well, you and Barbara get on with it, rehearse it through.' So we did the best we could with it religiously anyway.

The very irate author turned up. We assumed it went perfectly well but Ted demanded to know where Joan was and why she wasn't directing it? We said 'Well, we're just working on it at the moment.' And he said 'I'm not interested in you fuckers working on it, where's Joan?' Well, she was having lunch with somebody and I walked into this place and, in the best manner I could, I stalked up to her in my ragged clothes – it was a badge of honour to wear ragged clothing – and pointed my finger at her and said, 'There is an author waiting for *you* to do his sodding, bleeding play, while you're living it up with the last gobblings of the fatted.' Gerry blanched and I just wandered back.

We were bloody exhausted. We'd got varying temptations from the West End etc. but it didn't bother me because I'd been to that stick before. I'd also done a few nip aways from dear Workshop to bring some money into the kitty.

I came back and said, 'Look, are we still going on with it?' and she said, 'Yes, we're still going on with it.' And then she was talking about musicals. It seems facile now but it had been such a struggle – such a big struggle. George Cooper was married, which had become an impossibility under our circumstances, to have children – stuff like that. I can't answer for what George's reasons were but I knew it wasn't for me under the circumstances, I really did. So I said, 'Right, well I would like a break for a certain length of time.' I had a feeling that the Company Meetings had ended up with 'Well, come again next time – we'll start and those who aren't here, we'll assume you're not with us.' It was one of those things.

In retrospect, it was such a silly thing really, and we were all so tired and it meant much more than it sounds at the time. To do, to be expected to do, this kind of play – very good this kind of play, I'm not knocking this kind of play – but not what we'd all been sacrificing for. [12]

The final nail started as such a little thing – a favour for a friend – as Harry recalled:

Isla Cameron [film actress and folk singer]; who had a love/love relationship with Theatre Workshop, you know many times she was rejected by Joan for various reasons that I know nothing about, but she had an awful love relationship with the Theatre and tried to do a lot for it; came to me and said that a critic, I won't say who he was, a well known drama critic, would like to meet Joan Littlewood, 'Would you talk to him?' I said 'Well, to arrange a meeting?' She said, 'Well, he can't get to see her – he wants to talk to her desperately, would you see him?' So I then go, I had lunch with the man, said I'd do the best I could, came back to play the show that night and there was a letter for me. I thought it was the usual bunch of notes – in those days she'd do beautifully written pages of notes that went on for ages. In principle she said she was very overworked, the Workshop version was, 'Dear Harry, if this is the way you feel you should go and leave us all, and go off into the West End theatre.' Accusing me in a very lovely way of being an absolute traitor and a shit – but in a very lovely way and giving me my total freedom, actually, to do this kind of thing. So in high dudgeon I read this before I went on. And she had sent somebody down to get it out of the rack and I'd already read it, and, of course, spent the night in torture cause I'd gone on and played knowing it. I shot off that night; I was living with a marvellous teacher, a reader in English, in a caravan at the bottom of his garden, for nothing. And the next thing I know, thump goes the caravan and Gerry comes screaming in at 3 o'clock in the morning talking me desperately out of it, and I was thinking 'What have I done? It's all got slightly ridiculous.' [13]

It was hard to comprehend, on the one hand Joan dug in her heels and refused the critic's interview and on the other she was bending to commercialism, as Harry later told:

She did try hard to defend it from the encroaching whatever it was that had to come. This is what made a seeming volte-face to people like myself who were closely connected. So it was strange, because right to the last minute she was fighting one way then all of a sudden a switch of policy.[14]

I don't think there was any break up really of Theatre Workshop. There was a change, that's the best way to describe it. To us at the time it seemed like a break up, a complete smashing and ending but not really. It was a change. A moving in another direction that took the shows into the West End ... and I didn't wish to do that, personally, so mine was a very traumatic kind of break.[15]

But first Harry would honour his commitments to the company for the rest of the season. After all, the show must go on, and so it did. *Pepito* was received with classic 'mixed reviews' ... *The Stage* commented:

> Theatre Workshop undoubtedly add to their triumphs with this production, once again the chief honours go to Joan Littlewood, who can not only bring the best out of a group of players, but develops so well the visual side of a production. For all its charm, the story is slight, and comes second to the manner of the telling, but Mr Allan displays a certain *naïveté* in his dialogue, which is apt to become irritating. The acting is uniformly good, with Harry Corbett the essence of peasant simplicity as Pepito, the basket maker.[16]

Whereas Ken Tynan let rip in the *Observer*:

> Mr. Ted Allan, who wrote 'The Legend of Pepito' has a habit of sacrificing imaginative truth to propaganda, and he is lucky to find a company as anxious to save him as Theatre Workshop. This leftist comedy about the impact of American big business on a Mexican village is worth seeing for its sunbaked setting and for the performances of Messrs. Maxwell Reed and Harry Corbett [it was actually Maxwell *Shaw* – typical, get a good review and you can't show it to your mum]. Mr. Corbett's dazed, dreaming basket-maker is sketched with extraordinary skill. But some of the minor rôles are very crudely filled. Will Miss Joan Littlewood, the director, never realise that it is on artistic, not ideological grounds that

the West End shuns her players? If she would prune her company, strengthen and reinforce it, she could easily take the town.[17]

But first she would take … Barnstaple.

Harry would be happy; they were back on epic theatre, literally. Theatre Workshop had won the UK premiere rights to Bertolt Brecht's *Mother Courage*. The Devon Theatre Festival at Barnstaple would be the venue for this feather in the cap.

Written as a reaction to the invasion of Poland in 1939, *Mother Courage and her Children* is set during the Thirty Years War of seventeenth-century Europe. It follows a woman through some of those years as she pushes her canteen cart, trying to make a profit from the same destruction that will, one by one, claim her three children.

Bertolt Brecht, founder of the Berliner Ensemble, was the most prominent force behind, and gave the name to 'epic theatre' or 'theatre of alienation' … Right, let's have a quick stagger through the highlights of the history of theatre genres.

We start with conventionalism – open-air theatre, that uses masks and symbolic props with a rudimentary, if any, set and language usually in verse form, the actors represent their characters. A high degree of audience imagination is needed. This theatre includes ancient Greek, mediaeval religious and morality plays through to Shakespeare, who also used elements of…

Naturalism – a reaction to the above. Theatre moves indoors in the early seventeenth century and gets a proscenium stage. Its aim is now to create the illusion of real life with everyday language and more secular themes, along with detailed scenery, props and costumes. Innovations with lighting trap the actors behind the proscenium. Get too close to the candle, oil, and later gas, footlights and you'd go up like a rocket. But dim lighting on distant actors leads to a need for a big and bold spectacle, gestures and make-up – melodrama was born. However, the invention of electric light frees up the actors and their new techniques focus on 'real' performances requiring little to no audience imagination. This leads to…

Anti-naturalism – a reaction to the above. It includes the epic theatre or theatre of alienation (Brecht) and the theatre of the absurd (Beckett, Pinter). Anti-naturalism is a swing back to conventionalism but with better lighting.

Stanislavsky had sought to escape the hated, old-fashioned melodrama by taking the theatre of naturalism as far as he could. The audience were a fly on the wall to the proceedings onstage, and could become so involved that they forgot they were in a theatre. There would be nothing to distract from the spell i.e. there would be no breaking of the fourth wall, no contact with the audiences and the theme and style would be realistic. Prose not poetry; Darwin not God. Which does rather put the kibosh on naturalistic Shakespeare (you can only get away with that on film, using a voice over for the asides, etc.). Theatre Workshop used the techniques of the theatre of naturalism, but for Shakespeare; and works that included ghosts, fairies and asides to the audience employed, as Joan would say, a 'heightened' naturalism.

For Brecht, naturalism smacked too much of escapism, so epic theatre was born. This theatre of alienation used such means as addressing the audience directly, unrealistic props and sets, disjointed action and songs with disturbing lyrics set to jolly music, all to jar or to alienate the audience from becoming emotionally involved in the play. There would be no chance to escape the fact that you were watching – there was also no chance of escaping the author's message. The idea was to alienate you enough that you viewed the play with a critical eye, but not so much that you left the theatre.

Close cousin to this is the theatre of the absurd; Beckett's *Waiting for Godot* being its most famous play. Absurdist playwrights, again in a reaction to realism, reflect the philosophy of Albert Camus, who went looking for the meaning of life and found that there wasn't one, life is absurd. Instead of logically topping himself in a blue cloud of Gauloises, Camus felt the enormous freedom to be found after coming to this decision and that the choices one makes in defiance of this meaningless life, give life meaning. The plays of theatre of the absurd employ nonsensical dialogue, meaningless actions and absurd plots. They are not meant to be real. Most are tragicomedies; it is, after all, a funny old world. As such they can trace a direct line from Shakespeare and *commedia dell'arte* to Charlie Chaplin and Monty Python:

> For life is quite absurd
> And death's the final word
> You must always face the curtain with a bow.
> Forget about your sin – give the audience a grin
> Enjoy it – it's your last chance anyhow.

Life of Brian is pure theatre of the absurd, dahrlink.

Any production is somewhere on the pendulum from conventionalism to naturalism. No one style of theatre is better than another; it depends on current fashion and personal preference. In the end, good theatre is one you're happy to pay for.

So, if you already knew this, my apologies. If you didn't, next time you're stuck next to someone intoning that such and such is 'Pure theatre of the absurd, darhlink!' you'll know what they were talking about before they get deservedly beaten with their copy of *The Guardian*.

The Berliner Ensemble's *Mother Courage* had been named as Best Play and Best Production at the Paris Festival in 1954. Given *Arden of Faversham*'s success the following year, Brecht would have been aware of Theatre Workshop when Oscar Lewenstein made the first overtures to him on behalf of the company. Lewenstein was then general manager of the Royal Court but would later become its artistic director, shepherding productions such as *Look Back in Anger*, *Billy Liar*, *Loot*, and *Entertaining Mr Sloane* alongside his work as a film producer responsible for *Saturday Night and Sunday Morning*, *A Taste of Honey*, *Tom Jones* and *Rita, Sue and Bob Too*.

Lewenstein thought that Theatre Workshop should revive *Richard II* and present it with the Brecht premiere at the Devon Festival. He went to see the great man himself, as he remembered:

> I went to Berlin, saw Brecht and said I thought Joan would make a perfect Mother Courage and that Theatre Workshop was a company that ought to have his sympathy. He was very co-operative, and said we could use any of the designs, music and so on and he'd send a young assistant called Karl Webber to assist in the production.[18]

Such an auspicious start – you know where this is going, don't you.

Legend has it that Brecht demanded that the title role of Mother Courage should be taken by either Joan Littlewood herself or Gracie Fields. But as Gracie was busy, Joan it would be. That lasted for all of five minutes before Joan recast the role. After all, she was directing not only that play but also revisiting *Richard II*, and this was aside from trying to get a summer tour to Warsaw off the ground and worrying how, when and with what they would open their next season at Stratford. To take on the lead would have been a job too far.

The recast didn't go as well as it could, as Barry Clayton recalls:

That was a drama in itself because Joan had got a very butch actress who she said would be very good as 'Mother Courage' who turned up to rehearsals on a motorbike all in leather gear. Rehearsals would start and then Joan would be getting at her, in the end she said, 'Look Joan, if that's the way you want the fucking thing playing, then why don't *you* do it cause I'm pissing off.' And she left.

Avis was next in to bat. But how could Joan hide these cast changes from Brecht's assistant Karl Webber, who had arrived with detailed instructions on how exactly the production should be staged. Barry Clayton remembers:

We had a guy from the Brecht Company, he came with a big photo album of a 'minute by minute' of the Berliner Ensemble's production and said 'Zis is zer vay for der cart. Der cart vill look like zis, und zees are der props – vich ve vill have here und zat is der vay zey should be made,' and Joan said 'Get that man out of the theatre.' And so people were delegated to go and take this guy from East Berlin to see Madame Tussauds, the Tower of London or anything – or to take him to English pubs and get him drunk. And then eventually the whole theatre was locked up and he was not allowed to come in.

This got back to Oscar Lewenstein:

The next thing I heard from Karl was that he'd been refused admission to rehearsals and that Joan had decided to put another actress in the part of Mother Courage. This development had to be reported to Brecht who threatened to bring an injunction to stop the play going on unless Joan played the part. So, rather late in the day, Joan put herself back in the part and the play opened at the Tor and Torridge Festival at Barnstaple.[19]

All this did not make for a good atmosphere as Barry recalls: 'the relationship with Bert Brecht was never the same after that. I don't remember him being anywhere present when the thing was done in Barnstaple – and if you can imagine a less likely place to present

"Mother Courage" than Barnstaple [people of Barnstaple, he said it – don't write to me].'

It was dreadful; not enough rehearsal, not enough actors and too many cuts. *The Times* reported:

> Miss Joan Littlewood as a producer, takes curious liberties with the text and as an actress, while trying hard to intimate the character of Mother Courage in what she presumes to be the Brecht style, succeeds in only conveying a suggestion of dull, almost bovine placidity in the face of recurring crisis. Mr Harry Corbett is adequate as the lecherous chaplain who changes his religion as often as the occasion demands, but the production as a whole gives neither the company nor the play the ghost of a chance.[20]

This was kind compared to Ken Tynan's verdict:

> By any definition the play is an epic, a tale of endurance set in the open air (there are no interior scenes) of any war-bruised country. It is also a folk opera. Its earthy language, dotted with imagery as mountains are dotted with edelweiss, takes frequent flight into song, accompanied by Paul Dessau's trenchant music. Theatre Workshop, the company chosen to play it, was dismally unequal to the strain. Ants can lift objects many times their size and weight, but actors cannot. Mother Courage is a role calling for the combined talents of Signora Anna Magnani[21] and Miss Siobhan McKenna:[22] Miss Joan Littlewood plays it in a lifeless mumble, looking both over-parted and under-rehearsed. Lacking a voice, she has had to cut Mother Courage's song, which is like omitting the Hallelujah Chorus from the Messiah.
>
> As a director, she has sought to present, with fourteen players in a concert hall, a play which the author intended for a company of fifty in a fully equipped theatre with a revolving stage … Some of her blunders are attributable not so much to financial straits as to sheer perverseness. She adds music where Brecht indicates none, uses Dessau's score in the wrong places, and has it sung badly where she uses it rightly. The result is a production in which discourtesy to a masterpiece borders on insult, as if Wagner were to be staged in a school gymnasium. Miss Barbara Brown does well as the mute Kattrin, and Mr Harry Corbett's

decaying chaplain abounds in hints of the performance this actor might have given in more favourable surroundings.[23]

Ouch! For Harry, it was time to seek out those surroundings. He was 30 years old and the darling of the critics with a caravan for a home. Harry Greene and Marjie had gone. George Cooper was going, as was Joby Blanshard. It was either stay with an increasingly commercial company enjoying a dubious future, in which site-labouring and bouncing would feature heavily, or look elsewhere in the theatre. He chose the latter. Perhaps if the Arts Council had come up with some conkers earlier Harry would have stayed being the big fish in the little pond of Theatre Workshop.

But they didn't and he didn't.

The pied piper was changing her tune from jazz to oom-pah-pah. Even if she did go down fighting, reaching for ideals that were swept away on the tide of success, Joan must have found Harry's opinion an uncomfortable mirror. Though, ironically, he would have been the first one to defend her, shouting from the rooftops: 'At least she had a bloody go.'

Joan's account of Harry and George's departure makes for interesting reading:

> 'Harry's going,' said Gerry.
>
> 'To earn some money,' said Harry in his old between-the-teeth way.
>
> 'Will you be playing your Richard at the Devon Festival as planned?'
>
> 'Yis,' he said, after a slight pause, got up abruptly and left.
>
> 'Tynan's got at him,' said Gerry. He brought Peter Brook to see Richard II. They gave Harry a Soho lunch and promised him a part in Hamlet.' …
>
> Harry had hardly left the room when George Cooper walked in. 'You off too, George?' I said.
>
> 'Lovely money,' he was using his squeaky, baby voice. 'Lovely grub!'
>
> At that moment I swear I heard my heart crack …
>
> Why had they chosen to go now? Now, just when we could break through? We'd stood together through thick and thin. In any case what will happen to them, out there in the jungle? Well that's their lookout.[24]

Harry, had he lived to read that, probably wouldn't have raised much more than an eyebrow at the accuracy, though if he had he would have been in good company – including that of Joan herself. When coming to record the audio version of her book, she looked at the now abridged text and asked why the writer entrusted with the task had made so much up. 'You've got it all wrong,' she said, 'none of that happened.' She was answered, 'But Joan, that's what you wrote.'

No, Harry wouldn't have complained, he adored her. She was, for him, a genius. And genius, much like beauty, excuses a lot of behaviour. He would have said that it was 'just Joan'.

Another very 'just Joan' memory comes from Peter Rankin:

> then you get to 1955 when two of her best actors – Harry H. Corbett and George A. Cooper, I think probably simply worn out, because – from my own experience of working with Joan – it was fantastic, but very, very demanding, and there were times when you felt, 'I just want to go away and do something else, just for a little while, just to give me a break', and I think they'd rather slightly had it and so they went off, but it broke Joan's heart because she thought, 'That's the end of the company' and in her autobiography, she stopped at that point when she did the first draft and said, 'That's it, that is the story of Theatre Workshop.' And the publisher said, 'You must be mad! Because we haven't had *The Hostage*, we haven't had *Oh What A Lovely War*, we haven't had *Fings Ain't Wot They Used T'Be*, we haven't had Shelagh Delaney, we've had none of the big things!' She said, 'Oh those were just writing jobs.'

Harry later reflected that Joan was:

> an unpredictable woman … She always retained the feeling that a genius could walk in off the streets. She hurt many people … Someone at that moment in time was brilliant, then their time was over and they were finished with. I do not know Joan Littlewood, the director, I think I know Joan the Woman, or did in the past … She's a marvellous, warm, beautiful person to know, love and be with. I feel no sorrow for her, I really do not. She's a millionaire in terms of talent … I can find no negative qualities in her, not in a thousand years, because she gave people

an opportunity to do things they could never have conceivably done themselves – even if they were ruined in the bloody process. I can really find no fault or criticism of Joan, none whatever.[25]

Notes

1   Goorney, *The Theatre Workshop Story*.
2   Theatre Archive Project, British Library.
3   Harry, in conversation with Howard Goorney.
4   Theatre Archive Project, British Library.
5   Goorney, *The Theatre Workshop Story*.
6   *The Times*, 24/5/55.
7   *The Guardian*, 23/6/55.
8   Theatre Archive Project, British Library.
9   Harry, in conversation with Howard Goorney.
10 *Ibid*.
11 *Ibid*.
12 *Ibid*.
13 Harry, in conversation with Howard Goorney.
14 *Ibid*.
15 *Ibid*.
16 *The Stage*, 9/6/55.
17 *Observer*, 12/6/55.
18 Goorney, *The Theatre Workshop Story*.
19 *Ibid*.
20 *The Times*, 1/7/55.
21 Italian stage and film star, winner of best actress Oscar for *The Rose Tattoo*.
22 Distinguished Irish actress, toast of Dublin's Abbey Theatre. Select film but prolific stage career on the West End and Broadway. Won the Eire Society of Boston's Gold Medal for promoting Irish culture.
23 *Observer*, 3/7/55.
24 Littlewood, *Joan's Book*.
25 Goorney, *The Theatre Workshop Story*.

10

Go West Young Man

After leaving Theatre Workshop, the inevitable question was, could I act outside it? Having to work with other people and despising their way of working didn't make for a happy relationship. Also one had to take definitive attitudes, e.g., about the way Shakespeare should be played. Not realising that, to a certain extent, it was a passing phase with Joan – quite rightly because she was discovering new ways of doing things. However, you were left with an iron-clad attitude, and it took a long time to recover from it and realise there were other ways of doing things.[1]

Harry H. Corbett

Before finding out how his new director, Peter Brook, thought Shakespeare should be played, Harry took his first steps in front of a television camera. His first in front of a film camera had been a bit part the previous summer in *Passing Stranger*, starring Lee Patterson and Diane Cilento, two actors he would bump into again down the road. Fellow Workshop actors George Cooper, Joby Blanshard and George Luscombe also appeared in the film – it must have felt like a works outing.

In August 1955 he appeared as a boxer in *The Girl*, written by East End playwright Wolf Mankowitz. In September came *The Hole in the Wall*, a violent and murky tale of the East End set in the 1850s and starring Mervyn Johns. Harry played Blind George and was listed in cast as 'Harvey' Corbett – perhaps he was trying out a new name. He would have to: according to the rules of Equity, the actors' union, no two members could work under the same name, and to get work you had to be a member. As the children's entertainer and puppeteer Harry (Sooty) Corbett was already registered with Equity, Harry would need a new name. Maybe Jimmy Fraser, Harry's agent, had persuaded him to try Harvey on for size. Though as Harry so rarely kept any mementos from his career (press cuttings, programmes etc.) and had actually kept *this* cutting, it leads one to believe that he kept it simply because it was a misprint – something that would have appealed to him.

Both of these programmes were, of course, for the BBC; ITV didn't start transmission until 22 September 1955.

When the *Hamlet* rehearsals started, Barry Clayton remembered Harry popping in to Stratford East to report: 'They're all so polite to one another.' Perhaps, after Joan, that would be worthy of a comment. Harry was always going back to Theatre Workshop: it was his home, they were his friends, his family almost, and of course – most personally – Avis was still there. Though there was no more talk of wedding bells; her wedding dress had long been donated to the company's wardrobe. Shirley Dynevor poignantly remembers: 'I did the Bride in *An Italian Straw Hat* and my bride's dress was Avis' wedding dress that she never, of course, wore.' Shirley also remembers that production for Joan's babysitting, 'We had no one to look after Josh, who was about one at the time, and so Joan says, "Oh, I'll look after him." So she takes him up to her top room and she dressed up in black veils and netting and did dances for him to amuse him. All through *Italian Straw Hat* all I could hear were the screams of my son.' Not that Harry would have known, as by the time Josh was wailing and the wedding dress finally had an outing he would be in Russia.

Peter Brook's *Hamlet*, starring Paul Scofield in the title role, opened on 24 October at the Theatre Royal, Brighton, before going on to the Alexandra Theatre, Birmingham. Harry played the First Player, Lucianus, and the First Gravedigger and must have decided upon his name as he was billed in the cast list as Harry H. Corbett.

After Birmingham the production was due for a London run, but was delayed by an unusual invitation. In the midst of the Cold War, while most of the West was still gripped by fear of the communist bogeyman, the USSR invited the company to perform at the home of Stanislavsky, the Moscow Art Theatre. How could they say no? This headline-grabbing event was an extraordinary opportunity for a peek behind the iron curtain and after all those years at Theatre

Workshop listening to the virtues of communism, you can guess who was first on the plane.

One of the company members of what would be called the Moscow *Hamlet* was a young Aubrey Woods. As Aubrey was playing the Second Gravedigger and Player Queen alongside Harry, I thought, despite the passing of more than fifty years, he might have one or two memories of the event – I was wrong, it could have happened yesterday. With my gratitude, here are Aubrey's evocative recollections:

The visit was finally fixed during the first week or so of the English tour – we first learned of it when the Company Manager called us onstage after a performance to tell us that the final date had been altered and that we would appear instead in Moscow before opening in London.

Being the first full foreign company to visit Russia since the Revolution gave a strange, unreal atmosphere to every aspect of the trip. Harry was eagerly enthusiastic to see at first hand a regime he greatly admired, in its native surroundings. The flight to West Berlin – the transfer to the Russian sector via the Brandenburg Gate and the contrast between the West and East sectors of the city – the crowded roads of the West – the lack of any private cars in the East – one of the airport staff at East Berlin airport smoking away while refuelling an aircraft from a tanker – the reception at Moscow airport – we circled the airfield and could see on the tarmac a large crowd outside the reception building – a visiting dignitary perhaps – a Government official? – no, the crowd was artistes and staff from all the theatres in the city and outside to welcome us – touchdown – an exchange of embraces, presentation of fur hats and gloves to us from our fellow theatricals.

Waking on our first morning in the Hotel to a three foot overnight fall of snow – the dress run-through at the theatre – the first night – the endless applause and curtain calls – the reception afterwards – caviare by the kilo and vodka by the gallon – the welcoming concert – David and Igor Oistrakh duetting – Ulanova dancing the Dying Swan – the Red Army Choir singing 'It's A Long Way To Tipperary' – every performance and every day after that a revelation – a host of memories after fifty years.

During the dress run Harry sat himself on a chair next to the giant metal tank in which the detonators were set for the final scene and 'Go bid the soldiers shoot.' Someone threw the right switch at the wrong time. Harry was the one who shot – straight up from his chair – glassy-eyed, trembling and stone deaf for the next half hour or so.

The translators who were detailed to accompany us and who – whenever we ventured on our own in twos or threes off the main streets into the gloomier but more interesting side streets were always there walking towards us and leading us back into more salubrious and recommended points of interest.

Lenin and Stalin laid out in the Red Square Mausoleum and our party being ushered in ahead of the vast never-lessening queue waiting to file past their heroic past in respectful silence – Lenin's left ear looked a little moth-eaten.

Sitting in my Player Queen costume for the official photographer and his vast bellows enclosed plate camera 'Very still please.' No pressing of bulb or button, just the lens-cap removed, the photographer silently counting, then the cap replaced. The portrait was perfect.

Our movie cameraman, Douglas Slocombe the eminent filmmaker, having to discard the oil from his camera and replace it with graphite as the outside temperatures in Moscow froze the oil – then going south to Baku with Peter Brook to film a Russia production of Hamlet and having to replace the oil to suit the new climate – such was the size of Russia North to South.

Learning that a beggar had been found frozen to death on the steps of the Hotel one morning but removed by the street sweepers – all women wrinkled and tanned by the inclement weather – before Moscow awoke.

Being told one day that we were all to be in the theatre an hour before the half was called. The road from the Kremlin to the theatre was cleared of pedestrian and traffic occupants by the time we were bussed there and we noticed when we arrived that there were a dozen or so dark suited men with ominous bulges under their armpits or at their waists stationed backstage – not, we felt, Shakespeare enthusiasts. Five minutes before curtain-up someone was ushered into the stage-level box, seated at the rear out of view of the audience and behind two large bodyguards. After the show four of the leading actors were presented – in the

box – before the entourage was hastened into black limousines
and Mr. Molotov left at 90mph along the deserted road still out
of sight behind the bullet proof smoked windows.

Finally leaving with official gifts – a poster with our names
phonetically translated – I was Odpu Bygc [Обри Вудс. Harry
was Гарри Корбет] – a large tin of Beluga Caviare – even larger
for the principals – a hand-painted cigarette box and a hand-
somely illustrated book on the Moscow Underground – one of
the wonders of the world – many personal gifts from the friends
we made there – and so back to Berlin, the Brandenburg Gate –
West Berlin Airport and London.

There is footage of that arrival. The incomparable Paul Scofield,
who would be awarded with a CBE in the New Year Honours list
a few weeks later, is asked if they had a good time: 'Oh, Yes!' the
company chorus. Harry can be seen peeking over shoulders at
the back, camera lights glinting off his ear-to-ear grin. Seeing the
Soviet system up close and personal had been good for Harry. It
had confirmed him as a staunch socialist. Communism? You could
keep it.

Hamlet finally opened in London at the Phoenix Theatre on 8
December. The triumph in Moscow, while making enough of a
sensation to give the production an impressive 124-performance
run, proved a bit of an albatross in respect of the London reviews. An
air of 'yeah, so?' pervades. On Harry, specifically, Ken Tynan commented: 'Broad fun was never Mr. Brook's strong suit. Hence Osric
falls flat; Ernest Thesiger's praying mantis Polonious is annoyingly
restrained and the gravediggers, despite the earthiness of Harry H.
Corbett, miss their true *Galgenhumour.*' Brian Murphy disagreed:

> I saw him in Paul Scofield's Hamlet. He was wonderful. Of
> course, it was a commercial set up so there was, it seemed to
> me, another level that Harry had moved onto but all I could
> keep thinking was – I did love Scofield but you couldn't help
> but think that wonderful voice, if we're not careful, you're just
> hypnotised by it and we don't see what is behind it – but I kept
> thinking, I wish we could see Harry's Hamlet.

The production also has a small footnote in television history. It was
the first Shakespeare play televised by ITV. The heavily abridged

ATV production went out live across London and the Midlands on 27 February 1956.[2]

At the end of March, the next play in the season, *The Power and the Glory* from Graham Greene's novel, had a week in Brighton before coming into the Phoenix on 5 April. Scofield masterfully transformed himself from a Prince of Denmark into a whisky-soaked priest lying low in a fascist Mexican state where the Church is outlawed. Harry played the policeman on his trail, determined to trap and execute him. A reviewer commented, 'The burden of acting falls on Paul Scofield entirely; he is deeply sincere but apt to play on one note with a slightly mechanical quaver ... The other parts, with the exception of Harry Corbett who is excellent as the police lieutenant, tend to mere vehemence and simple type playing.'[3]

Last in the Phoenix season, opening on 7 June, was *The Family Reunion* by T.S. Eliot. Written in blank verse, it sets Greek Tragedy in a drawing room melodrama. The play bleakly tells of the redemption of Harry, Lord Monchensey (Scofield). While erroneously believing he has murdered his wife (he is only guilty of wanting her dead) he is summoned to take over the country pile by his dying mother (Sybil Thorndike). As in Aeschylus' *Oresteia*, Monchensey is hounded by the unlikely appearance of the Erinyes (the Furies) in Act I; later they transform into the kindly Eumenides in Act II, while assorted absurd aunts and uncles become a baffled Greek chorus. At the end Monchensey leaves the pile in the hands of a younger brother and escapes with his trusty servant Downing, played by Harry. Today it is held as an innovative masterpiece. When it premiered in 1939 it was a complete turkey. Eliot himself admitted that the inclusion of the Furies didn't work and that Monchensey was 'an insufferable prig'. Though better received in the '56 revival it still remained a bit of a hotchpotch for most. The chorus' incomprehension was a condition shared by the audience during the performance and by Harry during the rehearsals. Barry Clayton remembers: 'Harry used to come back from this and say "I don't know what the hell they're talking about, they sit there and they don't do any analysis like we do ... but the money's good" and that was the thing, I mean Harry went because they needed money.'

That is entirely true, and entirely misleading. Confronted by the enquiring, and thin, faces back at Theatre Workshop, home of suffering for one's art, he would never have said anything else. Breezing in to announce how marvellous it was wouldn't have gone down too well, and any compliments towards his new director would have been asking for it. Joan did not have a particularly high regard for Peter Brook – forty years later she was to say of him:

> I can't stand him, silly cunt! He has too much good taste. I was kidnapped by a friend and taken to his theatre, the Bouffes du Nord. The seating was monkish. The actors were throwing potato peelings at the audience. If that'd been Stratford, I thought, it would have been thrown back. But everyone was too busy admiring the great left-wing director. Left-wing, my foot![4]

You have to hand it to Joan; never in her entire life did anyone have to ask her what she really thought. But Harry's comments were not just for the sake of tact, they were innate. The embarrassment of success, learnt at Theatre Workshop, would never leave him. His level of fame dictated his level of guilt. To those inside the business it would be, 'Oh, it's awful, but the money's good', to those outside he had 'just been lucky'. Harry always saw himself as an uneducated kid from the slums that had made good. To others his talent was amazing, to him it was mundane – a very human condition and one that made him so likeable – you'd never go out to dinner with someone who thought himself wonderful, well not twice anyway.

The Phoenix season had also allowed Harry to fulfil Annie's hopes, as he later told the papers:

> She used to say 'One day my boy, you watch it, you'll walk down that road with a five pound note in your pocket, a whole five pound note, of your own; you will, you know.' … The first time he made a killing on the London stage, he changed his money into five pound notes. And then he went back and threw the notes all around the parlour. 'But I'd left it too late, she was too old, she didn't know what it was all about. I'd left it too long.'[5]

Having been absent from Manchester for such long periods Harry wouldn't have seen the first signs of Annie's dementia. With each visit she was to slip further away from him.

By August Harry had landed a six-part crime series for the BBC, *New Ramps for Old*. It starred Mervyn Johns who 'plays Philimore Sparkes, the gentlemanly crooks' outfitter. In each episode he is abetted by the old lag Kegworthy, played by Harry Corbett, a young actor who has made a name for himself in Theatre Workshop and appeared on BBC-TV in two of Wolf Mankowitz's plays.'

From there it was straight into rehearsals for Congreve's *The Way of the World* at the Saville, with Margaret Rutherford heading the cast, before Harry took the role of Salvatore Ferraro in an ITV production, *A Man About the House*, in February of 1957. The first of many swarthy/brooding/crumbling, sometimes menacingly heavy characters his looks and ability would lend themselves to: 'I did years of being cast as an American gangster, terrible stuff. Then years of being an Italian gangster. Those old films come back to haunt me,'[6] he later said.

Then came a call from Theatre Workshop, not from Joan but from John Bury.

After Harry and others had left the Workshop the replacements had required training, as Howard Goorney commented:

> The influx of new actors, some of whom had had conventional theatre training or experience, resulted in a change in working relationships. Much had to be re-learned, and the emphasis was now on learning from Joan rather than on learning together as previously. Consequently, her role, always a key one, now became predominant. So the focus from 1955 onwards tended towards Joan's work in the Company, without, I hope, minimising the contributions of those who worked with her.[7]

In 1956 Joan had had a great success with Brendan Behan's *The Quare Fellow*. By November, due to her now predominant role, she herself needed a break from Theatre Royal and left it in the hands of John Bury until July 1957. A few months into his season, Camel was in need of help. This was unsurprising, given that he was not only designing, building and lighting the sets but now directing too. Glynn Edwards, years before he would be wiping down the bar in *Minder*, remembers Harry coming in:

> John Bury, who was also our set designer, he did a season and he did an Elizabethan play, 'The Duchess of Malfi', anyway Harry helped me enormously because I was struggling with a romantic lead – I never played many romantic leads – I was struggling with this one and Harry gave me a lot of tips and took me through the lines. He was an actor's actor, very much was Harry. He would

always jump in and give you a helping hand. Avis Bunnage played
the Duchess and I was one of her lovers.

I said to him 'I'm worried about this,' and he said, 'Well, I've
got a bit of time off,' and he came in and helped me and then
when the show was on he came in and watched it a few times
and gave me notes.

Thanks to the money earned on TV, Harry could afford to do this.
All actors did this. You made a bit of cash on telly to subsidise your art
in the theatre. There was a rampant snobbery about TV; it was seen as
second best compared to theatre. Or rather third best, second being
film (or, at Theatre Workshop, fourth – Joan once told Michael Caine
to 'Piss off to Shaftesbury Avenue. You will only ever be a star.'[8]). At
the same time TV was criticised for being 'photographed theatre'.
All TV drama went out live. You would rehearse for a week in large
rehearsal rooms, with tape on the floor marking out the rudiments
of the set. Then on recording day you would get into the studio and,
after several run-throughs, would go out live to the audience. The
cumbersome nature of the cameras, and the fact that adaptations of
stage plays were the main drama fodder, gave a very staged effect.
One camera had a nice wide shot covering the action and a couple
would be trained on the actors for close ups: cut in between them –
Bob's your uncle. There were no interesting angles or tracking shots
and they wouldn't have known a montage if it bit them. But it was
the early days of the medium and things were about to be shaken up.

The BBC had been riding high as the home of high-tone drama;
ITV was seen as the home of cheap variety shows. Naturally they
wanted to 'up' the image. When ITV launched in 1955, few of its
companies had dedicated state-of-the-art studios or could afford
them – hence the abundance of cheap shows. ABC, serving the
Midlands at the weekend, had converted a cinema in Didsbury,
Manchester, into studios and Granada, which also started life as a
cinema chain and also served the Midlands (but during the week),
had commissioned shiny new studios of their own down the road
on Quay Street. Both companies wanted a slice of the artistic pie
and both were determined to put the North at the forefront of TV
drama. Very soon actors who had taken years to get to London were
heading back on the train to work in Manchester.

In the spring of 1957, Harry himself headed north. He did a
couple of Television Playhouses for Granada, playing Nik Ferens

in *The Crown of the Road* and James I in *The King's Bounty*. I'm sure it was good to see the family, though it could have been under better circumstances, for in March his brother William had committed suicide. Though they rarely saw each other, as Harry was in London and William lived in Stockport, it still would have come as a shock. According to family legend William stuck his head in the oven because he thought he had cancer. He didn't. He was 42.

In the early summer, Harry landed a feature film. He later remembered when:

> my agent, James Fraser – 15 years a good friend – phoned:
>
> 'Harry,' said the man who scorned a written contract between us, 'what about a part in a film? "Floods of Fear" is about to start shooting. They've asked if you are available.'
>
> The offer was manna from heaven. I had pounds, shillings and pence before my eyeballs when I started to make the film. I tried to save every penny – how Mr Callaghan would have appreciated my efforts. I was a one-man price freeze.
>
> I didn't see the point of having expensive meals in the studio. I used to sneak down to the canteen and eat with the technicians and extras for a couple of bob a time.
>
> But the other leading players were puzzled at my disappearance when eating time came round.
>
> They eventually found me in the studio canteen, and after that I got a stream of polite notes from the producer suggesting it wasn't the right thing for a leading player to use the canteen. It rather suggested they weren't paying me enough.
>
> I survived the flow of messages, and by the time the film was completed had saved just over £800.[9]

Floods of Fear gave its star Howard Keel a break from launching into song in Hollywood musicals and saw him cast as a convicted felon. Set in the Deep South during a downpour, prisoners are trying to shore up flood defences when the bank bursts. Keel rescues a fellow prisoner, Cyril Cusack; a doctor, Anne Heywood; and a prison warder, Harry. Cusack wants to escape, Harry wants the prisoners locked up again and Keel wants to wreak his revenge on the man who framed him for murder, all the time looking good in a wet shirt and battling the frenzied water. Battling water probably came easier to Keel than it did to Harry who recounted: 'I can swim a few strokes, but I'm not Tarzan. In the film "Floods of Fear," I had to spend a lot of time in a water tank. As soon as the cameras began to turn, something came over me. I swam like a champion. But when the word "cut" rang out, I started to sink in a flurry of spray.'[10]

By August, Harry was at the Edinburgh Festival. He was appearing in Sartre's *Nekrassov* for the English Stage Company before transferring in September to the company's home theatre in London, the Royal Court. A satirical farce, *Nekrassov* tells of a con artist passing himself off as a Kremlin defector while Parisian newspapers whip themselves into anti-communist frenzy on the back of his lies. The production was designed by Richard Negri. In 1954 Negri had opened the Piccolo Theatre on the site of the now defunct Chorlton Theatre Club. As attendance numbers at Chorlton had waned the club committee took management into their own hands and away from director Jimmy Lovell. Predictably the club closed and Lovell went on to become artistic director of Dundee Rep.

In *Nekrassov* Harry played the gullible newspaper editor. The con man was Robert Helpmann, who is better remembered as a dancer and choreographer. The play also featured a young classical actor, Ronald Barker, who is *much* better remembered as Ronnie Barker. A reviewer, while complimenting the splendid style of four of the supporting players said: 'The fifth, Harry H. Corbett, plays the ego-mad editor in quite a different style – the elaborately loose-jointed, loose-tongued style of certain American "method" actors.'[11]

If he were the journalist who would later dub Harry 'Britain's Marlon Brando', it would bring a whole new meaning to the title. A title those who knew Harry found risible, as Murray Melvin tells:

> Marlon Brando couldn't have done what Harry did, that's for certain. Look at those parts – could Marlon Brando have done that comedy, could he have done 'Juno and the Paycock'? Course he couldn't. He wouldn't have known where to start. It was just made up for a bit of a headline. He was a real company member and I'll tell you what, he asked for me. He did a pilot of a new television series – don't ask me what it was called – he got me a small part. I was a tailor and I had to measure him for a suit. You can imagine the fun we had, can you see the moment when I was taking his inside leg. I said, 'How long we got for this Harry, short scene is it? We could do the whole half hour like this.'

One medium perfectly suited to Harry's 'method' acting was television. The difference between theatre and TV, apart of course from the money, is that in the theatre you 'act' the part – on TV you 'think' it. Harry was called to Manchester again, this time to ABC's Didsbury Studios and the first of many appearances in *Armchair Theatre*.

Armchair Theatre was a pioneer of multi-camera shooting. Mixing live as the programme went out – a lot more cost-effective than post-production editing – they were leading the way in using different camera shots: size of frame (establishing, wide, two shot, close-up); angle of shot (eye-level, above, below); panning (camera swivels left to right); crabbing (camera slides left to right); tilting (up, down or Hammer Horror sideways); zooming (camera stays – shot focuses in or out); tracking (shot stays – camera moves in or out). All these sweeping multiple camera movements, aside from a few criticisms of frenzied camera work, meant the actors (who should be in shot) and the technicians (who shouldn't but often were) all had to keep their wits about them. Going out live could be extremely testing. Most famously testing for the producers and cast of *Armchair Theatre* would be the following year when, during a live broadcast, the actor Gareth Jones tragically suffered a heart attack and died off-camera in-between his scenes. The show went on, actors and crew improvising to the finish.

Having gone to all that technical trouble to get away from television being seen as 'photographed theatre', it would have jarred to then have actors giving 'theatrical' performances – cue the method actor. Harry's first performance for *Armchair Theatre* was as condemned murderer Mears in 'The Last Mile'. John Wexley's original stage play had launched the career of Spencer Tracy.

Though early live TV did give wonderfully edgy performances sadly not many survive. They are lost or were never recorded in the first place. Although videotape would start to become available the following year it would not be extensively used until much later on in the 1960s. Even then it was still prohibitively expensive and was regularly re-used. Television companies even recorded over their tapes of the 1969 Moon landing with, rumour has it, the 2.30 from Doncaster.

The shows that do survive are not the original 'live' performances. After those had gone out the actors would come in and do it again so the show could be tele-recorded onto film. Occasionally shows were recorded onto film at the outset. Harry's next job, *The Adventures of*

Robin Hood, was one of these. Harry would get robbed or rewarded by Robin quite a few times over the coming months. The show was filmed because there was an international market for British costume drama. We traded across the seas, selling 'Oh, Mr Darcy!' and buying 'Eat hot lead, punk!' We still do. The reason why so many early American shows survive is that they had no option but to record onto film due to the different time zones across the continent.

Harry's first appearance in *Robin Hood* was in the episode 'The Charter', playing a nobleman, Sir Bascom, who is scheming to steal an important Royal Charter from his dying uncle, played by an almost unrecognisable Paul Eddington, another regular on the show. Harry later played a peasant, Jason, in 'The Angry Village', needing Robin's help to stop their grain being stolen. In 'The Genius' he played a monk, Nicodemus, the deliciously over-the-top genius of the title, who designs a catapult for Robin Hood's gang.

Next up for Harry was the ITV Play of the Week, *Widower's Houses*. One of George Bernard Shaw's *Plays Unpleasant*, it is a scathing look at Victorian slum landlords. Harry played Lickcheese, the landlord's rent collector. The journalist Bernard Levin, perhaps not a fan of 'riding through the glen', reported:

> Harry H. Corbett has done some disappointing work lately; now he has capped his performance in 'The Last Mile' a week or two ago with a magnificent portrayal of Lickcheese in Shaw's play that makes it urgent and vital for some impresario to put on 'Pygmalion' (if Tennents and the Public Trustee will allow him to) simply so that we may see Mr Corbett as Doolittle.[12]

Harry followed this with a run of *Armchair Theatre* programmes. The studios in Manchester would get to know his shadow well. His brother Albert often accompanied him. Harry delighted in showing Albert life behind the scenes and Albert delighted in seeing his baby brother in action. In *Panther One-Forty* Harry played a man whose neighbour has bought a new car, the Panther of the title. Despite not being able to afford it, he orders one. 'Harry H. Corbett gave a brilliant performance – the measure of his success being that one could almost accept the corny dialogue he had to utter.'[13] In *A Gust of Wind* he played Emanuel Rigattieri, an unpopular man in an Italian block of flats. When the wind blows his door shut, locking him out wearing only his nightshirt, his neighbours get their revenge by charging him with indecent behaviour. 'Harry H. Corbett played the main part with great understanding – a comedy with just a tiny sprinkling of pathos.'[14] Hmm ... Harry would go on to corner the market in those.

His next appearance does survive. *The Emperor Jones*, written in 1920 by Eugene O'Neill, is a prime example of a classic play being translated into television. It is the story of Brutus Jones, an African-American escaped convict who has set himself up as despot of a small Caribbean island. He struts in an ornate military uniform and claims to have special powers. Kenneth Lee Spencer, the American bass-baritone, played Jones, and Harry played Smithers, the Cockney trader who warns Jones that his subjects are planning to revolt. Laughingly, Jones makes his escape through the jungle but is faced with a series of harrowing trials. To the rising sound of jungle drums he becomes lost, confronts past murders, and has to shoot his way out of a chain gang and slave auction. Finally exhausted, stripped of gold braid and dignity, he is slaughtered by the natives. His body is brought from the jungle and laid before his former subjects. They carry him away leaving Smithers to stare apprehensively into the dark jungle. Aside from the performances, the production is notable for its ambitious camerawork. Point-of-view tracking shots, the sound of footsteps being dubbed over, and fast pull-back shots show the ways in which they were pushing at the technical envelope and how accomplished television was becoming.

The next few months saw Harry playing a couple of heavies in feature films. *Nowhere to Go*, co-written by Kenneth Tynan, was a rare visit to film noir by Ealing Studios and marked Maggie Smith's debut. *Shake Hands With the Devil* was set in Ireland during the 'troubles' and boasted a starry cast headed by James Cagney and including Sybil Thorndike, Cyril Cusack, Dana Wynter, Michael Redgrave and Glynis Johns (Mervyn's daughter). Richard Harris, who had just had a stint with Theatre Workshop, can be glimpsed in an early role, as can Donal Donnelly – more of whom later.

The year 1958 had seen Harry making steady progress in front of the camera. It also saw him marrying Sheila Steafel. Sheila was born in 1935 in Johannesburg. She came from a middle-class home and, naturally, had African servants. 'I was brought up with nannies who really were wonderful motherly figures with big breasts and crisp white aprons you snuggled into – just like in the old films set in the southern states of America,' she would later say. She found school dull and stifling and was very nearly expelled for writing and performing what was deemed a risqué play. Though she had wanted to be an actress for as long as she could remember, she went to university to study fine art: 'when I got to university and found that Africans didn't have the warm feelings towards white people that I was used to, I was surprised and frightened.' Her theatrical ambitions proved too hard to give up and she soon dropped out, becoming a dental nurse to earn the fare to England where she could realise her dream:

> I also remember doing something rather cruel. I said to one of the women who worked for us: 'I'm going to a country where black people can go into the same restaurants as white people and they can sit next to white people on the same buses'. She didn't believe it. She said to my mother, 'Who is going to do Sheila's washing when she goes? Can she send it back?' When I arrived here, I remember writing home that I made my own bed.[15]

Several years later, her dream as yet unrealised, Sheila met Harry in a nightclub. She was there working as a waitress, dressed in a sari and serving curries: 'I wasn't a working actress when we met and I think he thought I'd get it out of my system.'[16]

They married on 10 October 1958. In line with Sheila's faith the ceremony took place at the Liberal Jewish Synagogue on St John's Wood Road. They settled into a flat in north-west London. Cynthia, Harry's niece, remembers coming to visit:

> We stayed with him when he lived in Hampstead, when he'd married Sheila. He used to take us to the Museums and he took me to my first Chinese meal. 'What do you want Cyn?' 'I've no idea, you order for me.' Once we were going for a meal, not at a posh restaurant just down a side street, and he bumped into this chappie and he said to him 'Hello, so and so, when did you get out?' and apparently he'd been a bouncer – because Harry had been a bouncer at one time round the clubs in Soho – This guy had just been put down for GBH. Harry said to him, 'Do you want some money?' putting his hand in his pocket but the guy said, 'Don't worry, Harry, such and such is seeing me all right.' 'Oh, as long as you're all right then.'

Harry loved Soho – it didn't matter where you came from, but where you were now. He knew everybody there from his days on the doors, only now he went inside. A favoured hangout was Gerry's Club, the Groucho's of its day. It was a place where showbiz movers and shakers could meet, greet and unwind after the curtain came down. Harry had been a member for years. A fellow member was Freddie Ross; in the mid to late 1950s she was a young woman moving and shaking her way into the world of PR management. She would go on to handle Tony Hancock. Handle? Reader, she married him. She would also handle Harry's career and remembers their first meeting:

> I met Harry in Gerry's Club in Shaftesbury Avenue and he came in as only he could, unshaven and with a cap and a tweed coat that had nothing to do with the cap – I mean he looked like a derelict; both of my clients, both Tony and he, I met when they looked like derelicts. Harry came in, I had no idea who he was, and he joined up with our table. John Junkin was sitting there and Willis Hall – we used to sit around at Gerry's and I was part of the gang. I always looked like the rich Jewish Bitch and I had a Mini Minor and lived with my parents on the corner of the street where Harry lived and so it was easy for me to give him a lift home. And so that's what I did. I gave him a lift home and so we became mates – and why we became mates is because whoever was working would pay for the next round of drinks and I always looked as if I was working, so I was always paying for everybody's drinks.

By 1959 Harry could afford to buy the rounds. He kicked off the year with another *Armchair Theatre* – 'The Sentry', a American Civil War drama in which he was reunited with Lee Patterson, but this time he wasn't a bit player to the American star, he was second billing. January also saw a piece in *The Times* bemoaning the lack of subsidy for theatre companies who were finding it impossible to find the wages to retain a permanent cast. The correspondent naturally got in touch with Stratford East and reported: 'Mr. Gerald Raffles, of Theatre Workshop says his company suffered from the loss of Mr. Harry Corbett, Mr. George A. Cooper and Mr. Howard Goorney, since returned, to other managements and media.'[17]

In February 150 leading lights of the performing arts, including Harry, were invited to exhibit their paintings at the charity-fund-raising Martell Art Exhibition. Sheila's brief study of fine arts would come in handy, though even the most loving eye couldn't have called his efforts 'fine' art. He didn't keep it up. For some unaccountable reason as soon as my brother and I were underfoot he never seemed to have the time ... His materials were stored under the bed, ready for action at a moment's notice. They eventually migrated to the attic – I think they're still there.

The month also saw Harry in a one-off production without décor at the Royal Court – these are freebies that showcase new work. The English Stage Company was giving a leg-up to new writer Alun Owen. Born in Wales but raised in Liverpool, Owen was an actor who was finding his true vocation. First produced on radio, *Progress to the Park* is a play set in Liverpool and shows the city's religious frictions through the love story of a Protestant boy and a Catholic girl. The production, directed by Lindsey Anderson, introduced Harry to Tom Bell, a young actor about to make a name for himself. It also reintroduced him to Donal Donnelly, born in England but raised in Ireland, who had worked on *Shake Hands With the Devil*.

Owen would go on to write prolifically for the small and big screens and for radio for over thirty years; two of his most memorable productions were *Lena, Oh My Lena* and *No Trams to Lime Street*, the latter including a breakthrough role for Tom Bell. Both were for *Armchair Theatre* under Canadian producer Sydney Newman, who had taken control in 1958. The freebie had definitely been worth it. 'A strong cast made the most of this very entertaining play,' said *The Stage*:

> Tom Bell and Margaret Tyzack were remarkably good as the young lovers, and Harry H. Corbett, an actor of the people if ever there was one, was excellent as the Welsh Liverpudlian who has escaped to the London literary world and is able to take a dispassionate look at his home town. Others from whom Lindsay Anderson drew fine performances were Donal Donnelly and Keith Smith, as seamen of contrasting types, and Gerard Dynevor, as Bobby Laughlin's [Tom Bell's] bigoted Orangeman father.[18]

Gerard Dynevor, Harry's friend from Theatre Workshop who had played Aumerle to Harry's Richard II, was still acting – but only just. He went on to become a television director, shepherding early episodes of *Coronation Street*. His fragility eventually got the better of him; he committed suicide in 1966. His wife, Shirley, remembering a get-together at Theatre Royal held in the mid-1970s, said:

> I was terribly glad going to the theatre for a gathering and I know my son Josh, who was eighteen at the time, had a lovely talk with Harry and I remember Harry saying to Josh that he thought Gerard was the greatest Aumerle ever. Which was such a lovely thing to say to him, because I'm sure Josh remembers that to this day.

Back in early 1959, Harry was hardly off TV screens. He played a producer in *The Bird, The Bear and The Actress*, an Italian café owner in *The Jukebox*, and Anthony Quale's son in *The Shadow of the Ruthless* – a young David McCallum also featured.

All of these productions had been for ITV. The new network was now leading the way, and not just with their technical camera work, as television history expert Professor John Hill[19] explains: "'Armchair Theatre' paved the way for new writing. It has a reputation for "kitchen sink" but most were very traditional. The BBC was slow to catch up. ITV stole the march on the BBC.'

In the hopes of stealing it back, the BBC allowed a few daring souls to set up the Langham Group. Harry would be one of its founding members and he later explained the group's experimental work:

> It was only experimental in the sense that it was attacking a certain hardness that had come into television; most television directors wanted basically to be cinema directors. They rooted you to a spot, they shot through your earhole, they shot up your nose, they shot everywhere possible to shoot; and intercut so much that you got a disjointed effect. So this experiment aimed at being absolutely the opposite of the cinema, returning to the pure days of early television when the artist moved around with the camera, was in complete rapport with the camera. The only really basic experimental thing you can get out of this one-camera technique is that if a scene needs to flow and every nuance needs to be observed from every character's point of view, you don't interrupt it with a close-up here, and a close-up there, or a line off camera that might lose import, or the look lose import.[20]

The Group's first production was an adaptation of Turgenev's *The Torrents of Spring*, and where Langham was truly experimental was with its writer – it didn't have one. A most unusual innovation for the 1950s as Professor Hill can testify:

> Then the director and the producer were the same person. Today they are separate. In Langham there wasn't a writer. Normally, in other dramas, the writer was the most important, the director only minimally serving the script. You'd be hard pushed to remember any director of TV. That was the oddity of the Langham Group because the person mainly behind it was Tony Pelissier, a cinema director. They were interested in the movement of the camera and the sound effects, trying to find a new language. It wasn't an actor's medium.

Not unless they could improvise a script; there would be no writer to give them the lines, something that would have been unusual for the more traditional members of the cast, one of whom was a certain Wilfrid Brambell – definitely more of whom later. Harry describes working on Turgenev's novel:

> We started basically with that and the idea of translating the story into contemporary life. Then we said, here's something that's usually done in a serial over a long period of time. But we wished to do it in a single play, get the essence of it. We'll call this the new television we wish to go for. So we more or less got hold of the content and the bones of the thing, threw it away; then we got everybody together in the room, improvised it, and we taped it. This experiment was carried out by Tony Pelissier who was responsible for the unit known as the Langham Group, helped by this marvellous man Mervyn, who was fantastic. He built a sort of mock-up camera so that we could work for the first time on the floor of the rehearsal room with a mock-up camera. We'd never heard of it before; we still don't see it today; we just have directors moving this way and that way; they do the best they can. But we actually got the feeling of moving with a camera, you see. It was the beginning of what I believe I'm known for, working with cameras.[21]

Professor Hill describes the production:

'Torrents' was shot live and had elaborate camera movements. It has more movements than any play of that time ... Harry plays 'Sonny'; it's a slightly odd role for him because he's the cuckolded husband. A lot of what caused controversy in the film was that Sandra Dome, who was his siren wife, liked other lovers – there was a seduction sequence. He's a put upon husband. So in some sense it wasn't a natural part because it doesn't play to his dangerous man persona – he was a brooding screen heavy. In Langham he's very seedy.

The experiment was short-lived – it wasn't cost-effective. The group was wound up in 1960 after just three productions. Only *Torrents* survives to show what could be done with ingenuity, effort and, most importantly, the luxury of rehearsal time. Time as always, but especially on screen, equals money.

Over the summer that followed *Torrents*, Harry resumed being a brooding screen heavy in a string of films. *The Shakedown* was a murky tale of pornography and blackmail starring Terence Morgan and Donald Pleasence, and was apparently banned in Finland. *The Times* had this to say:

> The Shakedown is constructed on American Gangster lines and shows Augie (Mr Terence Morgan) coming out of prison and determined to take back the prostitution 'ring' he has built up before his sentence. Another and even more repulsive thug, played by Mr Harry H. Corbett with a rich relish for the eccentricities of villainy, is in charge, however, and it looks as though Augie is beaten until he comes across a broken down photographer (Mr Donald Pleasence).[22]

In the Wake of a Stranger sees a sailor thwarting the attempts of killers who are setting him up to take the fall for a murder. Alun Owen made an appearance, as did David Hemmings in an early 'schoolboy' role. The leading lady was Shirley Eaton who, five years later, would iconically suffer death by paint in *Goldfinger*.

Talking of murdering young beauties, next came the film *Cover Girl Killer*; one of my personal favourites. Harry plays 'the man': a serial killer stalking young models who have appeared on the cover of titillating magazine *Wow*. There is plenty of disapproving dialogue on the sins of the flesh in these morally corrupting publications – nearly as much as there are shots of bikini-clad flesh for you to be corrupted by. Posing as a Mr Spendoza, disguised by a flasher mac, naff wig and pebble glasses, Harry sets about ridding the world of smut and filth by dispatching the monthly cover girls and posing them post-mortem as they had appeared on the mag. First on the list is Gloria, a showgirl at the Casbah Club. Spendoza picks her up from the club promising photo shoots set for that evening and 10 a.m. the next morning. '10 o'clock!' moans Gloria. 'I shall be dead!' Cut to her dead body the next day. The police suspect Johnny Mason, played by Spencer Teakle – now there's a name to see in lights. Mason is the owner of *Wow* magazine and an ex-archaeologist (but of course) who has been hanging around the theatre interviewing showgirls for his rag and has seen the memorable Spendoza.

He is soon cleared, so Harry, now dressed normally and posing as a Mr Fairchild, toys with the police by telling them he knows the identity of the killer – he is a Mr Spurling who has been renting a flat off Fairchild and burning copies of *Wow* before disappearing. Using Johnny Mason's girlfriend and Casbah Showgirl Miss July as bait, the police lie in wait to nab this Mr Spurling. But Harry is one step ahead. Now posing as a producer making a film about the killings, he sends an actor clad in flasher mac, naff wig and pebble glasses to the Casbah. Once the luckless actor is being grilled down the police station, Harry grabs Miss July backstage and starts to throttle her. Our hero Johnny Mason arrives in the nick of time but gets pistol-whipped. When he comes to, he sees Harry chasing Miss July along a high gantry. Mason unties the ropes and Harry falls to his death. Brilliant B-movie fodder; Harry is wonderfully unhinged and menacing. You can sometimes catch the film in the wee small hours on TV, keep a look out – it's a little cracker.

On 26 November Harry opened at the Princes Theatre in *Kookaburra* – a forgettable musical about an Englishwoman trying to settle in Australia in 1913. Although lustily sung, the songs and dialogue weren't lusty enough to escape a lukewarm reception in the papers:

> There are a few scenes which hit the mark, and have vigour and life, but these are overshadowed by masses of dialogue of exceptional dreariness. Too much is made of an English remittance man – a character straight from one of the lesser Victorian novels

of particularly revolting sentiment. Not even that clever actor Harry H. Corbett can make anything of him.[23]

When it closed in the New Year, 1960, it was back to the films. Harry appeared in crime drama *The Unstoppable Man* and was reunited with Donald Pleasance in *The Big Day*, the story of a man who had to choose between a love affair with his secretary or a promotion.

Then, in the spring, Joan Littlewood got in touch. According to Harry, Joan had been going through a period of being captivated by cabaret artists. He would say:

> Joan always felt that actors *were* singers, *were* dancers … she had changed round to say she was only really interested in people in cabaret and musical, those were the 'real' actors you know. She'd had a falling in love with the people from cabaret and musical, I won't mention names but there were several of them at the time and that was it. Unless you were cabaret or musical you didn't exist. You weren't possibly capable of working. I got a little bit of this from Joan, not a lot.[24]

As Joan had several productions running in the West End at once during this period, there were distinct advantages in working with performers used to cabaret. There was now little time for the extensive training of, and research by, actors. Joan needed people who could turn it on and improvise – the natural stomping ground of the cabaret artist. By 1960 Joan had fused Stanislavsky and cabaret, and now saw her actors as pure entertainers, or, as she put it, her 'clowns'. Brian Murphy, who had been at Theatre Workshop for the last five years, remembers this change:

> We used to do Stanislavsky and that was great, we all took it in turns to read a chapter. We approached the play through the reality of Stanislavsky but later on it was almost as if she turned her back on it because we were now 'clowns' and as 'clowns' we could encompass anything and everything in history. And, of course, Harry was so good he could switch instantly from one mode as it were into another and take you with him.

Harry returned to Theatre Royal for the lead in *Ned Kelly*, James Clancy's play about the Australian bushranger and outlaw. On the run from police after murdering three of their number, Kelly was finally captured during a gunfight. He was shot in the legs, left unprotected by his homemade armour, but he survived, unlike his gang, and went to the gallows in 1855, immediately becoming the stuff of legends.

'I was asked back,' Harry later remembered:

> I went to do Ned Kelly; I didn't go to do Ned Kelly so much I got stuck with it. I had a very successful theatrical life but something always pulled you back. Always things were going to be as they were. This was after Brendan Behan and all the rest had gone. The seasons were always going to go back and by golly they did. She started off, with 'Ned Kelly', to free the actors that she'd got together and it worked – of course we completely sacrificed the character and the part of Ned, because she would say 'These two policemen were being marvellous. Oh, let's have more of that' so Ned Kelly totally and utterly disappeared from the scene while we had more of that – which was really the point of it in a way. One didn't object or get uptight about it and say 'there goes my part through the window' because all of us were there in the season bringing on or trying to do what we'd spent five years doing before – a bunch of actors together.[25]

One of the bunch was Avis. She was to play Harry's mother. Joan would finally have to put romantic notions of a happy ending for the pair to one side when introduced to Harry's wife, Sheila. Another of the bunch was Brian Murphy who remembered:

> Later, when he came back to do Ned Kelly, I was standing next to Harry – I bumped into him, met him briefly and we exchanged odd words and things but nothing really, I'd not worked with him – and then it was, it was incandescent, it was extraordinary. I think overall what I remember was the intelligence of Harry in his acting. He could be flamboyant if the character required him to be, but it was an intensity that he had and an intelligence that drove, that reached you. You just wanted to listen to him. If he was giving any sort of lesson to a fellow actor it was in his performance, you learnt from what he was doing. There was nothing showy about it, he could be if he had to be but not as an actor personally – there was nothing luvvie about Harry at all.

When we worked in rehearsals it had taken me a long time to grasp anything of what Joan was saying, it was a slow process, but Harry was a prime example of what she meant and intended and there he was with you and it rubbed off on you. I seemed to think it rubbed off on you. I was doing better by working with Harry. He had that effect. He was generous on stage he provided support for you. You upped your game, as it were, coz his game was 'up' but you felt you could reach him – whether you did or not I don't know, I remember someone saying 'You're doing a lot better' and I was thinking 'Yeah, that's down to Harry.' The better the person you play opposite the better your performance.[26]

Overseeing the choreography of the police and the Kelly gang during fights and escapes was Jean Newlove:

I was taking movement classes there – it was at a time I had seen 'Seven Brides for Seven Brothers' and 'West Side Story' and I got them doing things on the stage at Stratford like that. I got Harry doing a run and running up the wall, the side of the shack or whatever it was, you can run up a vertical wall, and he was very good at it.

Which is more than can be said for whoever was in charge of special effects, as Murray Melvin remembers:

I was about when he was doing Ned Kelly. I was here for that run-through that went on for about 3 ½ hours and ended in a lot of smoke. I mean it was wonderful – we were falling about, Madam was furious, furious that we were falling about. The smoke went off no one could see anything – we were rolling about.

When it came to the reviews, if Harry hadn't objected to having his part thrown through the window then Ken Tynan did. In a piece entitled 'Ned Kelly and the Keystone Cops', he wrote:

James Clancy's Ned Kelly is a dashing attempt to make a play out of the extravagant career of Australia's most notorious bandit, who was hanged eighty years ago at Melbourne; and it fails on two counts. Whenever the hero is offstage, we long for a camera to show us what he is doing; and whenever he is onstage, we yearn for a better writer to tell us what he is thinking ... Miss Littlewood encourages her actors to improvise, which is all very well when the play in question is contemporary in idiom; but it is difficult to improvise speeches that fall from the lips of nineteenth-century Australians. In the crowd scenes one gets the impression of anxiety, as if everyone felt impelled to chatter, on pain of being sent out for not talking in class ... Harry H. Corbett, as Ned, gives a haunting and characteristically audacious performance; he plays the hero mock-heroically, striking poses that verge at times on fatuous fraudulence, yet never allowing us to forget that even frauds may be right. The conception is Brechtian; the dialogue, unfortunately, is not.[27]

The Times was kinder: 'Miss Joan Littlewood ... leaves the Theatre Workshop with the impression that she has not yet quite made up her mind what to do with her material. The only firm decision she seems to have made is that the Kelly gang shall be played as romantics and their pursuers as comic policemen.' After complimenting Harry as dashingly heroic it went on to say:

> Miss Avis Bunnage gives a lively impression of the old lady who is the mother of outlaws *par excellence*, and Mr. Brian Murphy has several delightful turns on his own, sometimes as an inept police sergeant and sometimes as a philosophical linesman in the telegraph service. But it will no doubt be a better evening's entertainment once Miss Littlewood has determined the sort of shape it ought finally to take.[28]

This last comment was a fair assessment of Theatre Workshop as a whole. More than most companies, their productions would be honed during the run. Each performance would be a refinement on the last, guided by Joan's constant notes.

Towards the end of that run, Joan started rehearsing Ben Jonson's *Every Man in his Humour*, the play she would take to that year's Paris Festival. In the cast was a young Victor Spinetti, a former cabaret artist who had been with the company since the previous autumn. He had joined the cast of Wolf Mankowitz's *Make Me An Offer* before taking over in Frank Norman's *Fings Ain't Wot They Used To Be* at The Garrick. In his autobiography Victor remembers:

Harry H. Corbett dropped in to rehearsals at Stratford East, took me aside and said, 'Don't work with her. Get out. Get away. She'll destroy you.' His best work, as Khlestakov in *The Government Inspector*, Ould Brennan in *Red Roses for Me* and above all, Richard the Second, had been for Theatre Workshop. I was in a state of shock. I'll guess. He saw us having a kind of fun he'd once known, a fun *Steptoe and Son* was not providing. Simultaneously he was remembering the exhaustion at the end of his Stratford East days brought on by Joan's relentless demands.[29]

Which was remarkably foresighted of Harry, considering he would not land the role of Harold Steptoe for another eighteen months. I am not entirely convinced Harry spoke out of either jealousy or remembered exhaustion; he was merely speaking from experience. Perhaps he had seen in Spinetti a vulnerability that, as Harry knew all too well, could lead to the young man being crushed – he needn't have worried.

A few years later, Victor would go on to win a Tony Award on Broadway for his performance in Theatre Workshop's *Oh What a Lovely War* before breaking into films. He told me:

First time I was aware of Harry I was on stage rehearsing the Ben Jonson and I saw him moving across the Dress Circle and Joan must have, in her usual way, said 'Oh you must come down and see how marvellous this actor is, since you fucking left – you bastard.' So down he came to see what she said was going to be the next Harry. That was typical of Joan. Anyway, it made no difference coz we just laughed about it and he said, when we got to know each other, he said 'Careful cause she can destroy you.'

Later still in 1972, Victor was collaborating with Joan and Frank Norman, the writer of *Fings* on a new 'Brits abroad' play about a package holiday to Spain:

There was a show called 'Costa Packet', and Frank and myself and Joan were working on it. The whole idea was that the Spaniard was all the same person – coz all Spaniards look alike. The Hotel Manager would be me, the Cabaret Entertainer would be me, the guy hustling them on the beach would be me. We worked for a few weekends on this over a period of months and then

when the show was about to go on, Joan and Gerry came to
the house, on my birthday, and said, 'Are you really going to be
with us on Monday?' I said, 'Well, yes – What's up?' Gerry said,
'Well. We're a bit worried about your Spanish accent, it might
sound Italian.' I said, 'I don't have an Italian accent, if I've got any
accent at all it's Welsh. Since when have you been worried about
accents?' I said, 'What's up?' 'Well,' said Gerry, 'Poor old Maxwell
Shaw hasn't been working, so we're giving the part to Max.' and
I was fired. Ages later in a pub Frank Norman punched me in
the back and said, 'You bastard!' I said, 'Well? I was fired.' and he
said 'Well Joan walked in and said 'Victor's getting too grand
to work with us now, since getting that award in New York, so
Max has stepped in at the last minute.' So, in a funny way, Harry
was right.

Back in 1960, as the company left for Paris, Harry returned to filming. In the summer he played Inspector Jock Bruce in an Edgar
Wallace Mystery, *Marriage of Convenience*. Howard Goorney played
an onion seller. When it wrapped, Stratford East got in touch again.
But this time it wasn't Joan – it was John Bury.

Bury had been left in charge, and in the lurch, again. Harry
remembered:

> Then I had a call, then [Joan] had started her worldwide travels –
> she kept nipping away to places, to France doing a bit over there.
> Then I had a call from Camel Bury to say that he was in a bit of a
> hole. Joan had not yet come back from wherever it was and he'd
> had to mount the season on his own and would I help out. I said,
> 'All right.' He said, 'I've got three weeks, I don't know what to
> put in.' and he'd already done the extremely successful 'Playboy
> of the Western World'. He'd got the whole lot on his shoulders.
> I saw him and said, 'Stick in a play by Alun Owen', it was called
> 'Progress to the Park'. But at that time it seems you were doing
> 'Sparrers Can't Sing' and Bob Grant had fallen out and they
> asked me would I take over his part to help them out on the last
> few weeks before 'Progress'. I said, 'Oh, all right.'[30]

Bob Grant had joined the Workshop in 1956. He would go on to
be best remembered for playing Jack Harper in the hugely popular
sitcom *On the Buses* in the 1960s and '70s. This was the height of his

career, but as work dried up he sadly slipped into depression. He made several attempts at suicide, finally succeeding in 2003.

Murray Melvin remembers Harry taking over in *Sparrers*:

> I forget what happened to Bob Grant, something dreadful, and, of course, as always when there was a crisis where did they turn to? Always to the old nuts and I remember because he came in. He didn't get any rehearsal, poor love, but he got his newspaper – reading the horses – and in his newspaper were his lines and you came in and you started and in true Workshop fashion if the line didn't come to him you walked around it. It was a wonderful time with him. He was my Dad in the play and it was so wonderful, that security. I'd had Avis, of course, but suddenly one understood what the security of working with somebody like that on stage was because you just looked at those eyes. That saying about Harry 'he was an actor's actor' – he was an actor's actor, which is the highest accolade I think you could give him, he just did the job.

When Harry had signed on for *Sparrers*, Camel had neglected to tell him that the company was due to take it to the Maxim Gorki Theatre in Berlin and to Copenhagen in October, just as he was about to do a few more plays for ABC. A feat of logistics that would not have been possible had *Armchair* still come out of Manchester, but in the summer of 1959 ABC had moved operations to the Teddington Studios in London. It was here where Harry appeared in an episode of *Police Surgeon*, the series that was the forerunner of *The Avengers*, and starred in *Armchair Theatre*'s *Pig's Ear with Flowers*, a comedy about Fred Harris, a butcher, and Maria, a tempestuous Italian domestic help, played by Isa Miranda. *The Times* noted that the director 'extracted admirable comic performances not only from those of his cast we might have expected ... but from such heavyweight players as Miss Isa Miranda and Mr Harry H. Corbett. Mr Corbett, indeed, expanded out of all recognition when given a rest from villainy as the amorous butcher.'[31] Harry also starred in Peter Yeldham's *Thunder on the Snowy*, a look at frictions inside the immigrant workers' camps on the Australian Snowy River Project. *The Stage* commented: 'Harry Corbett, now one of our finest all-round actors, plays Jan Radeck, a product of long years in the refugee camps of Europe who is soul-weary of "orders".'[32]

Harry was now free to begin directing *Progress to the Park*. The cast featured Brian Murphy, Roy Kinnear and John Junkin. Billie Whitelaw, a veteran of stage and screen at only 28 years old, triumphed as the Catholic girl. Sean Lynch was the Protestant boy, the part that Tom Bell had played at the Royal Court. The part Harry had played there, the Welsh Liverpudlian playwright commentator, was taken by Tom Bell, who incidentally had known Billie Whitelaw for years. They had both studied drama together at Bradford Civic Theatre.

'I expect great things of Mr. Bell;' wrote Ken Tynan, 'but even as I pen that sentence, I can predict and almost see his response – an ironic scoffing smile. To sum up: "Progress to the Park" is a beauty, rollicking, non-political lark, raised to a higher level by the writing, acting and direction (in that order) of half a dozen roles.'[33]

Tynan was not far wrong on Tom Bell: a couple of years later, with his film career just taking off, Bell was at an awards do. The Duke of Edinburgh was half way through a speech when a well-lubricated Bell heckled him. 'Tell us a joke,' he shouted. He was ignored. When he did it again Prince Phillip told him: 'If you wanted jokes, you should have got a comedian.'

Although HRH probably wouldn't have given a damn – after all not only had he come out of it rather well but the man has had to handle a lot more than drunken actors in his time – it was embarrassing for the bigwigs in the room and put a black mark against Bell's name. Harry, like most of the business, saw that as a major contribution as to why Bell's career never went as 'stellar' as it should have.

Progress to the Park ran at Theatre Royal until the January of 1961, by which time Joan had returned. Harry remembered: 'About 2/3rds of the way through the season Joan came back and it was all very matey again.'[34] Joan's good mood was down to being invigorated by her latest project. She was collaborating with the architect Cedric Price to create a 'laboratory of fun'. 'An enormous space framework would enclose many leisure pursuits and experiences,' wrote Howard Goorney. 'Included would be warm air curtains, vapour zones, optical barriers and a variety of new and exciting gadgets. Joan's own description was: "A place of toys for adults, a place to waste time without guilt or discomfort, to develop unused talents, to discover the fund of joy and fun and sadness within us."'[35]

Cedric Price's plans envisaged an open steel structure over which cranes hovered, ready to move prefabricated 'rooms' into new positions at the drop of a lever, and giving the building endless variations. Price said of his proposed building: 'Its form and structure, resembling a large shipyard in which enclosures such as theatres, cinemas, restaurants, workshops, rally areas, can be assembled, moved, re-arranged and scrapped continuously.'

Joan's 'fun palace', a title that would do it no favours, was a place where, according to Price, you would be able to:

> Choose what you want to do – or watch someone else doing it. Learn how to handle tools, paint, babies, machinery, or just listen to your favourite tune. Dance, talk or be lifted up to where you can see how other people make things work. Sit out over space with a drink and tune in to what's happening elsewhere in the city. Try starting a riot or beginning a painting – or just lie back and stare at the sky.

Joan was at the start of trying to bring this huge venture to the east of London. It was a venture that would increasingly take up more and more of her time, leaving long stretches when Gerry would have to helm Theatre Royal by himself. As she set about courting the press and battling the councils over funding and planning, Harry went back to filming.

He was reunited with Margaret Tyzack in the Theatre 70 production *Chance Witness*; he would follow this with another Theatre 70, *The Intruder* and then another Armchair, *The Money Makers*, written by Ted Allan. Harry then starred in the short film *The Wings of Death*, one of the Scotland Yard series, playing Scottish detective Superintendent Hammond.

By June he was again back at Stratford East. Joan was directing him in James Goldman's satire *They Might Be Giants*. Goldman came over from the States for the rehearsals. Harry played Justin Playfair, a former judge who believes he is Sherlock Holmes. Playfair's brother, wanting him committed to an asylum, arrives with psychiatrist Dr Mildred Watson, played by Avis. Playfair then ropes Dr Watson into helping him hunt down his nemesis Moriarty through the streets of New York, meeting plenty of 'sane' oddballs along the way.

Roy Kinnear played Playfair's brother; Glynn Edwards, John Junkin and Brian Murphy were amongst the odd balls. It was the last time Brian would work with Harry at Theatre Royal E15:

'I would have loved to have worked with Harry on more stuff because it was like being next to a battery in a way that charges you but without any loss to himself. You felt good working with him and you gained a great deal.'

As the opening night loomed Joan wasn't ready, as John Bury recalled:

> Hal Prince, the American impresario, was backing *Giants*. He had Princess Margaret coming down for the opening night and Joan wanted to postpone it. It wasn't a problem particular to that piece. In the early days when we were a repertory theatre it didn't matter so much. No one came on Monday, and by Thursday it would be quite good, and by that time we were rehearsing the next one. Now we were transferring shows and so everything had to be on the boil for the first night. Of course Joan was always late and she wanted to postpone the opening night of *Giants*. Gerry said, 'You can't, I've got the Press coming.' Joan's answer was 'I don't want the sodding Press.' Then he said, 'We've got Princess Margaret coming.' She said 'And we don't want Princess Margaret either.' Hal Prince didn't want to postpone either. I think he'd come to the stage where he thought he wouldn't get a better show even if he gave Joan another month. I think he'd written it off. He realised he wasn't going to have a viable London and New York success.

The reviews were universally bad:

> Miss Joan Littlewood underlines every point and makes what should be swift and light as air as painfully plodding and heavy as lead. Miss Avis Bunnage, a substantial actress with a part even vaguely suitable, is grotesquely miscast as Watson, and Mr Harry H. Corbett, more subtly miscast as Justin alias Holmes, is also decidedly heavyweight, though intermittently rather endearing.[36]

Joan had set a lot of store by this production and took the critic's rejection badly. 'We became quite obsessed with this scatty play and its secret poet,' she later wrote:

> It came as a shock when, to a man, the critics turned it down. Jim Goldman didn't fight back like Saroyan,[37] but rewrote his play

as a film with George C. Scott playing Holmes, and I'm sure he couldn't have been as good as Harry Corbett.

At first I raged against the critics, then I gave them up. London was finished anyway. We could do better anywhere else. We couldn't do worse.

What was the last straw that broke the camel's back? I'm not exactly sure. It could have been that night when I was sitting outside Olivelli's, in Gerry's car, and Tom Driberg joined us. A cynical remark was passed – about E15 – or the play ... All I remember is getting up and going, just going ... wandering about ... lost.[38]

Joan had left and, this time, she wasn't coming back.

It wasn't that Joan didn't care about the production – if anything she always cared too much. Glynn Edwards remembers:

Joan wasn't like modern directors who put a show on, see two performances and then walk away. I've known Joan call a Company for notes in between the matinee and evening performance on the last Saturday of a show's run. You could always see her in the audience, see her Gauloises on the go and her taking notes and once we got to the West End she couldn't cope with that. She had several shows running at once.

To the stress of overwork and the burden of expectation she also had to add the constant financial strain of keeping Theatre Workshop's home afloat. Joan could never make enough on West End runs to support Theatre Royal. The place was a money pit, always had been. Only now her favoured actors were getting a little long in the tooth to be working for two quid a week, wages had increased to £15. Actors not only acquire gravitas as they age but they also acquire families and extra mouths to feed; something that Joan could have a hard time accepting. Without a substantial grant, of which there was still no sign, it seemed a lost cause. She cracked, and packed for Nigeria, not saying when, or even if, she'd return. It was over.

Harry covered for her absence with the press:

Mr Harry Corbett, the leading man in Theatre's present production *They Might Be Giants* told the *Times* last night. 'She needs to go away and re-find herself, to find the new person she really is,' he said, 'what carried her through in recent years is not enough for her now. She has to go for her artistic need, it is as simple as that.' Her decision was 'an awful surprise' to the company.[39]

Joan's wasn't the only exit. During that year, Harry had invited Cynthia and her fiancé, Barry Whittaker, down to stay with him and Sheila at the flat in Arkwright Road. When they got there Cynthia found Harry alone: 'A few days before we arrived, she'd just left him. He did seem quite upset. I felt sorry for him. He wanted children but she wanted a career, she wouldn't have children so they called it a day.'

Sheila was still an unknown struggling actress at the time and having children would have rather cramped any ambition of making it to the top. In the early 1960s, as a rule, women did not have children and a career; it was one or the other. Of course, there would be many factors leading to Harry and Sheila's divorce but this first break-up marked the beginning of the end.

On Cynthia's previous visit they'd gone to the museums, but this time, understandably, Harry was in the mood for something a bit more lively, as Cynthia remembers:

> He took us to Raymond's Revue Bar, we sat with all these gang-sters talking shop and stuff, and Harry said, 'Cynthia, Barry, you must go through and see this show.' And we'd never seen a strip show before in our lives! We went in to see this show – they were putting these hats in all these special places as they were dancing with the fans, you know. And they brought us a bottle of whiskey with a mark on the side and they charged you for how much whiskey you drank out of the bottle – it absolutely floored me! And we went to the Celebrity Bar and that was a floor show – they were all dancing about jingling their bosoms.

Although today it sounds laughably seedy, back then this was seen as incredibly glamorous and sophisticated, and I bet it was a hell of a talking point when Cynthia and Barry got back up north.

In September Harry headed south. He had been invited to join the Bristol Old Vic for a season and had jumped at the chance to get out of town: 'I'd had a sort of bad mental time. I wasn't going bonkers but I'd had rather a lot of strain, a lot of overwork, and I was sick of being under the critical eyes of London. The opportunity came up, and I was very grateful at the time because it helped me enormously to play at the Bristol OldVic.'

Harry opened the season in the British premiere of Tennessee Williams' *Period of Adjustment*, a comedy set in Nashville about two marriages and their respective teething troubles. The reviews were good, *The Times* reporting: 'The cast, led by Mr Harry H. Corbett and Miss Elizabeth Shepherd, rise splendidly to the play's difficulties (notably that of accent) and the evening proves one of unexpectedly uncomplicated delight.'[40]

Period of Adjustment was so successful that backers wanted to take it into the West End. But Bristol said no – they wanted to keep the company together until the contracts ran out at Christmas. After that, who knew?

An 'uncomplicated delight' had been just what Harry needed. However, they were not words that could ever have been thrown at his next role – *Macbeth*.

The actor Milton Johns, newly graduated from the Bristol Old Vic Theatre School, was a spear carrier/assistant stage manager in the play and remembered, 'Harry was a delightfully unfussy man – easy and approachable for us menial ASM's – not a man to worry unduly about his place in the pecking order of life. He would slip into his cockney patter at the drop of a hat but there was, I always suspected, something a little sad and withdrawn about his eyes.'

Harry got that a lot, having inherited his large eyes – so do I. Large equals sad, in the way that light equals piercing and small equals piggy. Ah well, it's better than crossed. As for withdrawn ... yes, he could be, as already discussed. Besides, he was in a very different place than the young Milton Johns.

Milton would also remember the rehearsals, starting with the read-through:

Harry gave a reading the like of which I have never since experienced. It was spellbinding and one thought one was about to take part in one of those rare and special theatrical events that come on only a handful of occasions in life. Excitement was in the air! One realised, months after, that that morning was the peak of his performance. What caused the draining of his confidence over the next few weeks I can only guess at – though some of the guesses would be fairly obvious. Whatever the reason

Harry arrived at the opening night with about as much confidence as a man facing a firing squad.[41]

The play was to be set 'somewhere in the North', not specifically
Scotland, around AD 1,100. The costumes were also chosen to be
rootless and timeless. In the pre-production publicity the director,
Val May, had said:

> Macbeth is played as a pageant of demonology. Thus it becomes
> unreal, in my view ... I want to be sure that there is reality in
> everything that is done. That Macbeth is led to do his deed by the
> presence of evil that is very real ... I want the witches to be real
> old women; not spirits who believe they have powers. They are to
> be within the limits of human experience; rather like clairvoyants,
> if you like. But certainly not like three weird goddesses ... My
> overall main interest is to delve into the minds of the characters,
> and this is what I hope the production will show.[42]

When the curtain went up Harry was right to have been worried.
The set was criticised for being too overpowering, the costumes for
being too reminiscent of *Julius Caesar*, the witches for looking like
they were on day release from Bedlam and when Banquo's ghost
put in a blood-drenched appearance at the banquet, following
Macbeth around à la 'he's behind you', someone in the audience
started to snigger. Oh dear.

On Harry, the reviewers commented: 'While Harry H Corbett
is an extremely talented actor and has put an immense amount of
effort – and indeed passion – into the leading role, it is not really his
part.'[43] And 'Harry H. Corbett's Macbeth takes time to stamp himself on the audience. There have perhaps been more flamboyant and
physically dynamic Macbeths. But the actor is gaining force all the
time and from the moment he starts recoiling from Banquo's ghost,
his tormented soul is often brilliantly conveyed.'[44]

But not often enough – as the curtain came down Milton Johns
remembered:

> I was standing towards the end of the second row at the cur-
> tain call. The lines broke up and Harry turned to make his way
> towards the upstage exit. I stood back to let him pass and as he
> came level to me he stopped, put his arm around my shoulders

and we left the stage together. As we did so he turned to me and said, 'Milt, I was very nice to people on the way up!'[45]

Ah well, you win some … Anyway, the season would only last until Christmas and there was already an offer coming in for a new television play.

It was a bittersweet comedy about two rag-and-bone men …

Notes

1   *Ibid.*
2   *Observer*, 11/12/55.
3   Terris, O., 'The Forgotten Hamlet', *Shakespeare Bulletin*, vol. 25, no. 2.
4   *The Guardian*, 6/4/56.
5   Interviewed by Michael Arditti, *Independent Magazine*, 26/3/94.
6   *Daily Mirror*, 8/9/72.
7   *Weekend News*, 12/8/72.
8   Goorney, *The Theatre Workshop Story*.
9   *The Guardian*, 23/9/02.
10 *Manchester Weekly News*, 25/3/67.
11 *Ibid.*, 18/3/1967.
12 *The Guardian*, 19/9/57.
13 *Ibid.*, 23/11/57.
14 *The Stage*, 27/12/57.
15 *Ibid.*, 27/2/58.
16 *The Guardian*, 17/8/79.
17 *Ibid.*
18 *The Times*, 14/1/59.
19 *The Stage*, 12/1/59.
20 Head of Research, Department of Media Arts, Royal Holloway, University of London.
21 Burton, *Acting in the Sixties*.
22 *Ibid.*
23 *The Times*, 18/1/60.
24 *The Stage*, 3/12/59
25 Harry, in conversation with Howard Goorney.
26 *Ibid.*
27 In conversation with Brian Murphy.
28 *Observer*, 29/5/60.
29 *The Times*, 24/5/60.
30 Spinetti, V., *Up Front: his Strictly Confidential Autobiography* (Robson Books, 2006).
31 Harry, in conversation with Howard Goorney.
32 *The Times*, 3/10/60.
33 *The Stage*, 13/10/60.
34 *Observer*, 20/11/60.
35 Harry, in conversation with Howard Goorney.

36   Goorney, *The Theatre Workshop Story*.
37   *The Times*, 29/6/61.
38   William Saroyan, American dramatist, author of Pulitzer Prize-winning *The Time of Your Life*.
39   Littlewood, *Joan's Book*.
40   *The Times*, 10/7/61.
41   *Ibid.*, 5/9/61.
42   *The Stage*, 29/4/93.
43   *Evening Post*, 22/9/61.
44   *The Stage*, 5/10/61.
45   *Evening World*, 27/9/61.
46   *The Stage*, 29/4/93.

1. Harry and Beatrice Collins' small son, Rangoon, Burma 1926. (Author's collection)

2. Harry and his aunt, Annie Williams, Manchester, c. 1930. (Author's collection)

3. Harry, Earl Street, Ardwick, c. 1928. (Author's collection)

4. H. Corbett RM, 1944. (Author's collection)

5. Harry as Henry VIII in *The Rose Without a Thorn*, Chorlton, 1951. (Author's collection)

6. Barbara Brown and Harry in *Arden of Faversham*, Theatre Workshop, 1955. (Courtesy of Theatre Royal Stratford East Archives Collection)

7. Howard Goorney, Harry, Barbara Brown and Gerry Raffles in *Richard II*, Theatre Workshop, 1955. (Courtesy of Theatre Royal Stratford East Archives Collection)

8. Harry as the Cockney Trader and Kenneth Lee Spencer as The Emperor Jones, *Armchair Theatre*, 1958. (A.B.C. Television Ltd)

9. Harry and Joan Littlewood rehearsing *They Might Be Giants*, Theatre Royal, 1961. (Courtesy of Theatre Royal Stratford East Archives Collection)

10. Harry, Duncan Wood and Wilfrid Brambell during a break in filming *Steptoe and Son*. (Author's collection)

11. Alan Simpson, Ray Galton and Harry on the set of *The Bargee*, 1963. (Galton–Simpson Productions Ltd for Associated British Picture Corp. Ltd)

12. *Rattle of a Simple Man*, 1964.
(Associated British Picture Corp. Ltd)

13. Maureen. (Photo: Barry
Griffiths. Author's collection)

14. Maureen and Harry in Cannes, 1965. (Author's collection)

15. Harold Wilson, Alf Morris, Harry and George Wigg on the steps of 10 Downing Street, 1965. (*The Sun*)

16. Harry and Maureen at a charity fête in Tring, 1970. (*Gazette*)

17. Jonathan, Harry and Susannah at the house in Ginahgulla Road,
Sydney, on a day off from *The Last of the Red Hot Lovers*, 1972
(Photo: John Pinfold. Author's collection)

18. *Steptoe and Son Ride Again*, 1973. (Photo: John Jay. Author's collection)

19. In cabaret. (Photo: Mel Figures. Author's collection)

20. Harry, Wilfrid and Maureen on Christmas Day, Geelong, Australia, 1977. (Author's collection)

11

Delicious, Delightful, Cannot Wait to Work on It

It is ironic that I had appeared a hundred times on TV in the six years before Harold Steptoe came into my life. And I can't count the number of parts I have played in the theatre – most of them of a serious type.

It was while I was playing Shakespeare, in the early sixties, that my fate was decided by the scriptwriting team of Alan Simpson and Ray Galton.[1]

Harry H. Corbett

According to Ernest Hemingway: 'A man's got to take a lot of punishment to write a really funny book.' The *Steptoe and Son* writers, Ray Galton and Alan Simpson, met on a tuberculosis ward: Ern would have approved.

Ray Galton was born in Paddington, London, in 1930. His father spent most of his career in the navy and separated from Ray's mother during the war. Ray later said:

It was a traumatic time for me. I was kept in the dark about their separation for some time – I used to wonder where he was. In those days, it was such a disgrace to even contemplate divorce or splitting up. I used to pray every night that the war wouldn't end so that the kids wouldn't ask me where my father was. It had a terrible effect on me.[2]

Ray left school at 14 and spent time as a plasterer's apprentice and labourer, before ending up driving a desk at the London offices of the Transport and General Workers' Union. When he was 16 he was diagnosed with tuberculosis and rushed into Milford Sanatorium. Waiting lists for sanatorium beds could be as long as two years. Ray's queue jumping was not a good sign; he wasn't expected to need the bed for more than a fortnight.

Alan Simpson was born in Brixton, London, in 1929; his father was a draughtsman turned milkman. In 1947, while commuting to his job as a shipping clerk in London's city centre, Alan began coughing up blood. The hospital confirmed tuberculosis and he was sent home. That night he haemorrhaged. The following day his father died from Hodgkin's disease: 'In one swoop, my mother lost her husband, and her son was given the last rites.'[3] Alan was confined to bed at home for three months while waiting for a sanatorium bed, and a further year trapped in a staging post until space opened up at Milford. In 1948 he was finally in, as Ray remembers: 'One day a fellow walked past and the room went dark. I turned around to see the biggest guy I'd ever seen. I later found out it was Alan. Spike Milligan would go on to call him "He Who Blocks Out the Sun".'[4] Alan is 6ft 4in, and Ray is tall enough to look him in the eye, which explains why neither of them stoops in apology to the rest of us.

During the long months on the ward, waiting to see whether they would leave on their feet or in a box, the pair struck up a friendship. They had so much in common – not just height. They were Londoners, two of the only teenagers in the place, with a similar upbringing, social background and outlook on life, as well as a passion for the cinema and radio comedy. Their shared sense of humour meshed so completely that they could telepathically finish each other's punch lines. They were also very, very bored.

Ray's roommate, Tony Wallis, had an RAF 1155 radio. A select few inmates were hooked up and Ray and Alan would spend half the night listening to the American Forces Network. Tony was also an engineering buff and soon had the entire sanatorium wired for sound. Radio Milford was born. Broadcasting out of a linen cupboard, it quickly grew in popularity, progressing from music requests to panel shows. Ray and Alan were invited to join the Radio Committee and it wasn't long before the pair wrote and produced the first of their short comedy scripts, entitled *Have You Ever Wondered?*

This was the start of a relationship that has spanned sixty years, and changed the face of television comedy. They still meet up every

Monday for coffee and still finish each other's sentences, which makes them a bugger to quote.

Having found their calling, their first step on the road from hospital inmates to professional scriptwriters was to send a script to their heroes Dennis Norden and Frank Muir, writers of the hit radio series *Take It From Here*. Norden and Muir pointed the pair in the direction of the BBC Script Department, advice Ray and Alan used to pass on to anyone who wrote to them.

Alan was discharged from Milford in 1950; Ray had to wait another year for his release. Reunited in 1951 they finally had a chance to take the advice and sent a sketch to BBC script editor Gale Pedrick, he liked what he saw and called them in for a meeting.

They started writing for the show *Variety Band Box*, where they met Frankie Howerd; they would continue to write for Frankie for the rest of his career. They were also drafted in to help on the BBC flop *Happy Go Lucky* – within days Ray and Alan were writing one-liners, within weeks the whole show. One of the comics on that show knew a good thing when he saw it, as Ray remembers: 'Alan and I were at rehearsals and this figure wandered over to us with the script and muttered, "Did you write this?" We nodded. The figure said, "Very good!" and wandered off again. That was Hancock.'[5]

Ray and Alan started writing regularly for Tony Hancock. They got away from the variety format by creating the first radio sitcom, *Hancock's Half Hour*, in 1954. Instead of 'doing a turn', the comedy came from the situations Hancock found himself in. It was a slow-burning success, transferring to television in 1956, with Duncan Wood as producer. Hancock was huge. Whenever he was on, the streets would empty. The series continued until 1961. The same year Ray and Alan also wrote Hancock's film *The Rebel*.

Although well received in the UK and Commonwealth, the film didn't go down well in America where it was titled *Call Me Genius*. Determined to crack the States with his next feature, Hancock rejected several Galton and Simpson scripts over the following months. In an effort to update his image he took a break from his successful writers and entered a period Alan refers to as 'Tony's French Haircut': 'After we'd finished with him, to change his image, he had his hair cut short into one of these French Razor cuts, which was what he had for the rest of his life, in an attempt to modernise and get away from his East Cheam image. And it made him look very old and ill.'

Ray, however, differs in his opinion, 'Oh, I thought it suited him, he looked good – but he wasn't right up in the nut.'

The upshot of 'Tony's French Haircut' was that Galton and Simpson were free agents. The BBC, seeking to rectify that, made them an offer they couldn't refuse. Tom Sloan, Head of Light Entertainment, invited them in for a little chat. He dismissed their offer to write a series for Frankie Howerd whose star, he believed, and according to recent viewing and appreciation figures, was on the wane. Instead he told them of his pet project, *Comedy Playhouse*.

Ray remembered that: 'Sloan gave us five hours of television time with which we could do what we wanted. He said, "The only thing I insist on is using my title 'Comedy Playhouse' – that's all. The rest is up to you." Of course we jumped at the chance. It was a golden opportunity to fulfil an ambition: to write for actors. It really was an emancipation from being a comedian's scriptwriters.'[6] No writers had ever been given such freedom.

They began work on the ten half-hour, one-act plays and dried up on number four. After days of staring at a blank page and not coming up with any characters, Ray floated the idea of 'two rag-and-bone men', to which Alan replied: 'You'll never get a half hour show out of two rag-and-bone men.' Following a few more hours of zero inspiration, the idea began to have merit and they set to work. Ten pages in they realised that one of the men was old and stayed at home, and the other was younger and out on the round. 'Suddenly it hit us – father and son. That was the breakthrough! It gave what we'd written a whole new meaning, and everything seemed to click into place.' Alan recalled:

> We were literally half way through writing when the father and son notion came to us. We could then take an element from the first ten pages, where the young man has picked up a golf club on the round, and return to that. This one golf club was his symbol of a better life, a tangible symbol of his need to get away from his father and improve himself with a higher class of person.[7]

His 'need to get away' would be painted all the blacker when the son's age was placed at nearing 40. This was in the days when 40 was not the new 30 – it was middle-aged. For those of you who will turn it in at 80, it still is. Situation comedy could afford writers the chance to explore such tragic elements. But these elements

would not be the natural stomping ground of established comics –
they needed actors who could play the script, not personalities who
would play their image.

The script was entitled 'The Offer', it was the fourth of the
series and along with the first three would be given into the care of
Hancock's Half Hour producer, Duncan Wood.

Next, Ray and Alan set about casting the family firm of Steptoe
and Son, the name taken from a photographers' shop local to Ray
called Steptoe and Figge.

Alan explains: 'The whole idea of *Comedy Playhouse* was to try
and cast actors wherever possible.' 'Especially from our point of
view because we were fed up,' Ray added. 'We thought as long as
they had a sense of humour and the touch they'd be fine. We'd had
enough of people counting their lines to see how many funny ones
there were and actors didn't seem to do that.'

A shoe-in for the part of Albert Steptoe was Wilfrid Brambell.
Born in Dublin, on 22 March 1912, after leaving school he held
down a job as a reporter for the *Irish Times* while moonlighting
as an actor at the Abbey Theatre. During the war he toured with
the Entertainments National Service Association. After demob he
stayed in England, drifting through various repertory companies.
While trying to break into radio drama he supported himself as
everything from washer-up to postman. He soon landed minor film
roles and following his West End debut in 1950 joined several theatrical tours. He had married Molly Josephine in 1948 but they
divorced when she bore the child of their lodger, Roderick Fisher,
in 1953. By which time he had become a regular in supporting roles
on television, including *The Quatermass Experiment* and *Nineteen
Eighty-Four*. Always cast older than his years, by 1961 he had his
'old man' down to a fine art. 'At that time I was known by my less
fortunate fellow actors as "Old Neverstop".' He later wrote:

> I had for years been making a reasonable living from the box.
> One of the finest television plays in which I have ever appeared
> was a five-hander written by Clive Exton and entitled *No Fixed
> Abode*. The action of that Granada Production took place in a
> Doss House dormitory where, for some eight hours, four social
> drop-outs met and fused. It was a deep-thinking play with tre-
> mendous impact.[8]

It made an impact on Galton and Simpson, who not only wanted Willie for 'The Offer' but had also cast him in another Playhouse episode 'The Visiting Day'. The character of Albert Steptoe ran the gamut from conniving, vindictively evil, leering bastard to frightened, frail, sympathetic father. Aside from his talent and technical expertise, Willie had been around the game long enough to be a safe pair of hands.

The character of the son was even more complex. Close in age to that of the writers, he would be their voice. Harold Steptoe could be cruel, violent, passionate, stifled and above all dissatisfied. He was also loving, dutiful, insecure, and optimistically ambitious; prone to flights of fancy that gave respite from pessimistic reality. He was, unusually, a leading everyman, but one safely viewed at the bottom of society. The part also required the ability to flip an audience from belly laugh to pathos in a heartbeat. Ray and Alan knew exactly who they wanted.

'We phoned up Duncan Wood and said can you get an availability check out on Harry H. Corbett and Wilfrid Brambell,' remembered Ray.

'We picked them,' Alan continued:

we never met either of them, but we obviously knew of their work. Harry was very well known in the business. People in the street had never heard of him. You'd say 'Harry H. Corbett?' they'd say 'Who?' But in the business he was a star – an actor's actor we used to call him cause everybody knew his work, which was in a way experimental.

He did the Langham Group, I remember seeing him in *The Torrents of Spring*. I saw the Langham Players do two productions, *Torrents of Spring* and the George Bernard Shaw, and also he was obviously the big thing in Theatre Workshop. So everybody in the business knew him to the extent that, if he was on television in these things, every actor in London who wasn't working would be glued to the screen down in Gerry's Club. When Harry was on television, it was a bit like when Arsenal are on television today, everybody stopped to go and find a television screen … Halfway through writing 'The Offer' we both said 'Wouldn't it be wonderful if Harry H. Corbett would play the young man.' And we'd seen Wilfrid play a couple of old men. Wilfrid was only 50 years old, he was a bit like Moore Marriott in Will Hay, he played an old man of 80 when he was only 39, and we said 'The old man, wouldn't it be lovely if it was Wilfrid Brambell.' As Ray says, we got in touch with Duncan Wood, we put in a request, we sent them the scripts and they both said yes.

The availability request had found Harry during his run as *Macbeth* at the Bristol Old Vic. It must have been a welcome distraction after the production's lukewarm reviews. Harry agreed in principle and continued with the rest of the season. Next up was the premiere of *The Flanders Mare* by French writer Jean Canolle; a gay romp through the short marriage of Henry VIII and Anne of Cleves. Harry played the king. It must have taken him back to his Chorlton Rep days when he also played Henry in *The Rose Without a Thorn*. Though back then the national press hadn't turned up to pick over his performance. 'Harry H. Corbett makes a meal of a caricature out of the King. Generous of girth, lascivious of tongue, he oozes debauchery.'[9] *The Times* commented that Harry appeared 'to do most of what could possibly be done with the central character.'[10] Backers who had come down to see the play were making noises to take it into the West End.

He'd also been able to squeeze in the odd telly. 5 November saw the transmission of the *Armchair Theatre* production Roll on Bloomin' Death, a 'new officer struggling with command' war story. One critic commented that Harry had given 'another of his fine, in-depth performances – a convincing portrayal of the ex-sergeant who just wants the easy way out.'[11] Hopefully the out-of-work actors glued to the box agreed with him, and there would have been plenty of 'resting' actors about. The actors' union, Equity, had just gone out on strike against ITV on 1 November 1961. ITV had got knock-off rates when it had first lurched into life six years earlier and, now it was doing well, it was time for some payback, but negotiations broke down and so all new contracts were out of the window. *Coronation Street* would only feature the same thirteen characters for months, by 'eck. The strike wouldn't end until 3 April the next year, a situation that would do BBC productions, including *Comedy Playhouse*, no harm at all.

Harry had got that *Armchair Theatre* in just in time. The Bristol season continued with another chance for him to revisit the past with the staging of *Mother Courage*. This time he had a crack at the cook, not the chaplain. Last in the season was a musical

The Big Client, the story of an advertising man, Fred Cooper, trying
to land a deal. 'Harry S. Corbett [sic: the mistake proving that either
Simpson was right, Harry wasn't known outside of the business,
or the reporter had phoned the copy in on a bad line, while half
cut. Probably both], as Fred, works like mad to achieve the vigour
the evening needs, but although the chorus work energetically, the
support he receives from the rest of the company is not consistently
strong enough.'

It had been a bit of a 'Goldilocks' season at Bristol – not too hot,
not too cold. Still, it had been a nice rest from the London critics.
What he needed now was a job he could really get his teeth into
back in front of the cameras. As luck would have it Galton and
Simpson had finished the script of 'The Offer' as the Bristol Old
Vic season was drawing to a close. The producer, Duncan Wood,
sent it down to him. 'I understand from your agent that all will
hinge on whether you like the script or not. I hope you do,' he
wrote on 5 December. 'Perhaps you would let me know as soon as
you can. PS. I am sure the script is overlong, and we can probably
cut it to the equivalent of Macbeth.'

The actor Freddie Jones, who was in the cast at Bristol, remembers Harry saying, in his usual self-deprecating way: 'I won't get
too excited, who wants to watch a show about rag-and-bone men.'
Though truth be told, it was just what Harry was after:

> I had met Galton and Simpson slightly, and told them how much
> I really admired their work – I really did – and asked if they ever
> felt like writing anything separate. I never in a thousand years
> envisaged coming over to light entertainment: all the television
> I saw that was making any kind of good (what's the word) social
> comment (though I hate it) was the Hancock-Sykes kind of half-
> hour comedy programme. They remembered this conversation,
> obviously, took me at my word, and this thing about the rag-and-
> bone men thumped through the door. I read it and immediately
> wired back: 'Delicious, delightful, cannot wait to work on it.'[12]

Wilfrid was already on board. If he and Harry had turned it down
the writers had a back-up plan as Alan explains:

> 'In case the first choice wasn't available we picked Ronald Fraser
> and J. G. Devlin, who did one for us in *The Desperate Hours*,[13] but

he was going to be the old man if Wilfrid couldn't do it and we'd ask Ronnie Fraser if Harry couldn't do it.'

'It's a funny choice really.' Ray mused.

'What, Ronnie Fraser?' asked Alan.

'Yeah ...'

'Well, it wasn't really ... in as much as it depends how you look at it,' Alan continued, 'Ronnie Fraser used to play three ways – he used to play very posh, or he played Scottish, or he played Cockney – and his Cockney accent was very good, as good as Harry's.'

The test of Harry's Cockney accent came on the first day of rehearsals, 28 December, at the Sulgrave Boys' Club on the Goldhawk Road, just round the corner from the BBC studios.

'The funny thing about Harry was that you could always tell he wasn't Cockney and he was north country cause he always used to pronounce his g,' Alan, the Londoner, remembered. 'He would say "bang-ging". We had a sequence where the old man had been mending chairs and Harry came in and said, "What was that bang-ging? I distinctly heard bang-ging." That was the one thing that gave him away and certain vowels – but generally speaking, good.'

'It wasn't true cockney,' Harry later said, 'in Steptoe I use it as a weapon to show the emasculation of the man.'[14] He pitched it light and wistful with that distinctive sibilant affricate of '*dz*irty old man' that helped to take the edge off his rough appearance, clad in gumboots and hulking overcoat. The much impersonated voice was there on day one, as was Wilfrid's. 'Wilfrid was exactly Cockney,' remembers Ray. 'Wilfrid was Irish of course,' Alan adds, 'but he had the Received Pronounced King's English. You'd never have known he was Irish.' You'd never have known he wasn't royal – Willie's off-camera voice could have rivalled the Queen's, and this was in the day when HM still spoke like a cat with its jaws wired: 'Enn' not 'Anne'. Willie's attire could also have given the Royals a good run for their money, as Harry said: 'Our Wilfrid is the Beau Brummel of the acting profession. He's never without a natty bowler and a neatly-rolled umbrella. Those terrible teeth were specially made for his part in "Steptoe". He normally has a toothpaste smile.'[15] He was on occasion so dapper that the clothes wore him. Ray remembers the story of 'Wilfrid trying to get into the BBC Club, which was on the 4th floor – it was the best club in London at that time

…' 'After the show in his civvies,' interjects Alan. 'After the show,' continues Ray, 'and they wouldn't let him in, and I got a call. "Mr. Galton?" "Yeah." "Oh, there's a man out 'ere claiming to be Wilfrid Brambell." "Well, it probably is Wilfrid Brambell." "Would you care to come outside and identify him?"'

Harry would have had no trouble being recognised by reception. His off-duty ragged-arsed appearance by now had less to do with social commentary and more with rumpled laziness. He could go out in a Savile Row suit looking as sharp as 007 but his natural appearance was that of an unmade technicolor bed, as Alan remembers: 'We always said that Harry looked better on set than he did off.'

Harry remembered that first rehearsal:

> We went through the mutual admiration phase which lasts off and on for about two days: 'I just love your work, have another glass of wine, thank you very much.' And then we got down to cases … So then we began to build this relationship between us, of getting the points over. You see the rag-and-bone trade didn't mean a thing; I wasn't interested in a documentary about rag-and-bone men. I don't give a damn whether the prices are right, wrong or otherwise; that's dismissed, that's thrown out of the window. But it gave a perfect format and a set-up to range and slash all over the place. I mean with Harold the domestic work is over and done with in five or ten minutes. Then it's all politics, sex, general economics, the church: it's about a thousand and one things, but it's certainly not about the rag-and-bone business. That was of no interest to us.[16]

'The interesting thing about this show, always when we look back,' remembered Alan:

> is the complete contrast of styles of acting. Whereas Harry was forever searching for different ways of doing it, exploring, do it this way or that way, the old man did it the classical way – he decided on his performance and that was his performance every time he did it. The only thing was to try and remember the lines occasionally. Whatever Harry was doing, the old man's performance never varied.
>
> One thing I've got to say, Harry, like Hancock, never interfered with the text, never changed the text. All he did was change

the way he'd perform the text. Never paraphrased or cut it, never came up and said, 'Oh, this line's not right', he learnt it word for word but played with the way he performed it.

Sometimes Ray and I would say, 'Where did he get that reading from?' I know you can hit Good Morning, Good *Morning*, *Good* Morning – but he used to come up with variations on that.

'It must be very difficult for an actor,' adds Ray. 'Not being an actor myself, it must be very difficult that, to pick up sheets of paper and read it so precisely it looked as though every line had been discussed with the writer – but no. We didn't have to discuss the lines with Harry or Willie – sometimes with Willie, yeah, but never with Harry, cause he knew.'

Willie would later write:

Naturally the mode of acting changes with the times. A century ago the blustering ham actor was in vogue. Then came the revolution to the realistic and intimate form created by Sir Gerald du Maurier. A well deserved knighthood. Then came the magic of such theatres as the Abbey in Dublin, and the New York Theatre Guild, both of which miraculously contrived to combine the boisterous art of Burbage with the delicacy of du Maurier. Later came the method school of acting which also produced tremendous talent. Perhaps I'm an old fuddy-duddy in that my heart is out of tune with this method.[17]

The differences in their working styles didn't bother Harry. He had after all started out the 'classical way' himself and though he had changed his style to working a script 'til all possible nuances and inflections had been explored, he wouldn't have had a problem with those who hadn't, wouldn't, couldn't or didn't want to change. If he'd had a problem he wouldn't have been able to work with most of the business. It also didn't bother Willie, who later also wrote:

Harry H. Corbett's approach to his work is as different from Wilfrid Brambell's as is chalk from cheese, but there are few who will not agree that that strange fusion was not successful. It was a pleasant and unselfish (albeit unmentioned) game of 'put and take'. Also I think it was one of the finest of Galton and Simpson's creations.[18]

Harry would have agreed with him, especially on the last point.

For actors, a rule of thumb on the quality of the script is how easy it is to learn. Truly dire writing will have you cramming all the way to the set and sometimes beyond – on one occasion in my own career in an effort to get home I held the script in front of my face during an actor's close up when he just couldn't remember it. *Steptoe* was easy: 'With that ease that comes with, "My God, this is brilliant."' Harry later recalled: 'You see, good work is always easy. You don't even have to learn the lines. They're there, they're right, and they're the lines you should say.'[19]

Harry's favourite line from *Steptoe* was 'I didn't get rickets through overeating.' Coming out of the mouth of a 37-year-old, five years after 'you've never had it so good', it was a beautiful piece of social commentary at the dawn of the swinging sixties. It was rare for a comedy programme to make you stop and think. Harry believed that Tony Hancock, Eric Sykes and Michael Bentine had achieved this with their shows, but their style relied more on visual comedy. Steptoe was different, as he explained:

> We used words. Not one of our scenes, surprisingly enough, relies on double takes, joey-joey, grimaces or whatever you wish to call them. They rely on words and timing. Have you noticed the pace at which we play them? Very, very delightfully slow and true to the subject matter. Now in the hands of a couple of hack charlatans, bad managers or whatever, they'd have said, 'Come on now, speed, speed, speed, bang it over lads, let's get it over quick; chop chop, lads, get the laughs; kick high and smile at the gallery.' But we had the time to play it properly; that is the important thing that came out of *Steptoe*. There was no need for comedy to be fast-fast and joey-joey, or to be fast-fast and compensate by a pause while comic business was done. It could all go along in its own truthful flow.[20]

Ray, Alan and Duncan Wood, along with Wilfrid and Harry all contributed to this truthful flow. It was a piece of drama. It was billed as such and the actors were contracted under drama rates, which were significantly smaller than those of light entertainment. The only thing that gave it away as the latter was the surprising presence of the department's head at rehearsals, as Ray recalls:

We knew from the word go that it was a hit. Tom Sloan, who had persuaded us to do the *Comedy Playhouse* in the first place, then came down. He must have got the word straight away, coz he was down at rehearsals at the beginning of the week. He said to us 'You know what you've got here, don't you? You've got a series.' 'No' we said, cause we didn't want to make a series, cause although it was hard work doing a different show each week, at least we were working with actors instead of comedians. But we knew it was good and we knew he was absolutely right.

It's hard to imagine now how original it was, as many sitcoms have tried to ape it over the years; but to be offered a series on the first day of rehearsals – it must have been extraordinary. Although the writers were not keen on committing to a series Tom Sloan wasn't about to take no for an answer. 'For a whole week Sloan continually tried to persuade us to change our mind,' remembered Ray. 'The offer for a series was there on a silver platter even before "The Offer" had been screened.'[21]

After the rehearsal week they got into the studio for the recording. The junkyard, in all its grotty glory was ready for the family firm. Frank Muir was to later comment that Galton and Simpson set *Steptoe* in a junkyard to annoy the BBC props department. Ray remembers: 'I was knocked out by the sets and I said to Harry, "Look at these sets." He said, "Never mind the sets, what are all these chairs?" I said, "That's for the audience." He said, "I'll have to re-think my entire performance." I thought, "Christ, we've got an actor here."' 'They'd not told him,' Alan continued, 'he'd assumed it was a piece of drama. We'd not worked with many actors before.' Which explains why they wouldn't have known that having a live audience would affect the performance. 'Mind you,' Ray remembered, 'whatever he did to change his performance worked. It was beautiful to watch … it still is.'[22]

For those not of a thespian bent, imagine you have to give a best man speech – there's a hell of a difference between delivering it to the mirror and delivering it to the guests, and you don't have to stay in character. While you're at it, think on the difference between the father of the bride's speech and the best man's. No one ever says a loaded 'good luck' to the father, but then he has the simple task of being loving/poignant/sentimental or, on occasion, relieved. The best man has to be *funny* – poor bastard.

The brilliance of *Steptoe* is that it was both poignant and funny.

For Harry, who was always meticulous in his preparation, the late addition of an audience must have been a brief annoyance. But only brief, as he later said: 'When I first played to them I got quite a shock. But I didn't find them getting in the way.'[23] Nor did he find it a problem whether to focus on the audience or the cameras. He had, after all, had plenty of experience in front of the lens:

> I neither want them there nor do not want them there; I don't care either way. I can to a certain extent, assume where the laugh-points – or the ones I want to be laugh-points are going to be. Surely the lift of an eyebrow or the twist of a face can get a laugh of a fairly serious line if you wish it to. It's the control of this that is important. That's why I say, 'Look at the contact between Willie Brambell and me.' Willie is holding it, but the point has to go over without a laugh getting in the way, and I am holding back certain things. Remember the dialogue isn't screamed out and you've got gales of laughter sometimes, so it takes playing. The thing must register but not look as if we're shouting over our laugh, to get it over.[24]

So as an actor, Harry had to play to and work the crowd; a crowd that would be laughing, creating pauses in the 'truthful flow' that would need to be truthfully accommodated. He would also have to monitor the cameras peripherally, so that no aspect of the truth of the performance was lost.

'You could say this is being camera-conscious if you wish,' he later explained:

> but it's terrifyingly important to know … I'm not going to lose the most important point of the play by being off shot. For instance, reaction in comedy, at least this form of comedy, is a line. It is written in. I mean, if you say to me, 'The place is burning,' right, you cut to me; I've merely got to say in reaction, 'Is it?' Or I've got to say, 'My God!' – with a pause. But that is a line; the camera must cut to me; you must see the reaction. Or we mustn't see the reaction. So this must be planned, and the camera and the other actor must know this and be ready to hold it up so that this reaction can go in.[25]

Harry's scripts are peppered with his technical notations of camera angles and cuts. But watching 'The Offer' the audience were not aware of this technical side. They were having too good a time following the attempts of the son to escape his dreadful father and forge a better life. They laughed at every familiar comedic brush stroke. What was not so familiar, and what they stopped laughing at, was an ending full of pathos, as the son failed to get away.

Alan remembers:

> We watched that closing scene as Harry literally crumbles. He's trying to push his meagre belongings away and start a new life, and he can't do it. We were watching this scene and Harry actually broke down and cried and I thought, real tears! This is what it's all about … this is acting! We weren't used to it with writing for comedians. Usually it would be stylised, shoulder-lurching sobs when comics cried. Harry really got hold of that final scene. It was real drama to him.

It was real drama to the audience; broadcast on 5 January 1962 it had an overwhelmingly positive reaction from the viewing public and critics alike. But my favourite review has to be from *The Guardian*:

> Comedy Playhouse on the BBC's Fridays has shown Alan Simpson and Ray Galton trying various moods and mixtures. Their first two were semi-failures; their third 'The Private Lives of Edward Whitely,' was amusing; a light entirely frivolous piece to which Tony Britton lent his own particular touch of satire. Last Friday 'The Offer' was a tedious piece about an old scrap-dealer and his son; this kind of fruity characterisation and painstaking dialogue seems to me death on television. The titters of the studio audience, though not overwhelming, much exceeded mine.[26]

On 15 January Duncan Wood wrote to Harry, 'just a line to congratulate you on an outstanding performance in "The Offer". It is a long time since we had such a reaction to an individual show. Quite apart from this, it was one of the most enjoyable rehearsal weeks I have spent.'[27]

Tom Sloan, buoyed by the reaction, increased his efforts to commission a series. Ray and Alan finally ran out of excuses and told Sloan that if Willie and Harry were willing, then they would be too.

They thought they were on safe ground, believing that the actors were not only devoted to purely straight roles, but that Harry's reaction to the thought of a studio audience would put him off committing to a series.

By the third week of January the BBC were in negotiations with Harry and Willie's agents. As the series would be light entertainment and not drama, and the actors would be in starring roles, the agents wanted double the fee that had been paid for 'The Offer', for which Willie had received 100 guineas and Harry 75. 'I did it for peanuts, because it was a good part,' he later said. 'And when the series was contemplated, a lot of professional comedians tried to talk me out of it. "It will never work" they said. Don't forget *Steptoe and Son* was the first TV comedy show which used character actors instead of professional comics or personality players.'[28]

It needed character actors to make it work; the social commentary would have been lost without them. Having spent all those years with Theatre Workshop trying to break the working-class stereotype, trying to take socialist values to an audience that weren't bothered; having, eventually, to make a choice between political worthiness or commercialism, here was a chance to have both. It was also a bloody good part and a nice little earner. Besides it would only be a short series.

Harry and Wilfrid were on board, but then argued about who was to have top billing – each wanted the other to have it. Eventually it was decided to have Harry top one week and Wilfrid the next. By the way, Wilfrid's unusual spelling of his name was original, as he later explained:

> I had been called Wilfrid (with two I's) after my uncle, and Brambell after Wilfrid. Who in the world could possibly invent such an unusual combination of syllables and sounds?
>
> There is an inflexible rule in the profession that no two performers may masquerade under the same moniker. Naturally I was not obliged to alter a letter either of my given or inherited names. For the reason that Harry Corbett of Sooty fame was first in the book, Harry Corbett the actor was advised and obliged to ring a change. I fully appreciate his unwillingness entirely to abandon the name with which he was born in favour of some fantastic pseudonym. Wisely he summoned his agent and requested him to repeat the alphabet.

'A,B,C' repeated the agent until he arrived at the eighth letter
– 'That'll do,' said Harry, and so henceforth and forever more he
is billed and known as Harry H. Corbett, but to his friends – one
of which I hope I am – he is affectionately and monosyllabically
known as 'H'.[29]

Harry would later joke that the H stood for 'H'anything'.

At the beginning of February, Ray and Alan signed the contracts
for five new episodes. They would be shown following a repeat
of 'The Offer'. As the boys got back to work, so did Harry. The
Actors' Workshop had formed a student advisory board; Harry and
his friend Alun Owen would both serve on it. There was drama on
screen for the BBC with *A Quiet Game of Cards*, directed by Alvin
Rakoff, and there had been drama off it with the return of Sheila.

When Harry's niece Cynthia married Barry in February of 1962
he sent a congratulations telegram, signing it from both of them.
Though the major disagreement over children still remained, it
appears that if they were giving it another go they must have been
trying to work on their differences, either that or ignoring them, as
one of them was packing.

Harry was bound for Bristol. He would miss Cynthia's wedding
as he was filming the teen flick *Some People*. Kenneth More starred,
Angela Douglas mimed to a pop song, and Harry played the disapproving father of Ray Brooks' motorcycling rebel with a lilt (a
fellow brooding biker was David Hemmings). Amusingly Harry
was only fourteen years older than Brooks – either he appeared
to have had a hard life or they're a law unto themselves in the West
Country. After acclaimed roles in the early 1960s Brooks was a
voice-over artist for many years before enjoying more recent fame
on British television dramas.

In April Harry was in *A Voice From the Top*, playing a bigoted
landlord:

Mr. Harry H Corbett was on top of his form as the endlessly
talkative landlord, defensively reeling off all the clichés and com-
monplaces, the tangled history and blind prejudice about race
relations he can think of rather than say quite simply that he will
not let his room to a Negro, and Mr. Corbett on top of his form
is formidable.[30]

He was also nipping along to the Merton Park Studios for another
Edgar Wallace Mystery, this time playing Jack Burgess in *Time to
Remember*, Marjie Lawrence from Theatre Workshop had a cough
and a spit in it. Soon after he appeared in a reworking of Tolstoy's
Resurrection entitled *A Matter of Conscience* in which he was reunited
with Billie Whitelaw. A reviewer noted: 'Some of the casting was a
bit eccentric, notably Harry H. Corbett as the guilt-racked prince.
Fortunately the part of Nekhlyudov calls for a certain amount of
lugubrious stiffness.'[31] The reviewer, however, did not make it clear
whether the eccentricity was in casting Harry as 'guilt-racked' or in
casting him as 'a prince'; if it was the latter then he would have been
pleased at the return of the rag-and-bone man.

Rehearsals for the first *Steptoe* series started on 7 May, again at the
Sulgrave Boys' Club. Harry would have had to put seeing images of
himself as Harold out of his mind. To have watched himself would
shatter a necessary illusion, as he later explained:

> Harold looks nothing like that to me. I can see me in there.
>
> Let's begin at the beginning. You see, I envisaged a character,
> let's say (and I've had to play it before today) a romantic lead.
> Now I am conscious of the fact that I've had a broken nose.
> I wish this would have healed attractively like it did with Ian
> Fleming and a few others like that, but you see unfortunately it
> didn't. It's just grown big and flabby and it wobbles. I got a thorn
> stuck in my eye during the war which has scratched it, marking it
> indelibly. Now I can see all these fantastic imperfections. Shaving
> as a youth I accidentally took too much skin off here and the
> hair won't grow there. I'm aware of all these imperfections. So
> I envisage in my mind's eye what the author intended this man
> to be. Now the author is stuck with me, and I play him for that. It
> is that that gives me the ability to con you, with a bit of luck, into
> thinking that the nose is fairly aquiline, the double chin doesn't
> actually wobble, and yes, the teeth do sparkle and they are clear
> and white. If I were to watch any of the episodes, do a make-up
> test or anything, I'd be finished. I wouldn't be able to do it, I'd be
> so concentrating on trying to bend the character back again.[32]

For actors, in order for the audience to believe it, they have to
believe it themselves. The last image they see in the mirror before
they walk out of the dressing room should be as close to the

character as possible. Most people, unless they are truly photogenic, deranged, or French, are shocked by the way they look on film. Their image in the mirror has been compensated for over a lifetime. It takes a lot less delusion to be a pig than a playboy, and a playboy is what Harold comically aspired to be, but it couldn't be comic to him, it had to be real – that was the joke.

Harry did come off it in later years; not only was he, by then, very secure in the role, but once he had a family, we used to insist upon watching it. I remember Jon and I would pile onto our parent's bed and the four of us would watch the opening credits. This was always followed by Harry leaving the room … and us rolling our eyes and joking that he was going to watch it from behind the crack in the door. He never did, as he said: 'I'd spend the rest of the night gnashing my teeth.'[33]

The weekly schedule of rehearsing and taping the shows could be quite gruelling. As Harry later recounted:

On Friday the cast discussed the script with the producer and outside shots were taken.

Wilfrid Brambell and I sometimes had forty pages of script to memorise – not just a matter of having a photographic memory to repeat the words like a parrot. Every word had its own meaning – the right emphasis has to be placed on it.

The Wednesday run-through with the cast present ironed out all the faults. Time after time we'd go through the script until every word was spoken at the right moment.

Thursday was the day the show was recorded on tape.

We'd have at least four run-throughs before everyone was satisfied.

The resulting sketch always looked so life-like. Harold or old man Steptoe would seem to casually appear at the door with all the time in the world at their disposal.

In reality it was like an obstacle race – jumping over cables – dodging the crews – to appear at another part of the set seconds later.

Once I slammed the door a little too hard as I entered the 'House'. The set shook with the vibration, and I was knocked to my knees by a blow to the shoulder.

I looked around for the culprit. On the floor lay the head of a fox. It had fallen from the wall when I had slammed the door.

Even when you're eating, talking to friends, or driving a car, one
section of the mind is busy with the words of the next script.[34]

Something that Willie could sympathise with:

Television light entertainment is, I think, more tense than provincial weekly Rep ... One Monday evening in the early days,
dear old Duncan Wood (our original producer) flippantly told
'H' and me to be back at ten in the morning DLP which, in
our language means 'dead letter perfect'. In the language of the
uninitiated it simply means 'know it'. Despite the fact that it
was a sixty-eight-page (foolscap!) script, I, in an evil moment,
decided to take the mickey out of Duncan and old 'H'. I stayed
up with black coffee until the wee small hours of the morning
and arrived at rehearsal dead on time, and dead letter perfect.
How was I to know that my equally evil playmate Harry H
would have thought of doing precisely the same thing. He also
arrived at rehearsal minus script ... 'H' and I expressed surprise.
Duncan expressed nothing. So, for ever after, Harry and I were
obliged to 'know it'.[35]

Sometimes, when it came to the recording, Willie wasn't always
DLP. He would occasionally fluff his lines, which used to piss Ray
and Alan off something rotten – it would distract from the laugh. As
the takes could be twenty minutes long, you only had the one shot,
if you had to do a retake the audience wouldn't laugh the second
time. As a green actor, I once got a big laugh on a sight gag in front
of a studio audience. The star of the piece immediately forgot the
next line; we had to repeat – no laugh. That would never have happened on *Steptoe*, as they didn't get retakes. Although the shows
were recorded, and not live like *Armchair Theatre*, the live ethos was
still in evidence because the new medium of videotape was incredibly expensive and a bugger to edit. This added a certain frisson to
whenever Willie was having a wobbler, but on the whole any of his
fluffs could be excused by the fact that he was playing an old man.
And playing it very well.

After the re-run of 'The Offer', in which the *Comedy Playhouse*
intro of a typewriter with Ron Grainer's whistling soundtrack of
Happy Joe had been dropped and replaced by the familiar Grainer
theme tune of *Old Ned* (which won an Ivor Novello Award), the

first episode of the new series, 'The Bird', saw the emergence of a recurring theme for the Steptoes. The old man putting the kibosh on any chance Harold may have had with the fairer sex, and thus a shot at getting away. While the pair await the arrival of Harold's date for dinner, Albert has deliberately put the clock forward an hour, leaving Harold to believe the girl has stood him up, and so ruining the relationship.

Next to be recorded was 'The Diploma', showing Harold's unsuitability for any other trade when he fails to get a diploma in television repair. Albert, however, has no such trouble in mastering the technicalities. This provided another long-running theme of Harold being forced to return to the horse and cart, as his father bests him once again.

'The Economist' introduced the idea of Harold's lack of business acumen, when he buys 4,000 dentures and has to sell at a loss. Frank Thornton made his first of many guest appearances in *Steptoe* as the denture seller.

In 'The Piano' the Steptoes are hired to remove a piano from a toff's flat. It gets wedged in a doorway and is eventually abandoned. The episode's peculiar claim to fame is that it marks the first swear-word heard on television: 'What goes up can bleeding well stay up there', which was highly risqué for 1962. They got away with it, not only through the efforts of Tom Sloan refusing to budge on the line, but the series was billed as drama – thus dramatic licence came into force. If it were purely comedy it would be seen as salacious. Despite the fact that real totters would have been using much worse language, that one 'bleeding' still raised questions in Parliament on television's slipping standards.

'The Piano' was also memorable for Harry on a personal level; it was recorded on the day his brother Albert died. A few months after walking Cynthia up the aisle, Albert collapsed with a coronary on 6 June; he was 55. His son Peter was with him and tried resuscitation to no avail. Harry made it to the funeral. Cynthia remembers him being dreadfully upset, with good reason. The two brothers had been very close, Albert being more of a father figure to Harry than their own father ever was. Avis would have agreed; she wrote to Albert's widow expressing her admiration and sorrow.

Back in London 'The Holiday' was the last episode of the series to be recorded, and it too introduced a favoured theme: Harold's unsuccessful attempts to escape the dreadful annual holiday to

Bognor. To scupper any chance Harold had of escaping alone to
the delights of St Tropez, and ensuring that the pair would end
up in Bognor as usual, Albert fakes a coronary, yes, it's a funny old
world. This episode was Willie's favourite of the first series. Ray and
Alan wanted him to play the heart attack as comedy; the thought
of playing it for real would have been too much for a comedy audience. Willie disagreed and during rehearsals fought for the reality
of the attack – it had to be 'real' to Albert, he argued. 'Camera day
arrived' Wilfrid later wrote:

> and Galton and Simpson were, as always, watching from the con-
> trols. I could feel their disapproval even from that distance and
> through that plate glass. My efforts to avoid them at the end of
> rehearsal were in vain. They politely but resolutely requested me
> to alter my performance, but I knew my interpretation was right
> and I remember jumping up and down in desperation and saying,
> 'The trouble with you two blighters is that you don't know how
> bloody good you are.' The scene stayed my way and created quite
> a stir amongst viewers and critics alike. Since then my favourite
> episodes have carried moments of pathos in the midst of hilari-
> ous comedy writing.[36]

They were Harry's favourites too. He was later to comment:

> In 'Steptoe and Son', Ray Galton and Alan Simpson have evolved
> a character drama entirely new to television; deeper, truer, sadder,
> funnier than anything that has gone before. It's really tragic-
> comedy, which is the essence of everyday life. Most people have
> met a Harold or an old Albert at one time or another, and if we
> are honest there are bits of both in all of us.[37]

The series was wrapped up. There just remained the drinkies and
congratulations – Duncan Wood in thanking the cast and crew
wrote: 'Alan Simpson, Ray Galton, Harry Corbett and Wilfrid
Brambell are four of the most creative artists I have enjoyed working with. They should be contracted forever.'[38]

Filming finished in mid-June. Transmission of the first episode
had got underway a week before and the writers and producers
waited to see what the viewing public and critics would make of it.
They didn't have to wait long; the first three episodes were such a

success that Duncan Wood was busy making plans to secure Wilfrid and Harry for a second series before the fourth episode went out. Not that Harry knew – he'd already got on a plane to Africa.

He was shooting *Sammy Going South* with Edward G. Robinson. The film would be released in the States as *A Boy Ten Feet Tall*. Harry played Lem, a rough- and-ready crook, and had a wonderful time. There was nothing he liked better than far-flung horizons and new experiences – though he could have done without one of them:

> Once I had to take a trip in a light plane from Nairobi into Big Game country. The pilot was a woman, one of those Amelia Earhart types. I was terrified. She said to me 'Hold the door open while we take off. Otherwise it will get terribly hot in here.' So I held the door open and up we went. Ten minutes later she said: 'Close the door or we'll all fall out!' I've never forgotten that.[39]

I bet he didn't. God, he loathed small planes, in fact he hated anything that shook you about. When I was a kid I made him come on a fairground ride with me, but a minute in, he was so pale and sweaty that they stopped the ride to let him off – I never asked him again.

In that summer of '62, unbeknownst to Harry, the audience back in Blighty couldn't get enough of *Steptoe*, as Alan remembered:

> It was an immediate hit when it went on as a series. It was a hit and the BBC, they'd never done this before, they immediately repeated it the following week – so it ran for twelve weeks instead of six. And Ray had hired a villa down in the south of Spain for about two months, I think, and I was on my way down to join him with my wife and I picked up a *Daily Mail* which had said the BBC are repeating this series …
>
> The reason the BBC repeated it so quickly was after episodes three or four everybody was talking about it, and it was finished. So they immediately repeated it again. By the time they'd run it through again everybody in the country had seen it. Normally it takes time to build up an audience.

'I think they've done it recently,' Ray interjected, 'I mean, not with the same results.'

'The only thing I can think of in recent years that's had the same effect was *Gavin and Stacey*,' Alan continued:

that had an immediate success … Baftas. Anyway, that's the only one I can think of. *Blackadder* was a terrible flop when the first series went out; it was bloody awful, diabolical. It was only when Ben Elton joined the writing team that he turned it on its head. And *Dad's Army* wasn't a success to start with and *Hancock's Half Hour* on the radio wasn't, that took time to build but *Steptoe* – straight away, it was a hit straight away.

A hit that Harry was blissfully unaware of when he arrived back in London:

I'd just arrived at London Airport. As I stepped down from the plane and walked with the other passengers across the tarmac, I noticed there was a big reception committee waiting.

I looked around the plane's passengers for a Very Important Person who was causing all the fuss. Nothing less than a sheik, with a load of shekels in his bag, could command such attention, I reckoned.

Cameras were clicking and the staff at the airport had that sickly grin only reserved for potentates.

'Who's the big noise?' I whispered to my business manager, who had met me at the airport.

'It's you, you fool,' hissed Freddie Ross. 'You're a household name. The first *Steptoe and Son* episodes you recorded a few months ago were shown on television while you were filming in South Africa. They were a riot. You've become a celebrity. For goodness sake, wipe that bewildered look off your face and smile!'

I wasn't ready for fame. I didn't have a pair of sunglasses to hide behind.

I had left Britain a near nonentity to television viewers – and had arrived back on a summer day in 1962 as a TV star. It was confusing. I was like a spaceman returning from a trip to Mars to find the world had changed.

I was famous. The lad from Ardwick, Manchester, had arrived. I found myself with a new image, that of Harold Steptoe.

That hulking figure in the tatty overcoat and turned-down gumboots – and his wizened, unshaven 'Dad' – had walked into the hearts of millions.

Everyone was whistling the Steptoe signature tune of *Old Ned* to the clip clop of Hercules' steel-shod hoofs.

Over thirteen million people watched those first episodes in 1962. I'm told that it normally took a year for top comedy shows to reach those figures.

Two years later, 26 million people were tuned in to 'Steptoe.'

Harold was the turning point in my career – and my fortunes.[40]

Harry H. Corbett had arrived. He was an overnight success and it had only taken fifteen years.

Notes

1   *Manchester Weekly News*, 18/3/67.
2   Webber, R., *Fifty Years of Hancock's Half Hour* (Arrow, 2005).
3   *Ibid.*
4   *The Independent*, 4/1/09.
5   Galton, R., Simpson, A., with Ross, R., *Steptoe and Son* (BBC Books, 2002).
6   *Ibid.*
7   *Ibid.*
8   Brambell, W., *All Above Board: An Autobiography* (W.H. Allen, 1976).
9   *Evening World*, 18/10/61.
10   *The Times*, 18/10/61.
11   *The Stage*, 9/11/61.
12   *Ibid.*, 30/11/61.
13   Ronald Fraser (1930–97): Galton and Simpson cast him in their first season *Comedy Playhouse* episode 'Sealed with a Loving Kiss'. J.G. Devlin (1907–91), Irish actor: they cast him in 'The Reunion' and later as Leonard Rossiter's fellow escaped convict in 1972 episode 'The Desperate Hours'.
14   *The Age*, 7/4/72.
15   *Manchester Weekly News*, 18/3/67.
16   Burton, *Acting in the Sixties*.
17   Brambell, *All Above Board*.
18   *Ibid.*
19   Burton, *Acting in the Sixties*.
20   *Ibid.*
21   Galton and Simpson, *Steptoe and Son*.
22   *Ibid.*
23   Burton, *Acting in the Sixties*.
24   *Ibid.*
25   *Ibid.*
26   *The Guardian*, 8/1/62.
27   Galton and Simpson, *Steptoe and Son*.
28   *Listener*, 5/5/72.
29   Brambell, *All Above Board*.
30   *The Times*, 10/4/62.
31   *Observer*, 27/5/62.

32   Burton, *Acting in the Sixties*.
33   *Australian Woman's Weekly*, 3/5/72.
34   *Manchester Weekly News*, 18/3/67.
35   Brambell, *All Above Board*.
36   *Ibid*.
37   *Radio Times*, 28/10/65.
38   Galton and Simpson, *Steptoe and Son*.
39   *The Sun*, 3/6/72.
40   *Manchester Weekly News*, 18/3/67.

12

Hi-diddle-dee-dee

I'm still confused by this. I mean why should anyone be interested in me? Why should you want to interview me? Famous? I'm not famous. I don't think there's such a thing as fame anymore. Even Prime Ministers don't have it. Perhaps it's notoriety, I don't know.[1]

Harry H. Corbett

Harry stayed in London long enough to sign up for a second series before flying out to join Ray and Alan in Spain. 'The reason we were there,' Alan recalls, 'we were writing a film script, which we intended to put Harry in, which turned out to be "The Bargee" and so Harry came down and he said, "It's like a mad house back home, I can't go out. I'm being chased round the streets."'

Steptoe-mania was still in full swing when he got back and the merchandising soon swung into action. Pye Records released excerpts from the first series to compete in the charts with Ron Grainer's single of the theme tune *Old Ned* and Harry also released a single with Pye, *Junk Shop/The Isle of Clerkenwell*. The level of their fame really hit home when Harry and Wilfrid were asked to switch on the Morecambe illuminations. For someone who had spent thirty-seven years going unnoticed in the street it was a surreal experience:

Wilfrid Brambell and I were on our way in a chauffeur-driven car to switch on the lights at Morecambe. We faced a 60-mile journey from Manchester, but would we be able to stand the pace?

As our car stopped at traffic lights, people called, 'Got an old telly you want to flog?' or 'You'd do better with Hercules pulling that thing.' Children in overtaking cars waved gaily as their fathers got the last ounce of speed out of their motors.

We couldn't understand why everyone seemed to be recognising Steptoe and Son, despite our fast moving limousine. Wilfrid was his usual off-stage dapper self, and looked nothing like that rag-and-bone man. And I wasn't even wearing Harold's muffler.

After travelling some distance we stopped in a quiet spot to give our arms a rest from waving. I got in my day's exercise with a brisk walk around the car.

It was then that the agile mind of Corbett found the reason why we were receiving so much attention.

On the front of the car was a placard which read, 'Here are Steptoe and Son'. On the rear was another notice proudly proclaiming, 'You are following Steptoe and Son to Morecambe'.

No wonder so many had overtaken us. The motorists had been willing to burst a gasket so they and their children could say they had seen Harry H. and Wilfrid Brambell.

In itself it was a small incident, but it made me feel rather humble. It served to show the affection the public held for Harold and his Dad. These were the people who, by their appreciation of humour, had made me the television actor of 1962.

We left the placards where they were. What was a cricked neck and a muscle-bound arm compared to giving so much pleasure?

We eventually arrived in Morecambe, and were mobbed by thousands as we struggled to the platform to switch on the lights. Later, Wilfrid and I drove along the promenade in a totter's cart, piled high with all sorts of junk. The axles squeaked with the weight of old car batteries, scrap iron, rags, and battered radios.

Hundreds of kiddies skipped alongside of us whistling the Steptoe signature tune. Then one of them made a grab for a piece of junk sticking out from the cart. In case he should hurt himself by falling under a wheel, I gave him the bit of old iron.

That started a near riot. Everyone wanted to take something home to say it had been handed to them by Harold or his Dad.

Wilfrid and I handed out the junk. People staggered away with bits of rusty old metal, batteries, parts of washing machines, and wireless valves. In ten minutes the cart was cleared – not a bolt or nut was left. The horse was most appreciative of our efforts to lighten his load – but his owner was not at all pleased.

In the enthusiasm of presenting our 'gifts', we hadn't realised that the cart and its contents had been hired from a real rag-and-bone man. The 'goodies' we handed out represented a day's work to him.[2]

The real rag-and-bone men who supplied the horse and trolley for the filming of the series in London were brothers Chris and Arthur Arnold. Their horse, Hercules, was a 'real' working horse and could often be seen pulling a cart around the streets of west London. Though as the fame of the series increased, getting through the round took longer and longer as she ran the risk of diabetes from the amount of sugar lumps held out by chasing kids.

Harry had little trouble taking over the reins for the filming, as he said:

> I didn't really have to learn to drive because these horses are like the dear old milk horses of years ago. They go at their own pace, they know where to go and stop of their own accord. They know which lane to take and what to do at traffic lights. The only thing they object to is if you put them in the wrong lane for filming purposes – they know they shouldn't be there and it makes them nervous.[3]

Perhaps Hercules had been put in the wrong lane when she had her one diva moment, as Harry later recounted:

> We, of course, had our troubles – even with Hercules, our stalwart horse. Incidentally, I'll let you into a little secret. Hercules was a lady – and eventually died on us. She was replaced – and I don't think one viewer noticed the change. Both horses were so well trained by their owners that they'd respond to the slightest move of the reins. There was only one time when Hercules was a bit naughty. It was the beginning of a new series.
>
> She had just come back from a six-week holiday on a farm, and she was raring to go.
>
> The cameras were ready. Hercules stood quietly between the shafts. The actors took their places. The scene should have been the simple one of Harold driving Hercules solely down the street

on the look-out for bargains. But Hercules decided to play it differently. I had hardly settled down on the seat when she was off like a rocket.

For a quarter of a mile she went at full speed with the cart – and myself – bouncing along behind. The cast and technicians scattered like nine-pins. I held on like grim death as I heard yells of 'Ride 'im, cowboy.'

Finally, when Hercules was satisfied she'd shown her true paces she settled down to a slow jog.

It was a shaken Harry H. who fell, rather than jumped, from the cart. Hercules had a satisfied look in her eyes. She never acted up again – it was as if she were saying to herself, 'I've had my day.'[4]

Like the horse, Harry's head must have been spinning from this new-found fame. But unlike Hercules there was little acting up. His feet remained not only firmly on the ground but in his old haunts – literally. Gerry Raffles was still trying to hold Theatre Workshop together in Joan's absence, and that autumn the call went out for help once again, as Harry remembered:

Gerry asked me, 'Would I do this musical "What a Crazy World"'? So I said, 'Very well, I'll stick myself in it to correlate it together.' – because the way we worked, we'd kind of resolved a way of working like this, which came from the early period, in which I was more or less re-translating what she wanted, quickly, on stage to the people who had just joined. Especially in this case, we were handling a lot of young people.[5]

In Alan Klein's musical, Harry and 'Lovely' Avis played the parents of all-singing East End hero Alf. For Harry, it was a warm welcome home. Surprisingly, for actors, there was little jealousy of Harry's success with *Steptoe*. Murray Melvin remembers that the feeling was 'Isn't it great Harry's got that job. Everybody was very pleased.' Shame the critics weren't as pleased with the musical. 'There are two episodes in Mr Gerry Raffles' production that escape into the old world of Theatre Workshop … The mainstay of both these scenes is the Theatre Workshop veteran Mr Harry H. Corbett: and the brilliance of these passages suggests that good direction might have rescued the show as a whole.'[6]

It can't have been that bad, as Harry and Avis reprised their roles for a film version released the following year with Joe Brown playing their son. The soundtrack would follow soon after. One hindrance, or benefit, of being back at Stratford East was that Harry was unable to attend the television ball on Friday 23 November.

This was the annual bash of the Guild of Television Producers and Directors when they handed out their 'mask' awards. By 1962 the Guild had merged with the British Film Society and was officially known as the Society of Film and Television Arts. In 1976 they changed the name again to the British Academy of Film and Television Arts, and started handing out the now famous BAFTA masks to those working in film as well.

Harry won Best Actor and 'sent a delightful telegram expressing his hysterical joy and assurances that he would carry on working and endeavour to develop his hobbies.'[7] Duncan Wood won the award for Best Light Entertainment Production.

Being at Stratford meant that Harry missed out on another evening of note. On 6 November, as *Steptoe* was gearing up for its second series and Ray and Alan were working on a short *Steptoe* sketch for inclusion in the BBC's *Christmas Night with the Stars* special; the BBC held a cocktail party at Television Centre. Luckily Wilfrid was able to attend; unluckily he ended the night by being arrested for importuning at Shepherd's Bush Green.

When he appeared on remand a month later Wilfrid said in his defence:

> I was drinking large gin and tonics. At about 8.30 I went to the BBC club in the same building. I continued to talk and drink. I left at about 11 p.m. I was fuddled … I must have had at least a bottle.
>
> There was no sign of a cab. It was cold and I went into the lavatory at the Uxbridge Road end of the Green. I don't remember, but I imagine there were other people there. I took no interest in them. I did not smile or look at anyone. On coming out, I looked for a taxi but saw no sign of one. I walked to the other end of the Green. There, I went into the other lavatory because it was necessary. I noticed no one there.
>
> On coming out I stood on the corner. I had no intention of doing anything except going home … As far as I can remember, I was stopped on an island by two men who said something about being police officers, and they arrested me.[8]

Wilfrid had been nabbed by the 'Pretty Police', a crack team of
attractive officers who loitered in urinals waiting to be smiled at.
The unit's most famous 'collar' had been John Gielgud in 1953.
Though such a public 'outing' had personally devastated Gielgud,
his career and popularity had survived. Gielgud's case prompted the
Wolfenden Commission, set up to study prostitution, to also look
into homosexuality. In 1957 the commission had recommended
decriminalising private homosexual acts between consenting adults
over 21 years of age. This change in the law wouldn't be passed until
1967. So in 1962, when Wilfrid was arrested, even though the public's view on homosexuality was softening, nobody was openly gay,
not unless they liked prison and enjoyed being regarded as a sexual
deviant by some members of society.

Though Wilfrid, like Gielgud, worked in a profession with a
substantial gay population, where few cared about such private
preferences, it must have been mortally embarrassing for him. His
ears becoming attuned for the sound of sniggers from passers-by
and feelings of guilt would be a natural reaction; it would be hard
to escape self-loathing if the law of the land branded you a pervert.
For a man who could already drink like a fish the episode wouldn't
have helped his bar bill.

This incident didn't seem at all suspicious to Alan Simpson:

> Wilfrid was a very friendly man, in as much as when he was
> drunk he'd smile and chat to everybody. 'Good evening, dear
> sir. How are you tonight?' you know and when we were told
> that he was seen smiling at passers-by down the Uxbridge Road,
> I thought, 'Yeah, that sounds like Wilfrid', you know. He would, 8
> gin and tonics later, as they say.[9]

On 12 December Wilfrid was 'conditionally discharged for a year
and ordered to pay 25 guineas costs for persistently importuning
for an immoral purpose.' The defence that his conduct had been
mere innocent affability brought on by drink prompted the magis-
trate to comment that 'it might be accepted that drink had brought
out in Brambell, "in addition to excessive friendliness, some sexual
tendencies which normally are controlled or sublimated. It is not
necessary for a person to be homosexual to do this sort of thing."'[10]

The next day Wilfrid and Harry recorded the segment for the
Christmas special. Other than a few supportive words I doubt that

'this sort of thing' came up in conversation; it was a private matter that had no bearing on their working relationship – it would be drinks in the bar afterwards as usual.

Series two started recording a week later and aired on 3 January 1963, the same night that Tony Hancock's new television series started on ATV. There was a lot of interest from the press as to who would come out on top in the battle of the ratings: Hancock or his former writers. *Steptoe* was the winner with 8.79 million households, over half of those in Britain, watching. Over the whole year *Steptoe* was only beaten into third place behind *Coronation Street* with 9.70 million and, at number one, the Royal Variety Performance with 10.40 million – which also featured Wilfrid and Harry.

There was no animosity between Hancock and Harry. Freddie Ross Hancock, who would marry Tony in '65 and managed both of them, recalled:

> They liked each other, Tony and Harry. They both used to acknowledge each other and show their respect for each other in interviews. I represented them both and had no problems, when you consider that one week Tony was No. 1 and the next Harry was No. 1 there was no rivalry between them, and, not only that, Tony never thought that *Steptoe* was a rewrite of the rhythm of *Hancock's Half Hour*. He never saw it, as some critics wrote, as a sort of extension of Sid James and him – he never saw it as that, not at all.

Series two opened with 'Wallah-Wallah Catsmeat', in which the horse Hercules falls sick, so the Totting community help out the Steptoes, bringing junk to be bought at cost and sold at a profit. When the horse recovers the wily pair dose the vet with whisky to keep the scam going. John Laurie, who was a prolific Shakespearian stage and screen actor but is best remembered for playing the dour Private Frazer in television's *Dad's Army*, played the corrupt and drunken vet.

'The Bath' is high on the list of best-loved *Steptoe* episodes. With the arrival of new girlfriend Delia imminent, Harold returns to find the old man in a tin bath in the living room, eating his dinner. The image of Wilfrid dropping pickled onions into the bath water, and then replacing them in the jar has stayed vivid in the memory, as has Harry's reaction. His outcry of 'You dzirty old man' became a national catchphrase. Watching it was disgusting enough but reading Wilfrid's reminiscences of the occasion is even more stomach churning:

> When that bath scene terminated I had a quick change that precluded the possibility of a shower, and so I had to be content with a quick rub down. During this frenzied operation Duncan the director burst into the quick-change room and asked me what the hell I was doing half-way through the scene. I had been wriggling and writhing in that bathtub, so I informed him that the reason for these unrehearsed gyrations was that one of the larger pickled onions had bypassed my *cache-sexe* and insinuated itself into my anal orifice, and that I was not prepared to leave it there for the remainder of the episode.[11]

Yootha Joyce played the luckless Delia who ends up in the bath. Yootha, who would return to *Steptoe* on TV and on film and would go on to be remembered for *George and Mildred*, was an old friend from Theatre Workshop. An even older friend from the company played Marlene, the next girl Harold brings home. After installing a bath in the old man's bedroom and thinking he's safe from embarrassment, Harold arrives with Marlene to discover Albert bathing in the living room again – the new bath has fallen through the ceiling. Marlene was played by Marjie Lawrence. It is surprising how many Theatre Workshop actors would turn up in *Steptoe* ... no, actually it's not surprising at all.

In 'The Stepmother' Albert announces he is to marry and move to Cornwall, leaving Harold to fend for himself in a longed-for bachelor pad. It is a marvellous study in role reversal as Harold, waiting for his dinner, greets Albert's return with 'And where the bleeding hell have you been?' causing reviewers to comment that the Steptoes explored more of a mother and daughter theme than father and son, which made a nice change from them commenting that it was 'Pinter with shorter pauses'. In the end Harold scuppers the nuptials by goading the old man into showing his true colours and the prospective stepmother, played by Joan Newell, beats a hasty retreat. Both Albert and Harold are happy with the status quo.

'Sixty-Five Today' sees Albert's birthday. Harold gives him an expensive pair of gloves and takes him out for a cultured evening at a cocktail lounge, Chinese restaurant and the Old Vic Theatre with predictably disastrous results. The episode saw the return of Frank Thornton as the barman and was a favourite of Wilfrid's:

> Late in the evening the young man's patience broke and he travelled home by taxi leaving his Father to travel home alone by underground. When paying for his ticket the old man dropped the gloves of which he was inordinately, though secretly, proud. He reached home on the brink of tears and told his son what had happened. With a hug Harold replied, 'Never mind Dad, I'll get you another pair.' Moments of relationship such as this are all too infrequent in the life of an actor.[12]

In 'A Musical Evening' Harold and Albert clash over tastes in music. To escape Harold's classical choice, 'Wagner – a real eardrum splitter this!', the old man locks the record cupboard and throws the key ring, which includes the keys to the house and yard, into the junkyard. Finding the keys hours later, Albert threatens to drop them down a drain unless he can keep a gramophone to listen to his dance records. He then insists on playing them at the same time as Harold's Tchaikovsky. Harold throws the rescued gramophone back out into the yard, gets locked out and has to listen to ragtime played on his record player.

'Full House' sees Harold holding a poker evening. After his 'friends' have hustled him out of his cash Albert sends him to the pub to fetch a jug of bitter. Then, aided by a marked deck and some special glasses, Albert takes on the cardsharps and, after winning back Harold's money, cleans them out completely. Dudley Foster gave a wonderfully oily performance as the friends' ringleader. Making the first of several appearances in *Steptoe*, Dudley was a gifted straight actor who had also served in the ranks of Theatre Workshop – surprise, surprise.

'Is That Your Horse Outside' brought the series to a close. Patricia Haines guest starred as Dorethea, the lady of leisure who invites Harold in to her upmarket home. Observed by a loitering Albert, Harold emerges hours later. The old man warns that Harold is merely the bored woman's new plaything, a bit of rough, and that the same thing happened to him when he was young. Disbelieving, Harold returns to her house to find his place taken by the coalman – Albert is proved right again.

A week after the series wrapped, Harry flew out to New York in preparation for his next play. The Soviet Union visa stamps in his passport must have raised a few eyebrows at US immigration. The play in question was *Who'll Save The Plowboy* by Frank D. Gilroy. It had gone down well on Broadway the previous year winning the 1962 Obie Award for Best American Play.

The British premiere opened on 18 March and had short try-out runs in Oxford and Bournemouth before transferring to the Haymarket in London's West End. Harry played a mid-life failure, Albert, the ploughboy of the title, a nickname earned during the war when Larry, played by Donal Donnelly, had saved his life, much to the annoyance of Albert's uptight and adulterous wife Helen, played by the beautiful Maxine Audley. Larry turns up at their New York apartment dying from wounds sustained saving Albert years before and needs to see if it was worth the sacrifice. He brings a toy train as a gift for Albert and Helen's absent son, a son he later learns is severely disabled and living in a home. Unaware of Larry's discovery, Albert bribes a local boy to pose as his son. A painfully insightful piece, it was a little too painful for London; the critics liked the playing but not the play, deeming it mawkish and corny, full of American sentimentality – it would be interesting to see how it would go down today, considering how over the past few decades the British stiff upper lip has softened to a blancmange.

The play was directed by John Berry, a Bronx-born Hollywood film director whose refusal to name suspected communists to the House Un-American Activities Committee had seen him black-listed. He had been living and working in Paris in self-imposed exile since the early 1950s, though he would often work on this side of the Channel – the last time had been the previous year at Theatre Royal, Stratford East, not only performing in, but, in Joan Littlewood's continued absence, directing the play *Secret of the World* written by *Legend of Pepito* writer Ted Allan. Berry would return to New York in the 1970s. Donal Donnelly would also make his home there, and has enjoyed a long and acclaimed career; lovers of the silver screen will remember his performance as the financially inept Archbishop Gilday in *The Godfather III*, coming to a sticky end as his character gets chucked over a Vatican staircase.

Speaking of Joan, in early spring she came home to direct the film version of *Sparrows Can't Sing*. Barbara Windsor and James Booth headlined, and the supporting cast read like a roll call of

Joan's favoured faithful. Everyone was in it: 'Lovely' Avis, Roy Kinnear, Murray Melvin, Brian Murphy, Victor Spinetti, Glynn Edwards, Yootha Joyce, Marjie Lawrence and Gerry Raffles as a truck driver. Even May Scagnelli from Café L'Ange got a part. Harry got out of rehearsals of *Plowboy* for long enough to appear as a greengrocer. Gerry was working on a new piece for Theatre Royal at the time. He was collaborating with Charles Chilton who had written *The Long Long Trail* for radio, a musical about the First World War using the songs of the period. Gerry wanted to turn it into a stage play. Joan decided that she would direct the piece incognito; it was the first of many last gasps at Theatre Workshop – *Oh, What a Lovely War*. This particular gasp was chilling to behold. Joan dressed the actors as Pierrots, hoofing with rifles, singing *The Bells of Hell Go Ting-a-ling-a-ling* in front of a screen showing photos of the trenches as a ticker flashed up a tally of the dead. It played for a month at Stratford East and was a triumph, transferring to the West End for a year and then Broadway; later it was made into a film. The actress Frances Cuka, who created the role of the girl, Jo, in Shelagh Delaney's play *A Taste of Honey*, remembered:

> When I saw it at Stratford Victor Spinetti made the closing speech, which went something like 'The war game is being played all over the world, by all ages, there's a pack for all the family. It's been going on for such a long time and it's still going on. Goodnight.' This cynical speech, which followed the charge of the French soldiers, was quite frightening and you were left crying your heart out. When I saw it again in the West End, I was shocked by the change of ending. After Victor's speech the entire cast came on singing 'Oh What a Lovely War' followed by a reprise of the songs. All frightfully hearty and calculated to send the audience home happy. I think it was George Sewell who said 'The Management didn't take kindly to a down ending'. As far as I knew Joan and Gerry were the Management, having rented the theatre from Donald Albery ...[13]

The more things had changed, the more they had stayed the same.

The management, when they went to Broadway, replaced Avis with Barbara Windsor. Victor Spinetti, who won the Tony Award for his part in the production, remembers:

They fired Avis by shoving a letter through her letterbox. Avis had said to me, 'Oh, I'm so looking forward to going to New York with "Lovely War"', because we had a great time when she was there with 'The Hostage.' 'Oh, I'm so looking forward to it,' she said. Then there was the letter from Gerry and Joan firing her and they took Barbara Windsor instead. It broke Avis' heart. She was wonderful in it. She would have got the Tony Award if she'd gone. And I remembered Harry warning me about the kind of things that could go on. That could destroy you or upset you. It was like being thrown into a pool of sharks.

Harry Greene commented: 'I had never seen Avis so enraged and confused. It was to us all so inexplicable and utterly unprofessional. We saw it as a snide action on a lovable, talented and caring actress of esteem.' That's show business.

In May, towards the end of *Plowboy*, Harry and Maxine Audley took time out to present a one-act play by Emlyn Williams at the Green Room Rag charity fundraiser; Sammy Davis Jr topped the bill. Later the same month Harry began work on the film *Ladies Who Do*. He played James Ryder, a city financier. His cleaning lady, played by Peggy Mount, rescues a cigar from the bin and wraps it in a discarded telegram for her next client, Robert Morley. The telegram contains details of a takeover. Together with fellow charladies they make a killing on the stock market and in the end join forces with Ryder in a development scheme. Miriam Karlin, who had had great success on television in *The Rag Trade* and was yet another mate from Theatre Workshop (also appearing in *Secret of the World* with John Berry), played one of the charladies. It was a light Ealing-esque comedy and did as well as could be expected.

During the summer, Harry filmed *The Bargee* – 'the Casanova of the canals with a girl at every lock'. Written by Ray and Alan and directed by Duncan Wood, it was filmed on the Grand Union Canal and boasted a supporting cast of Hugh Griffith, Eric Sykes, Derek Nimmo, Richard Briers, Julia Foster and, already familiar to Harry, Miriam Karlin and Ronnie Barker. Ronnie remembered a lesson learned at the hand of Hugh Griffith:

Hugh Griffith was the heavy. We rehearsed a scene where I was trying to get him drunk to keep him out of the house while Harry Corbett had it away with his daughter. But he eventually drinks me under the table. I said some line and burped in the rehearsal and Hugh looked at me and said 'You gonna burp there?' I said, 'Yes.' So we did the take and about two lines before I burped, he burped. I said, 'You knew I was going to burp there.' He said, 'I know, but I just felt it, it just came out.' Bloody liar![14]

This is not the definition of ensemble playing.

Although the film would do well at the box office it wasn't critically well received, as Ray Galton remembers:

The thing that was basically wrong with it was that it should have been a French film, that's what it should have been, but, obviously, we're English. We thought it was a better film than the critics did but Harry was good and everybody else was good. It was a very enjoyable shoot, we spent the entire shoot there, we were with it every day. We spent a fortnight going up and down the canal before we wrote the script. We got booted off every night by the family who owned it, so we had to find hotels everywhere we stopped.

'It took us a week to get to Birmingham,' added Alan Simpson, 'and two hours to get back. Four mile an hour speed limit.'

Harry had his own take on the film's cool reception, 'Blame the censor. It started off with an X certificate and was then changed to a U. The censor's cuts wrecked the film, left me a cardboard character, instead of a lusty chaser of the birds.'[15]

The summer also saw Pye Records releasing *Steptoe and Son: The Facts of Life*, an audio compilation from the TV series, and Harry's recordings of the songs *Like the Big Guys Do/Green Eye of the Little Yellow God*, while the BBC successfully repeated the second TV series, keeping *Steptoe* firmly in the public's gaze. George Melly, in his guise as *Observer* critic, commented on what made *Steptoe* stand apart from rival sitcoms: 'The difference between the Steptoe half-hour and the others is the difference between a plant which has grown organically from a soil rich in situation and character, and two hat-stands with the jokes hanging on the pegs.'[16]

In the autumn of 1963 *Steptoe* was chosen for inclusion in that year's Royal Variety Performance. Marlene Dietrich was topping the bill, but it's now remembered for being the occasion when John Lennon told those sitting in the cheap seats to clap, and the rest to rattle their jewellery.

Due to working at either end of the country, Wilfrid and Harry could only manage one rehearsal, as Wilfrid later wrote:

> On the morning of that memorable day we got together in one of the many rooms of the Mapleton Hotel[17] for a quick word rehearsal which was not made any the more easy by the crowds of people in the street below incessantly chanting our signature tune, and demanding our appearance on the balcony. They only dispersed after it was explained to them that at the moment we were 'too bloody busy to be gracious'.

Royal Variety Performances are the front line of showbiz – hours of overcrowded anticipation punctuated by minutes of bum-clenching panic, where all concerned are waiting for it to blow up. Wilfrid had a minor blow up at the run-through:

> At 11 am that morning 'H' and I, wearing our full 'Steptoe' gear, sat in the auditorium eagerly awaiting our turn to rehearse on the stage of the Prince of Wales Theatre, and get it over with in order to rest before the show. We were scheduled to do our bit at approximately 1.30 pm but at 1.25 Marlene Dietrich arrived, wearing a grey tweed overcoat and kinky black boots. She frightened the director out of his patent leather shoes and, knowing more than most, she took two and a half hours to dictate her needs for her particular eight minutes. When eventually she left to slip into something tight, it was our turn. The director called Harry on to the stage where they both discussed the format of our sketch, whilst I sat seething in the sixth row of the darkened stalls. Eventually 'Sir' enquired of Harry as to the whereabouts of, as he called me, 'your side kick'. I do not think that my rage was justified, and when finally I was peremptorily summoned by microphone to mount the stage, I staunchly and silently refused to do so. Eventually, amid cries of 'Where is he?' the house lights were turned on. When I was so revealed, I was quietly angry enough to inform that director that the name of the show was not 'Son and Steptoe' and that I was also in it.

After they rehearsed the sketch the director suggested that at their curtain call Harry should be alone downstage bowing to the royal box after which Wilfrid would – ahem – *comically*, eventually join him. It was all too much for the royalist Willie who buggered off back to the hotel telling the director to apologise to the Queen Mum for his absence. But his feathers were soon smoothed when, 'the director came to my room and redressed. Later, I apologised to "H" for my necessary pomposity, to which he replied, "I'd have done the same under the circumstances." This I think is further proof that "H" and I work together rather than fight against each other.'[18]

The sketch entailed father and son totting around Westminster; Harold doing Downing Street and Albert, Birdcage Walk. When Albert reveals that he 'got a lovely load of junk out of that big house back there' Harold is outraged to discover that the old man has been in Buckingham Palace: 'I don't know what you're kicking up a fuss about. They've got junk in there same as everywhere else.' Unfortunately, it turns out that Albert has purloined more than junk. After being greeted by a fellow with a woman's name, Aida Camp, a little boy (Prince Charles) sold him a collection of priceless artefacts for little more than a balloon and some marbles. They are arrested by two guardsmen who discover that Albert has also made off with the crown.

The rather irreverent script was certainly brave, particularly in the royal presence, and would have been unthinkable a decade earlier. But this was the beginning of the swinging sixties and comical dis-respectfulness was now the rage. The sketch went down extremely well, which is more than can be said for Harry's appearance back at the hotel:

The theatre did not have enough dressing-rooms to accommo-date the whole cast – so many of us used bedrooms in a hotel just across the street.

The performance was over and I made my way back to the hotel to change into a dinner jacket.

I got as far as the entrance when a huge arm shot out and stopped me. 'Just where do you think you're going, my lad,' said a large door-keeper. 'You can't come into a respectable place dressed like that.'

'That's just it,' I said, 'How can I look respectable if I can't get inside to change?'

'What kind of fool do you think I am?' the doorman snorted.

It wasn't funny anymore. I got hot under the collar as I thought of the whole cast being lined up before Royalty with a gap where Harry H. should be.

'Look,' I said, 'I've just come across from the theatre where I have been working.'

'I suppose you're the boiler stoker,' grinned the doorkeeper.

I don't know how long the heated exchange would have lasted if my business manager hadn't come out of the theatre looking for me.

The manager explained to the doorkeeper that I was an actor dressed for a part and wasn't a real totter. Apologies were immediately forthcoming, but I wasn't annoyed.

I thought if a London hotel doorkeeper could be taken in, then I must really look the part.[19]

Harry made it to the line up in time for Princess Margaret and the Queen Mother. Her Majesty, according to Wilfrid, commented: 'I so enjoyed your sketch. Lovely local fun.'

She wasn't the only one to enjoy it; the soundtrack of the sketch released by Pye, *Steptoe and Son at Buckingham Palace*, did well in the charts for twelve weeks.

The RVP was one of many royal appearances (the ability to smilingly sit through each and every gala should qualify anyone for the Civil List), but my favourite was the time that Harry, after bowing to the royal box, stumbled going into the wings and blurted out a strangled 'fuck' as he lost his footing. During the line up he remarked to Princess Anne that he had nearly come a cropper: 'Yes … we heard you,' Her Royal Highness serenely informed him, gliding on down the line.

Harry was at the height of his stardom – but he wasn't very good at it:

You know, I once wanted desperately to be a star. I don't mean as a struggling actor, but when I had become a big name. I tried so very hard, but I just couldn't do it. I hired public relations people to build a star image, arrange big entrances into towns and told my PR people to keep people away from me when I left stage doors. The trouble was, when I came out and saw a little old lady with an autograph book being held back by my personal crowd pusher I just couldn't do it. I'd step down and undo all my PR people's work by telling them to stop pushing the lady about, and start signing autographs. I mean I couldn't even act the part of a star.[20]

He was still the same. People always are no matter how loud the applause, (those who go through life thinking fame will make a difference are to be pitied – but not as much as the people they live with) and he was finding out that when it comes to society, it's not just the cream that floats to the top. He also refused to be collected by newly chummy patrons of the arts: 'I can't be collected by anyone.' He said:

> I came up the hard way and one of the things I learnt when working as a bouncer at a pretty tough club – trying to get money to keep Theatre Workshop going – was don't let anyone buy you for anything. Not a lift home, not a bottle of champagne, if they buy a bottle – you buy one back. When I was very poor and sleeping in a dressing room and earning three pounds ten shillings a week, and living on Bovril at sixpence a mug, I was the toast of the doyens of the theatre at that stage. I was collected for my ability, not because I had isolated myself in some Swiss chalet and was leading a phoney life.[21]

By and large his default setting would always remain laconic, taking every opportunity to cock that snook:

> I was pretty well off, an established actor, a star in his own right. But I couldn't resist the sheer idiocy of the situation … I was dressed as a very lowly character, like something straight out of 'Waiting for Godot' and being given a lift by Freddie Ross, one of show business's personalities, to a television studio. She had gone out of her way to give me a lift and I was very grateful to her. But there I was earning all this money and dressed like a tramp. And there was Freddie all dolled up in fine clothes. I slowly climbed out of her very swish, low-slung coupe. Freddie walked over with me to the door where we chatted for a while and then she threaded her way across London's scurrying rush hour crowd to get back to her car.
>
> Imagine it! All those goodly people, going about their ways, involved deeply in their own minds with their own problems, the family back home, and so on. And there was this obviously well-heeled woman in the middle of them …
>
> And there was I, right behind her, grabbing up dog-ends from the pavement and gutter, yelling at the top of my voice: 'Look at her! That's a fine way for anyone to treat her father!'

Poor old Freddie. A deep beetroot, she crashed four gears and reversed into a taxi before finally getting away from it all.[22]

This wasn't the only joke at poor old Freddie's expense, as she remembers:

Harry was learning to drive and we practised in my little car and we used to drive down to Southend where I had an aunt. She couldn't believe I used to bring all these celebrities but they were mates. Harry would drive the car and I'd put the L-plates on and, of course, people would look round and stare at him and, of course, he'd get terribly embarrassed. But coming back we passed a kennels, a breeders, and we drove in and saw this little dog – and Harry bought it for me. It was a West Highland White, which was the kind of dog his agent Jimmy Fraser had so I made Jimmy the godfather.

Jimmy was Scottish and Freddie had often heard Harry use the word crumpet.

So I decided, as a reminder of Harry to call this dog Crumpet, cause it's Scotch as well. And Tony [Hancock] refused to let me call it crumpet. He said, 'If you think I'm going to let a woman of mine walk around Regent's Park shouting out "Crumpet!"' Coz then they had to explain to me what crumpet meant and Harry was hysterical coz he knew what it meant. I started calling the dog Crumpie.

Crumpet was not just slang for an attractive woman, back then, in certain circles, it was also slang for a specific part of a woman's anatomy …

By November of 1963, *Steptoe* was in preparation for a third series and was at the height of its popularity. So popular that an episode was chosen as the British offering for the London Festival of World Television. A critic noted that while the audience watched the best the world had to offer – stunned by the American footage of JFK's funeral, and delighted by China's artistic contribution about the River Li: 'The evening ended with one of the original "Steptoe and Son" programmes. There are some things we couldn't do but no one else can do Steptoe.'[23]

At the beginning of December Pye released Harry's single *The Things We Never Had* from the soundtrack of *What a Crazy World* as series three of *Steptoe* began filming location shots for the episode 'Homes Fit for Heroes'. Harold is out for a Sunday drive with Albert when they 'happen' upon an old people's home. Harold has plans to join a co-ed sailing crew and go round the world on a sloop. After dumping Albert in the home he receives a letter – the crew don't want him, he is too old.

During the episode, while ruminating on old age, Harold remarks: 'Hope I don't get as old as him, I reckon another twenty years and I'll turn it in.' Watching a repeat years later my mother turned to me and said simply 'He did.'

'The Wooden Overcoats' sees Harold bring back a load of coffins to the yard. This doesn't go down well with Albert: 'I'm a respectable rag-and-bone merchant, not a dealer in death.' He refuses to share the house with such evil omens and grumbles off to sleep with the horse. Later, with the lights in the house not working and a storm rumbling, Harold gets the willies himself and joins the old man in the stable.

Leonard Rossiter made his first appearance in *Steptoe* in 'The Lead Man Cometh' as a wonderfully dodgy lead-selling Welshman. Albert believes the lead to be stolen but Harold buys it anyway. After a policeman leaves a notice that lead thieves are in the area, the rag-and-bone men chuck the lot into the canal, only to discover on their return that their roof is leaking – they have just dumped their own lead. Rossiter's excellent turn saw him added to the 'invite back' list.

The man at the top of the list, Frank Thornton, returned to play a snooty butler in 'Steptoe A La Cart'. Harold is working a posh block of flats and after calling the butler a 'capitalist lackey' knocks on the door of French au pair Monique, played by Gwendolyn Watts. In love again, Harold begins to learn French and invites Monique home. Albert, annoyed at Harold, breaks out into fluent French learned during the war. Unfortunately, during the conversation, it is discovered that the girl is his granddaughter and Harold's niece.

In 'Sunday For Seven Days' Harold drags Albert to see Fellini's *8½*. The old man would rather see *Nudes of 1964* at the cinema next door, and so wrecks the evening by talking, slurping his drink and provoking a fight that sees the Steptoes chucked out. Albert gets his way and pays for a seat in the stalls of *Nudes of 1964*. Out of sight of his father Harold also buys a ticket, but in the balcony.

In 'The Bonds That Bind Us' Albert wins £1,000 on the premium bonds. Harold though gets nothing, as he'd sold his half of the bonds back to the old man in order to join a tennis club. Albert, after getting dandified, checks into the Savoy and hits Soho, where he meets Madge, played by June Whitfield:

> When I worked with him in Steptoe, which was great fun, I was the girlfriend of the old boy who'd come into a bit of money and he went up to town and came back with this tart. And it was great fun because of course Harry was absolutely mortified his father had come back with a floozy and I had to go up to him and pinch his cheek and say something like 'Watch what you say, I'm going to be your new Mummy.'

Harold ties and gags Albert and with the aid of shaving foam convinces Madge that the old boy has gone mad and has been spending stolen money – he will have to inform the police. Madge hands back her expensive engagement ring and begs to be kept out of it, after all Albert is her 'fifth one this year'. Albert may be crushed but he isn't daft – the ring was paste.

'The Lodger' was the last of the series. The Steptoes are in dire straits again. Albert, convinced Harold isn't pulling his weight, places a card in the local shop advertising for a lodger. Harold, having tailed Albert, surreptitiously removes the card – but is seen by his skulking father. Harold spends the next week working himself to a standstill on the round to impress his dad while 'innocently' asking how the search for a lodger is progressing. When Albert reveals he knew all along that the advert had been removed Harold leaves in a huff. A week later, after fifteen prospective lodgers have turned their nose up at Harold's room and Harold has sunk to being a sandwich-board man, they call a truce.

The series started airing on 7 January 1964, and immediately went to the top of the ratings, unthinkably beating *Coronation Street* and putting a BBC series at the top for the first time since the independent network gave viewers a choice of channel. It was seen in 9.71 million homes, over half of those in the UK, that translates to over 28 million viewers out of a population of 54 million, the biggest television audience of 1964. No other light entertainment series has ever got near that percentage, and given today's huge choice of media, it's doubtful that any ever will .

Unsurprisingly, in February of 1964 The Variety Club of Great Britain named Wilfrid and Harry as joint BBC Television Personality of 1963. The ceremony was televised in March. Harold Wilson, who had recently won the leadership contest to become Labour's new leader of the opposition, presented the awards. Wilfrid, in beautifully modulated tones, said:

> My trouble is that when I mean something I can't say it, so all the things I wrote down on the Christmas present that he [Harry] gave me have gone for a Burton. Incidentally this is it [brandishing a leather memo pad], so all that I can say is, I don't believe it. Thank you very much, everybody. And I'd like to say thanks to him too. Cause not only is he a terrific chap to work with but he's almost started to be the son out of the business. Over to you 'Arold.

Harry, for the benefit of Wilson, said: 'Er ... I don't want to be political, but I'd just like to say to these newcomers onto the scene, that I have been fighting for freedom for the County Palatine of Lancaster, Home Rule and nationalisation of the Manchester Ship Canal for some years now. Thank you.'

Wilson was gearing up for the general election that would be held that autumn; Harry was a popular TV star whose Labour sympathies were just outshone by those of his on-screen character. The only question would be how long it would take after the cameras stopped rolling for Wilson to ask Harry to lend his voice to the campaign?

The same month saw production of Harry's next film, *Rattle of a Simple Man*. Based on the Charles Dyer play, it starred Harry as Percy Winthrop and Diane Cilento as Cyrenne. Percy is a shy 39-year-old bachelor from Manchester up t'London for the football cup final, while Cyrenne is a lady of negotiable affection who overhears Percy's mates betting he won't be able to get her to take him home – so she does. Amazingly, for the time, it was directed by a woman, Muriel Box, whose films invariably had strong female themes.

It's a good film but Harry wasn't satisfied with his performance (a perfectionist's occupational hazard), not because he was concerned about making Percy different from Harold but, as he remembered, he was trying:

> to keep Percy away from going too far into what I know about the North; what I know about the lads, you see. There are vary-

ing accents around Manchester, there isn't a Manchester accent
… I tried to get this certain accent which comes from a certain
area, which is emasculated, back in the throat, almost a feminine type of accent, which would have suited Percy because the
accent is a weapon for the particular part … Now I see from a
dialect point of view I ought to have kept it away from that one,
but I failed miserably; I let it control me too much.

Personally, I disagree; his performance, and the accent taken from
about two streets worth of Manchester, was wonderful. The New
York Film Critics Circle agreed – they nominated him for Best
Actor. But Harry did love to dissect. This was natural enough, given
that he was an actor and not a film star, the latter usually dissuaded
from 'acting' for fear of disappointing the box office. The lines
between the two breeds are more blurred today, but both would
agree with him on one of filming's main aggravations:

It's terrifying working in films. It's not a question of me hating
the medium, but I hate the situation in which I have to work at
present. I formed a way of life in acting that requires rehearsal,
polishing. I can't give an instant characterisation, just like that,
and that's what I'm required to do. I'm expected to walk into the
studio at 8.30 in the morning and give an instant characterisation. With 'Rattle of a Simple Man' I asked for rehearsal time
and so did Diane Cilento – we both insisted, could we have at
least a week's talking and rehearsal together, to start with. But
we didn't get enough, in some cases we just had a little chat on
the set of no more than ten minutes, for the whole sequence;
a running-through of positions. Then all hell breaks loose with
hammers and lighting men who have fully two hours to light
the set – and they need it. Then they start shooting and you do a
take; in effect you rehearse on print. This is definitely bad for me
because I've either got it in the first take or it'll extend to about
39 takes before I'll get near it again. It's the business of creating
from inside, and spending the rest of the time trying to re-create
that marvellous thing you had at the beginning.[24]

Back then, as a lot of television drama was still 'live' it still had proper
rehearsal time – not now, it's the same as filming – so there was a
marked difference between the two mediums. If film actors seemed

to be the same in every part that's because all they had time for was the superficial. The little tricks of behaviour that had served them well, and safely, in the past. They, as it were, 'ran home to mama'. A course of action that Harry wasn't yet comfortable with:

> I could have done this if I'd have come straight out of rep. with my bag of tricks, because in repertory I used to be brilliant when I was rehearsing at home! I would get the script, I'd see the part, I'd learn it, learn all the movements, the matchbox would be crushed at the right moment like an eggshell – brilliant. I'd go in with it. And I'd be very hurt if other actors had done the same thing. [Shades of Hugh Griffith and Ronnie Barker.]
>
> But we had no point of contact like Willie Brambell and I, because I refused to listen to what they were saying. They were saying it with an entirely different intonation. That's not what I'd expected and it's just too bad, because my reply is going to be this way. When I became an actor I threw all this away. With Steptoe I'll go in knowing my play, not learning it, but knowing my play, knowing what it's about, know what I'm going to do – on the rehearsal floor I learn the play. I'm free. If Wilfrid throws me a line a certain way it'll shake me and I have to reply; this is known as contact. But, of course, there's not much time for this sort of thing in film. There might be for other actors but not for me. I've either got to go home and work on it all night and not take a blind bit of notice what anybody else is going to say to me on the set – consequently I'm going to be hard, factual, technically brilliant; or else I get into this terrible mess of trying to have the best of both worlds. I get into a terrible mess, waiting to discover what it's about. And by the time I've discovered what it's about, it's over; we've wrapped up. We've got to move on to the next set and 'Fellows, this is costing a fortune having this Rolls-Royce for three minutes, you know.' We've had it.[25]

Things were at least easier on the set of *Rattle* than they were off. His on/off marriage to Sheila was in its final death throes, as Diane Cilento, who would later build and run the Karnak Playhouse in her native Queensland, remembered:

> We had a lot of laughs but I'm afraid just at that time he was sort of going through a hard patch. Everything was going a bit

pear-shaped at the time. He was a bit distracted from having a
social time.

He was with my agent Jimmy Fraser and really this film that
we did was sort of one of Jimmy's little package deals where
he'd cast the whole thing out of his agency and so it was sort of
bizarre slightly.

The play had been done and it had been quite a success but it
had to be changed round for the film a bit and so I was made an
Italian – I think it was probably rather a good film. We took a lot
of trouble with it, we did try very hard, plays notoriously don't
translate well onto the screen.

Harry was going through a few things at that time, as I said,
and Jimmy Fraser was being very protective of him, of both of
us really, but we were part of his stable so we saw him a lot but
didn't meet socially.

It was not an unhappy shoot. Harry was grateful to be at work,
there was a lot of to-ing and fro-ing and people throwing up
their arms, that's what I remember and Jimmy saying 'Don't
bother him now, he's just in the middle of some awful thing.'
I think it was from both sides, you know. He had that special look
he had of looking as though he'd lost his last ten fights – he was
wearing that a lot.

The marriage was finished. By now the disagreement over children wasn't the only problem; while Sheila waited for her big break
Harry's stardom had caused tension, as she remembered: 'There
wasn't room for two dedicated actors in the same home, we were
so alike it was like living with yourself. And when his career went
ahead of mine I was vilely jealous … I was horribly arrogant, came
here to take Britain by storm and didn't.'[26]

This might account for the fact that Ray and Alan didn't
remember her coming to any of the *Steptoe* recordings, nor being
introduced to them. Ray remembered that some years later they
were 'at the BBC and we were with Harry talking somewhere and
we saw Sheila Steafel going in or coming out of a doorway there
and so he went over to speak with her and, well, we didn't. He did
and that was it. I think it was about the only time we saw her.'

Aside from these problems, the marriage appears to have been
'fluid' for quite a while. Cynthia recounts a tale of when her brother
and his friend Joe visited the couple:

When me brother went, Brian and Joe, Joe Tarrant – Brian's
wife's sister's husband – went with him to London, but Sheila
made a pass at Joe, and he was a real Catholic lad. This was in
the late '50s, around '59 I think. Brian thought it was hilarious.
Joe was a real church-going lad and wouldn't think of anything
like that.

I can only assume that Harry's eyes must have been roving too –
understandably the topic never came up in conversation. Freddie
Ross Hancock remembers that: 'He had no regard for her, but he
never did anything to show disrespect.' You can read a lot between
the lines of that one. He probably shagged half of London.

It was all over bar the paperwork. Sheila would move into a flat
nearby and the divorce papers were filed, citing her adultery. These
were the days before 'quickie divorces'. The decree absolute would
not come through until a year later in June 1965.

As Harry's stardom had helped the demise of his marriage, then
he might as well enjoy one of its fringe benefits. Fame is attractive, and it attracts a type who during the chase can fall over very
easily or don't bother running at all. Your grandmother was right:
there are those you have fun with and then there are those you take
home to meet your mother. It was the swinging sixties and it was
time for some fun.

Harry would have so much fun that Freddie remembers an occasion later that summer when he was abroad and she dropped off
one girl at airport departures and then went downstairs to pick
up another at arrivals. This would lead to a 'black ops' mentality to
dating as witnessed by Harry's nephew Martin, George's boy:

I remember I went up with a friend of mine to meet Harry in
London. He had a sports car. I think he hated driving, I don't
think he bothered much with it because he said, 'I don't know
where it's parked.' I always remember that. And then we went to
his flat and he said, 'Now listen boys, in case anybody ever asks,
you haven't seen anybody here.' And then he said 'Are you going
out for a drink later? Here.' And he gave us a tenner each. Now
can you imagine what a tenner was worth then. I have no idea
but I know it was something like £100 each. It was unbelievable
and I said, 'It's all right, we can share it.' And he said, 'No, no, have
one each.'

Wilfrid was also enjoying the fruits of fame. The Beatles were fans of *Steptoe* and had recruited him to appear as Paul McCartney's grandfather in *A Hard Day's Night*. Alun Owen, as scriptwriter, would be nominated for an Academy Award (The Beatles' American fans must have wondered why there were so many references to Wilfrid being a 'clean old man'). His performance opened Willie up to a legion of new admirers and surprised the hell out of Paul McCartney, who recalled: 'Wilfrid kept forgetting his lines. And we couldn't believe it. See, we expected all the actors to be very professional and word-perfect – couldn't imagine that an actor like Wilfrid could ever do a thing like forget his lines. So we were all very shocked and embarrassed by this.'[27]

Harry found a simple way of being able to catch any of Willie's stumbles on *Steptoe*: he learnt the old man's lines as well.

Wilfrid wasn't the only one trying his luck across the pond. In April, Ray and Alan sold the rights to *Steptoe* to the Embassy Picture Corporation. 'The agreement was concluded in New York last week' the papers reported: 'Episodes of the production, a BBC show, had been screened in America on Jack Paar's coast-to-coast programme the week before. Mr Paar described Steptoe and Son as "the greatest comedy show I've ever seen."'[28] Although a pilot show would be made, setting the characters in Chicago and starring Aldo Ray and Lee Tracy, it was never televised.

Unlike *The Night of 100 Stars* recorded at the Palladium in July. Harry and Wilfrid did a sketch, Shirley Bassey belted one out, Chita Rivera danced, the Beatles flew on wires, and Laurence Olivier and Richard Attenborough compered. Living up to the title, it was ridiculously studded with the stars of the day. All, however, dimmed in the presence of Merle Oberon and Gloria Swanson, and were snuffed out completely when Judy Garland took to the stage – *Over the Rainbow* brought down the house.

By the autumn Harold Wilson was trying to win a different house. As the general election loomed the Labour Party national rally was held at Wembley on 12 September. Ray and Alan had written a piece for Harry to perform at the rally. The writers were also strong, but not blinkered, Labour supporters, as Alan remembers:

> I was secretary of the Mitcham Labour Party for a year or two
> when I was in my twenties. There was a group of us who'd all
> been in the sanitorium who'd all been members of the Labour

Party and active during election time; coz I was down there going round in my Rolls-Royce picking up old age pensioners to take them down to the polls to vote Labour. And the Tory Party got the hump and said it's not right that a Rolls-Royce should be used – coz you get more people in a Rolls. And then I also got slated by the Labour Party for doing it – it was bad publicity. I thought I can't be bothered by this. The whole point was I can get eight of the old bastards in a Rolls and I can only get three in another car.

Luckily for Harry and Wilson they could be bothered to write for the rally. This first attempt at a convention spirit had also recruited Humphrey Lyttelton and Vanessa Redgrave, with varying success, as *The Guardian* reported:

They must have known that not even Vanessa Redgrave could stand on a stage, in white maternity smock and black glasses, read a political tract saying the man's needs go far beyond the satisfaction of his appetites, that man has his longings and his hopes, and so on – and get away with it.

Humph blew his socialist horn; and Harry H. Corbett (Steptoe jun.) assured his father on the telephone that they weren't going to nationalise him – 'I've had a look at the manifesto and you're not there.'

The longest applause of the day was for Mr Wilson. But the loudest cheers, I think, were for Mr. Corbett, for Aneurin Bevan (when his photograph was flashed on screen), and for George Brown when he said the Tories were so reluctant to go that it was even now not certain that they wouldn't hang on until Guy Fawkes Day. He could think of no better day on which to blow them up.[29]

They wouldn't have to wait until Guy Fawkes. Three days later Prime Minister Douglas-Home asked the Queen for a dissolution of Parliament. The date for the general election was set for the 15 October, which posed another little problem for Mr Wilson.

The BBC had started repeating the third series of *Steptoe* at 8 p.m. on Thursday 24 September. This would mean that an episode would be shown on election day while the polls were still open. Wilson believed that Labour voters, having got in from work and taken their boots off, wouldn't put them back on again to go out to the polls if *Steptoe* was going to be on. It would cost him votes.

Wilson asked the director general of the BBC to move *Steptoe*. This was not only rather bad form but incredibly biased – one can only suppose that it never occurred to him that even Tories enjoy a good laugh. The non-partisan BBC quite rightly refused to move *Steptoe* to a different night, but they did shunt it back to 9 p.m., giving everyone the chance to mark the ballot, get home and hang up their bowler hats or flat caps before the credits rolled.

Wilson won the election by four seats.

I'm sure Harry was happy, it couldn't get much better – but it did when the hand of fate pushed him onto the set of his next movie and smacked him straight between the eyes.

Notes

1   *Liverpool Echo*, 5/1/67.
2   *Manchester Weekly News*, 1/4/67.
3   *The Independent on Sunday*, 20/8/72.
4   *Manchester Weekly News*, 18/3/67.
5   Harry, in conversation with Howard Goorney.
6   *The Times*, 31/10/62.
7   *The Stage*, 29/11/62.
8   *The Guardian*, 6/12/62.
9   Galton and Simpson, *Steptoe and Son*.
10 *The Guardian*, 13/12/62.
11 Brambell, *All Above Board*.
12 *Ibid*.
13 Goorney, *The Theatre Workshop Story*.
14 McCabe, B., *The Authorised Biography of Ronnie Barker* (BBC Books, 2005).
15 *Mail on Sunday*, 31/10/65.
16 *Observer*, 11/8/63.
17 Now called the Thistle Piccadilly.
18 Brambell, *All Above Board*.
19 *Manchester Weekly News*, 18/3/67.
20 *TV Week*, 6/5/72.
21 *The Herald*, 20/4/72.
22 *TV Times*, 29/12/66.
23 *The Guardian*, 27/11/63.
24 Burton, *Acting in the Sixties*.
25 *Ibid*.
26 *Daily Sketch*, 26/11/66.
27 Carr, R., *Beatles at the Movies* (HarperCollins, 1996).
28 *The Guardian*, 8/5/64.
29 *Ibid*., 14/9/64.

13

I'm 21 and Married, Kindly Leave Me Alone

I'll have her, but I will not keep her long.

Richard III, Act 1 Scene 2

Maureen Blott was born on the 6 January 1943. Her first word was 'Doodlebug'. As soon as she would hear the drone of the V-1 rockets, she would grab the family dog by the scruff and toddle into the Anderson shelter. As in a lot of families, the shelter was the last thing Daddy built before he went away to war. Maureen's parents, Sydney and Patricia, had married in 1939 and moved into a new bungalow in Greenford, west London. When war was declared a few weeks later Sydney volunteered with the RAF, which was an obvious choice given that he was already taking flying lessons. But, due to the reflexes of one of his eyes not being up to standard, he was not selected as a pilot. Instead, he became a leading aircraftsman. He installed radios in Wellington Bombers, was involved with early experiments on radar and kept 'the few' flying. Pat always said his eyesight saved him. Most of the young men he had joined up with, whose eyes had earned them wings, never came home.

By 1943, when Maureen was born, Sydney was serving in North Africa in support of the Eighth Army in the fight against Rommel. Pat had stayed in London throughout the Blitz, and it wasn't until 1945 that father and daughter finally met. Maureen's brother, Malcolm, was born the following summer.

Before he went away, Sydney had worked as an administrator for the LNER. When he returned his job had not been kept open for him so he had to start at the bottom again, going to work in the head offices of the newly formed British Rail and going to the back of the queue behind those who had never served. Pat became a cook at the local school.

The war's forced foreign visits had left their mark on Sydney, and throughout the 1950s he would load the car and the family would spend their summers camping in the south of France. Maureen had a flair for languages and soon became so fluent in French that her teachers wanted her to go on to study at university. But she was having none of it. Having starred in all the school productions, she wanted to be an actress. Encouraged by her English teacher, at seventeen she auditioned for RADA and was told she was too young, to come back when she was older. Three months later she tried again. 'We've seen you before haven't we?'

'Yes, I'm older now.' They let her in.

During her first year at RADA her petite stature of only 5ft and a playing age even younger than her years saw her spending most of her time playing children in the seniors' productions. In her senior year she excelled in playing farce. Her natural comic timing, mind like a steel trap and unusual maturity were at odds with her cool beauty and bombshell figure; a face and figure that would pigeon-hole her as cheesecake.

She graduated from RADA in 1962, adopted the stage name of Maureen Crombie – no cheesecake could be called Blott – and that winter went to the Belgrade Theatre, Coventry, for panto and the play *Believe It or Not* by Edward J. Mason and David Turner. She was soon being sent to film castings and landed a role in the Val Guest movie *80,000 Suspects* in early 1963. The movie mixed romance, adultery and smallpox in a world gone mad. It starred Richard Johnson and Claire Bloom, the latter having an eye-opening shower scene. The scene was Maureen's main appearance in the movie and, thanks to the censor, wound up on the cutting-room floor.

That summer she appeared at the Regent's Park Open Air Theatre and in 1964 she landed the regular role of Nurse Maddox in the TV series *Dr Finlay's Casebook*. She also married Tony Boden.

Tony had also studied at RADA and had also worked with Maureen at Coventry. That summer he was spear-carrying with the Royal Shakespeare Company, so the newlyweds settled down to life in Stratford-upon-Avon. Tony's mother lived next door and she also worked for the RSC, but behind the scenes. Maureen followed suit and got a job as an ASM/dresser for the company.

The RSC was producing Peter Hall's *The Wars of the Roses*. For Maureen this meant quick-changing actors in and out of their armour in the wings and standing on a chair to ram the helmets down before rushing the actors back out onto a set designed by John 'Camel' Bury.

Camel had finally left Theatre Workshop the previous year and was at the start of his long and fruitful association with Peter Hall. He would go on to become head of design at Stratford-upon-Avon, before following Hall to the National Theatre where their great success *Amadeus* won him two Tony awards.

Back in 1964 this career was yet to come, as was Maureen's. She hadn't given up on it and was still auditioning, though this was not proving popular. Tony's ever-present mother had definite views that Maureen, despite having the better prospects, should stay at home, support 'our' Tony, and learn the delights to be found in preparing tripe, be it Honeycomb or Fatty Seam. Only a few weeks into the marriage Maureen was coming under more and more pressure and was repenting at leisure, usually by herself as Tony was invariably next door. When one of the auditions paid off, and she landed a plum role in a new Harry H. Corbett movie, she was given an ultimatum: Tony or the career. Well, to be exact, Tony and his mother and tripe, or the career. Maureen packed her bags, headed home to Greenford, leaving Stratford, Honeycombs and Fatty Seams far behind and walked onto the set of Harry's next movie:

'We met on the first day of shooting of a film called *Joey Boy*,' she later recalled:

> I had come down from Stratford, I was already married to somebody else – but we'll gloss over that.
>
> In the film I started, the character, started off at the age of thirteen and I had all the boobs bound up, you know, the liberty bodice and the whole bit – and finished at about age nineteen at the end of the film. But at the first day of shooting I was dressed as the 13 year old. Harry wasn't actually on the set that day. He'd just come to have lunch with Frank Launder and Leslie Gilliat, the producer and director, and he started speaking to me and hanging around and, in fact, it was beginning to get a bit embarrassing in that every time I came off the set he would be at my shoulder, 'You're a nice little girl, you're very talented, how is it I haven't seen you before.' And I said to myself that I would

have to stop this because, you know, the crew were beginning to [wink and say] 'You're in there!' you know, and so I decided that I would say to him that I thought he was married and it was sort of a bit embarrassing.

We were set up to do a shot and as usual before you actually turn over there was a hell of a lot of racket and he appeared at my shoulder again and I thought, Oh my God, I'm going to have to say something, I can't speak, and so I raised my voice to get above the din and I said quite loudly 'I'm 21 and married, would you kindly leave me alone!' and just as I opened my mouth they called for silence and my voice rang round the set. And Harry looked as if I'd slapped him or as if he'd been groping me or something, and the first assistant choked on his tea and the cameraman fell off his perch, it was hilarious.

I think it was the word 'kindly' that did it, 'Would you *kindly* leave me alone.' But it was like a red rag to a bull to Harry, you see, he just then followed me around all over the place and 'My car is at you disposal and will you have dinner with me *tonight,* and *tonight* and *tonight.*' That's how we met. So it was by default, really, because he shouldn't have been there on the first day. You see, if he'd come on the set, you know, sort of on day two or three I'd have known my way around and I'd have either sort of told him where to go or else I'd have been a bit more relaxed about it – but, as it happened, he thought it was highly amusing.[1]

Harry's persistence paid off, Maureen agreed to a date at a Chinese restaurant, 'Mind you,' she said, 'I realised at the time I was probably the seventh girl he'd taken there that week. He was a bit of a hell raiser before we married and was caught up in the "being a star" bit, but he has changed completely since then.'[2]

When they finished the shoot Harry went back to *Armchair Theatre*. He starred in the comedy 'The Hothouse' written by Donald Churchill, the play marking Diana Rigg's television debut as Harry's wife. 'The Hothouse' was *Armchair Theatre*'s greatest success so far, attracting the highest TV play audience figures for 1964. Then negotiations started for the fourth series of *Steptoe*. A series that nearly never happened.

Wilfrid Brambell's turn in *A Hard Day's Night* had upped his profile in the States and he had been offered the lead in a new sure-fire Broadway musical, *Kelly*, based on the story of a man who had jumped off the Brooklyn Bridge and survived. At the same time the BBC had not yet locked down another *Steptoe* series. Ray Galton and Alan Simpson were busy writing for Frankie Howerd, so any new *Steptoes* would have to wait until the spring. Willie said yes to *Kelly*.

'Wilfrid announced that he couldn't play the next series cause he was going to Broadway,' Alan remembers:

> He was going to star in a musical and it was expected to run for two years and so Ray and I seriously considered writing the fourth series starting off with the old man's funeral. We were going to kill him off.
>
> We had it all worked out – it would start in the cemetery and Harry would be all sorry for himself, feeling guilty and going back home to this empty house and almost in tears cause he thought he killed him and didn't look after him, and there was going to be a knock at the front door and he'd open it to 'Mr. Harold Steptoe?'
>
> 'Yes.'
>
> 'My name is John. I'm your son. My mum said that if ever I was in any trouble to come round and see you.'
>
> And it was going to be called *Steptoe and Son* and Harold was going to be the father with his 21-year-old son. We were going to ask David Hemmings to play the young man.

Hemmings, a year away from being hailed as a 1960s icon in the film *Blowup*, was already known to Harry. The two had worked together on the films *In the Wake of a Stranger* and *Some People*. Although Harry would probably have enjoyed the challenge of bringing a new dynamic to the show, he was not comfortable with the idea of killing Willie off and wrote to Tom Sloan to that effect. After all, maybe Willie would become available.

As 1964 drew to a close, Willie started rehearsals for *Kelly*, Ray and Alan ruminated on the next series and Harry looked at other offers. He also continued his pursuit of Maureen, taking her to his favourite old haunts around Soho and black-tie dos. None of it fazed her, even though she had long been an admirer of his work:

> 'I thought he was a brilliant actor,' she said. 'In fact when I was at drama school, I was at RADA when the first of the 'Steptoes' were shown, and all the students came in the following morning

having seen it and said 'Ah, what about that Harry H. Corbett – he's something else, watch it next week, it's compulsive viewing.' So yes he'd been a popular name amongst drama students because, you know, you had to watch him.[3]

The public agreed, with *The Times* reporting that, according to the annual survey of the *Motion Picture Herald*, 'The most popular stars of 1964 were, in this order, Mr Sean Connery, Mr Cliff Richard, Mr Stanley Baker, Mr Elvis Presley, Mr Peter Sellers, Mr Norman Wisdom, Mr Harry H. Corbett, The Beatles, Miss Sophia Loren, and Mr Dirk Bogarde.'[4]

Understandably, Maureen's family were slightly fazed the first time she took him home to Greenford. Her brother Malcolm remembered coming back to their small bungalow one afternoon to find Sydney and Pat entertaining a film star. A surreal experience to start with, but by the end of the visit it was all quite normal, apart from the twitching of the neighbours' net curtains.

By the end of January, Harry had signed on to star in a new play, *Travelling Light* by Leonard Kingston. Michael Crawford and Julia Foster (who had worked with Harry as Christine on *The Bargee*) co-starred. The play opened its pre-West End run on 15 February and that spring and early summer enjoyed good audiences. Which was more than could be said for *Kelly*.

Kelly opened, and closed, on Broadway on 6 February. Having cost $650,000, its failure became a Broadway legend. 'It was a stinking show,' said Wilfrid:

> It cost three times as much money to stage as My Fair Lady. We rehearsed for four and a half months – and the show lasted for two and a half hours. It was the first ever musical on Broadway to be taken off after only one night. But I was laughing all over, for I made a helluva lot of money out of it. I got grand notices and had a swinging holiday.[5]

He then immediately got on a plane for London, as Ray remembers: 'Wilfrid came running back saying I'm ready to do the series – and I think to the day he died David Hemmings never knew, at least we never told him, that he was going to be offered the part.'

So it would be business as usual. But the next *Steptoe* series would still have to wait. Ray and Alan had not yet put pen to paper on any new scripts, no matter who was going to be in the cast, and Harry was committed to taking *Travelling Light* into the West End.

Leonard Kingston's play had started life as *Edgware Road Blues* in a Sunday night presentation at the Royal Court in December of 1963. The comedy told the story of Brian (Harry), an ebullient travelling salesman, who persuades his room-mate Arnold (Michael Crawford), a shy, eccentric, wannabe-Buddhist, to give up his job as a waiter and join forces selling door to door; an enterprise doomed to failure when Arnold falls for Brian's girlfriend (Julia Foster).

If rehearsals were anything to go by, the play itself seemed doomed, as Michael Crawford remembers:

There was great turmoil doing the play because they changed things daily. One of those shows where nothing stayed the same from day to day.

Every day our schedule went from 9.30 in the morning until 9 or 10 at night. Everyone was trying to be enormously help-ful. Ann Jellicoe was directing. Michael Codron was producing. He was wonderful and patient, and then they replaced Ann with another director [William Chappell].

So we were now doing rewrites every single night. We started the previews and it didn't work, we weren't really prepared to start previewing at all. And we had, like an old music hall gag; we had lines written all over the stage. They were written on the mirrors, inside the suitcases – because we were travelling soap salesmen.

A lot of the dialogue is repetitive and if you get it wrong you go very wrong and Harry – I'm his protégé and he's teaching me how to sell soap door to door – he opened his suitcase, because I could hear him dry, he opened his suitcase and he went straight from Act I into Act III and I thought 'How do we get back?' And I looked round at him, and he always had the same expression on his face – *everything in the world is a nightmare and I daren't open another door in case something worse appears.*

And we were laughing so much we were crying. I played a character who had to cry anyway and I spent more time crying, I was actually laughing till I was crying at his ad-libs because I just didn't know where to come in. And it suited my character and it suited his character to do exactly what we were doing. Chaotic! This was very close to the opening night ... we got what are known as mixed reviews.

Amidst this chaotic time we had a lot of fun. We used to go out together every night to The Pickwick Club to have supper. Even when we were doing the show we would do the same, we did get on very well, and I kept looking at this girl who was putting the records on – they didn't call them disc jockeys then. It was a lovely club, the Pickwick, where all the artists from the shows would go afterwards. It was just terrific; they don't have anything quite the same anymore. I suppose Jo Allen's is the nearest but you get a lot of outsiders; The Pickwick was just for shows.

I fancied this girl who was putting the records on so much that I kept going on to Harry, 'Look, you can go and chat to her for me. You go and …'

He said, 'Fuck off!' all he ever told me to do was 'Fuck off!' I can still remember crying with laughter because he got so cross. Of course he wasn't really getting cross – it was a funny anger. He knew he was being funny, it was that kind of humour that he had.

In the end he said, 'Oh, for fuck's sake, I'll go and do it.' So he goes over and drags her out of the box and brings her over. He says, 'This geezer wants to ask you out. Now do you want to go out with him or not? Coz he's driving me fucking mad.'

In the end we did go out, and we got married. So without Harry I doubt I'd have made it across that room.[6]

As Crawford embarked on his marriage, Harry's officially ended. The decree nisi was issued in March of that year. His divorce had been a lot more straightforward than most, as Maureen had already discovered. Despite the brevity of her and Boden's marriage, Tony wasn't letting go without a fight. Either his Catholic religion had given him pause or he still believed that Maureen would return; a belief that must have been stretched to breaking point when Maureen appeared at the divorce courts. She wasn't coming back. Maureen's father, Sydney, also spoke on her behalf – though he was not a well man, having been diagnosed with a stomach ulcer. It was to no avail – Tony would not agree to a divorce.

At least Maureen's career had been going well: alongside being sent for more film auditions and continuing with *Dr Finlay*, she was starting to land comic roles and in May was cast opposite Roy Hudd in an episode of his new TV vehicle for the BBC. She was also seeing Harry on a permanent basis and that summer moved into his flat and was introduced to more of his friends.

Harry had a wide circle of friends from the shady denizens of Soho to the, perhaps shadier, leaders of the land. The MP George Wigg became a good friend; he was Harold Wilson's Paymaster General – though many would say that 'spymaster general' would be a more fitting title. Wigg had been an army man until entering politics aged 45 and shared a passion for horse racing with another of Harry's, and Wilson's, close friends – Desmond Brayley. Brayley was from a similarly poor background to Harry and, like Wigg, had been in the army, becoming the army boxing champion.

Brayley was a self-made man, his fortune coming from building up the Canning Town glass factory. His love of boxing stayed with him: he became president of the Amateur Boys Boxing Association and he would often invite Harry to watch the fights. Harry knew quite a few people from the boxing world; it was the only sport that he ever enjoyed as a spectator (the only sport Harry ever participated in was pistol shooting – a hangover from the war – and he would often shoot with friends in the police force at the Marylebone Rifle and Pistol Club, of which he was a member).

Brayley also knew how to spend his fortune, buying a country pile, a penthouse in Mayfair and keeping a huge and glamorous yacht in the Pool of London; Maureen and Harry were often guests on board. Permission to keep the yacht in the Pool was quite a rarity, but when you're chums with the PM … He would also use the yacht for political dinner parties; Ray and Alan remembered being invited to such a party and marvelling at the teak woodwork, gold plates and silver cutlery – very old Labour.

Brayley was also well known in the world of show business: he was a member of the Water Rats and of the Saints and Sinners Club, of which Harry was also a member. The Saints and Sinners, like the Water Rats, organised charity fundraisers. They are a discreet luncheon club that in Harry's time used to have charity race meetings. These days they organise golf fundraisers but still have their famous annual blowout dinners. Neil Benson, secretary of the club, remembers Harry, George Wigg and Brayley:

> Harry used to pal around with George Wigg, who became Lord Wigg and a seriously shady figure in the Labour government, and Desmond Brayley, now there's a real character. A friend of Desmond's brought me into the club as secretary back in '65, which I've been doing ever since. Now was he MI5? Who the

hell was he? I do remember once one of our members had a burglary and Desmond Brayley spoke to somebody, who spoke to somebody, who got all the goods back. One of the criteria for being a member of the Saints and Sinners is raffishness and if ever there was anybody totally raffish it was Brayley.

I remember, sometime in the *Steptoe* period when Harry was really cock-o-the-walk, I was walking down Park Lane to our annual dinner at the Dorchester and we met, he was there in his wonderfully grey sprayed-on showbiz DJ, and we wandered into the Dorchester together and in those days, as now, the only time we ever distinguish ourselves between Saints and Sinners is that at the annual dinner you choose either a white or a red carnation depending on which you think you are. We have pretty girls there with the carnations to give you a flower as you go in. And I walk in with Harry and, of course, no one wants to give me a carnation cause all these girls are vying to give him one and eventually he picks on this girl and she says to him, 'What colour would you like?' and he says, 'Oh, give us a white one, darling.' And she takes a white carnation puts it up against the revere of his new dinner jacket, which didn't of course have a lapel buttonhole, so she stuck the pin in the revere which split from top to bottom and without batting an eyelid Harry said, 'Oh fuck it! Give us a red one.' Which I always use as the real distinction between a saint and a sinner, the classification is that transitory.

Harry was also frequently to be found at The Savage Club, as the guest of a Brother Savage of high standing and low stature – Wee Georgie Wood. Thanks to his mother, George Wood was on the music hall stage before he was six years old. And thanks to his adult height of 4ft 9½in he played a boy his entire life. With his 'onstage mother' Dolly Harmer, he became the toast of the music halls and as huge stars they toured the world with ENSA, entertaining the troops in the Second World War. I wouldn't be surprised if Annie had taken her Harry Boy to see them back in the 1930s. Harry had a lot of time for Georgie Wood, and the feeling was mutual. In his later years Wood was a columnist for *The Stage* newspaper and frequently mentioned their friendship; a friendship that helped to re-kindle in Harry his boyhood love of variety and music hall. Harry began to entertain the idea of joining the variety world by doing one-man shows round the clubs and to that end became a member of the Concert Artist's Association.

Someone who would have met the association's membership criteria was another of Harry's good friends, Maurice Woodruff. Woodruff was a high-profile clairvoyant, frequently seen in cabaret and on television, and with a famous clientele – it was said that Peter Sellers wouldn't make a move without consulting him first. Though not as devoted as Sellers, Harry – wary of not giving the occult the benefit of the doubt – respected Woodruff's predictions. One of these had been that Harry would soon be heavily involved in sorting out the affairs of a new family. Woodruff said of Harry: 'He is a deep thinker ... far deeper than perhaps he would like you to know.' And Harry said of Woodruff:

> I come to see you out of interest. I'm not terribly interested in myself; I fool myself that I am the captain of my soul, the master of my fate. You've got the sixth sense that has been blunted in most of us by the commercial age ... You fascinate me with your international generalisations that are so often dead-on ... Maybe you get a sort of tremor that passes us by. You've got the sort of highly-developed instinct that animals have, the instinct that takes the drunk safely home. I believe that we will be accepting clairvoyancy more and more as the years go by. If I had a child born with this gift I should be as glad about it as I would if I had one with enormous intelligence.[7]

No to both, I'm afraid.

Harry was also keeping up his ties with Theatre Workshop, though this was set to change. The company had taken *Oh What A Lovely War* to Broadway in October of 1964, when the show closed in January of 1965 they returned to London and ran into the financial rocks once more. Theatre Royal, as always, could not be kept afloat without substantial aid from the Arts Council: aid that was not forthcoming. The company disbanded and the theatre was leased to outside management.

One member of the company, Margaret Bury, had started a drama school to carry on teaching the company's ethos. Lessons had been given to students at Theatre Royal but as this was no longer available, she needed other premises. She acquired the lease of Hatfields, a detached Georgian house set in its own grounds in Loughton, east

London, which would serve as administration and rehearsal rooms, but she needed funds to pay for a building large enough to use as a theatre. Thanks to his success, Harry was in a position to help, as Jean Newlove, who was responsible for running movement classes for the burgeoning school, remembers: 'Harry did an interview for the *News of the World* and got a hell of a lot of money for it and he was so embarrassed he bought this barn and he had it moved. He said something to me about it – he felt easier because he spent the money that he got, he put it to good use, which was very typical.'

The fourteenth-century barn was in Ditchling, Sussex. The following year it would be dismantled, piece-by-piece, and transported and rebuilt in the grounds of Hatfields. It was named the Corbett Theatre and for over forty years has seen productions by the students of East 15 Acting School (E15 being the postcode of Theatre Royal, Stratford East).

Gone were the days when Harry had begged Jean to send him a few cigarettes to keep him going at Laban camp, which was something that, due to the lessons learnt at Theatre Workshop, was taking a very long time for both of them to come to terms with. Jean remembers meeting up with Harry around this time when he came to visit her young daughter, Kirsty MacColl:

> I was going to have a big party with some of the theatre and Laban people because I had not been able to have a party due to Kirsty's ill health, which was pretty dire because she had asthma. I nearly lost her many times and I was going to celebrate because she seemed so much better – and then she hadn't been. She'd been rushed to hospital and we'd nearly been at death's door again and I had to cancel the whole party and Harry was the one person that said, 'I'm going to come anyway.' We were living in Selsdon, which was very difficult to find, I'd built a house there and it was an unadopted road. Kirsty was absolutely delighted he was coming, he came down and he had quite a nice car then [a 1965 Mustang Convertible] and we saw each other in a different light. He had quite a nice car and I had quite a nice home – suddenly, we were sort of different.
>
> He was very sweet. I remember he brought her a little plastic umbrella, and something else, and she was so thrilled and he told her all about how he'd had to use the umbrella to fight off Indians along this road because it was so wild.

When Margaret Bury sought help elsewhere amongst Theatre Workshop for her new school she was disappointed. Joan Littlewood had neither the inclination nor the time for Theatre Workshop, let alone East 15 Acting School; from now on she would be devoted to her 'fun palace' project. Speaking in 1967, Harry reflected on his history with the company:

> I never really left Theatre Workshop. It became more and more apparent that money was needed. I became popular. We started to get press notices towards the end, and television extended a sort of feeler in my direction, so I worked in television. This suited me perfectly because I was still able to work at Theatre Workshop; in other words, I could get the money to bring back to Theatre Workshop. The actors, as always, subsidise this kind of work.
>
> I then got fascinated by television, because remember one thing that did come out of Theatre Workshop was truth, absolute searching truth. This truth was tailored to a medium known as the theatre, in which the huge gesture is used, so that it can be seen, where the nod and the wink wouldn't suffice. Sometimes one had to sacrifice truth for the presentation of the theatrical effect. Television really allowed me to use this truth. I simply walked from one group theatre to another … But I stayed with Theatre Workshop while still enjoying the fruits of the truth in television – and the money – until about two years ago. Even when I was doing Steptoe I was going back there, doing shows, doing seasons, and building a building.
>
> Then finally the break came with Theatre Workshop. We had to break it up because of financial problems. The inevitable end of the avant-garde is when it becomes the classical, and another avant-garde should come in to attack it. This has always been so in the past, I think, through economic reasons. By the time an avant-garde theatre gets to maturity the money's fading. The period of any theatre of that kind is about fifteen years. It starts as an idea, it grows, it gets a highlight period towards the tenth year; then gradually it tails off, and I do not know any group theatre, any foremost repertory theatre of the past, which has not done that. It's at the end of that fifteen-year period it should burgeon out, and Joan wanted to do this with what she called her 'happydrome'. This was to take the form of a huge pleasure-park arena with a really fantastic theatre, theatrical conception.

Theatre Workshop could no longer carry the weight of these
ideas that were being propounded; that is why it finished, and
I finished with it.[8]

Joan's 'fun palace'/'happydrome' was never built. We got the
Millennium Dome instead.

Joan herself, would never have thought of television as truth-
seeking group-theatre. According to Galton and Simpson she had
little time for the medium, Ray remembering: 'We always said that
she thought of Harry as her crown prince.'

'I think she thought he compromised his art,' said Alan.

'Oh yeah,' agreed Ray, 'Not think – she did. Doing such a thing
as television.'

She was not alone in this opinion; at that time denigrating the
medium was par for the course in the theatre. Nicholas Amer, who
had been part of the Old Vic cast that came to see Theatre Workshop's
Richard II said of Harry: 'When I saw him doing *Steptoe*, oh, I thought
he was wasted in that, but that says a lot about me. As a theatre actor
in those days even the movie industry was considered second string.
Television was "Oh! I've been doing them a great favour."'

For Harry, it was television doing the favours. It had ended the
old theatre clichés that Theatre Workshop had loathed and fought
so hard against. 'Television broke it up, finished it off,' he said:

> What is the cry of the old show business personality? He doesn't
> get a chance any more. Where have all the musicals gone? Where
> have all the opportunities gone? The people who have survived
> are the artists. Artistry has nothing to do with show business.
> Quite honestly, artistry is truth, and if you've got a good truth,
> you can do it on an ice-rink, on television, as a ballet, do it as any-
> thing you want. So I don't see enough show business in evidence
> to be contemptible about show business.[9]

But Harry was always sensitive of the lowly image television had
in the business and was quick to be dismissive of the medium, and
his success in it, when talking with other actors, especially those
from the Theatre Workshop days. Barry Clayton tells a typical
story. Barry had left Theatre Workshop in the early 1960s, gave up
acting and after a few years with the Polish Film School was back in
England directing documentaries at Granada Television:

Who should I see in the canteen at Granada but Harry. So I went over and said, 'What are you doing? I'm directing a series of documentaries and I'm having a great time cause I can do whatever I like and they seem to like what I'm doing. And Harry said, 'Well, you're all right. Look at me stuck in this thing. Still, I'm making a lot of money.'

Back in the summer of 1965 Harry was spending money. He and Maureen bought a cottage in Benenden, Kent, a place to escape from London and the constant attention, and in August they went on holiday to Cannes; fitting it in before the rehearsals for the fourth series of *Steptoe* began that September. As Maureen's divorce was still some way off, they always regarded it as their honeymoon. Amongst their most treasured possessions, prominently displayed in subsequent houses, were two watercolours of the surrounding countryside and an oil painting of the boats in the harbour. Most precious of all was a little fish-shaped ashtray given to them by a restaurant.

Maureen's family were also abroad at the time, celebrating her brother Malcolm's 19th birthday in Corsica. As a treat, Sydney had left the car at home and they had travelled by train to Marseilles on Sydney's discounted tickets and then flown for the first time. But a few days into the holiday Sydney's stomach ulcer flared up. He was so ill in the night that the reception of the small hotel they were staying in contacted one of their fellow guests, a young French doctor, who took one look and arranged for him to be rushed into hospital, as Malcolm remembered: 'We got him to hospital and they did various X-rays, which he had to have standing up. They operated overnight and Pat and I were sitting in this waiting room all night long not knowing if he was going to make it or not – it was pretty touch and go.'

Sydney survived. Pat and Malcolm were told to come back the following morning when they finally found out what was wrong:

> The staff didn't speak much English and we didn't speak much French, but the nurses then explained to us that it was cancer.
>
> The surgeon asked what treatment he had been getting. He couldn't believe that in the UK they'd been treating him for a stomach ulcer – he was incredulous and he recommended that Sydney see this surgeon at St Bart's hospital in London for another operation. The cancer was so advanced that it really needed a top surgeon – it would be his only chance of survival.

Pat and Malcolm managed to contact Maureen and Harry in Cannes. As they waited for them to arrive they went to the British Consulate for help in getting Sydney home. 'But it was never open,' remembers Malcolm, 'When we finally did get through, they didn't want to know.' Of course the family didn't have travel insurance or enough savings to pay for direct flights or medical care.

Maureen and Harry arrived, checked into the main hotel in Ajaccio, and joined Pat and Malcolm in waiting to see when, or even if, Sydney would be well enough to travel. When there were signs of improvement, it was decided that Malcolm would return to England alone on his original ticket. As the days slipped by, Harry also returned; he had to get back, not just for the *Steptoe* rehearsals, but to make arrangements for Sydney's transfer.

While Maureen and Pat cared for Sydney, taking in all his meals, as was the Corsican custom, Harry and Malcolm went to see the recommended surgeon at St Bart's, who agreed to operate. Harry arranged the transfer and the five seats needed to get Sydney, who had to lie down during the journey, Maureen and Pat home. At the beginning of September they arrived at Heathrow and were finally taken to St Bart's. Sydney was very weak and would have to wait another two weeks before he was strong enough for the next operation.

Pat, Malcolm, Maureen and Harry visited every day, though Harry's visits would have to wait until the evening. From the second week in September he was rehearsing the new *Steptoe* series and doing the rounds of pre-publicity.

The first episode of series four, 'And Afterwards At ...' was recorded on 12 September. Harold is finally getting married. A sour-faced Albert gives it six months, and so is delighted when the bride, Melanie, jilts Harold at the altar. As Albert spats with the mother of the bride, played by Mollie Sugden (giving a wonderful battleaxe performance that was to hint at her later work in *The Liver Birds* and *Are You Being Served?*), Melanie drives off, leaving a broken Harold to return with Albert to Oil Drum Lane. Soon the extended Steptoe family descend for gin and sympathy and to give a fresh airing to long-standing feuds. Uncle Arthur, played by Harry's old chum from Theatre Workshop, George A. Cooper, leads the charge in asking for the wedding presents back. An incensed Albert and Harold chuck the gifts out of the window and Harold invites Albert on honeymoon: 'Go and get packed. You've had a wash, it's a shame to waste it.'

As there had been no new *Steptoe* episodes on screens for the last twenty months, Harold's wedding was just the kind of explosive storyline that was needed to kick the series off. The press hailed the welcome return of the rag-and-bone men and the BBC made them the cover stars of the *Radio Times* on 30 September. They were seen as the jewel in the new autumn line-up. There was also speculation as to why they had been gone for so long. There had been rumours that Harry didn't want to do any more series and was tired of playing Harold. Harry put the record straight. He just hadn't wanted to *extend* the series:

> Ray Galton and Alan Simpson, the scriptwriters, have always wisely insisted that no more than seven episodes are ever shown in a series. That keeps the ideas very much fresher – and there's still plenty of situations to be thought up.
>
> The point was there was considerable pressure to have the series extended, but neither Wilf nor I wanted that. 'Steptoe and Son' should have a limited annual run. Something that leaves the viewers wanting more. As long as that's the case I'm always happy to play Harold.[10]

So the lengthy gap had not been down to dissatisfaction but lack of availability and, most importantly, scripts.

'Crossed Swords', the next episode, opens with Albert getting trapped in the outhouse. Three hours later, Harold returns from the round with a rare piece of Meissen porcelain. After Albert grudgingly admits that it might be worth something, the pair take it to an antique dealer, beautifully played by Derek Nimmo (who had worked with Harry on *The Bargee*). Against the old man's advice, Harold greedily turns down the £250 offered and enters the piece for auction. In trying to bid up their lot, Albert ends up buying it and the pair are out of pocket on the auction house's commission. As a final insult, Albert drops the Meissen and hides in the outhouse as an enraged Harold thrusts swords through gaps in the door.

In 'Those Magnificent Men and their Heating Machines' Harold returns to the house to find Albert lying with his head in the oven. Fearing his comments have driven his father to suicide, Harold soliloquises his responses at the inevitable inquest before the old man 'wakes up' and reveals he was merely cleaning the oven. When calm is restored Harold shows Albert the old central heating system he has bought for him. Albert is delighted until he learns that Harold is going to install it himself. In a case of art mirroring life, it's a botched job. When turned on, the system shakes so violently that it brings the ceiling down and floods the house. Albert goes off to sleep with the horse leaving Harold checking the oven for a gas leak. When Albert returns he finds his son with his head in the oven and leaps to the same conclusion of attempted suicide.

'The Siege of Steptoe Street' opens with the Steptoes going through a mound of unpaid bills they have no hope of paying. From a butcher's bill Harold discovers the old man has been eating grouse while he has been making do with pig's trotters. While looking through Albert's purse for money he also discovers an old school report. Harold was such an inept student that his headmaster feared that he would turn out backward, an assessment the old man had kept to himself for years.

When the debt collectors come calling the pair barricade themselves in the house with only tins of snails and asparagus tips to see them through the siege. During the night Harold catches Albert eating a biscuit and discovers he has hidden a whole packet. A betrayed Harold surrenders, and the butcher and the bailiffs enter to seize the Steptoes' possessions, but in a tussle with the butcher Albert fakes a fall and is paid £250 in hush money.

Yootha Joyce made a return to *Steptoe* in 'A Box in Town'. She plays Avis, a girl Harold has brought home thinking the old man would be in bed. He isn't. Having had his romantic aspirations thwarted yet again, Harold finally leaves home. He moves out to a top-floor bedsit and starts calling old flames but he finds none of the girls are interested. Albert, on the other hand, is proving very popular with the local widows. Harold eventually gets Avis to come back to his new pad only for the landlady to break it up and throw him out. Returning home he finds Albert worn out by the constant female attention and the happily reunited pair tear up their little black books.

Dudley Foster also made a return in 'My Old Man's A Tory'. Harold is to hold the local Labour Party's meeting at Oil Drum Lane and hopes to be confirmed by Foster, in his guise as party agent, as candidate for the council. Albert, initially dismissive of both his son's ambitions and his politics, is soon gleefully anticipating the lucrative backhanders Harold will get as a councillor. When his comrades arrive, Harold, in homage to Wilson, is sporting a mac and pipe – and so is the agent, who condemns Harold's idealistic efforts at ending the Vietnam War by writing to world leaders and informs him that the party have not chosen Harold as candidate but instead a middle class doctor who will be more appealing to voters. Harold falls on his sword but an incensed Albert throws the hypocritical agent out of the house.

In 'Pilgrim's Progress', the last episode, Albert is preparing to see the First World War trenches of his youth once more before he dies. Harold bemoans having to give up the delights of St Tropez to accompany him and ridicules the old man's pride in a country that betrayed the working classes with empty promises of employment for all and homes fit for heroes. He is, however, sympathetic to the old man's horrific memories, the pair playing the scene with beautiful poignancy and impeccable timing. Once on board the plane taking them to Paris, Albert gets into an argument with an American and a Frenchman (played by a returning Frank Thornton). After accusing the Americans of being late for both wars and the French for surrendering, a fight breaks out. The Steptoes are arrested at the airport and deported as undesirable aliens. Harold will never see St Tropez and Albert plans to return to the scene of his action in the desert under Allenby.

The series started transmission on 4 October and again went to the top of the ratings, despite being put in competition with ITV's stalwart audience winner *Coronation Street*. This was something that delighted the reviewer Milton Shulman:

> The unbelievable had happened. Monday's episode of Coronation Street had not only been dislodged from its position as one of the most popular programmes of the week, but it was nowhere to be found in the Top Twenty ... Could this mean that the TV soap opera, with its continuing characters forever blowing bubbles of petty, domestic strife has finally exhausted the patience and tolerance of its followers?[11] One can only fervently hope so. Of course the giant killers who have brought about this much-needed revelation of what the British public actually prefers in TV – as opposed to what they watch out of sheer inertia – are those unique rag-and-bone men, Steptoe and Son ... Just why the erratic doings of a dirty old man and his uneducated son should make the nation catch its breath with laughter is something that will long be argued about by analysts

of humour. Almost devoid of the conventional gags and slapstick situations that dominate most TV comedy, these scripts by
Galton and Simpson derive their appeal out of a meticulously
observed and naturally plotted observation of character. Since
the parent – child relationship is one that we all suffer or enjoy
by turns, we can get some vicarious delight watching the alter-
nating spasms of love-hate that grip 38-year-old Harold Steptoe
as he tries to assert his independence of his wheedling, posses-
sive, cunning crocodile of a father … It is indeed this endearing
reflection of life – true enough to make us sigh as well as laugh
– that, I believe, accounts for Steptoe's phenomenal hold on the
affection of the nation. And of course, the warm, sure, uninhibited, outrageous comic performances of Harry H. Corbett and
Wilfrid Brambell.[12]

Shulman may have been happy with the transmission slot but
according to one reporter:

the Steptoe creators and actors are not happy about the B.B.C.s
planning. From their viewpoint the Steptoe figures have been
cut by nearly half for the capers of [*Coronation Street*] still command an impressive audience.

Ray Galton's view is: 'None of us, writers and actors, is happy
to have the show used as a weapon.'

This point may influence Galton and Simpson in deciding
whether the present 'final' series of seven shows is indeed the last.
They do say it would be possible to do another. It is to be hoped
that the B.B.C. will pay due regard to their views. Premature
death for old Albert and Harold would be a bitter end.[13]

Not everyone liked it:

At a conference of women's organisations in Nottingham
recently, Kenneth Adam head of BBC TV heard them described
as 'dirty, obscene and immoral.' Take a letter like this from 'Only
an Eastender.' This young lady – her own phrase – underlines like
Queen Victoria and is also not amused. 'What exactly do you
mean when you describe "Steptoe and Son" as a series of high
standard? I would never in a million years refer to love-making
as "Crumpet."' It is undoubtedly shocking to some good woman

that scriptwriters Simpson and Galton should get, for instance, £1 6s. 8d. last night for writing just four words; 'Toffee-nosed red pouffe,' a line they gave to Albert ...[14]

But for Harry and Maureen, ratings and reactions would not have been at the forefront of their minds just then. They were both busy at work. Alongside filming *Steptoe*, Harry was taking part in a short film about buskers, the timing of which was not wonderful but Harry had promised and his 'star' presence was the only way the makers could get a guaranteed distribution. He waived the fee in favour of a donation to East 15 Acting School. Maureen was also busy doing publicity for her next film *The Great St Trinian's Train Robbery*. But all of this was a sideshow to the ongoing hospital visits to see Sydney following his second operation, and to the news that they broke to the family on one of those visits in early October. Maureen was pregnant. The child was due in April and everyone was hoping like hell that Sydney would live to see it.

Contemplating birth and death had seen Harry in a reflective mood when he and Wilfrid were interviewed on the last day of filming the *Steptoe* series.

Willie talked about his and Harry's relationship: 'Harry and I got the parts, worked well together and have been firm friends ever since. We don't see much of each other off the set, though. Harry lives in North London and I have a flat in Pimlico.'

He also said they were all 'as happy to be back on another Steptoe series as hungry flies on a sleeping fishmonger's slab.' And that: 'Some people say we're a washout from the Steptoe part. But they're bonkers – just ask my bank manager. Films, plays, other TV appearances ... we get the lot.' Finally, touching on his turn in *A Hard Day's Night* he joked it was: 'Quite shattering to find yourself a sex symbol at 52. I think I prefer being Old Steptoe – and it looks as if he is going to be around for a long time. I hope so anyway ... what with my flat, my cottage in Essex, holidays in Greece and Italy and all these expensive clothes I keep buying!'

Harry agreed, 'Of course Steptoe is here for a while.' He also liked the financial benefits of being a Steptoe: 'Steptoe has been a godsend. In one series I make a year's earnings – and I'm a free agent after the 27 weeks it takes to make a series.' He also fielded questions about his private life: 'He regrets the failure of his marriage (In March this year he divorced his South African born wife

Sheila) "It just didn't work out," he says. "But I have lots of friends and lots of interests."' It being his private life he naturally didn't mention Maureen or the baby.

But when asked a question about his likes and dislikes he answered:

> As many as anyone else. But particularly I hate people who speak two languages. They make me feel such a birk. I feel like a real Charlie – and for a little while I would swap any success *Steptoe* has brought me for a decent education.
>
> Perhaps one day I'll be satisfied with what I am. But I doubt it. I think I am just one of those people who is destined to see himself as someone who could have achieved a great deal more – if only he had tried a little harder.[15]

Those distant dreams of healing the sick were still there. Buried, but there.

Five days after *Steptoe* wrapped, while Harry was working on his next film – Michael Bentine's *The Sandwich Man* – Sydney took a turn for the worst. He had recently been moved to a side room – never a good sign. But it was still a shock when the hospital contacted the family with those words you hope you never hear: 'Come now.'

Malcolm was first to arrive and Sydney managed to hang on until Pat got there, but died before Maureen and Harry made it. They missed him by minutes.

Maurice Woodruff's prediction had sadly come true. Harry had been, and always would be, central to the affairs of a new family. However, before you go rushing off to cross any palms with silver, Maurice also predicted that Harry would live to 80. So, you pays your money and you takes your choice. Speaking of choice – Maureen had to choose whether to keep working or not. To have a partner on location, and a packed suitcase and babysitter on standby in case the agent called, or give up the career and support Harry, so he could stay at the top of his game while enjoying the family that she would raise. Maureen had already found enough success in her career to satisfy her inner contender and, naturally, her father's death would have tempered her outlook on the future and how short it could be. She chose family, and as one that benefited from her raising, I will always be grateful, nearly as grateful as Harry.

She never lost her touch. Sometimes, when a 'fixed' shelf collapsed or he hadn't let the dog out in time, Harry would quickly launch into *Richard III*. Complete with hunchback and gammy arm, in cod-Larry Olivier voice he would decry, 'I'll have her, but I will not keep her long.'

She could always undercut him with the oldest look I have ever seen.

Notes

1   Interviewed by the *Steptoe and Son* Appreciation Society (SSAS). Video of the complete interview is available on their website.
2   *Sunday Mirror*, 10/9/72.
3   Interviewed by SSAS.
4   *The Times*, 1/1/65.
5   *Mail on Sunday*, 31/10/65.
6   In conversation with Michael Crawford.
7   *Reveille*, 7/9/67.
8   Burton, *Acting in the Sixties*.
9   *Ibid.*
10   *Manchester Weekly News*, 25/9/65.
11   Answer: No.
12   *Evening Standard*, 3/11/65.
13   *Evening Sentinel*, 3/11/65.
14   *The Sun*, 9/11/65.
15   *Mail on Sunday*, 31/10/65.

Bright Lights and Bacon Sandwiches

I wouldn't mind doing another series – it's been great fun. But the writers seem to have decided that this was the last one. If I had been asked to do another series while we were in the middle of recording the latest, I might have turned it down. There's no fun being out on a cold morning with an equally cold horse staring you in the eyes. But now I gather there is not to be another 'Steptoe' anyway. The BBC is always a bit slow in these things. It never seems to ask us for another series until the very last minute. [1]

Harry H. Corbett

Steptoe and Son was over. Having been at the top for four years, Ray and Alan wanted to bow out on a high. Besides, it was getting harder and harder to come up with storylines. Having come to the end of their exploration of the characters, they were moving on.

So was Harry, but not back to dramatic roles. Having made one of the first, and possibly the most successful, metamorphosis into light entertainment, he couldn't now go back to playing brooding heavies. The public, and critics, wouldn't have it and he was well aware and accepting of that. Amusingly, when he had first done comedy roles, the critics were amazed at his success; now it was unthinkable he should be capable of anything else. They and the viewers were also incapable of separating him from Harold. His performance was so believable that he would always be inextricably linked to the part. It was an association that was reinforced every time the BBC repeated the series, which they did, regularly.

In the past he had taken the money from TV and used the time it gave him to support Theatre Workshop, but since its demise there was now no siren call back to Stratford East. Hitting 40, with the new responsibility of a baby on the way, in a business he knew could be fickle and short-lived, he now needed the money himself. But he still gave his time to any cause that asked him. The same week that they buried Sydney, he and Maureen put in an appearance at the Metropolitan Police Flying Squad's Dinner Dance ...

And, of course, he was still supporting the Labour Party. In thanks for past efforts, Harry and Maureen, Ray and Alan and their wives were invited to dine with the PM at the House of Commons. The invitation coincided with that autumn's mounting crisis over Rhodesia, when Prime Minister Ian Smith issued the Unilateral Declaration of Independence. Alan remembers:

> Harold Wilson apologised and said he couldn't make it to the dinner, he was having a conference over the Smith affair in Rhodesia and he'd get there as soon as he could. Mary Wilson, who was there, went berserk because there were thirteen people instead of fourteen. She rushed out into the Commons and grabbed a passing Labour MP and dragged him in to sit down and make fourteen around the table. Then Wilson turned up about half past eleven or midnight saying, 'Oh, I've just been speaking to Mr. Smith about ...' – he was name dropping for us, we couldn't believe it.

Wilson also had work to do on the home front. Having won in 1964 by only four seats, he would soon need to call a general election in the hopes of increasing his majority. In November Henry Solomons, the Labour MP for Hull North, had died, thus prompting a by-election set for January. Depending on the results, Wilson would know whether the time was ripe to call the general and start rolling out the PR bandwagon. On 9 December Wilson invited Harry to Downing Street. After the meeting they joked on the doorstep that No. 10 had no old scrap but did have a touch of dry rot. When asked by the waiting press what they had discussed Harry simply said, 'the North' – where they were both from. Though it's unlikely that Wilson would not have taken the opportunity to make sure they could once again rely on a little touch of Harry on the hustings.

They were joined on the doorstep photo call by George Wigg and Alf Morris, the young MP for Wythenshawe, who had invited Harry to view that afternoon's debate:

> I was the Member of Parliament, that's how I met Harry. He was involved in Wythenshawe, it was part of him and there had never been a Labour MP for Wythenshawe until I was elected in 1964. We were in touch then because he was supporting – in an area where they would have known why they were supporting.
>
> He did help politically. Really speaking, Harry was anxious to use his gift of performing. He didn't have a great deal of time but what he did have he gave. Celebrities were not going out of their way to perform in politics for nothing. He was a very generous person, Wilson loved him.
>
> Harry came and we had lunch in the Commons and we talked about his past and my past and it was quite clear that there were not just parallels in every sense of the word but remarkably close parallels.

Alf Morris was brought up in Ancoats, a stone's throw from Harry's home in Ardwick. His father had been gassed in the trenches during the First World War:

> My memories of my father are of him sitting by the fire, he was very thin, he had a shocking cough. He was waiting to die. He died in 1935. They said they could bury him direct from Nell Lane Hospital, as Southern Cemetery was on the other side of the road, to save on the cost of a proper funeral, as we were so poor – that upset my mother even more.
>
> My mother was told that he hadn't died of war related injuries – he died of heart failure and they said 'sadly', in the word-processed letter of condolence, she didn't qualify for a war pension. Harry Thorneycroft, our member of parliament, pegged away for three years. He came on his pushbike in 1938 and told her: 'You're a War Pensioner.' I was 10, my mother turned to me and said: 'When you're old enough you'll be taking Mr Thorneycroft's leaflets out.' She wasn't in the Labour Party but she knew about leaflets. That's what I did when I was 14. I didn't join the Labour Party, I was volunteered by my mother.

Like Harry, Alf remembered putting his hand up in class for the free school dinner: 'The school I went to had a canteen for those who could pay – we went to the Methodist Hall, 600 yards away, for ours and we had something quite different. We had gruel – you never asked for more.'

Alf had also served in the military, in Palestine. But, unlike Harry, on his return he went on to further education. He studied at Oxford and Manchester Universities and became a teacher before entering politics and breaking his working-class stereotype: 'The assumption was that we were all daft, that people from the under-class were all stupid.'

He also loved *Steptoe* and he and Harry would joke that 'Oil Drum Lane was quite posh compared to Ardwick.' His one regret was that the only time he heard Harry's native Manchester accent was when they were chatting together and would slip into the ver-nacular – they were most probably unintelligible to the rest of the Commons dining room. Though I expect Harry would instantly flip into the London accent when needed. He had a pretty con-vincing one after all – during research I asked one of Harry's old schools if they could dig out some records only to be told: 'Oh no, he couldn't have come here, dear – he was a Cockney.'

Due to his own chronic ailments, Harry was very interested in the legislation that Alf dreamed of passing into law. As a mere back-bencher Alf would have very little chance of getting a bill through the House. But in 1969 he was entered in the Private Members' Ballot. Once a year the Commons holds a lottery and twenty winning mem-bers have the chance to get a bill of their choosing heard. But time is precious, as there are only five hours on thirteen days allocated to hear these bills. First come, first heard. Therefore if you are number twenty your chances are pretty slim. Alf came first in the ballot.

Most Private Members' Bills are anything but. However, Alf managed to fend off the intense pressure to adopt ready-made, fully supported bills that ministers and private lobbyists wanted to push through and stuck to his guns. His Chronically Sick and Disabled Persons Bill passed into law in 1970. It was the first piece of UK legislation to recognise the rights of disabled people.

It also put right the wrongs Alf had seen his mother suffer: 'What the act did was to make it impossible for them to say that anyone who died of a cardiac or thoracic illness, who served in a theatre of war where gas was used as a weapon, hadn't died of war-related injuries.'

The act has been used as a blueprint for similar legislation world-wide, and in 1974 Alf Morris became the first Minister for the Disabled in any country. In 1997 he was created a life peer and still serves in the Upper House. When I showed Alf a photograph of him and Harry with Wilson, the Rt Hon The Lord Morris of Manchester AO QSO remarked: 'Look at us on the steps of 10 Downing Street. How could you not be moved by Harry's gift? I look inconsequential … frivolous.' Yes, there are remarkably close parallels between them, as that is exactly what Harry would have been thinking of his own appearance on the steps of power.

Labour won the Hull North by-election in January of 1966, with Wilson's announcement during the campaign that funds had finally been found to begin work on the Humber Bridge helping enormously. The wind looked fair for the general election.

The same month Harry started work on *Carry on Screaming*, a spoof on the Hammer Horror films. Harry played Detective Sergeant Sidney Bung. Aided by sidekick Peter Butterworth, he has to foil the evil plans of mad Dr Watt (Kenneth Williams), avoid the blows of Mrs Bung (the lovely Joan Sims), while falling for Dr Watt's vamp sister, Fenella Fielding. 'I knew all about Harry H.' remembers Fenella:

> When I was a student everyone was talking about how wonder-ful he was as *Richard II*. I know he was a very fine straight actor. I think he came into *Screaming* in a part written for Sid James who was unavailable. I think the role was a bit of a stretch for him … something different.
>
> Normally when you sit about behind the scenes in the studio you just gossip but Harry just used to talk about his accountant and how inefficient he was, how he had to give him instructions on what to do – and that impressed the hell out of me. Actors always leave that to other people but he was talking very sophis-ticatedly about finances.
>
> He was very sweet to work with. We had a particular scene together where he was so laid back I had to do all the running, so I had a word with the director and we did a retake. It was all very amicable; I liked him very much and admired him.
>
> He got on well with all the regulars. Kenneth Williams himself was very different in *Screaming,* very pleasant and chatty – I do know Kenneth didn't like Sid James so it was probably bliss that Harry was playing that part.

According to Kenneth Williams, he and Harry didn't spend much time talking about finances, far from it: 'We had a newcomer to the team in Harry H. Corbett and when he told me he was suffering from a painful bunion I took off my shoe to show my own malformation. "Cover it up," cried Peter Butterworth. "This is a film set not a surgical ward."'[2]

At the end of February, Wilson called the general election and Harry called Wilfrid. He persuaded Wilf, who was not known for his Labour sympathies, to join him on the hustings in support of Hugh Jenkins, the MP for Putney. Harry had already helped out on Hugh's first successful campaign in 1964. This time around Hugh was receiving the support of such celebrities as Bernard Bresslaw, who had just appeared with Harry in *Carry on Screaming*, Alfie Bass, Harry Fowler, Kenny Lynch, Priscilla Morgan and Clive Dunn. Clive not only drew the picture of Hugh that was used on the campaign posters but also organised a fundraising dance that he remembers Harry coming along to.

All of this made quite an impression on Hugh's young agent, and later long-serving General Secretary of Equity (the actors' union), Ian McGarry:

> Before I joined Equity, I worked for the Labour Party. I lived in Putney and was the election agent for Hugh, who had been Deputy General Secretary of Equity before he was selected as a candidate and before I knew anything about Equity.
>
> I remember Harry coming down to work with us vividly. He came in character from Steptoe. I had to go and hire a horse and cart from some gypsies. We surprised the police a bit when we said there was going to be a cavalcade led by a horse and cart with Harry, Wilf and Hugh.
>
> I'm not sure Wilf was an enthusiastic Labour supporter but Harry had dragged him out, having celebrities was something new in an election campaign then. I always found Harry very chirpy and bloody good fun. Serious about the politics but good company and a good guy to be around.

On 31 March Wilson won the election, increasing his majority to ninety-six seats. Hugh Jenkins was returned to the house, went on to become Arts Minister, lost his seat to David Mellor in 1979 and became a life peer in 1981.

The 1966 general election also gave plenty of ammunition to a new satirical programme that launched on 1 March, *The Frost Report*. Fronted by David Frost, its roll call of writers included old hands Keith Waterhouse, Frank Muir, Denis Norden, Barry Cryer and up-and-coming talents Tim Brooke Taylor and Bill Oddie, along with every future member of Monty Python apart from Terry Gilliam. In the cast, and now on the road to fame, were John Cleese; stars of *The Two Ronnies*, Barker and Corbett; Nicky Henson and Sheila Steafel.

Sheila had finally got the success she had wanted, but soon found that fame was not all it was cracked up to be. Later that year she would tell the papers: 'I'd like to have children. That must be smashing. Even for a career, it wasn't worth it you know – breaking up and ending a marriage, I mean.'[3]

Harry and Maureen's marriage was still on hold, waiting for Maureen's divorce. With the baby's imminent arrival and Harry's old-fashioned views, they took matters into their own hands and changed her named to Corbett by deed poll, as Maureen's career came to an end. Her last engagement was to do the looping for *The Great St Trinian's Train Robbery*. Looping is recording a clean soundtrack of your lines during post-production. During the filming, playing Frankie Howerd's sexy sixth-former daughter, Maureen had been camping about in mini gymslip and fishnets. When, a few short months later, she turned up to the looping heavily pregnant, chins hit the floor. The cheesecake had, in fact, been a mother-to-be. Mind you, it didn't stop them asking her to also dub over many of the other parts; most of the girls you hear in the film are actually Maureen.

Maureen was under the care of consultant obstetrician Jack Suchet, father of journalist John and actor David. He had taken one look at her diminutive frame and recommended a caesarean. A good call, as the baby turned out to be breech. Before the operation, on the morning of 5 April, Suchet turned the baby to avoid the small chance of birth injuries a breech caesarean can bring. But the little bugger flipped back the wrong way before he had made it to the door. The baby, a boy, emerged unscathed, but Maureen had a reaction to the anaesthetic and caused many a sweaty palm for Harry, Pat, Malcolm and the anaesthetist as she proved extremely difficult to wake up. When she was finally recovered, she and Harry decided on the name Jonathan before visiting hours at the London clinic ended and Harry got chucked out. He went off to Soho to do a spot of celebrating.

The next day he arrived, bleary eyed, to find Maureen surrounded by congratulations telegrams. 'Who the bloody hell's Jason?' she asked him. Harry had done so much celebrating that by the end of the night he'd got Jonathan's name wrong. He knew it began with a J ...

Jonathan's middle name is Desmond, after Desmond Brayley. The new family would holiday with Brayley aboard his yacht in Tunis later that year. But Brayley never stood as godfather. Although Harry would have liked his children to be christened, Maureen didn't agree, believing that we should be left to make our own decision on the matter when we were old enough to understand it.

Brayley would always stay true to his raffish description. In 1970 when Wilson was booted out of 10 Downing Street, Brayley gave him the use of his Piccadilly apartment and chauffeured car. Wilson nominated him for a knighthood and Sir Desmond was later created a life peer as Baron Brayley of the City of Cardiff in 1974. The same year Wilson returned as PM and Lord Brayley became Under Secretary of State for the Army, selling his shares for over £1,000,000 in the Canning Town glass factory and resigning as chairman of the company to take up the office; an office he was to hold for only a few months as questions were asked about payments he had received while at the factory. Faced with a government inquiry Brayley handed Wilson his resignation. 'He was indicted for plotting to defraud the company, stealing from company funds and falsifying petty cash vouchers.'[4] However, no evidence was found and nothing was proved against him as he died in 1977 before the trial came to court.

Back in 1966, three weeks after Jon's birth, Harry and Maureen were once more dining at the Commons with George Wigg and the PM. Soon afterwards the couple headed north to Manchester, leaving Jon in the care of Pat. Since Sydney's death, Pat had naturally become a fixture in the Corbett household. She was still working as a school cook; she needed to, as Sydney hadn't lived long enough to be entitled to the British Rail pension (those years on active service had made the difference) so money was tight. Asking Pat to look after Jon was one way that Harry and Maureen could slip her some cash while everybody saved face. Given the amount of functions Harry and Maureen were asked to attend they would come to rely on her more and more. Eventually she was persuaded to leave the school and start 'working' for them alone. Harry adored her and she thought the world of him. To Jon and me she became a second mother.

Harry's visit to Manchester gave him a chance to see his own second mother. He and Maureen had headed north for the *Eamonn Andrews Show*, which was being recorded there, instead of London, to celebrate ten years of ABC. A fellow guest was Billie Whitelaw. Harry was a frequent guest on the chat show, but never on Eamonn's later show *This is Your Life*. Though not for the want of trying. The production office would ring Maureen and, in hushed conspiratorial tones, ask for her help in setting Harry up for the 'honour'. She would then call out to him, 'It's *This is Your Life*, do you want to do it?' and he would shout back: 'No, tell them to fuck off.' Having made sure they heard him she would then sweetly tell them, 'Oh, I'm so sorry, he's not interested. Goodbye.' For some reason they stopped calling after a while …

After they'd finished the recording of Eamonn's show, Harry and Maureen were getting into their car when a man tapped on the window. Harry let him in and they chatted for a while as they drove through Manchester city centre. A few minutes later the man asked to be dropped off and disappeared into the night. Maureen turned to Harry and asked, 'Who was that?' He replied, 'That was my brother.'

It must have been James. It came as a bit of an eye opener to Maureen, who was very close to her own brother, but circumstances and the fourteen-year age gap had meant the brothers were never close. James had, after all, enlisted in Bombay the year Harry was born and spent many years serving abroad. James' son Peter remembers Harry knocking on their door out of the blue in the early 1950s. It's the only time he remembers him coming to the house. Later on, Peter found programmes of Harry's shows signed by all the cast that James had been to see. James would die of a heart attack the following year in 1967, like their father, Sgt George, and eldest brother, Albert. He was 55.

Harry didn't go to see Annie. He wanted to, but on a previous visit she hadn't known who he was. 'It's me, Harry,' he'd said. 'You're not my Harry. You're not my little Harry Boy,' she insisted, before shutting the door on him. It was less upsetting for them both if he kept his visits to a minimum. Cynthia, Harry's niece, remembers that Annie had become more eccentric. She lived off oranges and chocolate and slept downstairs on a chaise longue. The upstairs was taken over by moths. Harry sent money and wished he could move her into a nicer place but she would have none of it. He realised that she needed the familiar to reinforce those rare occasions when she surfaced for long enough to recognise that Harry was grown and now had a family of his own:

> Today she still thinks of me as this little lad running home with his pay packet,' he would later say, 'She's 84 years of age, a proud woman who refuses help. I could set her up in a nice little house in the suburbs – but she is content with her old place. She refuses any financial assistance.
>
> I have to resort to dodges that even Harold Steptoe couldn't think of to make sure she doesn't want for anything.[5]

To make sure of that Harry made a will, leaving his estate to Maureen, who was asked to provide for Annie's care, and to Jonathan and 'any further issue' – me. I would sometimes sign myself as such on his birthday cards.

Back in London, Harry did another *Comedy Playhouse* production, 'The Seven Year Hitch'. 'One of the main reasons,' he said, 'was to work with Joan Sims again.' They played Londoners Ernest and Isobel Conway – husband and wife ballroom dancing teachers. During publicity for the show Harry was asked if *Steptoe* would be coming back, and he confirmed that he and Wilf were booked to do Ken Dodd's TV show from Blackpool later that summer, with Duncan Wood producing, 'But another series? There's no indication just yet. If another were written I expect I wouldn't say no to it.'

He was also asked if he was finding the *Steptoe* image hard to lose:

> The only way I can do it is to play a Hungarian peasant or an American gangster. But immediately I'm cast in a play that's set in London, there an automatic connection with Cockneys and *Steptoe*. Even though the Comedy Playhouse story has an entirely different setting and plot, no doubt viewers will think of young 'Arold when they see me in it.

Something he was not overly concerned with:

> As an actor there is at least 75 per cent of you in any part you play that cannot be eradicated or eliminated. Only in the theatre can

this happen because the audience is far enough away not to spot the small shadow movements that are basic to every person … Consequently I can assure you that I was never, at any time in my life, faced with the fact: God I must make this different, I really must make this different at all costs. I wouldn't have cared if they all came out like Harold Steptoe vocally or any other way, if it suited the character …[6]

Harry's next job, perhaps with a nod to his new-found father-hood, was for *Jackanory* – a children's story-telling programme. The producers were livening up the series by using well-known TV personalities to tell the stories and the stories themselves were now a bit more exciting than what had gone before, as Harry noted: 'At a time when kids of six get nicked for driving their dad's tractor, you can't give them Noddy in Toyland anymore.'[7]

All of his stories were of men and horses. *Pegasus the Winged Horse* saw him drop into the studio in parachute gear (Pegasus was then the Parachute Regiment's emblem) before changing into ancient Greek dress.

This was no gorblimy version of the ancient Greek legend but a tale beautifully told by an actor who might never have been within hundreds of miles of a Cockney junk yard for all the traces his accent bore of the 'Oh my Gawd' dialect we are accus-tomed to hearing from young Steptoe. So completely different was he in his role of storyteller that every last trace of Steptoe had vanished. His appearance, his manner, and voice were those of an ancient Greek prince rather than a modern rag-and-bone man with an eye for the birds.[8]

When asked about the programme, Harry had said:

I've no kids of my own but there were toddlers around the family when I was growing up. I always seemed to be pushing a pram. The thing about entertaining kids is that you must never con them. When I did my Red Indian story dressed up as an Apache that was real Indian sign language that I used. I got books from the research people and learned a few signs. I've always been crazy about Redskins and now I want to get the books again and really learn sign language.[9]

Harry had not admitted to having Jon because he was a private man and did not want his family to be followed around by the press. Also, perhaps he was a little worried that his children would carry the stigma of being born on the wrong side of the blanket. He needn't have been. I remember taking a perverse pride in being born a bastard and feeling quite let down when I found out my parents were married.

To keep their private lives just that, Maureen would, when answering the phone to a journalist, pretend to be a foreign house-keeper, doing a nice line in variations on: 'He not here – you call later.' Nice to know those years at RADA hadn't been wasted – she kept it up, even after there was no need, just for the crack.

And then the Steptoes came back – but on radio. The idea of adapting the existing television scripts for radio had been put forward during the previous summer of 1965 by Gale Pedrick, the man who had first called in Galton and Simpson to work for the BBC. After the fourth television series of *Steptoe* was broadcast, its high ratings gave a green light to production of the radio series. It began recording in February 1966, while Harry was working on *Carry on Screaming*, and started, as the television series had, with 'The Offer', recorded on the 6th. In all, thirteen episodes were recorded over six weeks (two episodes on consecutive Sundays and three episodes on the final Saturday). They were presented in costume in front of a live audience. The programmes had been kept in the can until the summer and were broadcast on Sunday evenings between July and September.

The successful transition to a different medium was produced by Bobby Jaye and the scripts were adapted, before Ray and Alan took over, by Gale Pedrick, who wrote that Harry was:

> the kind of man who would never approach the creation of a character without enormous concentration.
>
> Watching him at rehearsal, as I have done so often, I have been greatly impressed by what seems to be a compulsive necessity to master the characterisation to the last inflection.
>
> He is not an easy man to know, but once the brittle stage of mere acquaintance has changed to understanding, the honesty of the man shines through.[10]

In July, while the broadcast of the radio series was underway, the Steptoes returned to television in the one-off sketch written by

Ray and Alan for the *Ken Dodd Show*. In a reminder of Harry's early
television career, the programme was recorded live and saw Albert
and Harold sunning themselves in deckchairs on Blackpool beach.
They had made the journey to the seaside by horse and cart, causing a 31-mile tailback on the M1.

While in Blackpool, another insight into Harry's character came
during a publicity interview for the show:

> It is quite an admission to say that one's whole life is an act. But
> this, it seems, is the real Harry H. Corbett, younger member of
> the Steptoe and Son duo. 'I am not at all gregarious.' He said
> simply, 'When I'm with people I have to act. Nothing I say or do
> seems real.' ... Harry talks casually but he is a shy man, and one
> gets the impression that his acting saves embarrassment.[11]

After Blackpool, the family tried to get down to Benenden as often
as possible. In their absence Tom Short, who had been a dresser on
one of Harry's shows, looked after the place. The cottage afforded
more room than the London flat for family and friends to stay and
enjoy the new baby. Maurice Woodruff and his life partner Harry
Arnold were regular guests. Jon had been born with red hair, the
exact same shade as the Benenden butcher's delivery boy. When the
lad called, Maureen would chat on the doorstep while trying to
keep a straight face as she could see Harry, hiding round the corner,
mugging and shaking his fist at the kid.

Maureen's own domestic theatrical displays were always more
effective. Harry's upbringing had not prepared him for the role of
'new man' and Jon was not an easy baby. After several months of his
incessant crying and no sign of Harry at the 3 a.m. feed, Maureen
snapped. Harry woke one night to find her standing over him with
a knife, calmly informing him that his son was crying and what
did he intend doing about it. Harry got a lot better after that and
started pulling his weight.

In September the BBC once more repeated the *Steptoe* episodes
on television. Ray and Alan were asked, yet again, about the possibility of a new series and said, yet again, there would be no more,
despite the repeats being in the top twenty of the ratings. Harry,
meanwhile, was at work on his own project. That autumn, as the
family prepared to move into a new London flat in St John's Wood,
his weekends were spent opening fêtes and his weeks were spent

working for his recently set-up production company on a vehicle for ITV.

This new vehicle was *Mr Aitch*. The series would see Harry playing a London wide boy who funds his lavish lifestyle from the profits of a car park. The scriptwriters were Ian La Frenais and Dick Clement, fresh from their breakthrough success with *The Likely Lads*. Regular cast consisted of Gordon Gostelow and Norman Chappell, the latter becoming a close friend. As this was Harry's own production he was heavily involved in its creation. So was Maureen; she became unofficial casting director.

During pre-publicity a reporter commented:

> This Rangoon-born former timber stacker and plumber's mate is a master of that rapidly disappearing art, real conversation. He's an erudite raconteur, a thinker, a creator, an observer, a constant seeker after facts and perfection. A serious person. A clown.
>
> Describing him is like squeezing a coconut into a walnut shell … At the moment he's helping to sponsor what is temporarily known as the Corbett Theatre, a theatrical school being built out of a 14th century tithe barn in Essex. 'But,' he added, 'I'm fighting like mad to have the name changed. I mean, I might not be well known when it's finished.'[12]

Indeed he might not. It was an incredibly difficult move from one successful series to another, something that would apply to both Harry, Clement and La Frenais. And the more successful the original breakthrough, the harder it would be. But the series started very well. It reached number three in the ratings (the highest rated comedy show) and was being well received by the public, but not most of the major press. It was likened to *Steptoe* and, naturally, came up short.

Harry was even being likened to Steptoe during the recording of *Mr Aitch*. Barry Cryer, who was working on the show, remembers:

> When I was doing the warm up he said to me, 'Just introduce me to the audience, don't mention *Steptoe*. They'll know.' So I went ok, and said 'Ladies and Gentlemen, the star of our show, Harry H. Corbett …' and the loud speakers went da, da, da, di, da – the *Steptoe* theme. The look on Harry's face. They'd not told him. He didn't talk much about it but now and then there would be the odd remark about being haunted by *Steptoe*.

But that was tempered by his continued appearances in the role. In January 1967 he did a turn in full *Steptoe* gear at a charity gala in Sunderland in aid of the Doxford disaster. The same show had seen him do a ventriloquist act with Wee Georgie Wood as the dummy – a taste of the variety world he adored. And soon after *Mr Aitch* started airing he had said: 'My philosophy has always been the same. I will go out there and work but I never worry about an audience's reaction. If they like me, good. If they don't, well I've done my best. I certainly won't lose any sleep if they don't.' And even though he had his own new show he was not anti Harold: 'I would do another Steptoe series, but that all depends on the writers.'[13]

However, the return of the Steptoes was still looking unlikely, as he admitted a month later: 'They served their time. I think their time has run out. But again this is only my thinking, if it's possible to write more, I'm sure the authors will write them; they don't particularly wish to, themselves. Of course, they are the main inspiration for the Steptoes, so I can't really speak for them.'[14]

But he would have a chance to ask them. After the first few episodes of *Mr Aitch* went out the show was reshuffled. ATV's *Sportsweek* started and to beat the BBC competition would need a prime slot. It was given the number-one rated *Take Your Pick*'s slot on Friday at 7 p.m. *Take Your Pick* was, in turn, moved into *Mr Aitch*'s spot on Fridays at 8.25 p.m. and *Mr Aitch* was sent to Tuesdays at 11.05 p.m. This was a graveyard position that saw it slip down from its number three rating. To give the flagging figures a boost Harry called on Ray and Alan:

'He was doing *Mr Aitch* with a friend of mine called Alan Blakemore,' said Ray:

> Alan was a very unlikely property dealer, very funny, very eccentric man who was in partnership with an ex-boxer called John Arrow. The three of them were involved in *Mr Aitch*. We were approached to write it, we were just about to leave for America but because it was Harry we said all right, we'd do four episodes. It did come up and we made it much better, and we said to them promise you won't do any more – but they couldn't resist.

In keeping with the friends and family theme, Malcolm, Maureen's brother, was drafted in to help on one occasion:

There was this line where they had scripted they were buying shares from a company but they couldn't use the name because the company existed. My fiancé, Jennie, and I had turned up for the filming and Harry said 'Do you mind if I use your name?' So Mr Aitch ended up buying shares in 'M. Blott and Blakemore'.

After Ray and Alan left for the States, Clement and La Frenais returned and old friend John Junkin wrote an episode entitled 'A Star is Born' where Mr Aitch gets bitten by the acting bug (Ray and Alan would do their own version of this, including the title, in a later *Steptoe* episode). Given its rocky ride it was not surprising that the series didn't return. Two days after the last episode was shown, Harry started work on recording the second *Steptoe* series for radio.

Once again, Ray and Alan's existing television scripts were recycled, with Gale Pedrick making any alterations required for radio. A number of actors reprised their roles from the television series, including Robert Dorning in 'The Siege of Steptoe Street', Dudley Foster in 'My Old Man's a Tory' and Derek Nimmo in 'Crossed Swords'. In 'The Piano', Alan Simpson got in on the act, making a cameo appearance as the policeman.

It had been a busy spring, as Harry was also back campaigning for Labour. He had opened the new Dudley Labour Club in George Wigg's constituency, spoken at the Brierley Hill by-election and Harold Wilson had written to thank him for his efforts during the Greater London Council election. Unsurprisingly Labour had faired badly, as the elections coincided with the devaluation of the pound.

Summer saw the family in Benenden again and adding to the household. They bought a Labrador and named her Judy. To this day I can't think of that dog without seeing Harry play wrestling with her on the carpet (a regular occurrence as Harry's favoured telly watching position was lying on the floor, head resting on left hand, right flicking ash from ever-present fag – you could tell what he thought of the programme by the amount of noise he got out of the dog). It was a welcome interlude before he was back in rehearsals once more.

Fill the Stage with Happy Hours, a Charles Wood play about fading actors running a theatre, was due to open at the Royal Court on 6 September. It would follow an unlicensed satirical show called *America Hurrah* that was transferring to the Vaudeville. The Royal

Court, as a private members club, had not needed a licence, but the Lord Chamberlain threatened to prosecute the Vaudeville if the production went ahead there. So at the last minute, *Fill the Stage* was sent into the West End and *America Hurrah* remained at the Court.

> William Gaskill, director of the English Stage Company, said that the decision to exchange theatres would involve them in expense and inconvenience, but they did not expect to lose money.
>
> The *Fill The Stage* cast, which includes Hilda Baker and Harry H. Corbett, had agreed to play at the Vaudeville for the salaries they would have got at the Royal Court. 'A quarter or a fifth of the normal West End salary,' Mr Gaskill said.
>
> He described the decision as a: 'Necessary gesture of solidarity between theatre workers on both sides of the Atlantic.'[15]

Ray and Alan sent Harry a telegram saying: 'What a sneaky way of getting into the West End.'

A fellow cast member was Sheila Hancock:

> I can't pretend that I was ever Harry's closest friend. I found him quite edgy. Mind you, ours was a funny situation due to the censorship problem with *American Hurrah*. As a result we were poked into the Vaudeville. It meant that we were in the West End with a very odd cast of comedy people, i.e. dare I say, myself, who at that time was doing an awful lot of sitcoms, Harry, who was thought of as a sitcom person, there was Hilda Baker – an extraordinary cast but what we were doing was a very Royal Court show. It was a beautiful play but absolutely not one that people who knew us from television would have wanted to see, particularly. So it was a very strange event. A West End audience with that cast list would have expected a rip-roaring farce and they didn't get that. So it wasn't really a happy occasion. As it happened it turned out to be a very happy occasion for me because I made four women friends at that time. We all went on to read *The Female Eunuch*. We formed a women's group and as so often happens when you're in a flop you become very close.
>
> I didn't really have any great rapport with Harry. I admired him hugely but I always felt there was something sad – I think he was unhappy in the show quite honestly. It was disconcerting for all of us.

We all, I think, when we took the play, hoped that it would help us prove to people that we could do something else other than telly, that we could do a play at the Royal Court. Very often the theatre critics are very snooty about people who come from telly to theatre. Even when you've got a huge theatrical record behind you, they regard you as a telly actor. We all had it. My husband had the same thing with 'Morse' and it certainly took me a long time to shake off the titty blond 'Rag Trade' image. It's easier today but even for David Tennant, who had a big theatre past, it was 'Dr Who plays Hamlet'.

Harry's early career with Joan was so remarkable. They were pioneers, that company, I always maintain that Joan Littlewood broke down the working-class barriers much more than the Royal Court did, and before the Royal Court, with people like Harry. In the big Binkie Beaumont world of theatre he would never have been cast in the roles that Joan cast him in. His reputation was huge. Long before Theatre Workshop came down to Stratford East one had heard about this amazing actor Harry Corbett. But, equally, *Steptoe* was a highly regarded sitcom. I thought the series was absolutely wonderful. It was such a definitive character, for both of them. Wilf was the same. Wilf was a sad creature. I thought he was a lovely man. Of course he was gay at a time when it was illegal. For men like him, in that period, it was such a difficult life. I think he suffered terribly as a result of that.

Harry did get on very well with Hilda Baker. I remember him being very respectful towards her. They seemed to have a really great rapport. But he just used to keep himself to himself. Looking back I think he may have been a bit daunted by the band of women in that show because we were very into women's liberation. We were militantly feminist which must have been incredibly difficult for the likes of Harry, perhaps that's why we didn't gel or perhaps he was like John [Thaw]. When I was interviewing people about John there were several who said he was standoffish. But, in fact, he wasn't, it was the fact that he had his nose in the bloody script all the time and didn't enjoy chit chat on set, he wasn't that sort of man.[16]

Harry may have been unprepared for, and come late to, feminism, but he learnt, sometimes the hard way. Although Harry's style was

to invite friends from princes to bouncers back home for an equal-
ising bacon sandwich after an evening in Soho, he and Maureen
would occasionally hold dinner parties, and even more rarely Harry
would invite a business acquaintance to dinner. On one occasion,
after Maureen had spent most of the day in the kitchen, she and
Harry sat down with a man intent on making an impression. When
he, trying to be funny, made some derogatory remarks about the
food, Harry, trying to be pally, joined in. Without a word Maureen
collected the plates, scraped the food into the waste disposal, flicked
on the switch and left the room. As Harry sat listening to the grinding coming from the sink he must have known the times they
weren't a- changing – they had changed.

After *Fill the Stage* closed they were set to change again. Maureen
was pregnant; a pregnancy that would cause concern. Maureen's
blood group was O rhesus negative, Harry's O positive. A combination that can cause an incompatibility between mother and foetus
and result in RhD hemolytic disease of the newborn. During
delivery the child's 'positive' blood can come into contact with the
mother's 'negative' blood and the mother's body will see such blood
as a foreign intruder and fight it off with antibodies, as it would any
'disease'. This is not usually a problem on a first delivery but for
subsequent pregnancies the antibodies created during the first birth
will recognise another foetus's positive blood and seek to eliminate
it. This can cause the baby anything from mild jaundice to severe
anaemia, miscarriage and stillbirth. These days mothers are given
a dose of anti-D to stop antibodies being formed and protect the
child. But anti-D was not an option for Maureen, it would only be
licensed a few weeks after her due date – the family would just have
to wait and see.

In anticipation of the new arrival, Maureen and Harry started
house hunting. Their flat was rather inconvenient. There was
nowhere for Pat to stay over for babysitting duties, meaning frequent trips out to Greenford with a boot full of baby gear. Gear
that included a tank-like Silver Cross coach built pram. In the days
before buggies these prams were marvellously comfortable for the
baby and able to withstand a missile strike, but impossible to get up
the stairs to a flat. A flat that was equally impossible to enter, as the
new dog, when left alone, would rip up the hall carpet, jamming it
behind the door. If the dog and baby went out together Maureen
either had to steer the pram one-handed while being dragged along

by the dog's lead or tie the lead to the pram and watch it bounce sideways down St John's Wood High Street.

So a move was definitely on the cards, but not, as rumour had it, to Dudley. In November of 1967 Harry's friend and the MP for Dudley, George Wigg, was retiring from parliament and was set to become chairman of the Horserace Betting Levy Board.

> Since the rumour of Mr Wigg's retirement, political leaders in the division have suggested the comedian Harry H. Corbett of Steptoe and Son as a possible Labour contender.
>
> He has spoken for Mr. Wigg at the last two general elections and this year opened Dudley's new Labour club.
>
> Mr Williams (The Conservative candidate) is treating his possible opponent seriously. 'Mr. Corbett has made his views known before,' he said. 'He has supported Mr. Wigg and, I think, other candidates. I'm certainly not dismissing this as farcical.'
>
> But Mr. Williams is disappointed that he will not be having another crack at Mr. Wigg. 'I enjoyed fighting a strong man. It has always been more satisfying than fighting a weak one.'[17]

Harry did find it farcical, however:

> Me? Stand for parliament? You really must be joking. In the first place Col. Wigg hasn't been offered the new job yet. And I can say that in no circumstances would I think of contesting the seat if it did become vacant. A parliamentary candidate calls for someone local, who knows the place, the people, the problems. That is what impressed me most last time I was in the Birmingham area helping Col. Wigg.
>
> In any case, my main aim when I was working there during the last election was to try to persuade people to vote.[18]

George Wigg did become chairman of the Levy Board. He also served in the House of Lords as Baron Wigg of the Borough of Dudley. He died in 1983. Donald Williams, Harry's would-be Conservative opponent, won the by-election. Two years later he was voted out. He never returned to the Commons but became a county councillor. And Harry? He went back to *Steptoe*.

Ray and Alan had recently returned from the States. Their visit had not been a rip-roaring success; they had gone to oversee an

American version of *Steptoe* for the production company Screen
Gems and after taking four hours to 'Americanise' one of the
scripts, spent weeks loafing by a Hollywood pool waiting for the
production to start. Despite interest from Mickey Rooney and Jack
Benny as casting for Harold and Albert, getting the ball rolling was
proving to be a problem, as Ray remembers:

> They just couldn't make up their minds where to set it, where
> it wouldn't cause offence. If you put it in New York they'd say it
> was Jewish, if we put it in Boston it's going to be Irish and if we
> put it in Chicago it would be Italian and we thought 'Oh God!
> How many ...?' We said 'Why don't you make it black?' – and
> there was a big intake of breath. 'Oh, we daren't!' They couldn't
> dare put black people into such a terrible low profession. If you
> wanted to portray black people on American TV they had to
> be doctors or lawyers. Nothing was ever decided, so after two
> months waiting by the pool we came home.

During their absence the new adaptations of *Steptoe* on radio and the
regular repeats on television throughout the latter half of 1967 had
made the series as popular as ever. But Ray and Alan had no intention of writing a new series, and even if they had wanted to, they
were too busy writing with great success for Frankie Howerd. They
were, however, easily persuaded to reunite with Harry and Wilf for a
swansong sketch to be aired during *Christmas Night with the Stars* on
25 December. The sketch, recorded on 20 November, saw the boys
being arrested for being 'Brahms and Liszt in charge of a horse
drawn vehicle'. They return home on Christmas night to discover
that their dinner has been burnt to a crisp. After exclaiming he
has had happier times in a graveyard, Harold knocks himself out
with sleeping pills, and so misses the surprise party that turns up
moments later. The sketch proved to be the hit of the night and was
a fitting send-off for the *Steptoe* saga. Following its success the BBC
once more dangled a 'substantial cash offer' in front of the boys to
get another series – but they weren't biting.

Harry closed 1967 by releasing a novelty single *Flower Power Fred*
and opened 1968 by doing a guest turn on *Cilla* – Cilla Black's first
foray into hosting a TV show. Fellow guests were Tom Jones, Jimmy
Edwards and Roy Castle. Harry's contribution was a solo variety act.
'Those who thought Harry H. Corbett was just the dirty old son of

that dirty old man Steptoe must have been surprised to see his act. It was great. If losing the Steptoe series means we are to see more of Harry in "Cabaret" then I am all for it,' one critic gushed. However, the wonderfully acerbic Julian Critchley – an ex-Conservative MP who was spending his time as a TV critic while waiting for another chance to get back into the House – was 'disappointed by Harry H. Corbett whom I do not remember having seen before without Wilfrid Brambell.' An unusual admission from a TV critic.

Cilla, herself, was deemed by some to be a tad bland to host a fifty-minute show but, as her career will testify, most, including Harry, found her to be charming and unpretentious. Harry's young son would attest to that when she later came to the house. By that time Jon was a toddler and addicted to the children's programme *Tingha and Tucker*. His favourite song from the show was *The Wibbly Wobbly Way*, which was so much a favourite that he wouldn't go up to bed without it. Cilla was willingly press-ganged into singing it with him up three flights of stairs.

By February, Harry was back with *Armchair Theatre* recording 'A Second Look'. 'I play the part of a man left in charge of his boss's Rolls Royce. So he drives round to impress his mates and an old girlfriend'[19] – played by Nyree Dawn Porter of *The Forsyte Saga* fame. Barry Norman, the film critic, wrote: 'This character was nothing more nor less than Harold Steptoe in another hat, and though Mr. Corbett, naturally, played it very well, I'm not sure he was wise to play it at all. He's much too good an actor to get himself typed at this stage, and it would have been nice to see him in doing something entirely different.'[20] And, illustrating Harry's 'bum's on seats' mentality to the reception of his work, another critic commented: 'Harry H. Corbett showed that he hasn't been typecast by his Harold Steptoe role.'[21]

By March of 1968 Maureen and Harry had found a replacement for the flat by way of a house in Circus Road, St John's Wood. Or rather Ray Galton's eccentric property-dealing friend Alan Blakemore had found it. 'Alan Blakemore found the house for Harry,' Ray remembered, 'Alan had wild ideas that this would be a place for Harry to entertain and be in the centre of things. He thought that's how show business worked – Harry didn't of course and I don't think Maureen was at all interested in that kind of existence.' No, she wasn't and neither was Harry. That's what Soho was for. The house was purely domestic, as Harry later told:

I decided five years ago to spend every penny I had on leas-
ing one of the most beautiful houses in London – so I haven't
a penny left over for anything else. It costs us a fortune to live
in it, so why go out of the bloody thing. It's an old Georgian
house in St John's Wood – Paul McCartney's down the road –
and after furnishing it we don't have the money to flit away on
going out; I would say I'm very practical – my wife would say
I'm impractical. Before we got this house we were in a flat with
two bedrooms and a kitchen 6ft by 4ft. Jonathan was in nappies
– you could hardly get in the kitchen for nappies – there was no
room for a washing machine and Susannah was expected at any
moment. 'This is the bloody end' I said, 'We're going to have five
glorious years, girl' and I went out and fell in love with the best
possible house I could find. It has a kitchen 20ft by 30ft, deep
freeze, dishwashing machine, six bedrooms, central heating and
a garden for the children. I'm capable of doing this – one week
there's bread and butter, the next – champagne and caviar.[22]

I was born on 16 April at the London Wellbeck Hospital.
Unsurprisingly, it was by another planned caesarean – but that was
still a fairly unusual occurrence back then. Maureen remembered
sitting in the hairdressers and being asked when it was due: 'Next
Tuesday at 9 o'clock,' she answered to raised eyebrows. This time
the telegrams would get the name right as Harry was a little too
concerned to find out what RhD disease could have done to me
for wild celebrating. Maureen was once again under the care of
Jack Suchet and the same anaesthetist, who, on the morning of the
op, popped his head round the door to say, 'Ah, Mrs. Corbett …
I remember you.' Considering that the first time they'd met she
didn't look like she was going to wake up, I bet he did. This time,
to be safe, he only gave her a whiff of the good stuff – and she
woke up on the table. Feeling a breeze in the belly and starting
to gag on the tube she began kicking. Last thing she heard was a
nurse screaming, 'Oh my God, look at her leg, she's coming round!'
before she mercifully went under again.

I emerged looking like a 'skinned rabbit' according to one of
the midwives. My pallor was alarming enough to trigger concerns
of jaundice and anaemia and I was whisked off under the lights.
Whether I actually had need of any transfusions, Maureen could
not later ascertain. The staff were equally as shiftily reticent about

confirming her mid-op wake up, despite the bruising to her mouth that fighting the tube had caused.

Though they didn't know it at the time, any risk of RhD disease to me would have been very slight and brought on only by my own positive blood. Jonathan had turned out to be rhesus negative and thus had slipped by unnoticed. But I definitely queered the pitch for any following me. My 'jaundice and anaemia' could well have been down to inheriting Harry's sallow complexion.

Maureen, delighted that I was out of the woods, celebrated by shaving her legs in the bathroom sink – much to the admonition of the nursing staff. The next day she woke up and left all her hair on the pillow. I'd taken a lot out of her. In any other century she would probably never have made it past Jon's birth. She went to recover at a clinic while Jon and I were sent to Pat in Greenford, as Harry was working on the BBC play *The Fall of Kevin Walker*.

The play also starred Corin Redgrave and Judy Cornwell. Redgrave played a penniless Scot who comes to London to prove that anyone can get a well-paid job. He stays with bohemian artists, Harry and Judy, and is soon offered a job by the BBC as an interviewer. With an eye to the future, Harry commented, 'I've got this marvellous vision of the BBC gradually employing everyone in London, so that there'll only be one celebrity left – the only viewer, and he'll be interviewed every week.'[23]

Maureen was out of the clinic after a couple of weeks and Harry took a few months off work for domestic duties as, in June, the family moved into Circus Road. By now Harry had become so much the model new father that he had, on occasion, to be reined in. In those days babies didn't get lightweight disposable nappies – the terry nappy was half a sheet of towelling overlaid with plastic knickers. In order to stand upright with a full load a baby developed thighs that could crack walnuts. Harry, convinced that the necessarily tight-legged knickers were cutting off the circulation, was forever attacking them with scissors. Maureen would check on baby to find the knicker elastic in shreds and the latest development trickling down our legs. Eyeing another suspicious damp patch while the retreating Harry grumbled, 'Their legs were going white, Mo', it must have crossed her mind that it would be a relief when he went back to work.

Having a Beatle down the road might have afforded visiting adults a certain cachet, compounded by the family joke that Paul

McCartney had the idea for that summer's number one hit, *Hey Jude*, from the shouts at Judy, our Labrador, drifting over the fence; but it cut no ice with us kids. However, Mrs McCartney (childhood habit means I still find it odd to refer to her as Linda) was the epitome of cool. Not only did she have the exterior ornamental cornice of their house painted in multicoloured pastel hues that looked like a mini South Beach (rumour had it she did it to piss off an uptight neighbour), but she kept a horse in the back garden. I can remember watching, green eyed, as she led her kids up and down the street. The McCartneys garden must have had wonderful roses. Of course, horses were not an uncommon sight. The King's Troupe, Royal Horse Artillery has barracks in St John's Wood. Nearly every day you could see them trot by from the bedroom windows. And, yes indeed, there were regular visits from the rag-and-bone man. I don't think Maureen ever mentioned to him that Harry was in a similar line of work but the irony of the situation did not escape any of us.

Although Pat now had her own room for babysitting duties there was one bugger about moving to a house – the easy access it afforded paparazzi, who would scale the high wall trying to get a photo of young Steptoe. After finding one in the garden, Harry freaked, as any father of two small children would. He put a fence on the top of the wall round the back garden and, due to planning restrictions, had to settle for broken bottles set into the top of the wall round the front – which must have come as a bit of an eye-opener for the next pap who tried it.

On 17 June, Maureen's divorce finally came through. It would be made absolute the following month. In anticipation Harry and Maureen made an appointment at the local Marylebone Registry Office for their marriage to take place over a year later on Tuesday 2 September 1969 at 10 a.m.

With a future wedding booked, Harry would have a chance to reflect on one that never was when he took part in a royal gala in aid of the Cinema and Television Benevolent Fund, which was recorded on 22 July. Avis was also taking part. She was appearing in an excerpt from *Fiddler on the Roof*. Wilfrid, too, was on the bill – but not with Harry. Wilf was among the cast of *The Canterbury Tales*, a hit musical running at the Phoenix Theatre.

Harry took the rest of the summer off – well, apart from functions and charity gigs – and real work started again that September.

He appeared in a TV play, *The House that Jigger Built*, and started filming *Crooks and Coronets* with Telly Savalas, Edith Evans, Nicky Henson, Warren Oates and Cesar Romero – Frank Thornton and Clive Dunn also appeared. As he was coming to the end of shooting he heard that Annie had been taken ill.

Freddie remembers: 'Harry went up and looked after his aunt when she was dying. He would just disappear. He stayed with her and looked after her. He had the most quiet way of looking after people he cared about that I've ever seen in anybody. He never shouted about it. He never told anybody. He just disappeared.'

Harry never kept a diary – he wasn't overtly interested in himself – but I did find some scribbled notes that he made during Annie's last illness as she babbled of green fields. Perhaps he was trying to guarantee that he'd remember her in case Madeleine moments were few and far between:

When you're old you have time to think … what about our Jim and our Albert? … Have you seen these soups? … When's your Sheila coming? … That doctor wanted to touch my arm, I kicked him, he was sat where you are now … How much would I pay for a meal in a Hotel, for cabbage, potatoes and meat …

(She sings Sonny Boy) … Stood all afternoon to see Sonny Boy … Paper delivery boys get good money now. I think you better put that newspaper on the fire – it'll drive us to drink … I've been dreaming about you and me in the dugout. It was laughable eh? The zzzz bang! I suppose we won't have that next time there's a war … George is older than you – you couldn't blame him for being jealous over those bikes, I see him going past the shops in the cubs – he was carrying the cubs head … How dare you put that comb on the table, it's bad luck. (clears bits away for next door's cat) …

Oh, you got your memories to live on (clock ticks) … I was wondering if Miss White was still alive. Don't seem the other day since I was coming to the school to see you when you made them all laugh … I could do with a good cry and you know I can't cry (laughs) I must get someone to make me cry … One time I had only to look at you and I cried, it's comical …

… If I could get a new pair of legs and a new heart I'd be all right.

But she wasn't all right. Cynthia remembers Harry calling to let her know that Annie had to go into hospital, that it was time to come say goodbye. But Cyn was confined to bed herself with a suspected miscarriage so she never got the chance. Annie died a week later and with her went Harry's last ties to Manchester.

Back in London, he took on a new challenge by doing something old, as Maureen remembered:

> He liked to do absolutely everything. He juggled, you know, he would have done– well, maybe not an aqua show – because he would have got a bit bored with that, but he liked to do it all. He wanted to be in every field that he could. So he started doing pantomime because most of the stuff that he had done while the children were very small, they were a bit too young to appreciate, and so he thought 'That's a good idea, I'll do a pantomime and the kids can come and see me.' And then he got hooked on pantomime and so every Christmas it was 'Ooo, got to do a pantomime', it was great, he loved it.

Harry had been taught to juggle by none other that 'Monsewer' Eddie Gray. Eddie and his younger brother Danny had been professional jugglers since their pre First World War childhood and Eddie had gone on to star as part of the Crazy Gang. He earned his 'Monsewer' moniker appearing in Paris, where his Cockneyfied French accent was so atrocious, and comical, it became part of his act. When Eddie's regular juggling partner broke a leg Harry stepped in, and after six weeks of training joined him in cabaret. Harry and the brothers became firm friends, Eddie appearing in an episode of *Mr Aitch* and Danny becoming Harry's juggling partner. Danny's wife, June, had been a Tiller girl and later a trapeze artist and lion tamer with a circus in the States before she and Danny spent years touring together on the variety circuit. They eventually 'retired' to become stage door keepers in London's West End, I used to love hearing their tales of the music hall days, as did Harry.

As the inheritors of music hall, variety acts were still doing well in the late 1960s. There was the club circuit or 'summer season', a spectacular variety show in every seaside resort to attract holidaymakers. Then there were the TV shows, royal galas, *The Good Old Days*, *The Black and White Minstrel Show*, etc. Some acts could be seen on talent shows such as *Opportunity Knocks* – today you can see many would-be acts trying out on the revamped talent show format, *Britain's Got Talent*: it's a short walk from *The Tiller Girls* to *Diversity*, the dance troupe that won the talent contest and appeared on the holy grail of the variety world, the Royal Variety Performance.

'Sexed up' variety acts are still thriving in cabaret venues with a mix of burlesque, magic, comedy and song, but for many modern 'traditional' variety artists, a yearly mainstay is, and always was, pantomime.

The first time many of you will have performed for an audience will have been in a nativity play, and the first professional production you will have seen would have been a panto. Both of these are ancient art forms – though neither is usually accused of being 'art'. Nativity plays have come down to us through early Christian teaching tableaux and medieval mystery plays devised by the Church to more easily get the Bible message across to the illiterate masses. When the Pope banned his clergy from performing, the plays were taken on by the town guilds. This, naturally, led to more secular themes to tell the story of good versus evil – the morality play. Add in a clown and some thwarted love and you've got *commedia dell'arte*. Boy and girl want to marry but old codger disapproves. With the help of a comic servant they get a happy ending and the old codger is forgiven. Fast-forward a few hundred years and the boy/girl has a wicked stepmother/uncle/witch and friendly comic dwarves/servant/cow. With the aid of the genie of the lamp/fairy godmother/golden goose, good triumphs – finale ultimo and walk down. 'Get thee behind me,' had turned into, 'He's behind you!'

Although I love the old panto joke of 'Where's your career? It's behind you,' it takes a lot of skill, and a bit of innuendo, to entrance an audience made up of kids high on sugar and busting for the loo and parents who can't wait till they go back to school. It was a skill highly rated at Theatre Workshop, as remembered by Brian Murphy:

> As Joan always said, the simplest thing for an actor to do is to reach across the footlights and shake hands with the audience. Variety, of course, is of that nature — that's the extraordinary thing and many times, and particularly later, Joan's philosophy was to call us 'clowns' and make us actors/clowns so that we did break down the fourth wall that she had come to hate.
>
> Pantomime was always a potpourri. It was always made up of different types of talents – there were acrobats and people of

that nature but they were skilled people from whatever background, whereas today many of them aren't skilled in anything in particular. They're just put there because they happen to be so-called popular celebrities, even if they just stand there. I mean Ian Botham – what would happen if we turned up on the cricket field and started bowling? There would be an outcry.

But managements need a celebrity draw so that the audience, for whom this will probably be the only live theatre they see all year, will come to their show and not a rival's. Whether it's a sportsman, a reality TV contestant or Sir Ian McKellen in the sequins, the one important factor is always ticket sales. Panto is most theatres' biggest earner of the year – they rely on it to keep afloat.

In 1968 Harry was the celebrity draw for Bournemouth Pavilion's production of *Aladdin*. He played the evil Abanazar with a side step into a crowd-pleasing 'Uncle Harold', selling new lamps for old in his totting gear – 'Now I'm outside Peking's walls, I think I'll have a juggle with me balls …' God, he loved it, he loved that direct connection with an audience, with its nostalgic front legs of the cow connotations, and was determined to do more of the same.

By late February 1969, back in London, I caused my parents another medical drama by managing to go down with pneumonia, a bit dicey, as I was only ten months old. Dr Orton, the family GP, was called, stuck a tube up my nose and started sucking as we waited for the ambulance. Obviously, I came through unscathed, though it was touch and go. Malcolm received such a frantic phone call from Pat that it took him five minutes to ascertain that I was still alive. Unsurprisingly, from then on anytime a sniffle was heard from either of the kids, we were frogmarched down to Dr Orton's.

Being in close proximity to Harley Street might have tipped the balance when it came to deciding to sell the house in Benenden that spring. Having the new place in town meant that we hardly got down there anymore – moreover it was an expense that was needed to fund the 'five glorious years' in St John's Wood.

In April, Harry returned to the fold by appearing in an episode of *Galton and Simpson Comedy* for LWT. Ray and Alan had not long returned from another foray to the States where they had taken their hit show written for Frankie Howerd, *The Wind in the Sassafras Trees*. Tryouts of the show in Boston and Washington had been very well received, but on Broadway *The New York Times* slated it and it closed after four days. So they headed for Hollywood, where they had been asked to rewrite a film script for Universal Studios in the hope of bringing down the projected budget. Unfortunately their budget went up, and so, with no deal, they went home to write for ITV and asked Harry to be in an episode – an invitation due to either his talent or their guilt, 'I did feel very sorry for Harry,' Alan later said:

> because although in a sense we had made him a national and then an international star – or at the very least an internationally recognisable face and character – we did also kind of ruin his career. Even today, people forget what a brilliant, brilliant actor he was. Even watching Steptoe they tend not to notice how brilliant he is. To far too many he's just a silly comedy voice, a character actor. But at least we managed to give him some good light entertainment work as opposed to some of the stuff he was reduced to doing after Steptoe finished.[24]

Their episode 'Never Talk to Strangers' saw 'two exemplary, totally uncaricatured performances from Harry H. Corbett and Rosemary Leach'[25] playing the delectably named Basil Puddifoot and Olive Bunclarck, two residents of a boarding house who woo each other on a crossed telephone line. As she is a 'rubber goods packer' and he a rat catcher they invent more attractive glamorous lives, she as a *Vogue* model and he a pilot.

'It's marvellous to be back with them,' Harry said of his reunion with Ray and Alan to the papers – who, as always, asked if a *Steptoe* revival was on the cards. This prompted Harry's mantra of, 'That's really up to the writers. It ended because they felt they couldn't write any more. As long as I could be doing other things too, I'd quite cheerfully return to a *Steptoe* series.'

Which was handy, as games were afoot behind the scenes. The BBC had not fared well against ITV in recent comedy ratings and were on the warpath once more. 'Tom Sloan asked us about doing some more television at the BBC,' Alan recalls. 'He saw we were now back writing television and he asked us what about bringing back *Steptoe*?' As the boys' move away from television had not been a resounding success they were open to offers, and, by June, they had agreed to a series of seven episodes with an option of six more, all to be screened in glorious colour (the BBC would start screening in colour from 15 November). Their one proviso was that both Harry and Wilf were agreeable to a return – a foregone conclusion, really.

June saw the lad from Ardwick attending Royal Ascot and Trooping the Colour and in July, in a move that perhaps wouldn't have been approved of by Galton and Simpson, Harry fulfilled a long held ambition. He and 'Monsewer' Eddie Gray were booked as headliners for the Brighton Dome's *Big Star Show of 1969*. The local paper reported:

> 'I have a list of things in the back of my head which I want to do one day and this sort of show is one of them. I'm going to do a juggling act,' Harry confided with a friendly nudge.
>
> To compete with 'Monsewer'?
>
> 'Compete? I, compete?' came the incredulous Steptoe voice with its familiar wounded pride. 'I don't have to compete with him.'
>
> 'Monsewer' didn't bat an eyelid, but gaily announced: 'I don't feel a day over 42. Don't tell anyone now, but I'm 43-and-a-half!'
>
> Eddie Gray is the last of the Crazy Gang still working.
>
> 'Life gets boring if you retire,' he said with a twinkle in his eye. 'I work to keep me young.'

It was Harry's first variety show and, sadly, Eddie's last. The 'Monsewer' would die that September.

The late summer also saw Harry starring in a new series for ITV, *The Best Things in Life*. He played Alfred Wilcox, a man who has been engaged to the same woman for eleven years, but won't commit for fear of losing his chance for fast cars and fancy restaurants. 'After all,' Harry commented, 'how many husbands do you see in nippy little sports cars? They're all keeping to the speed limit in family saloons.'

He would know, as his own sports car days were a thing of the past. It wasn't a great loss. He was once the proud owner of a convertible Ferrari. He drove it away from the dealership with the top down, kept it down and the following Sunday got caught in a thunderstorm. Failing to get the convoluted top back up, and with the dealership closed and the footwells flooding, he got hold of the telephone number of the only other man in Britain to have the same model – Stirling Moss. I'm sure Sir Stirling's instructions were faultless but it was all too much like hard work for Harry. On Monday the Ferrari was returned.

Harry's long-suffering fiancée in *Best Things* was played by June Whitfield:

> I don't think it was a brilliant series but it was great working with Harry. I remember once he took my husband, Tim, and I to a nightclub in some basement and the music, even then, was so loud all you could do was thump the table in time to the beat – you couldn't speak. Poor Tim, who was nothing to do with the show business, sat all night with Harry going on and on, he couldn't hear a thing. It cured me of nightclubs.
>
> Harry was a lot more serious than I am about the work. I'm a little bit 'learn the lines and don't trip over the furniture' but I think Harry always had to find a depth – which probably made him a better actor. I admired his dedication.

June didn't think it was a brilliant series, but it still did well in the ratings: 'Last week's top show, according to figures from ITV's audience survey unit, was the Harry Corbett comedy series The Best Things in Life. There will be anxiety at the BBC with the repeated failure of BBC shows to make any dent in ratings.'[26] Not much anxiety as Tom Sloan had another *Steptoe* in the bag.

June had also noticed Harry's tendency towards nervous garrulousness. He put this to good use when he was required to go on and on promoting the new series. In August, while doing the Brighton summer season, he was the *TV Times* cover star; in their article, entitled 'Women and Me', he swung between reflecting on his life and career and 'puff-piecing' for the new character in *Best Things*:

> I had a strong feeling for social injustice but I think that victory has been won. Or else Shelter has taken it over. I'm not so rebellious as I once was.
>
> As you get on, you grow away from your roots. I don't see the people I grew up with. My friends are mostly in the business, or connected with it. But the other day a fellow stopped me in the street and said he knew me from school. I couldn't put a name to the face, but there he was – with a Rolls-Royce. No one at my school aspired higher than a barrow. It was encouraging somehow. There was someone else from the old background who'd made it with me.

One thing frightens me – when people ask me to explain my success. For once you've pinned down the formula, you're finished. After Harold, the junk man, had gone on no one would take me seriously. In a movie I was in with Edward G. Robinson, *Sammy Going South*, I was supposed to be a devil, and they just fell about with hilarity. I haven't tried villainy since.

After *Steptoe* became a success I had to take taxis. I was denied the simple fundamental right of every Englishman. The right to travel on buses and the tube and keep himself to himself. And I liked doing that. You see, I watch people. Everyone you see is just a fantastic act – putting on a performance for strangers, the boss, or the wife. You watch a woman haggling over the price in a shop. It's a great production, especially if she thinks she's been overcharged.

Success has meant that people listen to me a bit more. It's the money that does that. You look at two chaps in an office, one earning 50 quid and another 30. It's the bloke on 50 nicker who's going to get listened to. Yes, I've developed quite a bit of admiration for the chaps on the top of the heap. They've got the power. There may be a lot of idiots up there, too, but their voice is louder than anyone else's. To some extent, money has bought me that sort of freedom.

I've never been particularly ambitious. When I was a kid, I wanted to be an actor. But I soon forgot about it when I found out what the Royal Academy of Dramatic Art fees were. When the paint spraying firm I was with jacked it in someone said I should have a go at acting. I was knocked all of a heap when they took me on. It doesn't mean I don't take it all seriously, but if it all ended tomorrow I don't think I'd jump off a bridge. I'd take up something else.

It was his next comments that naturally caused the most guffaws at home – don't forget, he was selling something:

I don't believe in romantic love. That eternity bit. I think you feel it when you're about 13, then it wears away with the acne. But I've a great urge for strong, temporary attachments. The trouble with women is they tend to think in terms of centuries. I tend to look ahead just a couple of months. When I say 'forever,' I tend to mean 'til Christmas.' They think we're planning to go hand-in-hand for our pensions.

And, finally, his ambition? 'Maybe just one. To die at 90 with a jealous wife.'

A few days later he and Maureen were married.

So, why the year-long wait? Well, 10 a.m. on Tuesday 2 September was the very first appointment after the August Bank Holiday. As Marylebone Register Office had a celeb-filled catchment area, journalists used to scan the list of next week's forthcoming marriages so they could get the photo and the story. But *not* when they were knocking off early to beat the traffic and see their relatives over the long weekend.

The ceremony would have the smallest congregation possible: Maureen and Harry (who had left Brighton under the cover of a dentist's appointment) and their two witnesses, Malcolm and his fiancée Jennie. Jennie remembered that the day was planned with military precision:

> Pat had the kids at her house in Greenford, as we knew the first place the press would go would be to Circus Road. We didn't tell anyone where we were going. The four of us turned up together first thing in the morning at the Register Office. Malcolm parked the Zodiac right outside the door and we were ushered inside by the registrar. Fortunately the press hadn't picked up on anything, and afterwards we all left wearing sunglasses and went our separate ways. We saw Harry off on a train down to Brighton, where he was still performing the summer season, Maureen went shopping in Oxford Street and myself and Malcolm went straight back to work, not saying a word about it to anyone. It was fortunate that Harry was in Brighton as he could avoid the London press. I remember him telling us to keep a low profile for 48 hours, as after that the press would have lost interest.

They had managed to complete the nuptials without one reporter getting the shot. They'd avoided the bun fight and kept their privacy. Until it was posted on the notice board the next day, of course, then the papers let rip: 'Steptoe Weds in Secret!' they cried. It was revealed, disclosed and even discovered. Although some reported that the couple had known each other for some time, not one of them reported that they already had two kids.

There was little time for a honeymoon as, after Brighton, Harry went straight into rehearsals for a play, *Little Jack*. The play was writ-

ten by Ivor Burgoyne, an actor/screenwriter who was a friend of
Harry's and who had been moonlighting as a warden in a psychiatric hospital to make ends meet. Harry had got him some writing
work on *Best Things* and would now take his bedroom farce around
the country on tour. He would also take Maureen, Pat and the kids.
In charge of direction was another old mate, David Scase.

Joining them in the cast would be Chilli Bouchier, the silent
screen star, as a demented landlady, and Carmel Cryan as the
object of Harry's affection. Carmel had also had a stint at Theatre
Workshop and, during the run of *Little Jack*, got engaged to one of
its more famous members – Roy Kinnear.

As the tour came to a close, and before he started rehearsals for
Cinderella at Golders Green with Amanda Barrie and Freddie and the
Dreamers, Harry ruminated on the forthcoming return of *Steptoe*:

> 'The series is always progressing. If you look at the episodes we
> made seven years ago, then look at the most recent ones, you'll
> see big changes. Harold reacts very differently now to the same
> situations he faced at the start. He has matured and thinks in a
> new way. Because of this Steptoe is always fun to do and is always
> worth doing.'
>
> Is Corbett worried about being unable to return to 'Serious'
> acting should he ever want to?
>
> 'There's no problem,' he shrugged. 'If I wanted to play
> "Hamlet" or "Macbeth" I'd do it in a theatre where Shakespeare
> is accepted. Like the Old Vic.'
>
> 'Mind you, I think if I played "Hamlet" in a variety theatre,
> people would still accept me. The public are a lot more under-
> standing and a lot more sensible than they're given credit for.'
>
> Harry swithers if you ask him what kind of acting gives him
> the most satisfaction.
>
> 'There's nothing quite like the feeling you get when a thea-
> tre gives you a great big, slightly outraged belly-laugh. It sends
> prickles right down your bloody back,' he said slowly.
>
> 'On the other hand, there's the utter silence you get when you
> start on a big, serious speech from a great drama. It has the same
> effect, exactly.'[27]

He also got back on the Labour bandwagon. In a startling move
for the day, he appeared in their Party Political Broadcast on

15 October. Dressed in his *Steptoe* gear he assumed the stage at Brighton's Rank Centre after the departure of both Labour and Tory conferences, to amusingly wonder from the leader's podium if there were any tangible differences between them. The programme then cut to an in-studio panel of Labour MPs to defend themselves, not so amusingly.

'It so happened I was talking to some people concerned with making this Party broadcast,' he told a reporter:

Standing up shooting off my big mouth about one lot being as bad as the other, and who could tell the difference anyway?

Anyway, once I'd finished ranting on they asked me if I'd be prepared to say the same on TV – so I did.

I was brought up in the slums of Manchester, naturally that's bound to colour my personal politics. I knew what it was like to have no suit to my back and an empty belly. And what it was like to be envious of those with new suits and a full belly. Well, now I've got those myself – but I don't want anyone to be envious of me.'

With that end in view he visits about 20 hustings a year.

'I'm not up there to answer political queries. That's up to the guy who wants to be elected. My platform is to get people to use their vote.'

Would he be prepared to offer similar services to the Conservative Party?

'Sure I would, but I wouldn't be funny. I'd open a fête, or whatever, for the Tories tomorrow. But they'd never ask me. Because I'd stand up and have a real go at them.'

Harry comes back to television in the New Year with another batch of Steptoe.

'It's funny, you know, but everyone assumed I stopped being Steptoe because I was scared of getting typecast. The only reason I stopped was because the writers felt they'd exhausted the current possibilities.

Now they're ready to do another series and I'm quite happy to oblige. In fact I'm quite happy to grow old gracefully in the part.

It is, after all, a marvellous vehicle for me to express my own opinions.[28]

It was time to head back to Oil Drum Lane.

Notes

1 *Daily Mail*, 16/11/65.
2 Williams, K., *Just Williams: An Autobiography* (J.M. Dent & Sons, 1985).
3 *Daily Sketch*, 26/11/66.
4 *Toledo Blade*, 17/3/77.
5 *Manchester Weekly News*, 25/3/67.
6 Burton, *Acting in the Sixties*.
7 *Sunday Citizen*, 10/7/66.
8 *Glasgow Evening Times*, 28/6/66.
9 *Bournemouth Evening Echo*, 9/9/66.
10 *Glasgow Evening Times*.
11 *Burnley Evening Star*, 16/7/66.
12 *Liverpool Echo*, 5/1/67.
13 *Western Evening Herald*, 19/1/67.
14 Burton, *Acting in the Sixties*.
15 *Observer*, 3/9/67.
16 In conversation with Sheila Hancock.
17 *Worcester Evening News*, 10/11/67.
18 *Birmingham Evening Mail*, 10/11/67.
19 *Daily Mail Yorkshire*, 10/2/68.
20 *Daily Mail*, 22/2/68.
21 *Poole and Dorset Herald*, 28/2/68.
22 *The Herald*, 20/4/72.
23 *Radio Times*, 18/4/68.
24 Galton amd Simpson, *Steptoe and Son*.
25 Michael Billington in *The Times*.
26 *Evening News*, 20/9/69.
27 *Scottish Daily Express*, 21/11/69.
28 *Glasgow Daily Record*, 5/11/69.

15

Duty and Desire

After five years scratching around for a comedy series to unite the public in the way that Steptoe and Son managed to do in the early sixties, the BBC have come up with the laughter ingredient for the seventies – Steptoe and Son, the return of.[1]

'If it works, it works. If we fail, well … each of us will have to produce the best he can, and no one can be asked for more than that,' Harry reflected:

> When I was asked to do another Steptoe. I assumed, perhaps rather egotistically, that all the others would be there too. Without Simpson and Galton there would not be any Steptoe. The actors could be changed I suppose, although I could not play Harold without Wilfrid Brambell and I like to think he would not want to do the show without me.
>
> Steptoe is the sort of thing that happens only three or four times in an acting career, once every ten years if you are lucky.
>
> We have been to No. 1 in the ratings and can only go down. We will wait for the public to tell us whether they want any more Steptoe. I am not anti-critic, but it is the ratings – by that I mean the viewers – who will finally decide. Yes, I am looking forward to it, looking forward very much.[2]

As was Tom Sloan who, on 11 December 1969, gave a BBC lunch-time lecture in the concert hall of Broadcasting House entitled 'Television Light Entertainment':

I suppose it would be unfair of me if I did not let you into a few secrets of the craft. When Hancock decided to go it alone in films, his writers were, quite reasonably, upset. I talked to them, with a ten-week gap of programmes staring me in the face, I offered them the job of filling these ten half hours with anything they wanted to write and suggested we call the series Comedy Playhouse. It did not seem such a bad title at the time and represented my sole creative contribution to the discussion.

Enter Steptoe and Son

Galton and Simpson were delighted. They wanted to prove that they could work without Hancock and they did. Script number four came in and it was about two rag-and-bone men and it was called 'The Offer'. It was cast with two excellent but comparatively unknown actors and it was transmitted without much comment. The next day I asked Duncan Wood, the producer, if we could persuade the writers to do five more, giving us a series of six. He was doubtful. Ray and Alan were even more definite. 'I think,' said Ray, 'we have written a little piece of Pinter here and we couldn't possibly repeat it.' After a fair amount of persuasion, I got my five more and we launched the series. It was called 'Steptoe and Son'. We followed it quickly with a repeat series and it became part of television history.

Somehow it seems to take about three weeks for the word-of-mouth approval to go round about a new series and just as people were beginning to wonder what they had missed, the repeat series did the trick. In all, over three years, we still ended up with only twenty-six programmes, but they were classics in their time.

Was it a psychological study of old age and frustration? Was it a human story of the boy who never got away? Was it a real and tender interplay between a father and son? Maybe it was, but it certainly wasn't written as such. It was a series of well-constructed scripts involving two actors who breathed life into the words and made them real, and it was funny. Above all it was funny, hilariously funny. So much so that I am reviving it next year with seven new programmes.

As a final duty call the weekend before rehearsals started in February 1970, Harry and Maureen opened Steptoe's discotheque for the Stepney Jewish Youth Club. The club surprised him with a trophy for being their personality of the year and he surprised them with a cheque towards club funds. He wouldn't have wanted them to be out of pocket – thank God he had his chequebook on him. After signing autographs, cracking jokes and watching a display of Israeli dancing, he went home to work on the script. 'I expect to be up until the early hours.' he said.

Even though this was the fifth series Harry wouldn't have dreamed of being unprepared, as Maureen remembered:

> Well of course, by the time I knew him he'd made quite a few, so he didn't have to do quite such a voyage of discovery as it must have been to begin with. He knew what the character was and it was just a question then – not of just ringing the laughs out of it, because of course the laughs were always there – but of doing them justice. If you notice, Harry will very often begin a line [on one angle] or even a look and then will pause and then will take in three camera angles just on one inflection or something. Well, this isn't something that you're born being able to do. So the technical side of it he was always polishing, always polishing. You've got to have the feel for the timing of it. If you look at some of the earlier ones it's quite remarkable stuff really, and then, as he went on, that became second nature to him within the character.

The scripts could never come soon enough for Harry. He had already written to Duncan Wood asking to see more than the two available so he could 'do some proper work on them for once'.[3]

And the Youth Club trophy? It was displayed with equal pride next to the BAFTA and Variety Club Heart and all the other little mementos that people gave him for turning up.

Harry and Wilf's return was displayed on the cover of the *Radio Times*. Under a picture of the pair in the early morning scrapyard, the strap line read: 'The first new Steptoe series since 1965. In colour too.'

But Ray and Alan weren't happy about the colour. They thought the gritty dinginess of the Steptoes' surroundings was better served in black and white. They soon changed their minds – colour managed to make Oil Drum Lane look even worse.

The first new episode, 'A Death in the Family', recorded on Sunday 15 February, opened with the horse, Hercules, dying of a heart attack while out on the round. A distraught Albert, hearing that Harold had to send Hercules to the knacker's yard and proclaiming the horse to have been 'more like a son', takes to his bed. Harold, in his cups, buys a new horse and christens him Samson, but Albert will not be roused from his grief to either inspect the new arrival or see a new risqué film, *I am Curious, Yellow*. When Samson falls ill, Albert is finally persuaded to tend to him, and delivers him of a foal. Harold's powers of observation ridiculed, the Steptoes rename Samson Delilah and the foal Hercules II, before setting out for the cinema.

Real-life totter and Hercules' owner, Arthur Arnold, played the horse dealer who sold Delilah to Harold. Delilah was also his, though her real name was Dolly. Hercules was still alive and well, though she had retired from filming and was back on the round pulling lighter loads. In 1965, when the original series had finished, slum clearing had caused the Arnold brothers to lose their yard in Notting Dale (part of Notting Hill). They were moved up the road to a new one, which immediately had the Westway flyover built over it. Hercules II and Dolly fared better. When news got out they would be losing their stables, sacks of their fan mail arrived at the offices of the Greater London Council, which then built them, and their counterparts, a new £15,000 stable block.

'A Winter's Tale' sees Harold trying once more to escape the annual trip to Bognor. While suggesting Albert goes to relatives in Stoke-on-Trent, he plans to sample the delights of Obergurgl, skiing with mismatched equipment salvaged off the round. He rigs up a dry slope in the yard and on his first practice run hurtles into the house and breaks his leg. Albert takes his place in Obergurgl and Harold is left with a plaster cast and the delights of Stoke in February.

During the week following the recording, Harold Wilson, in a move that predates Blair's 'Cool Britannia' party by twenty-seven years, invited 400 media spotlighted guests to a reception for the Communist Prime Minister of Yugoslavia, Mitja Ribicic. Maureen and Harry were among those invited inside No. 10. 'Mr Ribicic was submerged in a group between Cliff Michelmore and Mr Bernard Delfont, and Harry Corbett and Julie Christie were practising pronouncing "Ribicic" which is even more difficult when you know how.'[4]

Harry returned to the studio for 'Any Old Iron'. Antique dealer Timothy Stanhope, played by Richard Hurndall, is browsing the yard and takes an interest in Harold. Albert proclaims the dealer a 'poof', an accusation levied at any man of culture. Harold, disgusted at the old man's attitude, believes theirs to be merely a platonic and business relationship and soon takes to wearing floppy hats and carrying man-bags. Albert, convinced his son is 'on the turn', threatens to make the 39-year-old a ward of court and, contrary to any other time, begs him to seek out the pleasures of a bird in the form of Dolly Miller. During a 'business' dinner, Albert's fears are realised when the dealer makes a pass at Harold. Fleeing the advances, Harold bumps into a policeman at the door who, contrary to Harold's belief, is not there to arrest them but is, in fact, the dealer's lover. A shaken Harold, meanwhile, has gone to give Dolly Miller a good 'seeing to'.

Though called offensive when repeated in more enlightened times, the episode was daring for 1970 (just three years after the Sexual Offences Act partially decriminalised homosexuality; 'partially' being the operative word), as it infers that an authority figure, in the shape of a policeman, could be gay. As such, it was reflective of society's changing acceptance.

In 'Steptoe and Son and Son', Albert answers the door to a heavily pregnant young woman, Daphne Tomlin, played by Ann Beach. She is looking for the baby's father – Harold. Albert tells her he's left for Australia but Harold soon returns home to face the music. Unfortunately neither of the prospective parents can remember their 'meeting', however, a quick check in Harold's diary confirms his sailor friend George took him to a party where the deed was done. Harold proposes to Daphne, much to the disgust of Albert who softens upon hearing the child will be named after him. Having bought a pram and new baby clothes Harold and his father look forward to the instant family, Albert even coughs up £500 for the happy couple. That is until Harold's friend George arrives. George has just returned home and admits he is the real father, that he and Daphne are to be wed and he wants Harold to stand as best man. The Steptoes go to drown their bitter disappointment down the Skinner's Arms.

George was played by Glynn Edwards:

> I loved doing the Steptoe, playing a handsome sailor boy. Harry
> and Wilf were both good to work with. It was the only time
> I worked with Wilfrid. I got on better with Harry, of course,

being a Theatre Workshop fella. Once you got into the Workshop, although people would go their own way and do different shows, you were always part of the team.

Harry was reunited with Carmel Cryan in 'The Colour Problem'. Carmel plays Murial Duddy, the latest girl of Harold's dreams. To impress her, he plans to buy a sports car instead of buying Albert the colour television he craves; after all, local hood Charlie Miller has bought *his* old dad a colour TV. Following the ensuing argument, Albert leaves in a huff and is picked up by the police in the early hours suffering from exposure. The next morning Harold has the new car and the promise of a weekend in Brighton with Murial when the police arrive to break the news. When Harold reaches the hospital he is told by the doctor, played by Anthony Sharp (who would return two series later as the vicar), that Albert has amnesia and the only things he can remember are colour television and Charlie Miller.

Though the doctor suggests putting Albert in a home, Harold refuses. Determined to see Albert returned to health, he gives up the new car and the chance of Murial to buy the television, which has an instantaneous and miraculous effect on the old man. Harold has been scammed once again.

Charlie Miller and scamming featured in the next episode, 'Men of Property'. After the old man has taken Harold to the cleaners playing Monopoly, they receive a letter – the ninety-nine-year lease on their house is up. They need £750 to buy the freehold but don't have it. Harold has heard that Charlie Miller has pocketed thousands by pouncing on green bank managers, opening a small account then arranging a hefty loan. The Steptoes will do the same. At the bank they bump into Charlie Miller, played by Michael Balfour. He tells them the new manager is a 'right carrot' and has given him a loan. Before the Steptoes can get one, the manager, played by Norman Bird, hints that he needs to get to know them socially. Harold takes the manager to a high-class restaurant and after paying a huge bill gets the £750 loan, which Albert immediately loses to the roulette wheel in the upstairs gaming salon. Harold now needs £1,500 to be back to where they were before the postman arrived – and more of Charlie Miller's 'carrots'. The pair settle down to another game of Monopoly.

The last recorded episode, 'TB or Not TB?', sees Harold return-ing home to find Albert coughing his guts up. They work out that since Albert started smoking, aged 8½, his lungs have got through 45 miles' worth of cigarettes. Having passed a mobile X-ray unit on his way home, Harold insists Albert comes with him for a check-up. When the results arrive Harold is in the clear but Albert's test was unsatisfactory due to a technical fault; a further test has been arranged. Albert panics but Harold convinces him that after two months in a sanatorium he'll be fine – that is until they discover the letters were in the wrong envelopes – Harold is the one who is unsatisfactory. Harold immediately develops a consumptive wheeze while Albert callously complains that he'll be left on his own and takes to wearing a surgical mask. Having made a will, leaving a small bequest to the Labour Party, Harold leaves for the hospital and certain doom. He returns, with an all clear, to find Albert has burned his bed and all his clothes.

During the recording of 'TB', Harold was mending a china figurine when Albert had to nudge his hand, so undoing the repair. Unfortunately, Wilfrid's 'nudge' became a grab and Harry caught his thumb on the jagged edge of the figurine and suffered a deep cut. Not wanting to ruin the take, Harry shoved his hand into his pocket and carried on – but he couldn't stop the bleeding. When he thought it was about to seep through the trousers and become noticeable they had to call a halt. This was the only time, that I know of, when they had to stop a recording (the one time I know they stopped a final dress run was when Jonathan came across a prop skull in Harry's dressing room and screamed the place down. Moments later a panicking Harry burst through the door having literally lost the plot). Malcolm remembers:

Jennie and I were watching from the audience when it happened. I went down to the set to see what was happening and he obviously had a bad cut. A doctor from the audience and a BBC nurse bandaged the wound as best they could to allow the recording to continue. As it happened, that day we were due to take Harry straight from the studio to Heathrow Airport to catch a plane to Spain, so there wasn't much time for delays. After the recording, we drove Harry to casualty, where he had a couple of stitches and a tetanus jab. Someone from the BBC may well have alerted them that we were coming because he was seen to the moment we arrived. And then we rushed him to Heathrow.

Harry liked having his family at the recordings; Maureen was always there, Pat often, and sometimes us kids when we were older. An added boon of Malcolm and Jennie being in the audience every week was a lift home. Harry would never have driven himself to the studios; being so absorbed by the looming recording he would have been a danger on the roads, and at that time Maureen didn't have a license, so they used to get a car in and Harry would arrange for Malcolm to have a parking space at Television Centre.

A parking place at the Beeb is harder to come by than a Nobel Prize and the parking tsars who control access are a force to be reckoned with. Every time a new one was on duty, even though Harry would give Malcolm's name and number plate, he often had to interrupt preparations to confirm identities and ensure his ride home. After Maureen got her license they used to try it on her. On one occasion, despite the necessary letters and with us kids rubber-necking from the back seat, the tsar refused to believe that Maureen was allowed in. She, not wanting to disturb Harry so close to going on stage, threatened that Mr Corbett would not set foot on the studio floor unless he knew his family were there and then questions would be asked! Complete crap, of course, but the officious little twerp manning the gate didn't know that and, eventually, the barrier was raised.

For someone with a 'great urge for strong, temporary attachments' Harry was managing to bear up rather well under family life. 'I'm very much happier being married than being a bachelor,' he commented during an 'at home' publicity piece for the series:

> Maureen has given up acting now to be my missus. Two people acting in the same family never makes for happiness. Not if one of you is a 'name'.
>
> I tend to alternate between a monastic way of life when I'm working, to playing hard and indulging my taste for whiskey when I'm not. I never drink when I work, not because of priggishness but because I'd go to pieces if I did.
>
> I'm so nervous before every performance anyway that I'd whip myself into a frenzy just to look relaxed on stage!

To try and relax at home Harry would disappear behind the newspapers: 'He liked reading the papers,' Maureen recalled. 'He read every paper he could lay his hands on. All the "Sundays", and if he wasn't working on the Sunday, or wasn't doing a charity, he used to just sit – in fact he sat in this chair – he used to sit behind the paper. And that was it, you didn't get a word out of him all day and just "A cup of tea?" – "Thank you."'

The chair Maureen refers to is an exceptionally wide and deep one. Harry would always lounge in it, left leg casually thrown over its arm, his face cupped in his right hand, little finger curling into his mouth. It is known as the 'dying chair', because Harry had pronounced it 'so comfortable, he could die happy in it' and it was always surrounded by a sea of newspapers, with Harry busily absorbing ...

'Absorbing, absorbing, but that was how he studied people, as well as watching them in the street,' Maureen continued:

> He locked them away for future use. And so he would be able to dredge them up or perhaps just a line that somebody said to him. Like the foreman that said, 'I'll see you never work in the building trade' – he's got in there somewhere, that bloke. It may have been twenty, thirty years, but they were all in there. He had a very retentive memory. Sometimes, he used to come home and say he'd seen something that was interesting or great, but mainly he used to sit and think, like Topsy, and I think that's what he was doing – he was filing them.
>
> I think most actors are [reclusive]. In fact, maybe all actors are. You can't really be giving 100 per cent to the job, which is after all what you should be doing, if you're out and about all the time. When preparing for a role, he didn't used to do more than he had to. If there was something that was already in the diary then he would turn up rather than disappoint people, but otherwise he used to cut it right down and we just used to get on with our lives and let him do it – he would sit in corners and mutter, going through lines and then I'd say, 'What would you like for dinner? ...What would you like for dinner? ...Would you like lamb chops for dinner?" – and it just used to go in one ear and straight through. 'Yeah – it'll be lamb chops for dinner, that's fine.' And an hour or so later he'd say, 'Oh, its lamb chops – that's nice.' It was quite obvious that none of it had gone in at all – and maybe all actors are like that – when I was working I think I was pretty much the same, not that my roles were anything like as demanding as his, but I'm sure that that is how you do it. You shut yourself off in your mind.

It was worth it. The return of *Steptoe* went out to good reviews and, more importantly, high ratings. The BBC would be picking up the option for another series. Sadly, Tom Sloan wasn't the one commissioning. A few weeks after the last episode aired he lost a brief battle with cancer. During that lunchtime lecture five months earlier, before he knew he was ill, he had reflected on his career in light entertainment:

> After fifteen years, and if I dropped dead tomorrow, I would not mind being remembered for having had some responsibility at least for the 'Black and White Minstrel Show', 'Hancock', 'Steptoe', 'Val Doonican', 'Death us do Part', 'Morecambe and Wise', 'Rolf Harris', 'The Likely Lads', 'Me Mammy', 'Harry Worth', 'Matty', 'Not in Front of the Children', 'Dad's Army', 'Oh Brother!', 'The World of Wooster', 'Monty Python's Flying Circus', 'Golden Silents', and dear old 'Dixon of Dock Green'. That's not the full list by any means, but it will do!

Tom Sloan OBE, died on 13 May. He was 50. Bill Cotton Jnr, who had been Acting Head of Light Entertainment during Tom's illness, took over.

One of Bill's first duties was to attend *The Sun*'s TV bash the following day:

> Within a few minutes of Harry H Corbett collecting one of *The Sun* newspaper's TV awards, presented to *Steptoe and Son* as the BBC's top series, he gave away the magnificent trophy.
>
> 'Harry said quietly to me, "I want you to let Tom Sloan's family keep it as a permanent memento."' explained Bill Cotton. 'You see, it was Tom's idea to start the Comedy Playhouse series from which Steptoe was born. So he was basically the instigator of it all.'
>
> 'I shall be giving the award to Tom's widow Pat this weekend,' said Mr Cotton. 'It was an extremely thoughtful gesture by Harry.'
>
> There couldn't be a more generous gesture from an actor in his moment of triumph.[5]

Peter Sloan, Tom's son, still has the award prominently displayed in his home. It has to be prominent – it's a whopper.

By the end of May, Harry was on to the second series of *Best Things*. It started airing on 1 June, and during recording he broke his rule for a few things already in the diary.

The first was to take part in a theatrical evening to aid American resistance on behalf of the Civil Liberties Legal Defence Fund. The evening's keynote speaker was Dr Spock, the paediatrician, who was a vocal opponent of the Vietnam War.

The second was to open Tring Junior School's fête – well, he had to, Maureen's uncle worked as caretaker at the school and he had nobbled Harry at Malcolm and Jennie's wedding a few weeks earlier.

The third was to be Jersey's 'Mr Battle' in their annual Battle of the Flowers – there was no tiara or sash, those went to Miss Battle. With up to 60,000 people lining the streets to see a parade made up of huge floats covered with dried and fresh flowers it was, and is, rather a big deal for the island, and quite an honour for Harry to be 'starring' in the event.

Not in the diary was a last minute panic call from the Labour Party. George Brown was the Deputy Leader of Labour and one-time Foreign Secretary. 'One time' because the man whose drunken behaviour had famously been excused as being 'tired and emotional' had been missing in action two years earlier when Wilson had called an emergency Privy Council meeting during the gold crisis. The 1967 attacks on sterling and the London Gold Pool had resulted in the devaluation of the pound. To stave off further runs on gold, and protect the dollar, in March 1968 the United States had requested that the London gold markets be closed. Wilson needed the Privy Council meeting so that the Queen could petition Parliament for a Bank Holiday, and thus close the markets. So having one's Foreign Secretary – ahem – 'incapacitated' was a tad inconvenient. The meeting went ahead without him. When George Brown found out he stormed into Wilson's office and started ranting. Unsurprisingly, a letter from Brown suggesting that he and Wilson 'part company' followed soon after. Brown remained as Deputy Leader, however, and by the 1970 general election was crisscrossing the country drumming up support, much to the detriment of his own seat in Belper. Brown had held the seat since 1945 but it was no longer safe. New housing developments had seen an influx of middle-class Conservative voters and Brown's continued absence had left the ground clear for his opponent. At the eleventh hour he asked Harry to tour the seat on the eve of the election. Harry agreed, he drove up, did the meeting and greeting and spoke at two rallies before schlepping back to London and the studio. All to no avail. George Brown lost the seat by over 2,000 votes, Labour's highest-profile casualty of their election defeat. 'I only wish the end results had been more rewarding and less lousy,' he wrote to Harry, thanking him for his efforts, 'I do hope that one of these days we can have a drink together.' Being in the midst of recording *Best Things* it's doubtful Harry took up such a gruelling invitation.

Besides he wouldn't have had time, having to also launch into the obligatory publicity for the new series, giving the reporters a necessarily catchy hook for their column, even if sometimes they didn't bite, as in this example:

He sat there, his suit covered in fluff, drinking a modest tomato juice. And he brushed off the obvious with typical Steptoe nonchalance.

The fluff? 'Well I've been rolling in bed with a bird, haven't I? With almost no gear on.'

Harry H. Corbett, rampant rag-and-bone man beloved of millions, was on to a favourite subject. The bachelor scene … 'Well, it's the joy of the chase, the pursuit, an' all that. That's where all the fun an interest is.'

But before you buy that for real let me put you in the picture. This was Harry H. digressing on the return of his ATV series The Best Things in Life, in which he plays – no prizes – a bachelor.

In actual fact, yer actual Mr. Corbett is well and truly hooked, married for the second time six months ago.

And in actual fact, he has very definite, non-bachelor views on women. Conservative views.

Says the real-life Harry: 'I like moral women – because I'm so immoral.' Then seriously: 'I don't like being with women who are in the forefront of fashion. I hate being stared at, and I'd shrivel if a girl turned up in a see-through.'

I was meeting Mr Corbett between rehearsals for his series, which made its come-back on Monday.

With his India-rubber face and fluffy, mousey hair, he looks, and is, a funny man.

He is also full of urges. Nice, mad urges.

'For instance, I get urges to sing the 'alleluiah chorus going up in the lift. Or to say loudly, "Somebody has just pinched my bottom" when there's only one other person in the room.'

Harry H. didn't have to explain his unconventionality. One look at him was enough.

I watched him walk away in his cornflower blue suit, primrose shirt, orange and brown chequered tie, brown wet-leather shoes, grey socks and red cufflinks – and knew Harry H. was somehow different.

And, as he passed a laundry van, he shouted: 'Are you the overland trip for Morocco?'

That's Harry H. for you.[6]

Why Harry should ever think that people were staring at Maureen's attire rather than his remains one of life's great mysteries. But Harry's fashion sense was nothing compared to his shambling gait. I can remember Jon and I following him down the street trying to copy it – hands in pockets, collar up, head down, rolling along. Maureen drew the line at all three of us shuffling down St John's Wood High Street and Jon and I got a well-deserved reprimand; she couldn't stop us following him, though. We knew that way we'd be ready to pounce on the crumpled pound notes that would absentmindedly fall from his pockets. It gave us something to do while waiting for him to talk to the passers-by that recognised him, and there were many – a five-minute walk to the park invariably took half an hour. He always had time for them – something you don't appreciate when you're dying to get to the swings.

We learned to wait patiently, watching him launch into the expected Harold persona. As Wilfrid was so diminutive, one of the most often-heard comments to Harry was 'I thought you'd be taller?' To which he would reply, 'So did I.' And if ever they were coy and asked 'It is you, isn't it?' he'd say, 'No, but I wish I had his money.' And every single one asked about the horse. They would leave happy, made up with having met him, and Harry would go back to being himself. I never once saw him annoyed by it. Resigned? Sometimes. Annoyed? No. Not only were they paying his wages, he didn't want to disappoint. But he never went out of his way to court it and would try to remain inconspicuous, sporting dark glasses and a selection of hats. That is when he managed to keep hold of them. On one occasion, he met a mate on the doorstep of Locks, the London hatters, where he had just bought a spiffy little number – the friend admired it – so Harry took it off, plonked it on the man's head, said 'There you go', before continuing on his merry way. He was always doing things like that.

Remaining inconspicuous, and thus able to study people, might have had something to do with Harry's dislike of a girl turning up in a 'see through', but probably more to do with a double standard. It was perfectly all right for others to go out in revealing clothing, but not his family. It was something that Maureen would never have dreamed of doing anyway. Once, on a topless beach, somewhere on holiday, she stood up to shake off her towel. Harry urgently whispered to her 'Sit down, sit down – everybody's looking at you.' To which she replied, 'Of course they are. I'm the only one wearing a bloody top!'

It was unusual for him to be sitting down on a beach. Unlike Maureen, Harry never sunbathed – as he could turn a rich mahogany inside half an hour, there wasn't much point. Moreover, he was always too restless, as Maureen related when asked for an anecdote (mind the name doesn't hit you on its way down):

We were on the beach, and Harry used to walk around looking at shells, he couldn't sit still on a beach – found it very boring – and so he was pacing up and down, hat on the head sort of thing. And from a distance I saw him stop and speak to another man, also with a hat on his head, also just standing with his hands behind his back looking out to sea and they spoke for quite a while.

And I thought, 'Shall I be nosy and go and see who it is, because we don't really know anybody here?' And then the man said, 'Well, goodbye,' and went into the water and swam out round the headland.

Eventually Harry came back and sat down and I said 'So? Who was that?' and he said, 'It was Larry Olivier,' and I said, 'Where?' – too late! Gone! He was staying quite nearby. He had been ill and was building up his strength to do quite a strenuous stage role, and I said 'So, what were you talking about all that time?' and Harry just said 'About had he seen this play and this, that and the other,' and apparently Larry said to him 'Oh, I saw you giving your acting lesson last week.' And so I said, 'Oh, that's what you're smirking about,' because Harry had always thought Larry was a great actor and it was nice that he said that to him, I mean he didn't have to, because I don't think they ever worked together

– that was nice – it's nice to know that you are liked and appreciated by other actors.

Harry was known as an actor's actor, he always had time for actors – I've never heard an actor say a bad word about him. They've always said he's very generous and would always take lots of time to get it right. And actors liked watching him because they thought he was worth watching, he could give them a few ideas. It sounds terribly pompous to say that they liked to see how it was done – but there was an element of that in it.

Having time for actors included signing up to support Equity's living wage campaign. That autumn of 1970, the union was aiming to take on provincial theatres and force them to up the weekly wage to £18. Of course Harry took part in the fundraisers, he'd been there.

In October he was back to work with the sixth series of *Steptoe*.

'Robbery with Violence' opens with Albert accidentally smashing Harold's prize collection of porcelain. To cover his tracks he stages a burglary, knocking himself out with a poker. When discovered by Harold, he concocts a story of valiantly trying to fight off six skinheads with a rolling pin. Harold believes him and calls in the police. Under questioning Albert 'remembers' that there were five skinheads and a Pakistani, prompting the inspector to comment that 'at least it shows that the races can work in harmony'. Albert becomes a local hero and is awarded a police medal for bravery. While hanging a congratulations banner, Harold finds the broken pieces of porcelain. Albert returns to find that Harold has been 'attacked by five skinheads and a Pakistani'. 'They' have taken Albert's stash of £150. Confronted with the truth, and the broken pieces, Albert decides to let Harold keep the £150 and save his reputation. But he's not out of pocket, as a reporter wants to pay him £250 for his life story. The marvellous Dudley Foster returned to play the police inspector; he would reprise the role four months later on radio. This was his last appearance in *Steptoe*; sadly, he committed suicide in 1973.

'Come Dancing' opens with a five and a half minute monologue for Harold. While Albert snores on the sofa, he roams from imagining the joys of Henry VIII's Hampton Court to getting away with murdering the old man – 'I was bored m'Lord, nothing more, nothing less.' When the cuckoo clock startles him he vents his frustration by nailing its door up. The noise wakes Albert who soon discovers that Harold is sulking over his latest flame, Jane. Trying to impress, Harold has agreed to partner her in a ballroom dancing competition – but he can't dance. Luckily Albert is an expert and gives Harold a crash course. Tango lessons are interrupted by the milkman, played by Tony Melody, who goes from raising his eyebrows at the pair to also giving Harold a few flashy pointers. On the evening of the competition Harold is resplendent in tails. Albert proudly waves him off, certain he'll win the cup, grateful he's been able to help. Harold returns without the cup or Jane. He was disqualified as Albert taught him the woman's steps. 'We both danced backwards. We ended up at opposite ends of the dance floor. The band couldn't play for laughing,' Harold moans. The only one he can dance with is Albert. The episode is the earliest to exist in colour, as such it is one of the most often repeated and best remembered.

In 'Two's Company' Albert has been dancing again, down at the Darby and Joan Club, where he has met a 42-year-old widow with whom he is in love – Daphne Goodlace, played by the 1940s film star Jean Kent. Much to Harold's chagrin, the pair are to be married. To celebrate, Albert has invited Daphne round to meet Harold before their engagement dinner. While Albert is out of the room phoning for a taxi, Harold and Daphne fall into each other's arms – they were lovers twenty years before, when Harold went by the name of Harry Faversham. Daphne's mother scuppered their relationship and they lost touch. The meeting rekindles the old flame. Harold breaks the crushing news to Albert who plans to move out. As father and son wrangle the problem, Daphne slips away. She leaves a note saying she can't come between them as they're already married. The taxi arrives and the pair head for the restaurant.

'Tea For Two' – It's by-election time and the Steptoes are supporting, and stuffing letters for, opposing parties. While Harold is out delivering, Tory Party bigwigs visit. The newly elected Conservative prime minister, Edward Heath, will be meeting and greeting in the area. To Albert's delight, they have selected him as the one to take tea with the PM. Harold is horrified. As teatime approaches, he threatens to dance the *pas de deux* from the second act of *Oh Calcutta* with Dolly Clackett, both of them stark naked. Blushes are spared when the Tory bigwig returns to say that Heath is running late and has to cancel. Harold gets £60 to recompense the old man's teatime spread and directs the bigwig to the outhouse, where he gets doused by bucket of whitewash laid as a trap for the PM.

In 'Without Prejudice' the roof is leaking. Running out of pots and pans and sick of living in a dilapidated house, Harold is determined to move upmarket. He talks Albert into viewing a property in a desirable suburb. With plans to keep the horse in the garage and the junk in the garden they agree to take it, much to the trepidation of their potential neighbours. As Harold dreams of the business deals he'll do on the local golf course, the residents' association, led by a returning Norman Bird, come calling. When they hear of the Steptoes' plans to buy some whippets to keep the rats down in the new junkyard, the committee offer them £500 to not move in. While Harold refuses to be party to such blatant social discrimination, Albert demands £1,000 – they settle on £850, money they can put towards repairs at Oil Drum Lane. To raise more funds they go looking at another salubrious property with, hopefully, the same results from some more prejudiced locals.

'Pot Black' sees Harold fulfilling his dream of having a billiard room 'à la country house'. He has bought table number eight from a closing-down billiard hall, the table he has played on twice a week for the last ten years. When delivered, Harold, decked out in waistcoat and bow tie, discovers that it takes up the entire front room. Ridiculed, he goads Albert into a match. Albert is winning easily, thanks to a combination of his cheating and Harold's foul shots. None of it is made easier by the lack of space. After having to leave the house, nip round the back to play through the open window, break a cue in half and still miss his shots, Harold admits the conditions have defeated him, but refuses to admit that Albert can. For once in his miserable life, he's determined to win. He has the table moved outside into the yard and the match continues through a thunderstorm and a blackout into the early hours. At last Harold is victorious. Promising to give Albert some lessons and with the old man's accolade of 'champ' ringing in his ears he puts the kettle on. Albert, meanwhile, goes back out to the table to tidy up – and puts on a solitary display of amazing trick shots.

'The Three Feathers' refers to the crest found on a Regency commode that Harold has bought from a woman on the round. According to expertise learned at antique appreciation evening classes, Harold believes it to have belonged to the Prince of Wales. Having bought the commode for £7 10s he plans to sell it at auction with a reserve of £200. Then the woman's husband calls, saying that his wife was unaware of the true value, and he wants to

buy back the commode. Harold wants £150. The husband reluc-
tantly agrees. Though Harold is happy to make a killing, for once,
Albert is unhappy at treating their customers so shabbily. Minutes
later an antique dealer arrives; he spots the commode and offers
£600. He promises to return in two days when Harold has dealt
with the original owners. Three days later, having bought back the
commode for £350, Harold is still waiting for the dealer. Albert
explains that he has been conned: the woman, her husband and the
dealer were all in it together. Their £150 cheque bounces and an
appraiser has valued the commode, and fourteen just like it, for £7
10s. Harold takes the pot and heads for his antique evening class;
he's going to hit his teacher over the head with it.

In 'Cuckoo in the Nest', the last episode in the series, the
Steptoes open the door to Arthur, Albert's long-lost first son.
Arthur, played by Kenneth J. Warren, has just arrived from
Australia, where his mother took him as a baby. Delighted to be
reunited, Albert insists he has Harold's room and makes him a
partner in the family business. Harold is bitterly jealous of the
preferential treatment, considering he has worked like a dog for
years. Believing Arthur to be a con man, he demands that Albert
choose between them. When the old man can't, Harold leaves.
Arthur is forced out on to the round and Harold takes to totting from a handcart. Three weeks later Albert tracks the starving
Harold down to his pitiful rented room. Having listened to tall
tales of how his son's new business is booming, Albert begs him to
come home. Harold was right. Arthur was a con man, and has sold
the Steptoes' horse and cart and disappeared. They agree to merge
their businesses and with the promise of a hot meal waiting at Oil
Drum Lane they set out for home to continue their talks. Albert
quietly pays Harold's back rent before the pair spot their cart in
the street and give chase.

After the series wrapped it was panto season again. Harry was
booked into Bromley for *Sleeping Beauty*. Danny Gray came along
for the juggling, and the box office record-breaking cast included
children's television presenter Brian Cant, singer Susan Maughan,
who had worked on the film *What a Crazy World*, and Lynda Baron,
who remembered:

> Harry being in the wings learning to juggle with Danny. I said to
> him, 'What *are* you doing?'

'I thought it might be quite good,' he said, 'I could make a feature out of it.'

Harry had such a childlike quality about him, as far as I'm concerned, that never went away. Here he was learning something new to do in a pantomime I don't know how many years down the line. He was always learning something new.

By January of 1971 the BBC had its audience figures for the latest *Steptoe* series. They had topped at 20.5 million.

One could reason a great many things out from studying these figures,' Michael Mills, BBC's head of comedy, wrote to Harry:

> but one result is, that 'Steptoe & Son' is still the greatest and most welcome entertainment offering in the United Kingdom today.
>
> If you accept that – and I don't see how anyone could gainsay it – then I think that we all should have both a duty and a desire to give the public more.
>
> Ray and Alan are very willing to write another 6 or 7 for us this year, and I would like to think that we were going to be able to achieve another 7 programmes in the Autumn of the year.
>
> The purpose of this letter is to ask. Are you agreeable to such a proposition?
>
> I think it goes without saying that I hope very much that you are.

Having agreed to the call of duty for the new series Harry revisited the old ones. The third radio series started recording at the end of January with a few cast changes due to unavailability. June Whitfield came in for the part of Daphne Goodlace in 'Two's Company' and Richard Griffiths landed an early role as the sea-faring George in 'Steptoe and Son and Son.'

After the radio, Harry took a few weeks of rest and relaxation with Maureen, Pat and us kids in Tunisia and Spain. Malcolm and Jennie joined us in Benidorm for Easter 1971. Jennie remembered how Harry was not overly impressed with breakfast in the hotel, and instead found a Brit-owned beachfront restaurant serving bacon and eggs. He went there every morning.

Holiday over; Harry began work on his next film, *The Magnificent Seven Deadly Sins*. It comprises seven separate 'sin'-themed vignettes, starring nearly everybody who was anybody in comedy at the time. Ray and Alan had written 'Pride', reworking an old *Comedy Playhouse* script. Harry's segment was 'Lust', written by Marty Feldman and Graham Stark, the latter also serving as the film's director. Harry plays a man who sees a girl on a payphone and chats her up while calling her from the adjoining phone booth. His wooing is successful and she agrees to a meeting as soon as she can get away from the disturbing man in the next booth with a face like a monkey – Harry. His monkey face crumbled beautifully. The scene ends with him abandoning the call and his hopes with the girl.

Then, after a quick aside for the *Des O'Connor Show* alongside fellow guests Jack Benny and Barry Cryer, it was time to pack the bucket and spade for Blackpool. Harry was starring alongside the singer Kathy Kirby in *The Big Star Show of 1971* at the South Pier, with Danny and June Gray also in the cast. It was a dream come true – headlining at Blackpool, the ultimate adrenaline rush. 'Harry is currently fulfilling what might well be the lifelong ambition of many of his contemporaries – a major summer season at Blackpool' reported *The Stage*: 'Obviously he is enjoying every minute of it, and with his crazy contributions – as a fortune-teller, deckchair attendant and eccentric surgeon – Harry blows up smilestorms that positively rock the South Pier twice nightly.'[7]

Helping him rock was Dave Dee, who was taking a break from Dave Dee, Dozy, Beaky, Mick & Tich in pursuit of a solo career. Dee and Harry were neighbours in Blackpool, having rented houses in St Anne's, overlooking the Royal Lytham and St Anne's Golf Course, for the duration of the ten-week season. In homage to the never-taken holidays of his youth, we also rented a beach hut. Harry would sit with cup of tea and sandwich, watching the world go by and his kids building sandcastles or going for donkey rides – though, perhaps, Jonathan wasn't enjoying every minute of it, as, on one occasion, the transplanted 5-year-old took to throwing everybody's clothes out of an upstairs window of the house to the promenade below.

It became the complete family outing when Malcolm and Jennie also came up to stay for a fortnight. Malcolm remembers that:

> whilst we were up there Maureen had always wanted to go, and had never been, to the Brontë Parsonage. Obviously it's a fair distance across the Pennines but as we were so far up country it was relatively close. Harry had hired a car and drove us all over.

He had a deadline by which he wanted to get back for the evening performance. We left in good time but ran into traffic. He was getting very agitated. It was an extremely nerve-wracking drive back.

I bet it was, Harry was probably tearing his hair out. He hated being late for a show – he would break out in a cold sweat at the thought of it.

In theatre you are expected to be there for the half-hour call, and most actors are there well before the hour, more if make-up dictates. Harry would invariably arrive two hours before curtain up. He was always the first in. He used to have a camp bed in his dressing room. Before every performance, after laying out his make-up from an old battered black tin that had been with him since Chorlton, he would lie down, put a towel over his eyes, right arm draped over his face and just switch the world off for a while. He didn't sleep; he was gathering his thoughts. Then it would be up, open the door ready to say hello and on with the slap – 'an actor prepares'. He was as punctual for rehearsals. Once, when it had become painfully obvious I was going to follow him into the family business, he was driving me to a play dress rehearsal at school and that bastard deliberately faffed about so that I would be late. As the minutes ticked by, past the deadline, I felt for myself the icy panic of not being on time – it was a lesson well taught, well learned and never forgotten.

By September, with the Blackpool season coming to a close, Harry was persuaded to take part in *An Hour With* … for the BBC. Michael Aspel fronted the programme that looked at its guest star's career, showed them in action, and then asked them to choose scenes from favourite films. It was an early foray into padding the schedule, as one reviewer pointed out:

> A repeat, old film clips … certainly it's an inexpensive way of filling an hour of television time. However, last night's 'An Hour with Harry H. Corbett' made an enjoyable item of viewing.
>
> The repeated programme was one of the gems of the Steptoe and Son stories, 'Come Dancing', still delightfully funny at the second seeing.

Hopefully it would be as funny at the third, as the BBC were about to begin repeating the sixth series in preparation for the arrival of the seventh in the New Year. Harry's *Hour* went to the top of the ratings and, according to the reviewer: 'His choice of film excerpts revealed fairly catholic tastes. They were of a dancing sequence, a duel, a Disney scene and an incredibly well filmed motor boat chase along the Amsterdam canals.'[8]

It is surprising that Harry's choices had omitted two of his favourite performers, as, according to Maureen, he thought:

> that Laurence Olivier was a very good actor – he thought he was very watchable – he was technically very good, and he had a similar approach to the work that Harry did. Larry Olivier used to spend hours with the nose putty and everything had to be just right; and when it was right, then he was right – and Harry was quite a lot like that.

He also thought that W.C. Fields was hilarious. I can remember him quoting Fields' proposed headstone epitaph – 'On the whole, I'd rather be in Philadelphia' – whenever we were dragged round a cemetery; an odd hobby, I suppose, but he always liked to see if he could spot a funny one. One can run out of things to do on tour and it does get you out of the hotel. As everything ceased in our house whenever Fields was on television, it's amazing he didn't make it into Harry's film choice; perhaps they couldn't get the rights, perhaps he had to choose from a list – you never know.

Films were still on the agenda that autumn when *Steptoe* prepared to hit the big screen with Ray and Alan's feature-length story about the rag-and-bone men. The movie opens with father and son leaving the divorce courts, having ended Harold's marriage, and then flashes back to a few years earlier, when the Steptoes had gone to an evening at the local football club. While comic Mike Reid does his patter, Harold nips to the bar where he meets Zita, a stripper. They hit it off and during her performance she slips Harold a note arranging to meet after the show. As Albert unwittingly chats up a drag act, played by Patrick Fyffe who was better known as Dame Hilda Bracket, his son sees Zita home. The next morning Harold returns to the yard and announces he and Zita are engaged, much to Albert's horror.

Steptoe senior does his best to ruin the wedding day and even accompanies the newlyweds on honeymoon to a half-built Spanish hotel, where Zita bumps into an old friend – the oily Terry. That evening, after waiting for hours for Albert to finish his lobster dinner and long after all the other honeymooners have disappeared upstairs, Harold and Zita are finally alone – until Albert starts groaning from the adjoining room. He has come down with food poisoning and begs to die in England. The Steptoes take the last two seats on the plane leaving Zita to follow. Soon Albert is better, but Zita hasn't come home. As the old man predicted, she has hooked up with oily Terry.

Months later, Harold hears that Zita is back in London; he tracks her down and discovers she is heavily pregnant. They agree to a fresh start and to settle down in Oil Drum Lane. But Albert refuses to live with her and Zita refuses to believe that Harold will ever leave the old man, so she decides that she'll be better off alone and departs.

After six months of Harold not talking to his father, the pair find a baby boy abandoned in their stable. They assume it must be Harold's son and the new father immediately starts planning little 'Jeremy's' future – a future that includes attending Eton so as to escape the family business. To this end Harold starts working extra jobs and, a few weeks later, comes home exhausted one day only to find that someone has taken Jeremy. He goes to confront Zita, who is dancing in a rugby club. The rowdy patrons make a grab for her, and Harold steps in to defend her honour only to have his body and pride severely beaten by the drunken rabble. Rushed backstage by Zita and her pianist, he finds Zita's baby, who turns out to be a girl fathered by the black pianist. Neither this baby nor Jeremy were ever his.

As the action shifts back to the opening scene of the film, it finds the Steptoes in a philosophical mood as they journey away from the divorce courts. A limousine, trying to overtake their cart, blares its horn behind them. They flip two fingers at it but when it passes they notice the Royal Standard. The car's regal Royal Navy-uniformed passenger, presumably Prince Philip, winds down his window and returns their vulgar salute in kind as the credits start to roll.

Translating a successful comedy show from TV into film was very much in vogue at the time. As previous attempts had shown it could be tricky taking away the live audience and trying a new format. One would need an experienced hand at the helm. However, Duncan Wood, who had guided every other *Steptoe*, was unavailable. He had recently been booted upstairs to be Head of Comedy at the BBC. The film's producer Aida Young, who had been associate producer on Harry's film *What a Crazy World*, suggested Cliff Owen, a director she had worked with on the movie *The Vengeance of She* a few years earlier. Cliff's credentials were apt. He not only had a background in directing many comedies for TV and film but had already taken *Morecambe and Wise* to the big screen. He also proved a popular choice with Galton and Simpson, as he had directed their screenplay for the film *The Wrong Arm of the Law*, starring Peter Sellers. But, according to Alan, he did not prove popular with Wilfrid: 'The old man would get very uppity with Cliff Owen. He thought he was a slob and an awful bully. Admittedly, Cliff would shout a lot and Willie didn't like that; he was a gentleman actor.'

'I think it was probably because Cliff found it easier to relate to Harry,' reflects Ray Galton:

> Both Alan and I found it easier to relate to Harry as well. It wasn't so much an age thing, although that probably played a part. It's just that Harry shared our cultural touchstones. Willie never went out of his way to engage us in conversation. He was a pro, he learnt the lines and did the job. That's fine. He was always pleasant company and fun on set, but there was no attempt to draw us into his life or his circle. Things were always on a purely professional level. Maybe on the film, with a longer, more intensive time together, that surfaced more than usual.[9]

Carolyn Seymour, who played Zita and now lives and works in LA, also did not have the best of times and 'hated doing that movie', though that was laid more at the door of having to portray a stripper rather than any ill feeling on set. 'Harry and Wilfrid were sweet to me,' she recalled, 'What a funny shy guy Harry was! Very funny.'

Harry himself never mentioned any great angst during the filming and obviously got on with Mike Reid. The comic had landed his biggest role to date when:

> The *Sunday Times* did three pages on me in their colour supplement. Producer Aida Young saw it, caught my act and gave me the part in her film. As I like to add my own lines of patter, the film rôle was half scripted and half ad lib. I hadn't met Harry Corbett before but soon found we were on the same wavelength.[10]

The final outcome of the production seemed pleasing but no one would know for sure until it hit cinemas in the spring.

That winter Harry released a single, *Harry, You Love Her* and appeared on the music programme *Lift Off* on 15 December to promote it. Naturally, he had to forgo panto that Christmas. However, he didn't escape promoting one. Jimmy Lovell, Harry's first director at Chorlton and who was still in charge at Dundee Rep, had written asking for help to publicise their Christmas show. As regional theatres lived and died by panto, any plug would help.

'On the eve of the "Jack and the Beanstalk" panto in Dundee,' the local paper reported:

> Mr Lovell got this greetings-gram:
> 'Some 22 years ago I saved your pantomime when I startled the world with my rendition of cow in "Jack and the Beanstalk" for you.
> I see again for the 22nd time I have been passed over! Your memory is short, sir!
> However, I bear no ill-will and wish only that the present performers have the same good fortune in their careers as I had.
> – Harry H. Corbett.'

The plug helped. Jimmy wrote to say: 'We are only a 300 seater but pretty well sold out for four weeks and I have just decided to run for a fifth – probably go down the drain but I need the time for the next show: "Arms and the Man."'

That must have tickled Harry, as it came twenty years after he and Jimmy had taken *Arms* to Platt Fields.

January of 1972 saw Harry and Wilf still in *Steptoe* mode as they were recording the fourth radio series. Yootha Joyce, Richard Hurndall and Anthony Sharp all returned to recreate their roles. Ray and Alan were also having a surfeit of *Steptoe* as an adaptation of the series was finally being aired in America. The US version was entitled *Sanford and Son*. As Galton and Simpson had suggested years earlier, two black actors were cast in the roles: Redd Foxx as Fred Sanford and Demond Wilson as his son, Lamont. *Sanford* proved an enormous success, featuring in the top ten of the ratings throughout its six-season run. For the UK counterparts, February 1972 saw them leave the radio studio and head straight on to Television Centre to record series seven. John Howard Davies, who had been a child star as David Lean's *Oliver Twist* and had grown up to become a TV director in charge of, amongst others, *Monty Python's Flying Circus* and *The Goodies*, took over from Duncan Wood as series producer/director.

In the episode 'Men of Letters', Anthony Sharp was back again, not as a doctor this time but in his more famous guise as the local vicar. The Steptoes are enjoying a game of scrabble, well Albert is, as he's winning thanks to a selection of vulgar words. The vicar comes calling and asks the Steptoes for a 'History of Rag and Boning' for the parish magazine. Both of them want to do the article, as Harold has the artistic streak and Albert knows the history. They toss a coin for the honour. Harold wins but Albert is asked to contribute anything he wishes to the mag. Thinking that this is the start of a new career and after interviewing local totters and his old man, Harold beavers away at the typewriter for seven nights like a Hollywood cub reporter. The vicar loves the resulting article and calls to say 5,000 magazines will be printed. The great day arrives. Harold comes home with a copy and reports how the vicar has been arrested for publishing obscene material and all copies of the parish mag have been impounded thanks to Albert's contribution – a pornographic, filth-laden crossword. The magazine, including Harold's article, is now going up in smoke. He has only three things to say to the old man: 'six across, thirteen across and twenty-eight down.'

'A Star is Born' sees Harold joining the local amateur dramatics society for their production of *Guilt! The White Man's Burden*. The episode offered plenty of in-house jokes as Albert, while denigrating his son's latest ambition, pronounces all actors 'poofs' and Harold recreates his audition speech: Marlon Brando's 'I coulda been a contender' from *On the Waterfront*. The audition lands Harold the leading part in *Guilt!* and hopefully will set him on the road to international stardom and away from the junkyard. The society comes to the Steptoes' house to rehearse. Trevor Bannister, who that September would star as Mr Lucas in the *Comedy Playhouse* episode 'Are You Being Served' which, like *Steptoe*, went on to several series, does a wonderful turn as the play's writer and director. He immediately casts Albert as one of his principals. This, and the old man's constant needling, enrages Harold so much that he loses all confidence (for a good actor, the hardest part to play is that of a bad one. It is a measure of Harry's expertise that he carries it off so well). Come the night of the performance, Albert is a hit and Harold a flop, yet again. Trevor Bannister recalled working on the episode:

> I always regarded the series as one of the few *true* situation com-
> edies. Harry and Wilfrid were of course exceptional in their
> characterization. The writing of Galton and Simpson was some of
> the best on TV. It was a very happy show to work on. Harry was
> a very generous actor to work with. I feel very privileged to have
> been a small part of it. Such quality is sadly missed on TV today.[11]

'Oh, What a Beautiful Mourning' reunites the larger Steptoe clan. Albert's brother George has died and Harold bemoans attending yet another obscenely grasping family funeral, at which there never seem to be any fewer graspers, as 'they drop like flies and breed like rabbits.' As George borrowed £25 from Albert in 1927, never repaid it and was 'tight as a gnat's chuff' the old man is determined to get first pickings of the deceased's hoarded goods at the wake. The wake sees actors returning from *Steptoe*'s other family episode, 1965's 'And Afterwards At …': George A. Cooper again played Uncle Arthur, Rita Webb played potty Auntie Aida, as opposed to Auntie Freda, and Mollie Sugden returned, not as Harold's prospective mother-in-law, but as Auntie Minnie. She, like all the other mourners, has noticed the only thing worth having from George is a small Limoges figurine. Even the shapely Caroline, one of Harold's dis-tant cousins, agrees. Harold is enjoying chatting her up until Albert informs him that she might not be that distant after all, as any of the Steptoes could be her father. After laying George to rest, tyres squealing, the family race each other back to divide the spoils only to find the house empty. According to his will, George has arranged that everything be collected during his internment. The sale of the contents and his entire estate he leaves to charity. Harold raises a toast to George: 'The only Steptoe I ever knew with a sense of humour.' As the rest of the thwarted family leave in disgust, Albert removes his hat to drink to the departed and reveals the Limoges figurine. 'Steptoe the clepto' has struck and reclaimed his £25.

In 'Live Now, P.A.Y.E. Later' Albert receives a letter from the Inland Revenue. Their inspector wants to interview him over the claims he has been making for his wife, a wife who has been dead for thirty-three years. He is expected imminently, so to avoid a fine or imprisonment they decide that Albert must feign senility. When the inspector, played by Colin Gordon, arrives, the Steptoes ply him with drink and Albert regales him with heroic war stories. As the inspector gets steadily inebriated he wants to know why Albert has not declared his wife's old age pension, as she's been entitled to it for the past six years and Albert has never claimed it. The inspector is appalled and will personally send a man from the ministry to see Mrs Steptoe the next day and help her claim. Albert is delighted at the thought of a cheque for £1,000 in back payments but Harold informs him he has now compounded the felony. The man from the ministry calls and Harold is about to confess all when Albert enters, in drag. He signs the forms as Gladys Steptoe and gets the cheque and pension book. While claiming the pension at the post office, a retired Fraud Squad officer, Peter Madden, takes a shine to 'Gladys'. After barely escaping from his advances with honour intact, Albert writes to the Revenue informing them of his wife's sudden death. They are sorry to hear it but now want to clear up Mrs Steptoe's estate and assume Harold and his sister Muriel will inherit. Albert has also been claiming for a fictitious daughter. To keep the old man out of the clink Harold drags up as Muriel and puts up with being chased round the house by the lascivious inspector.

Dragging up did not prove popular with either Wilfrid or Harry. Duncan Wood wrote to John Howard Davies with advice on how to smooth their feathers:

> Wilfrid has expressed reservations to me over the 'drag' bits. *Personally* I think the whole thing is very funny. It's not one of those scripts seeking 'truth'; it's just a romp. I'm sure that – treated on that level – it will go like a bomb. There's not much depth in the piece – in fact, I accept that it is a bit in Dick Emery territory. But it's very funny. Try to get them to see it in this light and go and enjoy it. I think page 52 could be treated a bit more subtly for Harry. There's a lot to be got out of his total incredulity at Albert's suggestion that he – Harry – does Muriel![12]

Although Wilf was disturbingly passable as a little old lady, Harry could never be the object of any inspector's desire, no matter how desperate or deluded. But that wasn't his problem with the episode. Unlike previous series, where there had been a delicate balance between poignancy and comedy derived from the touchstones of everyday family life, *Steptoe* was now heading into the realm of the silly.

Touches of this continued into the next episode, 'Loathe Story'. Harold once again has all the gear and no idea while father and son play badminton in the yard. After winning easily, Albert threatens to join the tennis club where Harold has made some high-class friends. That night Harold sleepwalks into his father's room and tries to decapitate him with a meat cleaver. Mortified, Harold seeks the help of a psychiatrist – Raymond Huntley delivering a superbly subtle turn as a breast-obsessed shrink, nonchalantly hiding girlie mags in his desk and doodling a topless beauty on his notepad. On the couch, Harold recounts a childhood spent waiting outside the Skinner's Arms for a habitually drunken Albert to be poured out and an occasion when the old man ruined his engagement to the poshest and richest bird Harold ever knew, Bunty Kennington-Stroud. Shown in flashback, she and her mother had called for tea so that mater could check out Harold's bloodstock before agreeing to the marriage. As Harold clumsily fawned, Albert was at his belligerent best, taking every opportunity to offend. In a final insult, the ladies become infested by fleas and run screaming from the house. Back on the couch, Harold is amazed he hasn't committed murder already; the unperturbed shrink prescribes tranquillisers and, armed with these, Harold is able to return home and not rise to the bait when he finds Albert is trying to rent out his room. However, no medication could stop him wielding a knife when he hears the old man has joined the tennis club.

Joanna Lumley played Bunty and recalls her time on the show:

It was an extraordinary week for me: for a start, it is very rare that the writers attend every rehearsal. Galton and Simpson did just that, honing each line Harry and Wilfrid spoke. Wilfrid used to turn up looking immaculate, in a tie and crisp shirt with matching socks and a breast pocket handkerchief. Harry, I was relieved to see, looked much more like an 'actor', in old jeans and a shabby shirt always untucked and flapping out at the back. They were both very kind to me, an absolute beginner: Harry in particular made sure that all our small moments together were well rehearsed. The show went out live in front of a studio audience. I don't remember much of it as I was offstage most of the time; but I hope it won't be disloyal to say that Harry 'grew' in front of an audience, whereas Wilfrid was assailed by nerves and wasn't nearly as funny as he had been in rehearsals when he was much more secure.

The series was back on top form with the next recorded episode, a perennial favourite, 'The Desperate Hours'. Starving and shivering over a game of cribbage in a house colder than the Russian Front, the Steptoes have fallen on hard times again. They've already pawned the telly and, with no money for the electricity meter, are now listening to the radio by candlelight. A news flash reports that two dangerous criminals have escaped from the local prison. As Harold roots around for foreign coins to feed the meter Albert answers a knock at the door, it's the escaped partners in crime, Johnnie and Frank. The younger partner, Johnnie, demands food (Albert is despatched to the kitchen), a car (they haven't got one, just the horse), and the telephone (it's been cut off). His demand for Harold's money results in a measly 3½ pence. Johnnie berates Frank, the older man, for choosing such a rotten house. He says that ever since Frank's trousers got caught on the barbed wire during the escape he's been holding him back, and he would have been free and clear without him. In fact, Johnnie says, Frank has always held him back, and he'd be better off alone. It is an opinion Harold can sympathise with. When Albert returns with all the food in the house, cold porridge, green cheese and rock-hard bread, it's the final straw – 'You'd be better off inside,' Johnnie tells Harold. The two form a bond over chances thwarted by their respective old men, as the old men form an equal bond over the ungrateful youngsters. When a police siren wails near the house Johnnie decides to make a break for it, and Frank begs to be taken along. Albert supports him, questioning the honour amongst thieves; while Harold pleads with Johnnie to go it alone. Guilt-racked, Johnnie cracks. As he'll never make it with Frank in tow, he resigns himself to them both returning to prison. Harold and Albert promise to visit. The electric meter clocks off again, empty of coins. Johnnie gives Harold his last shilling and the prisoners disappear into the night. Albert is pleased they stayed together. 'Yes, I expect you are,' Harold replies through gritted teeth. He closes the episode summing up the bleakness of his situation, 'Oh well, better go and lock the cage up.'

Frank was played by J.G. Devlin, the actor who had been alternate casting for Albert on 'The Offer' had Wilfrid been unavailable. Coming in for Johnnie, in what has to be the greatest contribution from any guest star, was Leonard Rossiter. Since Rossiter's previous turn in *The Lead Man Cometh*, his star had continued to rise and his reputation continued to impress. It certainly impressed Duncan

Wood, who was soon to leave the BBC and become Yorkshire Television's Head of Light Entertainment, where he was responsible for turning Rossiter into a household name with the series *Rising Damp*. Harry would have been impressed with the actor's dedication and perfectionism; in Robert Ross' book on the series, Alan reflected on the effects of Rossiter's arrival:

> When Leonard Rossiter came on board for 'The Desperate Hours', Harry raised his game completely. Leonard came in for the first day of rehearsal and played his part perfectly straight, and it was brilliant. Harry realised immediately that he had got a fight on his hands. It was amazing to watch. It just unfolded before your very eyes. It was like witnessing two stags in the glen coming together. For my money it's the best performance Harry ever gave.

Ray Galton concurs:

> Harry was getting very lazy. I thought he had coasted through a few of that series, to be honest. It's not surprising. I mean, after ten years of playing the same part, he was getting stylised. I think he was probably getting bored and a bit frustrated by that stage. It wasn't a challenge any more.[13]

Certainly, episodes that included 'dragging up' and boob jokes would not have provided much of a challenge, so to return to the usual standard of Galton and Simpson's scripts and play off an actor as remarkably talented as Rossiter must have given Harry a glorious respite from the easy gag.

'He had certainly picked up little coat pegs along the way,' continues Simpson:

> little tricks of the trade that he knew would assure him a laugh. And if anything, the old man was even worse. Willie realised quite early on that he could get a laugh by doing the leer before saying the line. When in doubt or desperation, do the leer and you get a laugh! It became very easy for both of them. They had both examined these characters so deeply that they could play them on autopilot and still get reasonable results. However, Harry in particular wasn't about to let 'his show' get pinched from under his nose.

> It was clear from the very first day of rehearsal that this was going
> to be a good episode… that's probably why we, or the powers that
> be, wanted to put it at the end of the series so it wouldn't be lost in
> the shuffle. Leave the punters wanting more, as they say.[14]

Last recorded, and penultimately shown, was 'Divided We Stand'. As
John Howard Davies was ill, David Croft – the prolific writer and
producer whose credits include *Dad's Army*, *Are You Being Served?*, *It
Ain't Half Hot Mum*, *Hi Dee Hi!* and *'Allo, 'Allo!* – was brought in to
oversee the episode.

Harold is determined to decorate the house, making it light
and airy and doing away with Albert's choice of 'dark green and
chocolate' paint. Nothing he chooses finds favour with Albert,
whose only contribution is to want flock wallpaper in the khazi.
Having reached an impasse, Harold snaps and refuses to live in
the old man's filth and squalor any longer. He decides to set up a
partition, dividing the house down the middle, even going to the
extent of installing a penny-operated turnstile in the shared hall,
so that Albert can access the kitchen and Harold the stairs. When
the border is closed Harold has freedom at last. It comes at a price,
though. Having spent all his money on the dividing wall he cannot
afford his own TV. So the apartheid is extended to the family set,
father and son each able to see half of the 21in screen. Harold wants
to watch the ballet; Albert can't abide it and switches over to a
horror film. Harold is incensed; they have already agreed it is his
night to choose the programme. Demanding that Albert switches
back to the ballet, Harold calmly reminds his father that he has 'the
law of contract on his side.' 'I have the knobs on my side,' Albert
retorts, in one of *Steptoe*'s most quoted lines. They compromise on
watching the football, but peace is short lived as they tussle over
who has more of the screen. Harold shoves the set at Albert and
following the wire back from the set pulls the plug on the old man's
enjoyment. Quick to get his own back, Albert beats his son to the
outhouse, but has his comeuppance when Harold pulls the chain.
His joy at his father's discomfort is brief, however, as he goes to bed
having left the gas on. The resulting fire, made worse by the firemen
losing time having to put pennies in the turnstile, lands the pair in
neighbouring hospital beds.

This episode is often voted the favourite amongst *Steptoe* fans. It
is certainly one of the most memorable. It is memorable to me on

a purely personal note – I can distinguish various members of my family in amongst the gales of laughter.

To promote the new series the *Radio Times* once again had Wilfrid and Harry as their cover stars and ran an 'at home' feature on the pair. Wilfrid reportedly marvelled at the show's popularity in far-flung corners of the world and defended it against those who thought his character's crudeness was merely gratuitous.

Harry touched on the difficulties of playing a maturing character: 'He's had enough gazumphs in his lifetime, he's been taken apart so often that he's got to be a little more circumspect now, a little more knowledgeable. Consequently, the naivety he displayed ten years ago is no longer quite valid in the sense that the times have moved as well.'

The reporter, Russell Miller, also addressed what effect being Harold must have had on him:

> Harry admits that Harold has changed his life completely, but he is ambivalent about whether it is for better or worse. He has earned more money and public recognition out of *Steptoe* than anything else he has ever done, but he is acutely aware also of the restrictions the role has placed on his career …
>
> Harold has probably had a greater effect on his life than Albert has on Wilfrid Brambell's. For Harry H. Corbett is incurably shy and claims to be tongue-tied without a script. He rarely ventures out of doors without a hat or spectacles, in the vain hope that they will prevent him from being recognised.[15]

Series seven finished its run on 3 April, a day after *Steptoe and Son* the movie officially opened at cinemas. The film became a runaway success, helped, no doubt, by being on the back of the TV series. It would win Ray and Alan the Writer's Guild Award for Best Screenplay and according to Alan, 'It was the biggest box-office sensation of the time. It broke 84 box-office records throughout the country.'[16]

Promotion for the film had coincided with recording at TV centre. By this time Harry and Wilf had been living and breathing *Steptoe* without a break for over six months. Understandably, Harry was a little more candid than usual when it came to the oft-repeated questions:

Is he worried about becoming typecast in the Steptoe mould?
'Yes,' he admits. 'It's not really good for an actor to play one role
for so many years, I can't go into a pub without some lads going
on about last week's episode on the telly. When we started the
series, we'd no idea it would catch on like it did. So far we've
done 42, all of them repeated, and we're just making seven new
ones. There are good reasons why it's caught on like it has but
I don't intend living in Harold's shoes for the rest of my life.'[17]

To slip out of Harold's shoes Harry jumped at the chance to take the
Neil Simon play *The Last of the Red Hot Lovers* on tour to Australia.
Harry had loved his previous visit there, even when he ended up in
the clink. Not only would it be a new challenge in a new horizon
but it also gave him the chance to show his family the world, and
one or two of his more salubrious old haunts.

   Three days after the film opened, on Jonathan's sixth birthday, we
boarded the plane for Melbourne.

Notes

 1   *The Independent*, 8/3/70.
 2   *Halifax Evening Courier*, 3/11/69.
 3   Galton and Simpson, *Steptoe and Son*.
 4   *Daily Sketch*, 26/2/70.
 5   *News of the World*, 17/5/70.
 6   *Daily Sketch*, 6/6/70.
 7   *The Stage*, 12/8/71.
 8   *Leister Mercury*, 9/9/71.
 9   Galton and Simpson, *Steptoe and Son*.
10   *ABC Film Review*, April 1972.
11   Galton and Simpson, *Steptoe and Son*.
12   *Ibid.*
13   Galton and Simpson, *Steptoe and Son*.
14   *Ibid.*
15   *Radio Times*, 19/2/72.
16   Galton and Simpson, *Steptoe and Son*.
17   *ABC Film Review*, April 1972.

Under the Blue Gum Trees

I've had 23 years in the business, and I still don't know where I'll be tomorrow. I have no control over my artistic life, no plan, no ambition further than the present. I would, however, like to make a lot of money. With money I can buy time and peace and comfort. Look I'm bloody 45 and I want to see the world in which Empires were lost and won before they're wiped out completely – Rangoon, the Taj Mahal, Samarkand.[1]

Harry H. Corbett

There was a chance to spy on Rangoon while flying over Burma on the long haul to Australia. But Harry didn't. He was asleep and no amount of prodding could rouse him, even to see his birthplace. Unsurprising, given that not only was sleeping a favourite pastime but the haul was longer than usual thanks to terrorist activities and the Vietnam War. This resulted in flying from London to Rome, to Bahrain, to Bangkok, to Singapore and finally Melbourne Tullamarine. Where the press were waiting:

Reporters and an impressive line-up of television cameras were poised ready to catch the comedy sketch they expected to appear from behind the door.

Two big blue eyes peeped through the door – 'Oh Gawd! What's all this? This is glamour,' he said, overawed by his reception at Melbourne Airport.

Just what you need after a day's flight with two small children. Of course, having only seen the tarmac, the journalist's first question

– 'So, what do you think of Australia?' – was a bit of a poser. This was quickly followed by the expected questions on being Harold: 'Surprisingly enough, Corbett isn't sick of Harold. He has just finished filming a new Steptoe series. "Harold is a wonderful character," Corbett said, "I like playing him. But it isn't what I like about the boy that's important. It's what the public think of him."'[2]

After sating the *Steptoe* interest it was time to bring attention back to the job in hand and Neil Simon's *The Last of the Red Hot Lovers*, with its handy built-in headline:

'Simon is a brilliant writer – he's a genius,' said Harry. 'He can turn the most trivial phrase into an hilarious comment.' He couldn't see any reason why Steptoe couldn't be a red hot lover: 'I AM a red hot lover.'

Wife Maureen sighs and smiles as Harry begins to shepherd his family out of the Tullamarine Press Room.[3]

Out of the pressroom and on to a rented house on Grange Road in Toorak, an upmarket suburb of Melbourne, where more interviews had been set up. I managed to escape the lure of basking in reflected glory: 'It was easy to see that Corbetts senior and male junior had plenty of personality. Susannah's was impossible to assess. She spent the interview sound asleep on a sofa, covered by a coat, while reporters photographers and television cameramen went about their noisy business.'

No doubt Harry would have been pleased, he was always wary of the damaging superficial attention his fame could bring. 'I want my kids to be ordinary kids in a normal family,' he said, 'I don't want them to feel special or different.'[4]

This was fairly easy to achieve considering that, at home, he was so ordinary and so shy. I can remember him steeling himself just to make a business call, never mind an appearance. He would sit by the phone with his usual bucket sized cup of tea, lit cigarette in the ashtray and a packet of Players on standby. Most of us have a phone voice – he had a phone character. As kids we loved it. To see him grasp the receiver, set his shoulders and then suddenly turn into a luvvie and start calling the grown man on the end of the line 'darling' would have us in hysterics. I couldn't say how much his performance was despite of, or playing to, the sounds of our snorting from under the kitchen table but I do know that it taught us to see his fame, and the resulting press attention, for what it was.

In a country as uninhibited as Australia, Harry's modesty caught the attention of interviewers that first day in Melbourne:

> Harry H. Corbett's parting shot seemed to sum up the man and the actor. 'All these interviews,' he said, 'makes me feel like a pools winner.'
>
> It seems the star of Steptoe and Son isn't an accomplished performer in interviews. He keeps apologising for not performing and, sitting in his newly rented house in Toorak yesterday he confessed that interviews were new to him.
>
> 'You see, in England you would never get me to give an interview,' he said. 'It sounds conceited, but I prefer to let my work do it for me. But here I'm an unknown quantity, especially on the stage.'
>
> Corbett explained earnestly what he intended to do in Australia while he is here for the Neil Simon play The Last of the Red Hot Lovers.
>
> 'I want to become a Commonwealth actor,' he said. 'I want to commute regularly to Australia and other Commonwealth countries and work hard in each. I don't want to do this business of getting in, getting out fast and making plenty of money. I hope we will be here until the beginning of next summer and I intend to become part of the local scene.'
>
> I don't know if we will do anymore of Steptoe. It's a bit like salmon spawning – we come back to it.'
>
> Acting and his family are his only interests, 'I've been lucky as an actor,' he said. 'The main thing is to work – and I've always been able to work. I haven't always been paid, but I've always worked.'[5]

Press done, family settled, kids enrolled in Christ Church Grammar School in South Yarra, Harry could get back to that work and started rehearsals, meeting director, Alfred Sandor, and his fellow cast.

The 'red hot lover' of the play's title is 47-year-old New York restaurateur Barney Cashman. Worried that life is passing him by, he decides to throw caution, and twenty-three years of married monogamy, to the wind, by having an affair to prove he's still got it. He tries to have it in his mother's apartment, during three afternoons spaced over three years, with three women in three acts.

Barney's first potential lover, played by Leila Blake, turns out to be a married man-eater with far too much experience to be interested in his amateur attempts at seduction. The second, a pot-smoking flighty actress, played by Anne Lucas, frightens him with tales of her bizarre past lovers. The third, played by Betty Lucas (no relation), is his wife's best friend and a neurotic pill popper, determined to get back at her own unfaithful husband but unable to follow through.

Betty had worked with Wilfrid prior to meeting Harry and gave her opinion on the differences between them:

> 'While I admire Wilfrid and enjoyed working with him, I feel that Harry is the finer actor.'
>
> Miss Lucas toured the UK with Wilfrid Brambell in a production of 'Twelfth Night.'
>
> 'I played Maria and Wilfrid played Andrew Aguecheek,' she said. 'He used to entertain us with a most wonderful repertoire of Irish Ballads. This was before he went into 'Steptoe and Son' … Steptoe was a lucky break for Wilfrid. He was out of work at the time.'
>
> Miss Lucas remembers Wilfrid Brambell as a very serious person, perhaps a little lonely. She really warmed to the subject of Harry Corbett.
>
> 'He is wonderful to work with – a fine actor and very unselfish.' Miss Lucas said. 'Some stars can make the other actors feel very unhappy on stage, but Harry gives so much all the time that if one is not good, it is one's own fault. Harry can be very serious, but he has a fine sense of humour and he's a splendid raconteur. He's also very much a family man.'

As they were working together, even if Betty hadn't liked Harry, she was hardly going to rubbish him. But such an obvious vote of confidence from a cast member would have helped to bolster his nerves, which, with the looming opening night and an unknown audience, were starting to fray.

He had also come down with a cold, which gave the self-confessed hypochondriac something else to worry about: 'I'll guarantee that before the week is out I'll be consulting ear, nose and throat specialists. I'm the worst in the world when it comes to ailments, but only when I'm starting a new play.'[6]

A cold is never great news for an actor but for Harry, it would help bring on the chronic catarrh he had suffered with for years –

his dressing room was never complete without an industrial sized bottle of Olbas Oil.

And then he started worrying about his New York accent: 'I sound halfway between a cockney and an Irishman at the moment. You know when the idea was first put to me I was overjoyed,' he said:

> But I know me, between now and opening night I'll get so many doubts that I'll end up thinking I'm mad to come 13,000 miles to perform in a flop. And I will be completely convinced of this right up until the day after opening night ... Then I'll be all right.
>
> Deep down I must know that the play has a great chance because it is a very beautiful play and very, very funny. It's the rehearsals, though, which always bring on my worries. When I start, things always look so bad that I can never imagine being ready for the night.

Of course, there were always the comparisons: 'One of my main problems is Harold Steptoe. I know, for instance, that the advance bookings for Melbourne are tremendous, which should be a great morale booster. But it isn't, because I also know that the people who have booked are hoping to see me do Harold.'

Even when he turned up specifically to be Harold at a charity gig, complete with authentic costume kept for that very task, he was still concerned with letting people down and his preparations would be meticulous. He would delve into joke books and research the locals to make sure his patter was up to snuff:

> But after I've made my appearance I feel like crawling away because I'm not really Harold. You see, I am not a comedian. I am an actor. To get Harold to the heights he has climbed I have had to work like a Trojan. I need a script first, and only then can I get into character. When people come up to me and say 'do 'Arold then', I'm lost, because I need the words. This is the main reason I like to do other things, so people can see that I am purely an actor.

An actor who, despite his success, still didn't rate himself too highly:

> You see, I have never had any formal training. I just drifted into the game really. I left school as soon as I was able, and so my

education is purely formal. This makes me feel uneasy when I get
among the actors who have spent years at school learning the
theory as well as the practice. When they start talking technical
I get completely lost, and so, I suppose, it makes me feel as though
I'm not as good an actor as them, despite the fact that I am probably making more money. I suppose this makes me work harder.
I don't really know how good I am as an actor.[7]

It's very nerve wracking … the theatre is all pressure and polishing. I very rarely booze with the boys and I'm not extremely
close friends with old Steptoe – I don't have close friends as
such because I have more home life than friends. I'm such a shy
person that even if only two strangers are around I feel uncomfortable and I'm inclined to shut up or go over the top and chat
my head off and be witty, gay and amazing. Mostly I work and
watch TV – because I'm lazy basically and the effort of going out
is far too much.[8]

Having waited so long to have a family he wasn't going to squander
his time with them: 'I prefer to stay at home with my wife and
family. It's beautiful to shut the world out when I get home from
the studio. Then I can forget all my worries and inadequacies and
just be 'Dad'. The family is the great stabiliser in my life. I think.
Without them, God knows, I'd probably be a raving neurotic.'

Even with us, he was having a fair crack at being one. But
Maureen, having lived though quite a few plays with Harry by this
time, had seen it all before and was not concerned: 'He does worry
a lot,' she said, 'but he also handles himself very well with people.
He will work harder than anyone else to ensure that things are right
on the night – and I can't remember a bad opening yet.'

While Harry fretted, Maureen was the rock that he needed to
keep him in the game. This was something he was well aware of:
'I don't lean on my wife as a morale booster … I look to her for
giving me a home. She can be tired and yet she'll still help me
to read my lines back … she'll give me a cup of tea at the right
moment … have the washing organised … our lives organised. This
is the way I lean desperately hard on my wife.'[9]

He never could have done it without her. She wasn't perfect,
though she seemed it. And thanks to all the line running she could
even do a very passable 'Albert'. Maureen's main fault, and a very

irritating one, was that she was always bloody right – this occasion proved no exception, and the reviews couldn't have been better:

> I don't know if Mr. Simon had Mr Harry Corbett in mind when he first wrote this situation comedy. He might as well. For I cannot think of any other actor who would have portrayed the difficult part of Barney Cashman with the eloquence and humility of Harry H.
>
> Mr. Corbett may be, or may not be the last of the red hot lovers. But there's no doubt on that score – he is the best of them. As the final curtain descended, and the roar of the applause thundered up, it was quite clear – the women in the capacity audience were all just wild about Harry.[10]

After three months in Melbourne, the tour moved on to Her Majesty's Theatre in Adelaide. It was a three-week run, not long enough to warrant finding a school, but plenty of time for the family to head out from the rented house on Northgate Street in Unley Park and get to know the city. In Melbourne the whirlwind of press, rehearsals and fine-tuning during the run had left little time to find the 'real' Australia, with the city's veneer of international metropolis making it more elusive. The glimpses we had caught had been thanks to tourist days out, when we turned into one of the attractions. Harry was asked to appear at the Echuca Steam Rally. Echuca is an historic port on the banks of the Murray River, its Aboriginal name meaning 'meeting of the waters' as it lies where the Campaspe joins the Murray and is also close to the Goulburn River. Its steam rally is a huge annual draw celebrating the past. You can also celebrate it, as we did, by taking a trip up the Murray on one of the old paddle steamers, floating past the river red gum trees that line the banks and that once provided the town's industry. Certificates for having steered the PS *Canberra* and a miniature red gum log buggy, which were presented by the rally's organisers, were packed into a suitcase along with mementos, cine film and seemingly every book on Australia's Aboriginal tribes, history, geology, archaeology, art, and flora and fauna that Maureen could find. Such suitcases were regularly sent back to Pat, who was looking after the house in St John's Wood.

The stay in Adelaide gave us a chance to quietly see some of the country for ourselves. It was a beautiful city, with wide boulevards, grand colonial Victorian architecture and a burgeoning arts scene. Its natural surroundings were unparalleled: minutes from the city you were in the bush, looking out over the Mount Lofty Ranges, feeding wallabies or cuddling koalas in Cleland National Park. A ferry ride took you to Kangaroo Island, huge areas of which had remained untouched by civilisation.

No Australiaphile's visit could be complete without a trip to the heart of the country and before the tour headed on to Perth we took a couple of days out and flew up to Alice Springs. Everything about the town paid homage to its isolation. As you came in to land at the tiny airport you could see the vast open expanse towards the gap in the MacDonnell Ranges, the gateway for the river, road and railway connecting Alice to the outside. This feeling of space continued inside the town. From our base at the Riverside Hotel, now renamed the Todd Tavern, we walked along the few wide-open roads past squat buildings pinned to the land by the winter sun in an unending blue sky. The occasional car threw up clouds of red dust that settled on signposts pointing out to the population of less than 12,000 how many miles away everything was. 'Adelaide – 1070', 'Darwin – 954', 'Mount Isa – 732', 'Ayers Rock – 300'.

The rock was our next destination. It had been discovered in the nineteenth century by explorers who named it after the then Chief Secretary of South Australia. Had they just asked the locals, who had revered it for millennia, they would have also discovered its name was Uluru, the name by which, along with Ayers, it has been officially known since 1993. We flew out of Alice on a fourteen-seat 1950s-built Connair Heron. There's nothing like a small plane for tackling the red centre's thermals; Harry was white knuckle the whole way. Today Uluru boasts a resort with five star accommodation; in 1972 it was a prefab motel one up from a campsite, which only added to the adventure and the majesty of the place. After landing at the tiny airstrip we were shuttled to Kata Tijuta/The Olgas, then onto the rock itself.

Maureen and Harry, by now spell-bound by all things Aboriginal, spent hours pouring over the cave paintings. Had they known that the ancient custodians of Uluru, the Anangu, weren't that keen on visitors trampling all over their sacred site I'm sure we would have stayed off it. Back then there weren't any around to ask. Unsurprisingly they had gone walkabout to get away from the circus. They have since returned to the off-limits areas of Kata

Tijuta to recommence ceremonies, placing a polite sign at the foot of Uluru asking you not to climb. Obviously, there was no such sign during our visit. Maureen had been asked by the press in Adelaide to snap a photo of Harry on the rock. Having looked at the steep climb and felt the gale force wind blowing across the face, Harry pronounced it too bloody dangerous. We went about 30ft up, got the pics and came back down sharpish to wait for the obligatory photo op at sunset when Uluru changes colour.

The photo of Harry was dispatched to the papers along with his impression of the place:

> Harry took a very serious view of Ayers Rock and what it represented.
>
> 'It's fantastic,' he said. 'The last piece of genuine wilderness left in the world. The flight alone was worthwhile … to see one single road in the middle of nothing. It made me think: "My God, how did people travel there with only horses?"
>
> The Aboriginal paintings are absolutely marvellous. It's not so much the Rock as the people who led their strange lives there … these people from so long ago who survived in the wilderness. The wonderful relics of their existence make you realise they had a fabulous religion. They firmly believed in an afterlife. That's shown in the paintings.
>
> This experience has fulfilled my image of Australia.'
>
> One funny comment from Mr. Corbett to the masses of tourists who busily used up the 30 seconds available late in the afternoon to photograph the changing colour of Ayers Rock: 'You realise it's made of plastic don't you? I saw them pop it up this morning.'

Pre-dawn the next morning, in sub zero temperatures, Maureen tried to drag us all out of bed. Having come thousands of miles she was determined we should see sunrise over Uluru. She was disappointed. As we and the other tourists snored on, she was the only one to make it to the bus. Over an hour later, as the driver who had seen it all before stayed behind the wheel in the warm, she witnessed the spectacle alone.

Back in Adelaide, with a suitcase of Aboriginal art winging its way home to Pat in London, we packed for the three-week run in Perth. The city afforded another foray on the tourist trail, this time to clamber through Mulka's Cave and marvel at Wave Rock. Maureen and Harry's rapidly expanding knowledge of all things Australian came as a bit of an eye-opener to the local press, most of whom had never set foot into the outback. When it's on your doorstep you never seem to have the time. After a quick respite staying at Yanchep Village, as guests of its colourful creator Alan Bond, we headed for the last stage of the tour and Sydney.

Here, Harry came into his own, showing us round his wartime haunts, singing snatches of remembered songs:

> Under the Blue Gum trees
> I hear you calling me
> Coo-ee, Coo-ee, Coo-ee.
> Till I return
> My love will burn
> Coo-ee, Coo-ee, Coo-ee.

We played footie on the grass of the Domain, and went for strolls round Darlinghurst and the docks at Woolloomooloo. Harry opened at the Metro theatre, King's Cross, in the second week of September. When it had last seen his shadow it was the Minerva cinema and he was a 19-year-old on the run.

Nostalgia was in the air that September. News came from England that Harry's last remaining brother, George, had died. He had suffered a heart attack. He was 54.

In Sydney, we settled into a colonial cottage in Ginahgulla Road, on the fringes of Double Bay, and were joined by Pat, who'd had an eventful first solo trip. During refuelling the passengers were informed that their pilot had 'slipped in the shower' and no replacement would be available for twenty-four hours. Pat was alone and at large in Singapore – it was enough to give Maureen and Harry palpitations. She arrived unscathed; she'd had a marvellous time, and was soon holding the fort – only slightly taken aback by her grandchildren's Australian accents.

One of Pat's first duties was to keep us from getting underfoot as Maureen launched one of the Bronte Beach Surf Club lifeboats. It being spring, the beaches were uncrowded, even the world-famous Bondi. Our favourite was Manly, to the north. We'd spend days on its pale golden sands. Further north took you to Waratah Park, a nature reserve that had been the set for *Skippy the Bush Kangaroo*, the show that introduced Australia to the world. Of course Jon and I had to be taken there, we were devoted to all things Skippy: 'If I could get even a small part in that, I would be making the big time,' Harry commented. 'They can't get enough of it.'

There was no real need to go and find nature – it came to you. The trees in the garden of Ginahgulla Road were home to possums. During the night when they went on the search for food they would scrabble through the open windows. I woke to find one sitting on my chest. I wanted to adopt it, but Harry, on the constant look out for deadly snakes and spiders, and relieved it hadn't clawed my face off, was having none of it.

We all loved Australia, and Maureen and Harry knew how much of a wrench it would be to leave. 'You know, the kids have not once mentioned back home since we've been here,' Harry told the papers, 'They eventually want to settle here – probably somewhere in northern NSW. I'm hardly game to break it to them that we've got to go back home in a couple of months.'

He had been booked into panto that Christmas, and on hearing the news Jon and I apparently proposed they should go home without us. Although Harry dearly wanted to stay – he had been offered TV shows during the tour but none appealed – he knew that realistically he could earn more in the UK. These days, earning a decent wage was important to him. At the Sydney press reception someone had asked 'Is acting more important than making money?' 'Money is the most important,' he said. 'I have two children to feed and to raise. I've managed to walk the tightrope so I get the money and the acting too. My career is too fragile to knock work back. I feel my future is here. I've got to go to England, but I feel I will be back.'

The five of us took the long way home, stopping off along the way on the trip of a lifetime. We arrived in Fiji on 16 October. Five days later Hurricane Bebe hit the Ellice Islands, now known as Tuvalu. Its capital, the atoll of Funafuti, was wiped clean. Bebe headed south and, if she didn't change course, was due to hit Fiji. We thought the hotel had been quiet.

We were staying in the Reef Hotel on the Coral Coast of Viti Levu. It was a paradise. Lush gardens swept down to the Korotogo beach, where you could wade out into a shallow lagoon. The Fijian staff of the Reef were the friendliest people we'd ever met and as Bebe approached, most decided to stay on to take care of their guests. A true act of kindness.

On the 23rd the hotel issued this statement:

HURRICANE WARNING NOTICE
To All Guests
Please keep your balcony glass door closed and the wire screen
closed also until further notice tomorrow, Tuesday due to
weather bureau hurricane warning for this afternoon, Monday,
and this evening.
Note
Windows and doors are hurricane proof.
Thanking you.

We checked lamps, filled anything that could hold water, moved
the mattresses into the bathroom and, like everyone else, waited for
it to hit. When the weather reports grew worse, the call went out to
assemble in the main building. They had strung a rope between this
and the outlying accommodation. Harry ferried over Pat and Jon,
and then came back for Maureen and me. I can remember watching his hands straining at the rope, the force of the wind lifting my
legs up and away from his back as I clung on round his neck.

In the foyer, one of the staff was entertaining the kids.
Unfortunately the window he was standing in front of wasn't as
hurricane proof as thought. It blew in, pebble dashing his back with
shards of glass. As first aid was given, the guests were shepherded
away to watch an impromptu cabaret, arranged as a distraction from
the howling around us.

We were lucky, but others were not so fortunate. Moments
before the eye made landfall at Lautoka, the winds registered 180kt,
207mph. The roof of the hospital in Lautoka was blown away, forcing 150 patients to evacuate and, 15 miles to the south, Nadi town
was flooded under 8ft of water.

In the aftermath, while the airport and hotels around Nadi were
closing, 30 miles further south the Reef stayed open. The staff
waited desperately for news of relatives; as the roads were blocked
and phone and power lines were down, wait was all they could do.

The lush gardens were gone; trees were uprooted or grotesquely
twisted and palms were stripped and limp. After putting the rooms
back to rights we watched some local lads battling with the bloated
corpse of a cow in the lagoon, pushing it out and over into the
breaking sea. Bebe left the Fijians with eighteen dead, 100 injured

and 3,000 homeless. But in our memories, and the photo albums, they are only ever smiling.

Next stop on our circumnavigation was Tahiti. We spent a week at Maeva Beach, waking up to views of Moorea, an island lying off Tahiti's north-west, and justifiably known as 'the last paradise'. From here it was on to Acapulco, watching the cliff divers, skimming over the submerged statue of Our Lady of Guadalupe in a glass-bottomed boat, going for midnight swims by the pool bar of the Hyatt and indulging in moustachioed fantasies courtesy of staying in the El Presidente suite.

Onto the last leg: manic taxi rides in Mexico City, clambering over Fort Montagu and swimming with green turtles in Nassau, nosing at the bobbing yachts of the super rich in Bermuda. We gravitated to harbours wherever we were, and Harry's time on motor torpedo boats in the Pacific Islands during the war meant that wherever there was water, he would find a boat for hire and skipper us around the coast searching for coves off the beaten track. Back in London, he would keep a 19ft launch moored on Regent's Canal. We spent so many days picnicking on the *Cressida V*, pootling through locks on the quiet hidden waterways of the capital.

By the time we made it home to St John's Wood, we had been away for eight months. It took the dog two weeks to forgive us.

As Maureen started hanging the Aboriginal art, Harry went straight into panto rehearsals, opening in *Robinson Crusoe* at Lewisham on Boxing Day (the show would break the box-office record). He also put some of his Australian earnings to good use. The Brigade of Gurkhas held a luncheon in Henry VIII's wine cellars, located underneath the Ministry of Defence, to thank those who had helped their appeal fund. Harry had 'appeared at fundraising events and gave the £6,000 he was paid for an Australian advertisement on television.'[11] Although quite a sum in 1973, Harry would have thought it small change considering the debt owed by his younger self. The Brigade presented him with a silver-mounted kukri, the Gurkha knife. This precious memento found a home near the bugle, kept for the Royal Marines, and the prints of Indian Army uniforms, kept for his father and his Rangoon childhood.

The newly hung paintings of blue gums and the red centre served as a reminder of how much we adored Australia, and how determined Harry was to see us return. But this ambition would have to wait. Thanks to the success of the *Steptoe* film, it was time for a reunion with Ray, Alan and Wilfrid and to begin work on a sequel.

Notes

1   *The Herald*, 20/4/72.
2   *The Sun*, 7/4/72.
3   *Ibid*.
4   *Woman's Day*, 17/4/72.
5   *The Age*, 7/4/72.
6   *TV Week*, 6/5/72.
7   *Ibid*.
8   *The Herald*, 20/4/72.
9   *Ibid*.
10 *The Entertainer*, 22/5/72.
11 *The Times*, 2/2/73.

17

Rides Again

Life has not only been kind to me, it's gone out of its way to ignore me.[1]

Harry H. Corbett

The second Steptoe film, *Steptoe and Son Ride Again*, had its own Australian connection in the form of director Peter Sykes, who originally hailed from Melbourne. According to Ray, the new director came as a welcome relief to Wilfrid: 'Willie was much happier with Peter and the entire film was a pleasure from start to finish.'[2]

'Oh, they enjoyed them, they enjoyed making them,' remembered Maureen. 'I think they enjoyed watching them. They were fairly simple to make – there were no problems with it, apart from obvious weather problems – standing round waiting. No, I think they thought they were good.'

The film opens with the Steptoes in familiar dire straits. Unable to afford two hot meals a day, Harold is reduced to taking Albert's unlovingly prepared cheese and fag ash sandwiches to work, and Albert is down to smoking tobacco that stinks of horse manure and bus tickets. The only one eating well is the horse, Hercules; who has been resurrected from his TV death.

Out on the round, against the bleak backdrop of 1970s graffitied London, Harold is called up to a high-rise flat. The lift is broken but, desperate for business, he makes the long climb to be presented with only a carrot for the horse. After sharing this meagre fare he is invited by a miniskirted vamp, played by screen siren Diana Dors, to take her dead husband's clothes … and herself. Quivering, Harold declines the invitation but wants the clothes. During the vamp's excessive advances they tussle on the bed and dislodge the cover from her dearly departed husband laid out next to them. She has been a widow for less than a day. Horrified at the thought of what nearly happened, Harold leaves the clothes and flees.

Back on the cart and dozing, he is unaware that Hercules has got on board a removals van bound for York. It's 200 miles and three days later before they return to Oil Drum Lane, but Hercules is lame. He gets the end Albert longed for and retires to a rest home.

In another familiar theme Harold's purchase of a replacement horse is spectacularly unsuccessful, even down to species. He drunkenly buys a greyhound off local hood Frankie Barrow, menacingly played by Henry Woolf. He still owes Frankie £160 for the dog, which is not a worry as this is a pedigree racing dog. The pair name the new member of the family Hercules II – and thanks to him the Steptoes will soon be rolling in cash. Or not, as on its first outing, the dog refuses to come out of the trap. The Steptoes will soon be rolling into hospital unless they can pay Frankie the balance.

They decide to train Hercules II themselves and soon discover the reason for its poor performance – it's blind. Newly equipped with contact lenses, they enter it for another race. Having sold everything they own, they back it to the hilt. This time the dog not only leaves the trap but is in the lead, right up until it smells the homely aroma of Albert's horrid fags. It leaves the track and leaps into Harold's arms.

Left with nothing but the looming appointment with Frankie's heavies the Steptoes come up with a desperate plan: they will fake Albert's death to claim his life insurance. Encasing Albert from the neck down in the body of a mannequin, local drunk Dr Popplewell, played by Milo O'Shea, rolls in to pronounce death and provide the all important certificate for the insurance company.

Having bought time with Frankie, Harold's plans for a quiet funeral are undone by well-meaning local totters. While Albert listens from upstairs, they drink to his memory over his junk-filled coffin. They are determined to give Albert a traditional big send off in homage to their dying profession. They present Harold with a fait accompli: all the arrangements have been made and soon the entire totting community descend upon the house. These included Yootha Joyce who had graduated from playing Harold's love interest to playing his Auntie Freda.

Another returning actor was Frank Thornton, who played the insurance agent. During the impromptu wake he arrives to drop the bombshell that Harold is not the beneficiary. In 1949 Albert assigned the policy to a Mrs Eileen Pyecraft, his one-time flame, and she will cop for the £1,000.

To salvage the situation Albert needs to be brought back to life. Harold moves the coffin into a curtained alcove and, unseen by the raucous mourners, Albert shimmies down the drainpipe and into the coffin. At Harold's signal of three raps he will emerge – a plan utterly ruined by the old man immediately taking a nap. Harold is left knocking on the lid to no response. It is time for the funeral and as the coffin is carried out to the waiting cart and driven to the cemetery, an increasingly desperate and drunken Harold repeatedly tries to wake Albert up. Sobbing at the predicament, he doesn't notice a van door swinging out into the road, takes a crack to the head and is knocked out cold. He is taken to hospital and the sleeping Albert's funeral continues.

Ten stitches later, Harold, now heavily bandaged and in a white hospital gown, escapes in a taxi and races for the cemetery. Vaulting headstones he theatrically flings out his arm and stops ... the wrong funeral. Finally, he sees the right mourners gathered around the grave. Sprinting, he loses his footing and ploughs headlong through the door of a mausoleum. Meanwhile, Hercules II has been scraping earth onto his master's coffin and, at last, the noise wakes Albert. He lifts the lid, takes one look at the faces staring down at him and starts screaming – as does everyone else. The vicar hot foots it away from the grave only to come across Harold stumbling incoherently from the mausoleum, white gown and bandages in tatters around him. Seeing Judgement Day upon him, the vicar faints.

Back at Oil Drum Lane, with order restored, Albert surrenders the insurance policy for £876. Harold spends £80 on a new horse for the business. The rest he invests, courtesy of Frankie Barrow, in a half share of a racehorse. Done up in Ascot best, on the way to the racecourse Harold divulges who the other share belongs to – a chap by the name of H.M. Queen. As the penny drops, in an echo of the first film, the Steptoes join in the royal carriage procession down the course and wave regally at the crowds before falling to bickering once more as the credits roll.

The reviews were good, better than for the first film, but it flunked at the box office. It lost money, which is always far more

important than critical acclaim. Favoured TV shows have never had
a great track record when turned into films. The first *Steptoe* feature
was probably the most financially successful of them all. Perhaps, as
Alan commented, those who had seen the first film didn't like it,
so they didn't turn up for the second. Plans for a third movie obviously never materialised.

In April, Harry appeared on *The Bruce Forsyth Show*, a variety
format produced by ATV. 'He was a guest on a show that I did up in
Leeds,' Bruce remembers:

> In that week of getting to know him, we did a few rehearsals in
> London before we went up, I found him a very pleasant man
> indeed and I enjoyed my time with him very much. He used to
> make us laugh, because he used to turn up every day with a car-
> rier bag with a few odds and sods in, a few bits to eat. It always
> looked like he was going on a simple little outing. He was lovely
> to rehearse with. I enjoyed his company. I didn't know at the
> time that he was such a good straight actor. I loved the *Steptoe*
> series, you couldn't not watch it and I was thrilled when the
> booking people said they had managed to get him on the show.
> He had a wonderful sense of humour, this lovely manner about
> him, which I took to right away. Because you never know with
> comic actors, which he was, sometimes comedy actors can be
> very dark, very much in a world of their own unless they are in
> their 'character' that they are playing at the time. Peter Sellers was
> a bit like that. Peter Sellers was 'in a character' that he played in
> the same way that Benny Hill was, although Benny was more
> light entertainment. You never knew who Benny Hill really was.
> They always felt more comfortable in characters. But Harry had
> a natural wit about him and you always accepted him as Harry
> H. Corbett. You didn't think of him as somebody playing a part.
> A lot of actors are like that, unless they're playing a part there's
> no real them. But he was real. We had a lot of laughs. I wish I had
> tapes of how we'd rehearse and the enjoyment we had. We hit it
> off straight away.

In the summer, Harry took the title role in a production of
Ionesco's *Macbett* for the Bankside Globe Playhouse, a temporary
theatre built by the Thames for a summer season to raise money
for the Globe Playhouse Trust. The Trust's aim was to recreate

Shakespeare's Globe Theatre, the 'wooden O', and was the brain-child of Sam Wanamaker.

This was to be *Macbett*'s London premiere. It rehearsed and opened at the Belgrade Theatre, Coventry, with Terry Scott playing Duncan, Victor Spinetti as Banquo and Frances Cuka as Lady Duncan. The play's director, Charles Marowitz, described it as: 'A Surrealist Comedy with Political Overtones and Parodic Undertones Set in an Absurdist-Satirical style with Tragic Implications.' At the beginning of rehearsals, according to Victor: 'He turned to us and said "Now then, you three, I don't want Theatre Workshop from you, Victor, I don't want Steptoe from you, Harry, and I don't want Terry and June from you, Terry."

"Darling, you better recast." I said, "That's all we've fucking got."'

'We had a blast,' Victor continues:

We loved doing that show, we had a great time. I played Banquo and whatever Macbett said, I'd say the same. So, Harry would come on and make a speech and then I'd come on and say exactly the same speech. Ionesco's point was that you never knew what anyone was talking about in Shakespeare anyway. It all sounded the same. Well, it was a surrealistic piece. It really was wonderful stuff to work on.

Harry, Terry and I shared a dressing room. I used to joke and call Harry 'Sir Harold', you see. I'd say 'Good evening, Sir Harold' and he would go 'Ah, young Victor, how are you,' because we're the same age, that was our game. And Terry Scott used to scream, 'Don't call him Sir! He's not a Sir. He's not knighted.' He used to go mad. So, of course, we used to have a great time winding him up, Harry was perfect at that. At one point Harry said, 'Ah, young Spinetti, how much did you get for that commercial you did for Jaffa Cakes?' and I said 'Oh, £20,000.' And Terry would jump up and say, '£20,000, £20,000! I only got £5,000 for Curly Wurlys and you're a nobody.'

Poor Terry, to be sharing a dressing room with such unmitigated bastards, still, it's good to see the 'surrealist comedy' onstage being mirrored behind it. There were even touches of 'tragic implications' when one member of the cast, who for obvious reasons shall remain nameless, recounted the following, as Victor remembers:

This was one of the most horrendous stories that Harry and
I had ever heard in our lives, this chap said 'I've given up smoking, my wife said,' "You've got to give up smoking," and I said "I
will, providing I can have sex twice a week." And then he said,
'She agreed, and then I'd save them up and maybe have it twice
in one night! Ha Ha!' It was the worst thing we'd ever heard.

For Harry and Victor, both enjoying living life to the full, one can
believe it. Apparently, Harry's only comment was a mumbled, 'Oh,
fucking hell.' Victor's was to offer to buy a carton of cigarettes.

Another potential 'tragic implication' happened a few weeks later
when the trisail canopy above the stage collapsed. The canopy had
been borrowed from the Royal College of Art, and adapted for the
temporary theatre. This did not prove entirely successful as the mod-
ifications affected the rain runoff. A man was despatched to walk the
pools of water to the edge of the canopy, which promptly ripped,
plummeting the man, water and canopy tatters to the stage below.

This was just one of the many setbacks Sam Wanamaker had to
deal with during his quest for the rebuilt Globe. He had started
the Trust in 1970. Many members of the profession gave time and
money to the project, and Harry was no exception – he must be
responsible for one or two of the timbers – but for over two decades Wanamaker worked tirelessly to turn his dream into a reality.
He was made an Honorary CBE in July 1993, as construction on
the theatre was underway. He died in London in December of that
year. The completed Globe was opened in 1997. It is his monument.

When *Macbett* closed, Harry signed on to appear in panto at
Aldershot that Christmas. He also signed on for a *Steptoe* Christmas
special, and he and Maureen started house hunting again. After all,
not only were the 'five glorious years' up but they had missed having
a place out of town, somewhere the kids could run about, somewhere to retire to one day. During the late summer of 1973 we were
endlessly bundled into the car in search of 'the one'. This turned
out to be a tiny sixteenth-century cottage perched on a hill in the
hamlet of Ashburnham, in the High Weald of East Sussex. Maureen
took one look at the view and fell in love. Harry, waiting in the car
at the bottom of the drive, agreed with her. He didn't tend to get
out and inspect that much. Not only was it far easier and quicker
if Harold Steptoe stayed out of sight, but it was cheaper. The price
invariably shot up as soon as people knew who was interested.

Despite being a TV star, money was always an issue. There was the lease on the house in St John's Wood, Harry's predilection for giving away as much as he could to good causes and to a regular supply of friends in need. There was also the expense of having two kids at private school. 'The only thing you can leave your kids is an education,' Harry used to say. He was always determined that Jon and I should have one that he could have only dreamed of, at school and at home. Our bedtime stories were wonderful. Yes, it does help having talented actors delivering them, but the choice was interesting. Most often we had our vocabulary expanded and giggled ourselves to sleep courtesy of the collected newspaper columns of Alan Coren.

Money was tight for everyone in the 1970s, time of high inflation, pay caps and the three-day week. Top earners were paying 83 per cent tax, many fleeing abroad into self-imposed exile. Naturally, funding for the arts was not at the top of the government's agenda. That autumn, as Harry and Wilfrid returned to the studio to record the fifth series of *Steptoe* for radio, Theatre Workshop had its back to the wall once more.

The late 1960s and early '70s had been challenging out at Stratford East. After *Oh What A Lovely War* closed on Broadway, the company had been disbanded and Theatre Royal taken over by outside management. Joan had gone to work abroad and concentrated on her fun palace project, the grand design that had driven a wedge between her and Gerry. In 1967 she had returned to a very different East End. A massive redevelopment plan was underway. As the bulldozers closed in on the theatre, Joan directed four plays with two successes: a satire, *Mrs Wilson's Diary*, that transferred to the West End, and *The Marie Lloyd Story*, with Avis taking the title role. By all accounts it was the performance of her life.

Outside the theatre, Joan had been campaigning for the children's playground project, her plan to turn rubble left by redevelopment into a centre for the local kids. Over the next few years several demolition sites were cleared and playgrounds were built. The project was run under the auspices of her Fun Palace Trust. At the end of 1967 the company had been disbanded once more and Gerry began pleading with the council to build, instead of the planned office blocks, an entertainment complex with the theatre at its heart. He was ignored.

By 1970 development was in full swing; all the shops and houses that the company had known so well in the 1950s were gone or going. Never one to take it lying down, Joan returned to stage a production highlighting local authorities. The playwright chosen for the piece was Ken Hill, who during his time as a journalist had reported on local government corruption in his native Birmingham. He and Joan used this as the basis for the play *Forward Up Your End*. The production prompted a suggestion that Theatre Workshop should focus on councils nearer to home, thank you very much. Joan's next production, *The Projector*, obliged. In 1968 the nearby Ronan Point tower block in Newham had partially collapsed, killing four people. As it would have been illegal for Joan's notes from the subsequent trial to be used in any new play, an eighteenth-century one was invented to highlight unscrupulous property development.

In the same month, Newham Council had threatened the theatre with partial demolition. Gerry started a campaign to save the building and asked for a grant from the Arts Council. No monies were forthcoming and the theatre closed.

Two years later, he had finally got Theatre Royal listed with the Historic Buildings Council, now known as English Heritage. He had also secured a grant. But, by then, Joan had lost heart. Over the next eighteen months she would only direct four productions, her final being *So You Want To Be in Pictures*, by Peter Rankin, in November of 1973.

Meanwhile, Harry had spent the autumn of that year appearing as a guest on an episode of *The Goodies*, the popular comedy show starring Tim Brooke-Taylor, Graeme Garden and Bill Oddie. Harry played a hypochondriac hay fever-ridden Minister for Health, blowing his nose on a box of disposable 'Sootys' – the puppet made famous by his namesake Harry Corbett. He also recorded the LP *Only Authorised Employees to Break Bottles* – a collection of songs from the British Isles. At the start of December he was reunited with Wilfrid and the pair went into rehearsals for the *Steptoe* Christmas special directed by Graeme Muir.

This opens with Harold visiting a snooty travel agent, played by Frank Thornton in his last outing for *Steptoe*. Harold has come to pay the balance on his forthcoming holiday to Majorca and is delighted when he finds a well-to-do couple in the shop who have just booked into the same hotel. Ever on the look out to go up in the world Harold plans a Christmas Day knees-up with them and offers to save seats on the plane. Once he leaves the horrified couple immediately change their plans.

At home, Albert is reminiscing on Christmases past, grateful that he and Harold always spend them together. When Harold comes home and drops the bombshell that he won't be there and has booked his father into an old folks Christmas dinner held by the vicar, Albert gives a master class in guilt. He will spend the day going down to the cemetery to sit with Harold's mother; after all, it will probably be the last Christmas before he joins her. He makes his way to bed 'accidentally' dropping a bottle of pills, recently prescribed by the doctor, and clutching at his heart.

It has the desired effect. Harold cracks and will stay at home, admitting to himself that escaping was only ever a fantasy. But he will cash in his ticket to Majorca and blow the money on the biggest party Oil Drum Lane has ever seen, with all his friends and neighbours invited – anything but be alone with the old man.

Preparations are under way, Albert has spruced up the decorations, Harold has brought home the festive fare of goose, turkeys and hams with more delicacies to be delivered and a lethal punch is being concocted in a po. On Christmas morning Harold is eagerly awaiting his guests when Albert drops his own bombshell – he has come down with chicken pox. He has also managed to infect Harold and the party is cancelled, leaving the two to enjoy a Christmas in quarantine.

After the recording, in early December, Harry headed out to Aldershot and the panto *Robinson Crusoe*. The special would be shown on Christmas Eve and proved a huge hit. *Steptoe* was on top once again and enjoying a success that unfortunately was not being repeated across town at Stratford East.

By the new year of 1974 the detritus of development was at door of Theatre Royal and, yet again, the cash had run out. Gerry went on the warpath. The Minister for the Arts, Norman St John-Stevas, was invited down. Photographs of the minister and Joan amid the rubble made a grand splash in the papers, shining a spotlight on the theatre's plight. Gerry presented him with an outline of their needs: more money to raise a permanent company, space to be allocated for sets and costumes, the environs of the theatre to be cleared and pavements laid, and leisure facilities to be built close to the theatre to encourage an audience to come to a building now in danger of being hidden by office blocks. Without all of these needs being met, Theatre Workshop, he assured the minister, could not continue.

The minister would see what could be done, and then promptly lost his job. In February a general election was called, which resulted in a hung parliament. Edward Heath resigned and Harold Wilson returned as prime minister. To secure his position Wilson would have to call another election that autumn. Fluctuations such as these rarely result in cash-spending decisions, but Wilson's new arts minister was Hugh Jenkins, for whom Harry and Wilfrid and many actors had turned out; perhaps all was not lost.

Gerry needed a subsidy of £110,000 a year to keep the theatre running. The decision came down from the Arts Council. They were willing to offer half. The remainder would have to come from local authorities. It was a plan of action supported by Hugh Jenkins. Bitterly disappointed, Gerry resigned and passed the baton to Ken Hill.

Before taking a back seat, Gerry went out with a bang, holding a short season of variety nights. There had often been fundraising evenings that the old stalwarts would take part in. Signing up for this final season were Harry and Victor doing a mind-reading act, Roy Hudd, Frankie Howerd, John Junkin, Hinge and Brackett, Barbara Windsor and Rita Webb.

The variety call had found Harry busy at Elstree Studios on the set of his latest movie. He had left the panto at Aldershot and gone straight into filming *Percy's Progress*, playing Prime Minister Henry Snope, a dead ringer for Harold Wilson. The cast included Leigh Lawson, Elke Sommer, Denholm Elliott, Vincent Price, Barry Humphries, Anthony Andrews, Ronald Fraser, Bernard Lee, James Booth and Milo O'Shea. The film, for which Harry got a writing credit, was a comedy about the only man left unaffected when a contaminated water supply renders all impotent.

In March, Harry got out the juggling clubs and took to the stage of Theatre Royal. He was there to take his bow on the very last night of Theatre Workshop. The variety turns were a resounding success, caused a flap in the papers and started a rumour that Hugh Jenkins would review the Arts Council's decision. The Workshop may have been hanged but it was still twitching.

It was a time of endings, for that spring Harry heard that Carrie, his only sister and last surviving sibling, had died. She was 66, a grand old age for a Corbett.

That summer, Harry continued in the variety vein. He took his one-man show on the club circuit and persuaded Wilfrid to appear with him in panto that winter. The pair had met up again at the start of rehearsals for the eighth series of *Steptoe*.

The series had a new producer, Douglas Argent, and kicked off with the episode 'Back in Fashion'. The Steptoes' yard has been booked as the backdrop for a fashion shoot. On the day, Harold appears in dark glasses and smoking jacket and, with cane in hand, greets the models, who immediately presume him to be blind. The misunderstanding is only cleared up while the girls are changing into their 1920s-themed frocks, prompting them to think of him as a peeping Tom. A view reinforced as Harold is repeatedly caught in the act while trying to stop the actual peeping Tom, Albert, from getting a good eyeful. During the shoot he wangles his way into being a male model and, lacking any 1920s clothing, he goes to get changed into his work gear. At that moment Albert appears in full gangster get up, steals Harold's thunder and is photographed surrounded by the beauties. When the magazine comes out Harold rips out the photos of the old man and shoves them in the outhouse.

The episode was not the strongest start to the eagerly awaited series that it could have been, and thus had a weak reception. Standards were seen to be slipping a bit, in writing, production and performance. Of course not everyone could be a winner, but it was not an auspicious beginning.

Happily, the next episode was seen as a return to top form. 'And So To Bed' revisited a perennial theme, that of Harold being thwarted in love. He and his latest flame, Marcia, are uncomfortably canoodling on the sofa. They are waiting for the old man to finish cobbling in bed and go to sleep before they can creep upstairs. When they finally get there, Marcia, played by Lynn Farleigh, discovers bed bugs and runs screaming from the house. Harold, refusing to have another bed off the round, visits Bayswater Bedarama. There he spies a waterbed. Seduced by the salesman's tales of the effect of its undulations on the act of congress he slaps his money down. When the bed is delivered it is missing its electric plug, but Harold needs the water to be warmed as Marcia will be calling that night. Albert offers to fit one while Harold is out on the round and, during the fitting, manages to plunge a knife straight through the mattress. Later, when Harold and Marcia passionately throw themselves onto the bed they are drenched. An incensed Harold tries to attack Albert through the door of his barricaded room.

The series was back to its glorious best with 'Porn Yesterday'. After a stinking hot day, Harold returns from the round with a What the Butler Saw machine and laughs himself silly at the antics of the risqué three-part reel, *Fifi et la Fotographie*. Albert is desperate for a peek but when it come to part three, Fifi has been replaced by another story, that of a woman in a bath and a trouserless milkman. Suddenly, Albert isn't as keen on the show and describes how a desperate, penniless young man might have all too easily fallen for the easy money offered by pornography. The penny drops – Albert was the milkman. Harold's 'You dirty old man' was never said with such feeling. Full of hypocrisy and revulsion, Harold will destroy the evidence but not before Albert has a last look. The old man's face crumbles as he beholds the images of his younger self. Harold offers the comfort that old age comes to us all, the pair delivering the poignant moment with the lightest of touches. Harold is about to burn the film drum when the vicar arrives. Played once again by Anthony Sharp, he is asking for donations to the church fête. Harold is persuaded to part with the now-empty machine. But on the day of the fête, the vicar has found a replacement film and the machine is doing a roaring trade. Albert is recognised as the film's star. Harold tries to take the drum away from the crowd and in the fracas the offending photos are scattered, leaving the old man to sign autographs for his adoring fans.

The next episode, 'The Seven Steptoerai', sees Albert joining the kung fu craze that was sweeping the country. Having just seen *Enter the Dragon* at the pictures he comes home to find Harold unloading a large Chinese vase. It could be a rare Ming but, as usual, turns out to be a fake. Undeterred, Harold decides to sell it at auction for a couple of hundred. Just then Frankie Barrow arrives with his heavies. Frankie has entered the protection racket and will, for just £15 a week, make sure no little accidents happen. One of his heavies smashes the vase as a telling example. The Steptoes sign up, but Harold is determined that Frankie won't get away with it. Inspired by *The Seven Samurai* he decides they need some hired muscle. Albert will make the arrangements and when Frankie is next expected Harold returns home to meet Albert's boys – every one of them an OAP. They have, however, been taking kung fu lessons and give Frankie and his gang a pasting.

Frankie Barrow, the godfather of Shepherd's Bush, was played once more by the actor, director and, later, professor of drama, Henry Woolf:

I thoroughly enjoyed myself on the Steptoes. It was a very happy atmosphere. I'd always admired Harry; he brought a breath of fresh air into theatre and television. Joan Littlewood had once said to me, 'He is the best actor we ever had in this company.' But Harry was the least grand chap you could imagine, terribly natural, humorous and serious about his work. He didn't just take it for granted that it was all just going to happen. He created a very natural, relaxed atmosphere, we all had a terrifically funny time – and Taxi drivers still recognise me as Frankie Barrow!

Whereas episodes in the series so far had featured pre-recorded outside shots and a large additional cast, the next, 'Upstairs Downstairs, Upstairs Downstairs', was a return to the classic, simple two-hander. Harold is stuck with domestic duties as Albert is ill in bed with a bad back. The doctor, played by Robert James, advises an unsympathetic Harold that his father will have to remain there for some weeks. Harold rails against his forced position of nursemaid by callously telling Albert that he has but three days to live. Harold, meanwhile, will pack for a holiday in Cornwall. Joking over, reality bites and Albert promises not to be a burden, Harold assures him that all will be well but over the next two weeks is run ragged by the constant demands. The ungrateful old man is ensconced upstairs surrounded by TV, phone and liqueur chocolates, endlessly screaming his son's name. Eventually, Harold cracks. He bans Albert from calling for a whole fifteen minutes, forcing him to turn up the TV sound himself. As he makes a move for the set, his back snaps into place. He dances a Charleston to celebrate but has no intention of letting Harold know – he wants to milk it for all it's worth. Later, returning home from yet more errands, Harold notices two empty cans of lager. This, along with the disappearance of his liquorice allsorts, reveals the malingering of 'that perpendicular ponce' upstairs. His revenge is sweet. He gives Albert a blanket bath, dousing his nether regions in surgical spirit. It is a 'miracle cure'.

The episode was a master class in two-handed situation comedy, and has become one of the best known, mainly for Albert's persistent shouts of 'Haaarooold!' from upstairs. This is the only episode where Albert does this, and yet it has become the defining impersonation routine for *Steptoe and Son* ever since.

The last episode, 'Séance in a Wet Rag-and-Bone Yard', sees Albert returning late, having been at a spiritualist meeting. He recounts having made contact with Henry VIII, Dan Leno and Gandhi, all thanks to the medium, Madame Fontana. Harold dismisses the woman as a con artist but Albert will hear nothing against her, having been introduced to her by his new flame, Dorothy, played by Gwen Nelson. He has invited the spiritualist group to meet at Oil Drum Lane, for he has an important question to ask Harold's mother. The group arrives, greeted by a love-struck Albert and a cynical Harold. During the séance Madame Fontana, given full theatrical reign by Patricia Routledge, channels Dorothy's dead husband who tells her to remarry. Madame Fontana next conjures up the spirit of the late Mrs Steptoe. Harold is disgusted by the display, refusing to believe his mother is there. Albert asks to marry Dorothy and conveniently gets a yes. Harold has had enough and breaks up the séance. In the aftermath Madame Fontana is revealed as Dorothy's daughter – the whole thing was a fix to marry off her mother. A disappointed Albert goes to bed leaving Harold to reflect, longingly, how nice it would have been to talk to his mum; a beautifully pitched moment. As he switches off the lights, a woman's ethereal voice softly calls, 'Goodnight Harold'. Frightened out of his wits and reverting to a little boy, he rushes upstairs to sleep in his dad's bed.

The series wrapped and was being well received, despite some niggles that had been creeping in behind the scenes. There had been a little disappointment with plotlines that, on occasion, had been veering towards the silly end of the spectrum. There had been fewer moments of pathos that the two actors had enjoyed playing so much and that had given previous series such rich texture. When they had started writing the first series, Galton and Simpson had kept a sheet with a list of half-formed ideas for future episodes. By the eighth series that list, naturally, was exhausted, encouraging the shows to vacillate between the usual classics and occasional forays into somewhat thin plots with the resulting thin characterisations. 'The old man would just go "Yeeargh!" and get a big laugh,' Alan points out. 'We used to feel sorry for Harry. He was working his arse off and the old man would just grimace and go "Yeeargh!" and get the laugh. That never bothered Harry, didn't seem to bother him.'

On occasion, Harry himself could be seen going for the easy option. There would have been moments of which he was no longer proud.

There was also an 'atmosphere' in rehearsal, though this was not down to any grand falling out, as there had never really been a 'falling in', as Alan continues: 'Ray and I knew Harry quite well. We used to socialise with him after the shows, whereas we never went out with Willie once.'

'The old man didn't socialise much in the bar,' agrees Ray:

He would go home or go to a gay place or whatever – we didn't know. Harry, we saw. We used to go out and eat with Harry before or after the shows. Willie never seemed a particularly tragic figure at all but he showed no inclination, as far as we knew, to start a friendship up with us in any way. The show ended and boom, he was out. Not always, a quick drink sometimes. Sometimes when we rehearsed we used to have drinks which got on Harry's nerves a bit towards the end.

'When we first started the series,' Alan interjects:

Harry used to come at lunchtime and he used to have half a Guinness in the pub and Wilfrid would have a gin and tonic. Then, as the series went on, Wilfrid used to come back to the rehearsals rooms 'not fit for purpose' as they say, with his old nose throbbing and forgetting his lines. We nearly always had to finish rehearsals around 3 o'clock. One day Harry came in with a tin of sandwiches. 'You coming down the pub, Harry?' 'No, I think I shall sit here and read the script,' he said; and the old man said, 'Right, I'm going to have an extra gin and tonic. Sod him! I've been in the business years before he came on.' And that sort of attitude. Wilfrid's attitude didn't make much difference to Harry, there were never any rows, it just used to get on Harry's nerves when Willie fluffed as it did ours. I used to think the old man had ruined the show completely because of his fluffs or when he couldn't remember the lines. I used to go mad.

Wilfrid, too, had his cross to bear. 'There was a different attitude,' thinks Alan Simpson:

Harry was always exploring the part and experimenting with different ways of doing it, while Wilfrid was of the old school of acting. He would learn the lines, decide how to do them and do

them the exactly same way every time. Then suddenly he would
be confronted with Harry, who would try something new every
time they went through it. The old-fashioned actor against the
method actor. It was a contrast that worked wonderfully well
for the show, but the cracks were beginning to show. I think
Harry was sometimes under the impression that it was his show.
It wasn't![3]

The 'atmosphere' between Harry and Wilfrid was not obvious, certainly it didn't interfere with the work and was so slight that visiting
actors, attuned as they usually are to even the most minor of squab-
bles, didn't notice. Henry Woolf remembered: 'As far as I knew, the
brief times I worked with them, they got on perfectly professionally
and perfectly amicably. It was very hard, as far as I could see, not to
get on with Harry.'

The series director, Douglas Argent, who would have been there
throughout rehearsals and performance, had rather fond memories
of the show:

I was in television for over thirty years and that was one of the
best programmes I ever did – no argument. You could ask my
wife, she used to say it was one of the few times I wasn't in a
bad mood. She said I used to come home quite happy instead
of cursing and swearing about somebody. I can't think of any
incidents. We just worked rather happily together and that was
it. We had no problems at all, not that I was aware of. We used
to come in, do the show, go home. I never had any problems
with them. I wouldn't say that the old man was the sunniest of
people. Wilfrid wasn't the type to socialise, and I wouldn't say, to
be absolutely honest, that Harry would have said Wilfrid was a
lovely man. He was very, very professional; both of them were,
always. Always came in about the second or third day dead letter
perfect – no messing about – every word, every syllable. The two
writers used to come to rehearsals, the scripts, of course, were
absolutely superb. I don't think we ever changed a word. We just
sailed through the series, we were way up in the ratings, and so
was the Christmas show. It was, without any doubts, one of the
most successful shows I ever did.

That Christmas *Steptoe* would turn out to be the last: 'When we had written the series that was to become the last one, we didn't realise it was going to be the last one!' explains Alan Simpson:

> There was always a chance that the BBC might want some more. But, to be honest, the atmosphere during the making of the eighth series, although not tension-packed, was different. You could tell that Harry and Willie were getting a bit fed up with it. We would see Harry a lot, both during production of a series and not. He would come for lunch and, although he never slagged the old man off, the irritation was clear in his voice. During the making of the eighth series Harry had made it clear that he didn't want to do any more. He just couldn't go on.

'It wasn't as bad as grumpy old men,' jokes Ray Galton:

> but something was turning sour. Don't forget, they had worked together a lot and over a long period of time. They were also firmly paired in the public's eye. That's quite a strain for anybody. Besides they lasted a lot longer than most marriages these days! Apart from the Harry and Willie situation, we had also got to the stage where we couldn't think of any more plot lines. Our cup of ideas had been drained. More to the point that sheet of half-ideas had been used up. We had written nearly sixty half-hours, the films ... life was too short to drag it down to arguments and half-hearted plot ideas.[4]

The Christmas show opened in the same way as the previous year's offering – Harold returns home to find Albert putting up the tatty decorations and, just like last year, he is determined to escape a festive season stuck at home in front of TV Christmas specials that were recorded in October (just as this one was). He is so determined that, this time, he will take the old man with him. With £80 saved in the swear box, the world is their oyster. Harold wants to feel the sun on his bones; Albert, as ever, wants Bognor. They finally settle on Christmas in the Alps, and they will take the night ferry to Switzerland, it being one of the few countries in Europe that would let Albert in. Now he needs a passport, but his birth certificate is lost, buried in the clutter of the under-stairs cupboard. An unwilling Albert is forced in to find it. The cupboard contains memories of Harold's childhood, not just for being the place he sat through the Blitz alone but his no. 9 toy bus and his school cap, complete with motto 'Know thy place and be grateful'.

Albert finally finds his certificate and the reason for his reluctance to find it becomes clear as the certificate lists his father as 'unknown'. The dirty secret is finally out and the picture on the wall Harold was told was his grandfather, is exposed as being that of Gladstone. Although Harold has difficulty seeing the old man as a love-child, he fantasises Albert is the illegitimate son of a lord. The notion is quickly dispelled by Albert mentioning that his mother was dreadfully upset when the muffin man died. But the revealing of Albert's shame is a relief; he is now looking forward to the holiday and a closer relationship with his son. With a new passport, the Steptoes arrive at the station just in time to catch their train. Albert goes through, but Harold is held back – his own passport is out of date. Albert selfishly leaves Harold at the gate, gleefully waving goodbye from the train. Harold is crushed, his dreams of escape in tatters once more. He makes his way to the exit, his leaden footsteps suddenly picking up as he dances towards the door and the waiting dolly bird in a sports car. They had been booked into Bognor all along.

Though it was not an absolute certainty that this would be the last outing for the Steptoes on television, in hindsight it is wonderfully fitting that Harold finally managed to get one over on the old man.

Harry and Wilfrid threw a wrap party and said goodbye to the crew and to the characters that had made them household names. Harry would miss doing *Steptoe* but, as Maureen pointed out:

> I have a feeling that there was a sort of general consensus that they'd said it all. I think Ray and Alan, at least for a while, maybe now they may think they could have written some more, maybe they are going to write some more, maybe they've already written some more. I think there was a kind of general feeling amongst them all that this is probably it, for the foreseeable future. We have said it all, we have done it all and from here on we don't want to go down, so perhaps best to leave it now. So I think there was perhaps an element of acceptance. It was not a sad thing that they didn't do any more. It was time – there's a time.

Life went on. In fact, pretty much as it always had been, for, a few weeks later, Harry and Wilfrid opened in *Cinderella* at the Casino Theatre in London. The lavish production marked Twiggy's stage debut as Cinders, and featured Nicky Henson as Buttons with Roy Kinnear and Hugh Paddick as the ugly sisters. Harry and Wilfrid played the Broker's men – Harry sidelining into a juggling act with Danny Gray, it would be Danny's last performance before he and June 'retired' to become stage door keepers. After the panto closed it really was the end of an era. Not of *Steptoe*, but of Theatre Workshop.

On 11 April 1975 Gerry Raffles collapsed and died at the age of 51. His diabetes and heart condition got the better of him while on a solo boating holiday in his beloved France. Joan's grief was absolute. She blamed Theatre Royal and vowed never to set foot in it again. A grand memorial was organised, with the old nuts meeting up to take part in a show that said goodbye to Gerry and, in a way, to the company and all that they had been. Harry acted as MC; he opened with:

> On Joan's behalf I would like to say welcome. We thought the place for this meeting should be Gerry's home, where else – on a boat – on the sea – in the mountains – deserts – on the roads? He was a roamer – always. He died roaring up the Rhone, against advice and caution without giving a thought to his health. He was hurrying back to try a new and splendid notion of theatre – suddenly his heart failed. He fell in a beautiful place, Vienne sur Rhone. For him it was sudden, for this house it was the agony of unbelievable loss
>
> Sorrow, who to this house scarce knew the way,
> Is Oh! heir of it, our all is his prey.

Joan was never the same. Shunning the home that would bring memories of her lost love she began camping out on friends. A year later, while visiting the spot where Gerry died, she met the vintner Baron Philippe de Rothschild, himself a recent widower. The pair entered a close consoling friendship, Joan staying with him at Château Mouton. She never directed at Theatre Royal, or in England, again.

The name of Theatre Workshop was used for a few years, while Joan kept tenuous links with the theatre, erratically helping and hindering the directors that came after her. Eventually, a fresh start saw the name removed from the posters outside. For some, the company had finished in the 1950s when they went commercial, for others it died in the 1960s when *Lovely War* closed. But there was never any coming back after Gerry's death and Joan's resulting miasma. Theatre Workshop faded away and entered the history books.

Notes

1   *TV Guide*, 28/7/72.
2   Galton and Simpson, *Steptoe and Son*.
3   *Ibid*.
4   *Ibid*.

18

Walkabout

I'm a compromiser more than a fighter. If one door closes I won't kick it down. I'll just walk up the road and find another that's open [1]

Harry H. Corbett

In the summer of 1975 Harry found open doors in television, playing a shop steward in one of the last episodes of *Comedy Playhouse*, Johnny Speight's 'For Richer, For Poorer', and in theatre, as he was preparing to take over in *Entertaining Mr Sloan*. While Harry and Maureen were overseeing extension works to the cottage in Ashburnham, making it ready for the day we could get out of town, Joe Orton's black comedy was running at the Duke of York's in London with Beryl Reid leading the cast as Kath. She had already played the character in the movie version. Harry would be playing her brother, Ed, the closet homosexual; he was replacing Ronald Fraser. Also joining the cast and taking over as Mr Sloan was a young Kenneth Cranham:

> What I often thought about Harry was that I mustn't do what he did. Later on, when I got *Shine On Harvey Moon*, I only did four series of that. They wanted me to do a fifth but I managed to steer clear. If you get too associated with one role it's very hard to be thought of in anything else. I think the *Steptoe* fame got out of hand. Other than *Hancock's Half Hour* and *Steptoe*, Galton and Simpson never really hit it again. They hit something with that. *Steptoe* was so successful, but the days of getting 28 million have gone. *Harvey Moon*, at its height got 13 million and now they are pleased to get 6 million.

There was something quite tragic about Harry's life for me. I saw him once on the Palladium with Bruce Forsyth, he was wearing his *Steptoe* costume. I thought, 'Don't appear as 'him' – keep 'him' in the show.' But fame is an odd area. I remember Ian McKellen was desperate to be well known and famous. Ian was appearing in Strindberg in the West End and in the next-door theatre was Dawn French. One night she made an unannounced appearance at the curtain call in his show and the audience lapped it up. He made a return visit and went on in her curtain call and nobody knew who the fuck he was. The only fame he has had is as Gandalf. It's odd how famous one is in one guise. So when I saw Harry in variety at the Palladium, I thought it was a mistake – but then if he liked that sort of thing …

As it happens, I've worked with a lot of people who had one foot in stand up or the variety world. What comedians do is they work in isolation. Actors come with half-formed ideas and blend it with other actors and the director in rehearsal, whereas comedians hang onto their stuff. I always regarded Harry as an actor, never a comedian, though he'd done a lot of comedy. He was perceived as an actor. At one time he was one of the new young actors in town and I often used to wonder, there he was getting the train down to Sussex, 'Was it worth it, doing 'Steptoe' for that long?' I'm sure the BBC didn't pay him very much – they never did.

When I did *Mr. Sloan* with him we were patching up a show. It's always slightly demoralising being cast in a takeover because you don't get properly rehearsed and Beryl Reid would only run the 1st or 2nd act so we had to rehearse it with the female understudy – we could never get Beryl. It took about three weeks playing to audiences for it to fall into place. Beryl was fantastic; me and Harry just towed the line. We used to sit in her dressing room in the interval. She used to stick a couple of Courvoisier down her face before she went on so she could get that hit. By the third line every night she had the audience in the palm of her hand. She wasn't a drunk; she just had a hit to kick off. Sometimes she used to jump two or three pages and the first couple of times it happened I was completely distraught and then I got to look forward to it. It was like one of those puzzles where you shift the squares around.

So we didn't really rehearse it properly because we had the enormous ego of Beryl Reid to deal with, that's what we dealt with and the show got pretty good. Harry and I took something like 17 minutes off the running time – that's a lot. We both had a good feel for pace. I think we did it rather well.

I felt Harry was quite a shy man. What really endeared me to him was that my mum and dad lived at Hastings and he went on the train with them. He was really nice to them and talked to them. I've worked with famous actors who behave appallingly. People say they're wonderful actors but, so what, if you don't cut it as a person. Harry was very friendly. It warmed you to him. That, to me, means an awful lot.[2]

As the first 'classical' actor to have such a success in a comedy role, Harry's situation was rather unprecedented, so, aside from serving as a warning to others, he spent his career – as most actors do – cutting his coat according to his cloth. And – as most actors are – he would never be satisfied with his lot. If you find a satisfied actor ask for their prescription. However, as Pat pointed out: 'He would only take jobs that let him be with the family, he wanted to be there and doing Steptoe gave him so much time off.' He was offered roles at the National Theatre and the RSC but, as Maureen would always say, 'they couldn't afford him'. Harry's success, while undeniably limiting, had left him in the extremely unusual and enviable position of being able to have the choice to spend time with his family; we were more important to him. So, as he came home to us on that train to Sussex, he would have been fully aware of the difficulty the *Mr Sloan* audience would have had disassociating him from Harold. 'It could have been a bloody disaster,' he later said, 'but the play was so good it grabbed the audience in the first few minutes. By the time I came on Steptoe was the last person on anybody's mind.'[3]

Mr Sloan closed in October and three weeks later the *Steptoe* crew were reunited once more for the sixth and final radio series. Episodes were taken largely from the final television series. Once again, many of the supporting actors returned to reprise their roles, including Anthony Sharp as the vicar, Henry Woolf as Frankie Barrow and George A. Cooper as Uncle Arthur. In the penultimate episode, 'The Seven Steptoerai', Ray and Alan made uncredited cameo appearances as Eric and Robin, Frankie Barrow's thugs. Alan later admitted that they were only cast 'when the producer couldn't afford a real actor! It was wonderful to ham our way through.'[4]

January 1976 turned out to be quite a month for Harry. His take-over in *Mr Sloan* had been so well received that he was Michael Coveney's pick for the 1975 Plays and Players London Theatre Critics Award for Best Actor. He also received an OBE for services to acting in the New Year Honours. He was listed alongside the puppeteer, Harry 'Sooty' Corbett. This gave rise to the rumour that either Whitehall mandarins or Harold Wilson had forgotten the 'H' when Harry's name was put forward and sent the good news to the wrong man. When the mistake was realised, they could hardly take it back so added them both. Though it's entirely believable, I hope it isn't true as Sooty deserved a gong for twenty years of kid wrangling. Of his own 'gold star', Harry was astounded and inordinately proud.

After a couple of quickies – the Louis Ife play *Murder in Mind* with Linda Thorson at Harrogate and an episode of the children's TV show *The Chiffy Kids* – we spent the spring in Sussex before Harry started work on another feature film, *Jabberwocky*. Alongside Michael Palin, the film featured a host of 'comedy' stars, both established and up and coming: Max Wall, John Le Mesurier, Warren Mitchell, John Bird, Bernard Bresslaw, Rodney Bewes, Annette Badland, Gorden Kaye, Neil Innes, Terry Jones and, the film's direc-tor, Terry Gilliam:

> I just got obsessed about casting as many great British comedi-ans, it was an extraordinary collection. What intrigued me about Harry was that his characters always seemed to be neurotic, so I wanted him to be a heroic character, one that Mike [Palin] looks up to. I was also intrigued by the fact that it had been for-gotten that he was a seriously classically trained actor – though he'd fallen into the lucky business of doing comedy. It's much harder for a serious actor to be a comic and I loved the fact that he had all that stuff to play with.
>
> Having worked with 'Python' and co-directed *Holy Grail* with Terry Jones I, very quickly, realised I was the 'monosyl-labic Minnesota farm boy that did funny pictures' and when it came to working with actors, Terry Jones was more comfortable. I worked better with the crew. So suddenly on *Jabberwocky* I was faced with all these extraordinary actors and comedians – and they did what I asked them to do, that's what was really weird.

A feeling that resonated with Michael Palin:

I knew Harry from *Steptoe*, of course, and was a great admirer of the way it was done. Galton and Simpson were terrific writers; I'd grown up with them. I began, as I got older, to realise that what they did so well was to create really good characters and once you've got strong characters you can do anything. *Steptoe* wasn't afraid of the emotional side; it wasn't all grinning and gags. It had to be played very carefully and I thought Harry's performance was terrific – it moved me a lot and as I began to think about comedy and why I like comedy I thought 'That's what I like'. Writers like that and a situation like that. I so much prefer that to the relentless barrage of jokes. When I started writing with Terry I thought this is the kind of thing I'm interested in. The very first thing we wrote together was similar to Galton and Simpson – but it never got made. So I was very excited when Terry said that he'd got Harry for *Jabberwocky*.

I hadn't worked with a lot of classically trained actors up till then because we'd carried on our undergraduate training through to *Python*. We hadn't done the *Ripping Yarns* where Terry Jones and I got to work with proper actors.

I think Terry Gilliam and I must have talked about our favourite actors and people we thought would work well in it. I hadn't worked with those actors who had come out of Theatre Workshop and the great things we remembered from when we were young, something that was very different from the plummy West End 'Noel Coward' kind of work. So it was interesting to meet someone who had been part of all that. One can't remember how fossilised the entertainment world was in the '50s and early '60s.

I didn't know what I was expecting Harry to be like but I remember I liked him very much and straight away. I think because he wasn't theatrical at all. There was nothing grand about him, in fact rather the opposite. He came across as someone a little bit uncertain of himself and why he could do what he could do. I could relate to that myself because I always thought acting was an odd thing. You go up there, you put this amazing performance on and then you go back to being yourself and everyone thinks you're an amazing extrovert and most actors aren't extroverts at all, quite the opposite.

He was a legend for us lads. Here I was talking to, and about to work with, someone who was a great hero. I'd had a certain amount of confidence from doing 'Python' but not much. We weren't terribly well known. We hadn't done *Life of Brian*. We'd done *Holy Grail* which had been a bit of a mess. Basically, I had only worked with a small team who larked about together. But within that group you had to have quite a strong image of yourself to get things done. It was quite competitive with six of us there. So to see somebody come who had carried so many shows with enormous audiences and so loved by everybody, I was a little bit worried – and it was rather nice to find that he wasn't grand.[5]

Though perhaps slightly demented as Terry Gilliam recalls:

The strangest story about Harry was when my wife [Maggie Weston], who was doing the make-up and hair, came to see him to talk about what he should look like. There in his flat the lights were dark, 'he kept it dark' he said. She said, 'Do you want to grow your hair long?' 'Yes. Let's grow it, or maybe we could get a wig.' As she's talking about his hair she's feeling his head … and he's wearing a wig. She didn't know what to do. She said, 'Err, have you ever had a wig made?' 'No,' he said. So she ended up making a wig to fit over his wig. Here's a man working in two wigs.

God, I want this story to be true. Unfortunately, I should point out that I can't confirm it. Aside from the trifling points of not having a flat or an aversion to lights, Harry never wore a wig at home. If he had you can bet we would have dressed the dog up in it. Of course he would have worn them for filming, in such a remarkably hirsute decade it was the norm. But at home he wasn't bothered. Even on stage it was too much like hard work and would counteract the lights bouncing off his bald spot by dabbing on boot polish. In a competition between vanity and laziness the latter always won, which might explain his predilection for hats. But who knows, perhaps he was going through a phase or taking the piss – perhaps he had a secret stash for just such an occasion.

Bi-wigged, he was ready for filming. 'Harry was dangerous,' Terry continues:

You didn't know what was going to happen all the time – that's what I liked about him. He was shameless in a strange and wonderful way. There was no sense of embarrassment with him; he'd go for it – whatever it took. He was bawdy and he milked it, it was wonderful to watch. On 'Python' there wasn't much ad-libbing but Harry would do things and you didn't know what was going to happen. I loved it. He was always coming up with stuff, that's what gave it real life. He wanted to make it more 'actory', I kept saying: 'We're only doing low comedy – but you can dignify it as best you can.'

The directive of 'low comedy' combined with the positive reaction to 'coming up with stuff' had worrying results for Michael Palin:

Harry and Max Wall were becoming quite creative, I think they just wanted to join in. Harry had this wonderful idea that as he was a lusty knave showing me the world, his codpiece should glow each scene – a very good Pythonic idea but I was a bit disturbed as it wasn't a 'Python' film, it was a 'serious' comedy. It was funny to find myself, as a 'Python' being nervous about that sort of inventiveness.

'It was great to bring all these people together,' Terry enthuses. 'They were working with their heroes – that was the atmosphere on set, it was exciting.'

It was friendly and relaxed off set too. They were shooting in Wales, near to where Harry's brother George had settled. Martin, George's son, remembers a visit to the location hotel:

He came down and stayed in the biggest hotel we've got with all the rest of the cast. I rang the hotel, said I was his nephew and turned up to see him. I was shown upstairs to this room and they're all in there, Max Wall, John Le Mesurier, 'Pythons' and all these stars having a drink, most of them were on Guinness. Harry didn't know I was coming. I walked up to him and said 'Hello, my name's Martin Corbett, you're my uncle.' And they all pissed themselves laughing. 'Oh, come on in, come in.' he said. 'Harry, you never said you had family here,' they cried. 'I didn't think anyone would come,' he answered. Harry was wonderful. I had an absolutely fantastic time with them all. I went to get a job as an extra thinking, 'I'm going to be in this bloody film with my uncle!' and they said no, I wasn't ugly enough.

Before they left, Harry came to the house. We were quite hard up for money at the time but a friend gave us a lobster and we all sat down to dinner. The next day he wasn't filming and we spent the day with me taking him round where my father had worked and the places he'd known. It was lovely, that time with him.

Unfortunately for Harry, the script didn't lend itself to him sharing a lovely time with the cast on set. 'Harry's scenes were kind of separate from all the others,' Terry remembers:

He didn't have scenes with Max Wall or John Le Mesurier. That was the thing with Harry, he kind of kept to himself and the others ganged up.

I felt he was frustrated, that he was desperate to be taken seriously. I used to say to him, 'Go off and do theatre, then.' But they couldn't afford him. He was a star.

That's the problem with being successful on television. Millions of people want you to do that again and again and again.

I would have liked to have worked with Harry again. The first time is always difficult – you're getting to know one another and, also, I would say that Harry wasn't the easiest of the lot because he did moan. I always felt he was never quite confident at the end of the day. Others were saying 'We did a great job'. He went away thinking he could have been better. His energy is what always amazed me. He would come onto set, after usually making a nervous meal out of his preparations, but once he was there – Boom! – all this energy would explode. And Mike and Harry didn't get much rehearsal time, we had to work it out on the floor.

'They were some of the first scenes I did,' Michael remembers:

It just wasn't difficult at all. Harry knew how to do it and related to all the other actors. There was never any question of 'this is *my* scene and I'm going to be like *this*.' Though I think he was quite worried about how he came across but that was more concerned with his performance. I would have thought someone who was 'Steptoe Junior' wouldn't have cared but, no, he wanted it to be special for the film. It was a completely different challenge. His past record didn't matter.

That's what I liked about him, and sometimes worried about him, he took it very seriously. He thought about every take. I remember one scene that had a real touch of intimacy about it; he played it very nicely so I could respond to it.

But the critics and audience didn't respond to the film. Gilliam recalled that:

With *Jabberwocky* I was so in my own head, so desperate to make my first film to prove things. I had these good people doing the scenes quickly and bang, on to the next scene and the next scene … Thank God they were all so brilliant, they could pull it off. But the critics ripped us apart, they hated it. Brueghel and Bosch were my two great heroes and I made a fatal mistake in New York. I wrote something to the critics saying 'this is not a Python film' – I didn't want it to be judged on that level – 'in some way it is more of an homage to Brueghel and Bosch.' And they just ripped me apart for that. 'How dare I compare myself to two of the greatest artists in history?'

The problem was that it wasn't a Python film and yet there was Mike Palin, Terry Jones and myself – it sounds a bit like a Python film and we got caught in that trap. It wasn't as funny as Python because it wasn't trying to be. It was more of a fairytale. Where it worked was in countries that didn't know Python … or with kids. The best screening we had was for kids – it's rude, it's crude. Kids love that.

'People weren't quite ready for the film,' thinks Michael Palin:

People are very slow to move from an established position. Suddenly along comes Terry Gilliam, known for his animation, he decides to make a film that's got this mixture of British actors that hadn't been in any other films apart from the *Carry Ons* and people didn't know what to make of it. It was different, fresh.

Holy Grail, at the time, people didn't understand it and thought it wide of the mark. Now they say 'Oh, great British comedy', it comes in the top five. By the time we did *Life of Brian* they'd got used to it. Now, when 'Jabberwocky' gets repeated, people are amazed because it looks absolutely wonderful.

It was a very interesting group of people. John Le Mesurier I loved, he was fantastic. Max Wall was an odd one. He had these terribly fascist views, whereas Harry and I were politically to the left. But Harry's performance, particularly, in *Jabberwocky* gave it something which makes it watchable again, time after time. There are human beings involved. It's not just a silly romp where we're all just doing jokes. There are moments where it's quite touching.

'Touching' was not something that could have been said of Harry's next film, well, apart from literally. This was *Hardcore*, a little-known oeuvre of the British sex-comedy cannon, a genre of film that has not only been swept under the carpet of history but firmly nailed down. Harry would have cameos in a few of these over the next couple of years. Seeing mainstream actors in such films was becoming a regular occurrence. The previous year Harry had been asked if he would be joining the bandwagon: 'I've got no snobbishness about show business,' he commented:

> I've never felt I've been bigger than the show. If I were offered an ice show tomorrow I'd be hysterical with delight. I'd be strapping on skates up at the local rink, practising until I could stand up on the damn things.
>
> The only thing I won't do is witless pornography. Sadly there seems to be a trend towards that. But if a soft porn show had wit, style and panache I'd certainly do it. Hard porn that never ventured from the sexual act itself, that wouldn't be on. There would have to be a good reason for a porn show – laughter.
>
> It would have to make them laugh. It would have to say: 'For God's sake, don't take this too seriously.' I wouldn't turn down a porn show out of any moral reason. It would be simply that it wasn't entertaining.[6]

Mainstream actors appearing alongside him in *Hardcore*, the fictionalised life story of glamour model Fiona Richmond, were Graham Stark, Victor Spinetti, Graham Crowden, Ronald Fraser and Adam 'Batman' West.

A surprising number of artistes would give a leg up to their careers or mortgages by getting a leg over in these films; names such as Willie Rushton, Christopher Biggins, Lynda Bellingham, Stephen Lewis, Roy Kinnear, Christopher Timothy, Jon Pertwee,

Diana Dors, Ian Lavender, Irene Handl and even Elaine Paige. The other side of the camera marked the debut of *Silence of the Lambs* Academy Award-winning director Jonathan Demme. Why, oh why, would leading thesps and future Oscar winners be jobbing in soft porn? Well, because it was the only gig in town.

In the late 1950s the Eady Levy on British Box Office receipts had given an incentive for foreign investors to make 'British' films in UK studios. But the chancellor of the exchequer's budgets of the mid-1970s had seen not only an exodus of British stars, but the foreign money too. In 1976 the government introduced a 75 per cent tax on those foreign producers who were resident in Britain. With only a few mainstream films qualifying for the few financial incentives offered during the global recession, the UK film industry was kept afloat by the James Bond franchise (which eventually bailed to make *Moonraker* in France in 1979), the continuation of the *Carry On* films, TV spin offs such as *Steptoe* and *Python* and – thanks to a concurrent relaxation of the censorship laws – that saucy seaside postcard of films: the sex comedy. Though, for the most part, sex and comedy are notable by their absence.

But there must have been something about them that appealed to the nation's psyche – they were the biggest draw of the decade, regularly beating artistic masterpieces at the box office. Some were even seen to be artistically worthy themselves: in 1974 Robin Askwith, star of the *Confessions of a ...* series, won the Evening News British Film Award for most promising newcomer.

Ah, it was another time, those far-off days before video recorders, DVDs and the internet, when one's jollies were found in a high-street cinema showing slightly racy films. It was commonplace; as such one rarely gave it a second thought. 1970s Britain was a country few would recognise or admit to.

By Christmas 1976 Harry was once again handling 'Dick'; this time *Dick Whittington*, the panto at the Congress Theatre in Eastbourne, with Anita Harris and Dora Bryan. The successful show managed to break the theatre's fourteen-year-old box office record in its first week. Playing at Eastbourne had the added attraction of being close to the cottage in Ashburnham; we could make the theatre in half an hour's drive. And I mean 'we', as that was the first year that I became Harry's dresser. Of course, Maureen, Jon and I had always been backstage and, bitten by the bug, I had usually wormed my way into finding something useful to do. But at age 8, I was now mature enough to be allowed to roam the wings without a minder, getting ready to assist in quick changes and being on standby to catch the buckets kicked off by the pantomime cow. I had always loved seeing him in panto, and if Harry had wanted to avoid my perfected 'last puppy in the shop' look, he knew that come November, I expected to see him practising with his juggling clubs over the sofa. But from the moment I was allowed to dress him, and spend every minute off school backstage; we had a pact – he would make with the panto and I would stop asking to go to stage school. Mind you, when I met some of the stage school kids hoofing as the chorus, I no longer wanted to. Any prepubescent ambition was firmly squished when Harry took me aside once to point out an actress playing the princess: 'She was a child star,' he said. 'And this is the only job she can get now.' Message received.

He was an incredibly patient and clear teacher and he always told me the truth, even if I was young enough to not want to hear it. 'Do you ever think we'll work together when I grow up?' I once asked him. 'I shouldn't think so,' he replied. 'The business will have given me up by then.' There was no melodrama in that, no self pity – it was merely a statement of fact on how the business worked and was another lesson learned for someone who wanted to join. It's a parent's job to prepare. He knew show business was fickle, hard work and, for women, prone to be short. But both my parents also knew that, as actors themselves, they didn't have a leg to stand on, and all they could do was give fair warning and, of course, considered criticism of performance.

That Christmas also saw the final *Steptoe* special on the radio. Ray and Alan adapted the 1974 television Christmas special into a 35 minute episode entitled 'Away for Christmas'. It was broadcast as part of David Jacobs' *Crackers* on Christmas Day morning.

By spring of 1977 'Steptoe Jr' was touring with 'Dad's Army's Captain Mainwaring' in J.B. Priestley's *Laburnum Grove*. Arthur Lowe played the suburbanite with a murky past, Joan Cooper his wife, both on and off stage, and Harry played the planter back from Malaya, sponging off Lowe's hospitality. Harry's wife was played by Gwen Cherrell, who wrote to Maureen after his death with her memories of him:

> I worked with Harry in the revival of 'Laburnum Grove' and for
> me every rehearsal was like attending a master class. His energy

and inventiveness and beautiful good manners made him the greatest pleasure to rehearse with.

Once we'd opened he never stopped wanting to try something new that he'd been thinking about since the previous performance. His joy when his ideas were confirmed by that night's audience was big and gleeful and generous.

His performance of *Richard II* at the Theatre Royal Stratford was the finest of his generation. I went to the first night with Kenneth Tynan and on the train journey home afterwards we sat in that entranced state – how rare – of knowing that we had seen great acting.

After the tour ended, Harry appeared in *A Hymn for Jim*, part of the 'premier' season on television that spotlighted new directors, in this case Colin Bucksey, who went on to forge a career in Hollywood. The play was written by Richard O'Brien, fresh from his success with *The Rocky Horror Picture Show*. Then Harry was on to discussions about a new tour.

A promoter, Kevin O'Neill, had mooted the idea of taking a stage show version of *Steptoe and Son* to Australia. Given how he felt about the country, and with Wilfrid eager to get on board, Harry was jumping at the chance. He approached Galton and Simpson to write the show. Although they hadn't worked together for a few years they met regularly. 'We saw Harry a great deal,' Alan Simpson remembers:

He used to come round the office and after we'd finished the series. We used to see a lot of Harry because we were discussing with him the idea of him redoing all the 'Hancock' shows. Tony Hancock had been dead ten years or more and we were going to remake all the shows with Harry – but it never happened. [Some of the *Hancock*s were eventually remade in the mid-'90s as part of the *Paul Merton in Galton and Simpson's* ... series, starring – unsurprisingly – Paul Merton.]

Of course it was not yet a done deal that *Steptoe* wouldn't reappear on television. The previous summer, when asked if it would be back, Harry had replied: 'The only definite thing I can say about the future of Steptoe is nothing's definite. It depends on how free we all are and when Ray Galton and Alan Simpson come up with more scripts.'[7]

'When it finished in '74, we thought that was it,' Alan continues, 'Then we thought they'd start again but then Harry amazed us by saying would we write a cabaret act for him and Wilfrid. We wrote about a sixty-minute cabaret. We never saw it, never rehearsed it with them. We spoke to Harry and he did the rest of it.'

As Harry didn't want to go without Maureen, Pat came to look after us kids at St John's Wood and see us through school until the Christmas break when we would be joining them. Harry, Maureen and Wilfrid flew out for the tour at the end of September 1977.

'We went via Singapore,' Maureen later remembered:

> We liked a particular hotel in Singapore and had a really good relaxing time listening to the jungle birds calling in the morning. So we said to Wilfrid, we'll stop in Singapore so we can pull ourselves together because there's bound to be a barrage of press when we get there. It's a bit silly trying to go all the way through.

Arriving in Perth on 5 October, they were immediately launched into that barrage to drum up publicity. Harry, of course, was an old hand, but it was a new and sometimes unwelcome experience for Wilfrid. The show opened at the Perth Concert Hall on the 16th and meshed Ray and Alan's script with humour tailored for the Australian audience.

Maureen gave an outline of the show:

> Cockney songs and one or two Australian songs thrown in, lots of gags, lots of gags, and some lines from *Steptoe* that are so well known that everyone was thrilled to hear them and see them delivered in person – and then there were people who travelled with us, like singers. Sometimes they changed from state to state, you know, they went off and did other things and someone else took over for another part of the tour. And we travelled with a band because, of course, they were singing these songs – we had our own roadies! Good fun.
>
> It was designed to be played on trestles at the end of the runway, the Opera House and everywhere in between. And so it was well received by everybody because you could adapt it to any kind of venue or any kind of surroundings. So lots of people got to see it and they all liked it.

The schedule started off being very clean, with no crossings out or amendments of any sort. It didn't last long. We opened in Perth and from then on it was somewhere else almost every day. We played some really marvellous places, there was always plenty going on. And, of course, in addition to just doing the show and travelling about there was the early morning radio shows and stuff like that and lots of press.

It was a very gruelling, very intensive tour. We enjoyed it, but we didn't get to do a great deal else because of all the travelling.

We mainly travelled about in convoy, from place to place, over-land … We were busy flying around or in the venue, out of the venue, in the cars, off to the next one or back to the hotel, get some sleep, off to the airport – we took off and landed forty-six times. And we kept criss-crossing the same country as well. You might be in one town in the River Ena and then a month later you'd be in the next town in the River Ena having been right across the continent in the meantime. Oh, it was a good tour.

It is quite tiring. But then the schedule was designed mainly that one didn't do anything else on that day. Especially if it were from side to side of the continent, if it was just upstate or in the neighbouring state it's not too bad but, yes, it is quite tiring, I think Wilfrid probably suffered the most from that, you know. It took its toll on him after a while.

[The show] was very adaptable – so you would go into a venue and you would do the sound call, or whatever, and I would stand at the back and say 'I can't hear you' and so we were very self-sufficient as a group. We went in, we asked for what we wanted, if it wasn't there we made sure it was and then that was it – out. And then we could spend the rest of the time going to whatever the local attraction was. Like if we were in Mount Gambier, there's the wonderful blue lake that turns a light blue on particular days of the year, right. It wasn't the particular day of the year when we were there, but nevertheless it is a lovely thing. And so I sort of got hold of the pair of them and frogmarched them up to the Blue Lake – it was like that. It was sightseeing, but it was all quite rushed. Except that when we had a day or so off then we would do a day out, if it was a day in the same town. So if you were playing, say, three venues in the same town it was great, because then you'd have the whole day up until show time to have a look around.

[I think Harry would have liked to have lived in Australia], he was very fond of it. He didn't have as much time to spend looking around at the scenery on this particular tour as he would have liked but every opportunity I made sure that we did ...As we were going along in convoy, I would say 'Wait a minute,' looking at the map, 'here's something I recognise, and I've definitely got to get out and photograph it,' and the whole cavalcade, half a dozen cars, would have to stop and they'd all have to get out while I did whatever and Harry thoroughly enjoyed it, because he wouldn't have had the chance otherwise. He loved the countryside and the towns.

[And the wildlife] he particularly liked kangaroos. He had a fight with one kangaroo, a great big red who walked up to him and started eyeing him up and he was saying 'Yes nice, nice kangaroo, lovely roo' and then it got a bit more familiar and he was saying 'Get down you bastard.' And in fact they're actually quite dangerous because they come up with their back legs and they can, have, scratched the insides of a man out, you know, if they get really cross. So, I mean, I suppose he'd read this and had it in mind. Oh, anything to do with animals – we were there.

We kids arrived to join in the cavalcade just before Christmas. A few days later we flew up to Surfer's Paradise on the Gold Coast. Harry and Maureen rented an apartment in one of the skyscrapers that looked out over the sand stretching off into the distance. This was to be our main base during the month-long stay. Harry and Maureen's letters to us had mentioned their trips out with Wilfrid; a postcard from the Tantanoola Caves of Mount Gambier describes going cave hopping: 'I dragged "the boys" 75ft down and up again to see the stalagmites and fossils. I'm sure they'd rather have been resting up in bed!' Maureen wrote on one after capturing the event on her ever-present cine film. In a cave or feeding parrots, an incongruous Wilfrid was impeccably dressed as always. Wilfrid's day trips took a back seat while we were with them. There were plenty of times we did all go out together, a trip to Phillip Island to watch the penguins marching up the beach sticks in the memory, but we naturally wanted to spend time away from the job as a family. Besides, although I found Wilfrid to be perfectly polite and always very nice to me, one had the sense that he was not comfortable around children. Nor did he seem particularly comfortable around the fans, which came as an eye-opener as my only experience had been seeing Harry in action at the stage door.

During one show, Wilfrid had an unbelievably grouchy moment. A woman in the audience, so much the worse for drink it was a miracle she was upright, lurched from her seat and started to climb up onto the stage directly in front of him. Just as she had got some purchase with two arms and one knee, the horrified Wilfrid, not used to the unexpected frisson of the cabaret world, planted a boot firmly in her chest and sent her flying back into the auditorium. She hit the floor just ahead of 1,000 jaws. While audience, band, roadies and theatre staff stood caught in the headlights, Harry leapt off the apron to come to the woman's aid. He picked her up, escorted her backstage and then returned to the abandoned Wilfrid and carried on.

In the wings the woman did not seem to be suffering from any injury, though it was hard to tell as she was so well anesthetised. She was most concerned with getting back to the show. 'I've come 2,000 fuckin' miles to see fuckin' Steptoe,' she bellowed, swinging for anyone who came near. Not that many did. The burly roadies were too taken aback by the full force of Outback womanhood in front of them. It was left to Maureen, all 5ft of her, to face up. 'How dare you use such language in front of my daughter.' She intoned in her best RADA voice (now was not the time to remind her that I'd heard far worse at home). The woman was eventually persuaded to be led away for a little lie down in a quiet room. As she left, turning away from belligerence and towards melancholy, she was explaining tearfully how much she 'Just fuckin' loved Harry', so it was a shame that she was too pissed to notice she'd just been in his arms. You know, travel really does broaden the mind.

When the show ended, a mortified Harry went to see how the woman was doing. Wilfrid was seemingly unrepentant, though he must have been embarrassed by his actions. He was lashing out to all and sundry, at one point even castigating Harry – 'You and your fucking kids!' he said to him. Now, to be fair to Wilfrid, who had no children and did not get to spend a great deal of time with any, being suddenly plunged into occasional rumbustious family life would have come as a trial, especially with a daily hangover. But he should have realised that a wise man never comments on a person's kids. For Harry, who loved us dearly, it was a step too far. Even then he could see that Wilfrid was not himself, so simply took him by the collar, drew him close and quietly said 'Never my children.' Nothing more was said. The next day Harry had 'forgotten' the matter; it was water under the bridge. Wilfrid certainly never brought it up. But then, he could have been a tad hazy on what had happened.

Obviously that incident stays in the memory as it was so outrageous, but for the most part the tour ticked along while we were there – get in, do show, get out, enjoy being back Down Under. And we did enjoy it. It was a wonderful experience. For Jon and me it was over all too soon and we had to return to London and school. As the tour continued on, Maureen and Harry's letters home mentioned no further problems with Wilfrid, but then they didn't mention him much. The letters were full of where they'd been, the old friends they had met up with – Betty Lucas from *The Last of the Red Hot Lovers* amongst them. When we spoke to them later on, one got the impression that Wilfrid had increasingly found the relentless pace of the tour very hard going.

Maureen recalled:

My job really, apart from being backstage and generally making sure that everything ticked over from our point of view, was making sure that Wilfrid got ready on time and got to the airport because sometimes he could be a bit cross, especially if he hadn't had a terribly good night – and he used to bite everybody's head off. So they used to send me along and I'd knock on the door and say 'Hello Wilfrid, it's Maureen.'

'Oh, right Darling, I'll be with you in a minute.'

So I was terribly useful from that point of view … One day we thought he was having a heart attack – in fact it was too many gins – but it was all right – we got him on the plane, he was in one piece.

Kevin O'Neill remembered an occasion when Wilfrid went AWOL. Harry had opened the show as usual but no Wilf came in on cue:

I walked to the side of the stage and Harry looked at me. I said 'I can't find Wilfrid, so be funny until I get back.' I ended up driving round to this lady's house and there's her, her husband and a kid and Wilfrid, in his stage outfit mind, and he's sitting at the dining room table and they're just about to serve roast beef and

I've gone, 'Wilfrid, what are you doing here? We've got a show to do. Harry's on stage.' 'I don't care, I'm not working tonight.

Harry did actually come to me at one stage, this was after about nine weeks, and said, 'Look, this is just too hard for Wilfrid, it's just not working,' and to be honest, he would have gone home had Maureen, his wife, not been here with him.

I find it doubtful that Harry would have actually walked. He had a contract, he would honour it. Most importantly, he would not have wanted to let the audience down, no matter how hard the tour became. The diary was rather oversubscribed. Aside from television specials, a couple of commercials (one for Ajax cleaner was shipped back and shown in the UK) and a Royal Variety Performance, there were extensions and extra dates to fit in the crowds that flocked to see 'Steptoe' in person and, always, the endless promotion, of which Wilfrid was never a fan. When the tour reached Christchurch, New Zealand, in March, the running time had been reduced. Tina Cross, the then up-and-coming singer, was booked in as opening support act and remembers:

We'd been contracted to do half an hour but were asked to extend our set. On the night the audience were chanting: 'We want Steptoe, we want Steptoe'. My final song was the Dolly Parton number *Here you Come Again*. Now the last line of the song is 'Here I go', so we're at the end of our 45 mins and I sing out 'Here I go-o-o' and somebody shouted out 'Well, fuck off then!'

Harry and Wilf came on and did their act. I think the audience were a bit pissed off that it was a bit short. I can't remember how long it was. However, Wilfrid was interviewed on the radio the next day and all we heard back was that either the DJ or someone had called in to have a go about the length of the show and Wilfrid basically said 'I hope your fucking cathedral falls down'. He was actually quoted in the press. This was the start of the tour. That's what I remember most, the kerfuffle we caused in Christchurch. Wilfrid was probably drunk; I remember he used to have his little hip flask.

Unsurprisingly the show did not have the warmest of receptions in the local papers. As a country that in the 1970s could have been compared to Scotland in the 1950s, New Zealand was possibly the very worst place Wilfrid could have chosen to have his meltdown, but anywhere would have been justified in being extremely insulted. Harry would have been so embarrassed. He and Maureen adored New Zealand; it was, for them, the most beautiful country they'd ever seen. Remarkably, Wilfrid's behaviour, yet again, didn't lead to an irreparable falling out; I was certainly never told of one and Tina couldn't recall 'any angst or bad vibes between the two of them'.

The tour came to an end and they finally returned home in April. I don't know if they all travelled back together – I don't think so – Wilfrid may have gone for one of his regular trips to the Far East. As Maureen later said:

> He had a lot of friends in Hong Kong, which he liked very much. So he used to get on planes and go to Hong Kong quite a lot to see his friends. He had a very wide circle of, sort of, colonial type friends, they had names like the 'Poncenby-Smythes' and things like that – it was a good crack. And we used to wind him up over it.

The tour had been a success. For Harry and Wilfrid, after being on and off work colleagues for fifteen years, to suddenly be seeing so much of each other was a novel experience but, by and large, one they enjoyed. They had always got on well at home when they had seen each other. Maureen commented:

> They did get on terribly well. We used to do lots of different things, like there was always me and there was always the kids and every weekend there was lots of charity stuff and lots of functions we used to go to and Wilfrid did other things, is all I can say. So, you know, we didn't have a lot to do with each other socially outside of doing a series. But Wilfrid just had different interests – that's all. And he liked drinking in pubs, and things and we didn't so … That's why our paths didn't cross perhaps as much as they might have done but certainly, yes, they got on terribly well. In fact we had a really good time when we toured Australia together.

Wilfrid and Maureen had not really known each other before Australia but, during the tour, became good friends. As an unexpected parting gift he gave her the most ridiculously whopping black opal to remember him by. Being tired and emotional may have occasionally made him feisty, but we could all see that underneath it, he was a sweet man.

Within days of landing in London, Harry was into rehearsals of his next play. He had been asked to take *Rattle of a Simple Man* to Rhodesia and South Africa and so had a brief tour of the UK playing opposite Kate O'Mara in preparation.

Just before leaving for Africa, Harry and Wilfrid got together to record a *Steptoe and Son* segment for an 'entertainment prelude'[8] to the 1978 Football World Cup in Argentina. The England team had failed to qualify, but Scotland were going, and the programme entitled 'Good Luck Scotland', and hosted by Ernie Wise, aimed to get the nation involved – as Albert says: 'You've got to support the Jocks', to which Harold replies, 'thought they had straps for that'. The twelve- minute *Steptoe* sketch was entitled 'Scotch on the Rocks'. Albert is planning on going to watch the football in Argentina with his friend Angus McLeod, using a combination of hitchhiking, canoe and banana boat, but doesn't end up going after a punch-up at the embassy.

A few days later, Harry left for Rhodesia with *Rattle of a Simple Man*. He couldn't wait to show us Africa – but he drew the line at taking us to Rhodesia as there was a civil war going on. It was the only time he went by himself. He opened opposite Dilys Watling in Salisbury (Harare), and throughout June and July toured the country. In Australia he had toured with roadies, in Rhodesia with armed guards, some of whom he remembered being irritatingly gung ho; one particular mercenary always offering to teach him how to shoot his sten gun, so he could manfully protect himself. After several days needling, Harry asked for it and a blindfold. After he'd stripped, rebuilt and handed it back in competent time, no more was said.

Maureen joined him in South Africa, and we followed on in the school holidays. It was another opportunity to expand our education, not just with the extraordinary landscape, flora and fauna but with its politics. South Africa was still in the grip of apartheid and Harry, as a firm supporter of Equity's stance on equality, had signed up for the union's declaration that none of its members would perform there if forbidden to play to multi-racial audiences. Permission aside, economic viability meant that one rarely saw anything but white faces in the audience. Coming from cosmopolitan London, and attending a school where WASPs were in a minority, it was a bit of a shock. On the way in from the airport a black man was trying to cross the road. He was paralysed but without a wheel-chair – instead he hunkered on a wooden board fitted with castors, affording him a good lungful of the exhaust fumes. He knuckled his way over the crossing. When the green man stopped flashing the cars started hooting their horns at him for being in the way, like he could go any faster. It was quite an introduction.

By now Harry was acquainted with a few Afrikaners. I remember having a conversation with one. Listening to the stuff coming out of the guy's mouth, I was convinced he was winding me up. 'No, he believes it,' Harry later said. 'And, more importantly, now you'll recognise it if you ever hear it again.' A dramatic lesson, perhaps – but then he had fought Nazis. It was, unsurprisingly, extremely difficult to fit in. On one occasion Harry took me ice skating, after a while a claxon sounded and the other skaters left the rink. But the place wasn't closing, it was mid-morning and no Zamboni came out to resurface. Around the edge more children waited to come on. Skating over to Harry, who was watching from the side, I asked why they were just standing there. 'They're black,' he explained. 'They can't come on until all the whites get off.' I broke an Olympic record leaving that ice. On the flip side, after being beaten up in a park for playing with the wrong sort of children, I had to ask Maureen what a 'Kaffir lover' was – but at least I had a new word to take home to my classmates. The memory of my best friend saying 'So, I'm a kaffir then' has stayed with me always.

We stuck to the theatre after that, at least the show was going well. During the evenings, as there were no quick changes to attend to, Jon and I were allowed into the lighting box to make the occa-sional cue. Jon, misdirected, threw the switch too early one night, plunging Harry and Dilys into darkness – he sends his apologies to any who saw it. During the days, while trapped in the city, we would seek out cinemas showing English-language films as the TV only seemed to air Afrikaans variety shows and one precious weekly viewing of *Charlie's Angels*. Maureen and Harry had to sit through Disney's *The Rescuers* seventeen times.

Matinees allowing, we took every opportunity to get out into the country and visit the big game reserves. Attempts at meeting indigenous peoples were not that successful and were confined to the tourist trail. We went to see the tribal dances put on by men working in the gold mines for a segregated audience; the ticket pointing out that: 'Tribal dances are arranged primarily to provide recreation and entertainment for the Black mineworkers, and not for the entertainment of the public.' Well we were entertained, dammit! The men were glorious. After the show some of the guys came over to the white end of the stand for the obligatory photo op. Posed next to one of the dancers I couldn't help but think how he was so dignified and I was so bleeding embarrassed. South Africa was beautiful but did leave one feeling slightly soiled. Harry was right, it had been an education.

As summer drew to a close and the run came to an end we flew to Spain to take a family holiday before the autumn term started. It was pointed out that Harry had been abroad for nearly a year and been earning good money throughout. If he came back now he would be faced with paying the usual 97 per cent tax bill. Paying 97 pence in every pound was the reason most big earners left Britain in the 1970s, they actually couldn't afford to stay there. Returning home meant Harry would probably make a loss on the year. Jon and I flew home; Maureen and Harry waited, much to their irritation as Maureen remembered:

> When we got back, [Harry] said, 'This is ridiculous! I've had to spend a month of my life sitting on a beach somewhere that I didn't really want to do – I'd have much rather come back – to save the money, the only potential money that one could save, to keep two homes standing. What's the point of that? Why don't we get rid of one of them?' And so we said 'Well, which one?', and then there was this problem about well is it really right to take the children away from London when they're just about to be teenagers – isn't that a bit mean?

Not really, we were already spending every weekend and school holiday in Sussex. London was great, but we were starting to feel more at home in the country. Maureen had always preferred it there. It was ideal for Pat, Malcolm and Jennie and their newborn children to come and spend Bank Holidays and Christmases and, besides, Harry's priorities were changing. '[The place in Sussex] was just a weekender to begin with, because we lived on the job in St John's Wood', Maureen explained:

There wasn't the motorway then and it took longer to get out of London so in those days one had to be nearer because, and especially from our point of view, when [Harry] wasn't actually in the studio or in the theatre, about three or four nights a week we would be at the Dorchester, at some Flying Squad do ... and, also, he liked to go round the clubs and see Danny La Rue and people like that and we were out a lot, and so you couldn't really live anywhere else but London. But then there came a point in his life – especially when the communications got better – one could get to the country faster, it became possible to live down here.

We decided to get off the wheel and get out of town. With all the touring we rarely seemed to be in one place anyway and it fitted in handily with our lives. Jon and I had just started our last year in juniors so it gave Maureen and Harry a year to find senior schools, sell up and build another extension to the cottage.

We'd had a great run in London. The five glorious years had turned into eleven, but, as with most things, it was time – there's a time.

Notes

1   *Titbits*, 18/3/76.
2   In conversation with Kenneth Cranham.
3   *Ibid*.
4   Galton and Simpson, *Steptoe and Son*.
5   In conversation with Michael Palin.
6   *Titbits*, 18/3/76.
7   *Ibid*.
8   *Radio Times*, 29/5/78.

19

Cardiacs and Coal Bunkers

Closed down for renovations, be back shortly.

Harry H. Corbett

The autumn of 1978 was a turbulent time in Britain. Maureen and Harry had arrived back just in time for the start of 'the winter of discontent', the roots of which could be found in the summer of 1975 when inflation had hit 27 per cent and sterling had trembled. To drive inflation down, the Labour government made a series of pay capping deals with the trade unions. These were made even more necessary as part of the belt-tightening conditions set by the International Monetary Fund when new prime minister James Callaghan secured a humiliating £2.3 billion loan.

By 1977 a weakened Labour Party had been forced into a pact with the Liberal party in order to maintain a working majority and, in July, announced a phasing back in of collective bargaining while keeping the pay caps in place. By the summer of 1978 inflation was below 10 per cent and both the pact with the Liberals and the agreement with the TUC were up. But the Chancellor only offered the unions a 5 per cent pay increase, which was dismissed. The unions also wanted the promised free collective bargaining back. They were in a strong position. Labour were ahead in the polls and Callaghan expected to call an autumn general election. He didn't. He would keep to the 5 per cent, impose sanctions on government contractors who broke that limit and wait for a better economic clime in the spring before launching his bid for re-election. Big mistake.

Ford Motors, who were government contractors, kept their pay offer within the 5 per cent limit, immediately prompting a strike supported by the Transport and General Workers Union just as the Labour Party Conference rolled into Blackpool. The conference voted for the government to keep its nose out of the negotiations. Negotiations that were looking increasingly like Ford were about to significantly up their offer. This prompted the TUC to try and work out a pay policy and avoid further strike action but no decision could be agreed. Ford and its striking workforce settled on a 17 per cent increase.

Back in London the Labour government tried to impose their sanctions on Ford. A motion of no confidence was called in the House. Labour, bereft of Liberal support, narrowly defeated the motion thanks to a temporary deal with the Ulster Unionists. But the damage had been done. Callaghan knew he couldn't make sanctions, and thus the 5 per cent, stick, and the TUC had no pay policy in place. It was a perfect storm for strike action.

First out were the lorry drivers. As most of the country's goods were transported by road, the strike bit quickly and hard. Petrol queues were magnificent, before the pumps dried up. We queued in Poole where that year's panto saw Harry in *Cinderella*, trying to get a laugh out of audiences running out of supplies and patience, shivering in the below-zero temperatures that ravaged the country for weeks. The drivers got their increase. After these successes the public sector wanted a slice, culminating in a 'day of action' on 22 January that saw 1.5 million out. Many didn't return to work. Hospitals only took emergencies, and schools and airports were closing. In Liverpool striking gravediggers saw bodies being stockpiled and burials at sea contemplated.

Callaghan, himself, was reported as saying: 'When I am shaving in the morning, I often look in the mirror and think if I were a young man I would emigrate'. Harry agreed with him. The country he loved was going to the dogs. The most visual confirmation of this was the refuse collectors' strike. Returning to London after the panto, Harry took us to Leicester Square to play 'spot the rat' amongst the huge piles of rubbish. The Conservative Party used images of the rubbish in their broadcasts. By February they were 20 per cent ahead in the polls. In March a referendum on devolution for Scotland was narrowly won, but not by enough for the government to grant it. The Scottish National Party withdrew its support and another motion of no confidence was called, which the government lost. Callaghan called the general election.

Harry didn't do much campaigning this time round. Not because he was leaving a sinking ship but because he was too busy. He was on location, filming an episode of the detective series *Shoestring*, playing a malevolent brooding heavy, a return to his first 'type casting' – his performance prompting reviewers to be astounded, again, at how remarkably convincing he was away from comedy. God knows what they would have made of his next performance in *The Basil Brush Show*.

But away from work Harry didn't care about politics, only raising an eyebrow at the inevitable prospect of new Conservative leader Margaret Thatcher, the woman who as Health Secretary had 'knocked off the milk' for school kids in 1971, sweeping to power with a promise to tame the unions. For Harry the world was a rapidly receding point of contact. Maureen was ill. At first she had ignored the abdominal pain and excessive bleeding – she was trying to get the house ready for sale. But then she found a lump in her breast, and there was no ignoring that. With the history of her father and two aunts dead from breast cancer, both she and Harry were not unaware of what the future could hold. Once more under the care of Jack Suchet, at the age of 36, she went in for a hysterectomy and potential mastectomy. Surprisingly, she woke up symmetrical: the lump had been benign, as had the uterine fibroid that was the size of a grapefruit. It was a lucky escape. When she came home from hospital, Harry carried her upstairs to bed with Jon and I saucer-eyed satellites, the only telltale sign of the pain each step was causing her was the whitening of her knuckles clutching at Harry's shirt. I can remember his face as he laid her down. His expression was one I hoped never to see in the mirror.

He was on parent and nursing duty as spring turned to summer and Maureen recuperated. Eventually she was strong enough to show prospective buyers around. It was a job not trusted to Harry as he would have taken the first offer out of embarrassment. A deal was done, she started packing the house and packed Harry back off to work. He was shooting the television remake of Eric Sykes' *The Plank*, an almost silent slapstick comedy that went on to win the International Press Prize at the 1980 Montreux Festival of Light Entertainment. Then it was on to his next series.

This new vehicle was *Grundy*, Harry playing a freshly divorced puritan newsagent out of touch with the permissive society displayed by his daughter, Julie Dawn Cole, her boyfriend, David

Janson, and the boyfriend's mother, Lynda Baron, who had taken
a shine to him. Written by Ken Hoare, Stanley Baxter's award-
winning writer, the series started shooting for Thames Television
in August and managed to get one episode in the can before the
'summer of discontent' hit.

The previous winter's strikes had rumbled into television.
Trouble at the BBC had threatened their Christmas line up, a prospect not to be borne in the ratings war. The Beeb, unhampered
by shareholders, had stumped up 15 per cent for technicians, but
throughout 1979 faced wildcat strikes at embarrassingly high-
profile events. During *A Song for Europe*, the show that picked the
UK entry for Eurovision, cameramen walked out and the show finished in audio only. Not to be outdone, a sound engineers strike
caused a global hiatus in that year's *Miss World*.

When strike action hit ITV there was no messing about; the
network ground to a halt for ten weeks during the summer, only
coming back online in October. For ITV it was disastrous. By
the time the nation was once again offered a choice of program-
ming they weren't concerned with having one. They were already
hooked by the BBC, and the turgid fare offered by ITV in lieu
of not being able to produce anything new kept them away for
months afterwards.

Harry was irritated; he'd been enjoying working on a new series
before the strike sent everyone home. Lynda Baron remembered:

> We all loved doing it, Harry was a delight to work with. He
> absolutely loved the business – he never had any of that down in
> the mouth nonsense of regret – his attitude to the business was
> joyous. He loved his house in the country and was going home
> to chop logs which I said wasn't a good idea, which it wasn't.

'I was feeling frustrated,' he later said, 'so I threw myself into some
heavy chores around the house.' The silly sod stacked a ton of wood
and single-handedly put together a ridiculously heavy concrete
coal bunker. 'Suddenly I felt a sharp pain. It was like very bad indi-
gestion. They took me to hospital.'

You bet we did, but that was a struggle. To protestations of 'Really,
I'm fine Mo,' while clutching his chest and groaning, Maureen
firmly persuaded him into the car and down to the local cottage
hospital where doctors firmly persuaded him that he was actually

having a coronary. They would take him by ambulance to the cardiac unit of St Helen's Hospital, Hastings. He even walked to the damn ambulance. At St Helen's he was hooked up to the monitors and reality started to kick in. He recalled:

> A woman kept yelling at me not to cross my legs. They're dead set against you crossing your legs, you know.
>
> I couldn't believe I'd had a heart attack. Later I found that a quarter of the nation were fellow sufferers. In my ward were scoutmasters, businessmen, fat people, thin people, smokers and non-smokers. It gave me macabre comfort.
>
> The family were scared. It was grapes on the hour. But I wasn't worried. All my life, I've rolled with the punches. I've never plotted or planned anything. I felt that this was just another punch that I could take.

New arrivals to the cardiac ward occupied beds closest to the nurses' station and the jump leads. As you improved, your bed was moved nearer and nearer to the doors, until the joyous day when you were deemed able to go home and got a cheerful send off from the other patients – another one had made it. Harry's heart attack had thankfully been mild and he made steady bed-hopping progress. When he was about halfway down, the young man in the last bed was leaving to go. I remember his family coming in to collect him wreathed in smiles; his children were of a similar age to Jon and me and we'd become friendly. As the young man picked up his coat from the bed the ward called out its goodbyes, he raised his hand in answer, suddenly froze and collapsed. White coats and machines hurtled towards him; curtains were drawn, all to no avail. He'd been dead before he hit the floor.

One was naturally disposed to reflection, sober and irrational. We blamed that concrete bunker for years. But, in reality, it wasn't that, or the stress of Maureen's illness, or the recent house move, or dealing with builders on the new extension, or the interruption of the new series. Every male member of Harry's immediate family had died of a coronary in their mid-50s. It was just his time. Of course, none of the other things, or his being a smoker, helped, and we still hated that bloody bunker.

Harry was out of the ward in record time. He spent a couple of weeks building his strength in a recuperation home. We would have liked it to be more, but he was already booked into panto at Bromley and nothing would stop him making opening night: 'I felt that if I could survive a season's panto I could survive anything,' he later said. 'Besides I didn't want to let anyone down.'

His bounce back was so remarkable that he even found time to record a new single, *Old Fashioned Christmas* by 'Harry H and the Kids' – Jon and I were two of the kids on backing vocals, fame at last. On the advice of his specialist in London he changed his diet, or rather Maureen did. She changed everyone's. Overnight she cleared out the cupboards and when you opened the fridge 'low fat' screamed at you. She had less success in getting him to give up his forty-year smoking habit, though not for the want of trying. Harry saw hypnotherapists, who pronounced him unsuitable material, and acupuncturists, who sent him home twiddling needles in his ears. Through a combination of will power and nagging he got his daily fix down from over sixty Player's Navy Cut to fewer than twenty Silk Cut red, a short aertex fag seen in those pre-nicotine patch times as being the healthy option. He did his best and we were proud of him.

Maureen had no success at all in getting Harry to cut back on work. He could have as easily cut back on breathing. Aside from making good on charity appearances, over subsequent months he honoured commitments working on the movie *Silver Dream Racer*, completing *Grundy* for Thames and began filming for the BBC on Arthur Lowe's new comedy series *Potter*, playing the regular character of local gangster Harry Tooms. Due to an uninterrupted line up, *Potter* was aired first, going out in the spring. *Grundy* had to wait for a gap in the summer. For most of the reviewers, it wasn't worth the wait, especially when it was compared to *Steptoe*, as was inevitable. I'm sure Harry was disappointed, though not surprised, by its reception. The series was not recommissioned, which came as a blow to Lynda Baron:

> I was mortified I never did any more series with Harry, as he was a joy to work with. Whether they hated us I've no idea. Nowadays, I'd ring up and ask why but back then one didn't. We loved doing it. All of us had a nice time – that often happens. It doesn't take off being the huge hit you'd hoped because you're enjoying yourself. Harry was delightful, that's all I can say about the man.

Harry rolled with the punches. While the Beeb once more repeated *Steptoe* during prime time, he reunited with Ray and Alan for a segment on Thames Television's *Comedy Tonight*, and guest starred alongside June Whitfield and Roy Kinnear in that year's Dick Emery Christmas special, *For Whom the Jingle Bell Tolls*, and was further reunited with the *Steptoe* writers and Wilfrid to film a Kenco coffee commercial as the year turned and panto once more beckoned; this time *Aladdin* in Croydon with Leslie Crowther.

By 1981 we'd been happily settled in Sussex for over a year. Maureen was in her element, now enjoying space and time to give her green fingers exercise. She'd had a minor hiccup just after Christmas: she'd found another lump. Once again, luckily, it was benign and come early spring she was back in her beloved garden, turning it into one that could rival those at Chelsea, with us kids earning pocket money hoeing swathes of veggies and unhooking birds from the fruit netting that protected that year's jam crop – don't talk to me about gooseberries. Harry didn't have a clue as to what any of it was, but he appreciated it. Freezing in the March winds he would call out to Maureen to 'Come in, you silly girl!' – his blood still thin after all those years.

He was the content squire, welcomed by the locals who politely contained their rubbernecking until he was out of the shop door. To complete the picture of country life, we even had donkeys. While working on a job Harry had got chatting to the animal handler. She was trying to find a home for a rescued donkey now retiring from a stint in show business carrying Joseph, Mary and the baby Jesus; she'd had a photogenic cross. Harry called Maureen to check it would be okay. 'Yes, that's fine.' Five minutes later he called again – 'It's got a friend.' 'Yes, that's fine, two's fine.' The phone went again, 'The friend's got a foal ...' As he would be banned from mucking out, the line was drawn at three.

The lunchtime get-togethers with Ray and Alan had taken a back seat now he was commuting, but he still regularly went up to town on business or to meet with his agent or friends. One occasion was the reunion at Theatre Royal, Stratford East, to mark the publication of Howard Goorney's book on Theatre Workshop in May. Many old lags turned up, putting on an impromptu variety show – Brian Murphy was in charge of the bar, doling out the drinks to raise toasts and share memories. Joan was notable by her continued absence. Still living in France she had recently sent a telegram on the opening of the theatre's production of *Hamlet* – the first she had sent for six years. She had signed it 'Petitbois'.

Harry's own variety wanderlust had gone unsatisfied for too long, and he spent the summer and autumn playing the clubs with his one-man show. He also signed up to appear in panto at Swansea that Christmas and to take his show to the Channel Islands the following summer before he and Wilfrid were due to return to Australia for another *Steptoe* tour.

It looked like 1982 was going to be another busy year, and that was without the planned series of *Potter* and any other TV or film roles. To take a break before it all kicked off, that September we flew to Corfu. We had been there years before when the island afforded few hotels and a smattering of hippies camping rough on deserted beaches. Now those beaches were teeming with holiday makers recovering from last night's partying. We rented an apartment in the hills. As ever, Harry skippered us in boats to seek out inaccessible coves or drove us through inland ghost towns now blind to the distant sparkling Ionian. One evening, stopping in a small hamlet, we were greeted at the door of a bar with astounded cries. In the background a TV was playing an episode of *Steptoe* dubbed over into Greek. It's hard to say what amazed the locals more, that Harold had popped in for a drink or that, in reality, he couldn't actually speak the language.

Back in the UK Harry filmed a couple of guest spots on the game show *Give us a Clue* and the Bruce Forsyth variety show, *Nice to See You*, before starting work on an episode of *Tales of the Unexpected* entitled 'The Moles', starring alongside Bill Owen and Fulton Mackay. Then it was off to Swansea and the panto.

He was starring in *Dick Whittington*. Traditionally, pantomimes at the Grand Theatre, Swansea, opened on Boxing Day and enjoyed a very long run. We had joined Harry in Swansea for the Christmas holidays; he'd only been away a few weeks but we could notice a change, he wasn't looking well. Maybe it was down to the dreadful blizzards that ravaged the country that winter. All too soon we had to return to Sussex and school, leaving Harry to carry on with the show until the end of the run in early March.

The actor Desmond Barrit, now the toast of the RSC stage, who has given pantomime workshops to classical actors entitled 'Wherefore art thou Romeo, he's behind you', was playing the dame and remembers:

Harry used to have a chair just in the wings and he'd sit and he'd watch everything that was going on onstage just to conserve his energy before getting up and strolling on for his cue. I remember thinking how terribly relaxed he was, because pantomime is so terribly difficult to do. I knew he'd had a heart attack and was on lots of tablets but I didn't know too much about it, at that time one didn't publicise one's health. Harry had a gentle relaxed approach to pantomime; he was an actor not a speciality act and the audience really warmed to him.

One of the panto's speciality acts was the Chuckle Brothers, Barry and Paul Elliot, a few years before they found lasting TV fame. Barry remembers:

Even though Harry wasn't in the best of health at the time he was a great trouper and every performance was exceptional. We didn't know how poorly he actually was until we'd all finished the panto because you would never have known from his performances.

We had a great rapport and it was so easy to work our routines with him. We only wished we could have worked together again.

Another of the specialities was the magician, Duval. 'He was one of Harry's old friends,' Desmond continues:

Duval had recently survived cancer; I remember it said so in the programme. Harry got him a job in the show because he knew Duval hadn't been working much. We took time out to do a charity gig for Cancer Research. A very young Catherine Zeta Jones sang in this concert, she must have sung about twelve songs, we did the curtain call about three in the morning.

Harry knew pantomime. That's what I admired about him. I found it a huge learning curve. I hadn't been in the business long and was quite young to be playing dame. One night my family came to see me. I was so embarrassed, a coalminer's son camping about in frocks. During the finale you always have to come on dripping with sequins. I came on with Harry, he took one look and said 'What the fuck's wrong with you tonight?' I was walking all butch and bowlegged coz my parents were in. I didn't want to mince on as usual. When I told Harry afterwards they were watching, he started pissing himself laughing. I had a great time working with him. I loved it. I learnt a hell of a lot watching him.

The show finished on 6 March. Harry could finally come home. He needed a rest if he was to get though the season in the Channel Islands and then the tour of Australia with Wilfrid. Maybe this trip Down Under would see Harry and Maureen buy that property they'd always hankered after. But duty first, while renewing his handgun license he got nobbled to appear at a Policeman's Benefit Dinner and he had to keep his appointment in town with his heart specialist, who, gratifyingly, gave him a clean bill of health.

A week later we were sitting watching the box when Harry felt a mild pain. I'd like to report that he was in the dying chair at the time, but he wasn't, I was. I asked him if he'd had his pills. Yes, he had. We thought little of it, distracted, as we were, by my packing for a first solo adventure, a school trip to Paris that was leaving early the next morning.

I have never forgotten the tone of Maureen's voice when she woke me later that night saying Harry was ill. As she warmed the car, Harry sat by the door. He had got himself dressed but was in great pain. He asked me to fetch his shoes. I gave him a pair, 'No, not them,' he gasped, 'the others.' He wanted the ones with the split for his bunions. In later life, when I have caught myself planning future possibilities, I remember that, amusingly, the last thing I did for Harry was to give him the wrong fucking shoes. It was not something I could have seen coming. Equipped with the right pair and aided by Maureen, he made his way to the car and was raced away. It ran through my head that that could be the last time I saw him; as such the image has stayed with me. I rang the hospital, warned them he was coming and waited. Some time later Maureen rang, they were doing all they could but Harry was insisting that I go on the trip to Paris. He knew I'd been looking forward to it; he didn't want me to be disappointed. I would rather have stayed but, in hindsight, perhaps they thought it best to have me out of the way.

So I was spared all the hard realities of the hospital. I was later told of his long fight, his bravery, and that his last words had been of Maureen. When his heart finally gave out, she collapsed. Malcolm had to carry her from the room.

One of the hospital staff immediately broke the story. It appeared on the late- night news. Having it publicised was, of course, expected but inconvenient as I was, as yet, unaware of Harry's death. Malcolm was dispatched to Paris to collect me the next morning. The poor bastard would have to make sure I didn't see any 'Steptoe Dead' newspaper billboards in the airport. He finally told me when we got back to his car, but I had already guessed.

The condolence telegrams and letters flooded in; Wilfrid's was brief – he couldn't really cope with it. The news of Harry's death had come on his birthday and it had hit him hard. Alan remembers: 'Wilfrid burst into tears when he was interviewed on the television the day after Harry died – he was in tears.' Many of the letters were from people who had never known Harry, just appreciated him. Maureen took great comfort from them, marvelling at the ones that had made it despite being addressed simply to Mrs Harry H. Corbett, Sussex, U.K. The papers ran his obituary. *The Guardian* reported:

> Two of the warmest tributes came from his Steptoe colleagues Alan Simpson and his co-star Wilfrid Brambell. 'I can only say that he was a brilliant actor and comedian and a very good friend.' said Brambell. Simpson described him as the 'Marlon Brando of the London stage. He was the most inventive actor I have ever known – always looking at a line, a word or an inflection to bring out a better meaning in it. He was an actors' actor.'

A few days later the same paper printed Joan Littlewood's recollections of Harry's time with Theatre Workshop. She couldn't help having another pop at the establishment, '[Harry] went on to a series of magnificent performances when we grounded at Stratford-atte-Bowe,' she wrote:

> After a long time the critics came. Then the maneaters. Our enduring poverty and their flattery won the day. He accepted a part in the West End, only a small part. They had detected a 'northern' accent.
>
> Harry had worked our way for a long time. Working with a 'genius' director who gave him 'moves' shocked him, and he didn't get over it. He abandoned theatre and went for telly and the bread.
>
> For me it has been a bitter pill to swallow. So many of my old company, so many beautiful clowns type-cast in their dull

brothel, the endless repetition of the act, and the spurious success which kills.

Cheers Joan. A long resident of the 'dull brothel' is Brian Murphy:

> With Harry, I know it will be looked at and scoffed at – all our work on television has to be taken with a pinch of salt because obviously it gave us our so-called fame and everything of that nature, but if you look at what Harry was doing in some of that *Steptoe*, you wouldn't find it anywhere today because he actually managed to instil, with his own integrity, some class into that role. He gave his sort of veneer of the working class, but he was almost like Hamlet – He could be a working-class Hamlet as it were. He had this strong vibrant intelligence and integrity about what he did, he didn't just slum 'Oh, now I've got to earn some pennies' cause we do, at the end of the day – you've got to eat you've got families.
>
> Joan was always looked after, she could be looked after in the lap of luxury or she could be quite happy down the mines to be perfectly honest. She didn't need to have money or pennies in her pocket. If she wanted a packet of fags she'd call up to Gerry.
>
> After I'd come back from a bit of telly, she'd say, a week into the first rehearsal, 'Oh yes, well, of course, Bryan's been doing that television hasn't he?' And I knew what she meant – but there was nothing to be ashamed of. But her family had gone, the people she needed to break down the barriers with.
>
> She could talk a load of rubbish sometimes. Howard was the best one for pricking that balloon. And when there were people like Howard and Harry on the stage it was priceless. I don't know where they would find that sort of actor today.
>
> You practice in whatever market place you can find, you adapt. There's no good being high-faluting because, as Joan once said when the Political Workers' Party came round thinking they'd get her support, she said 'Well. I think, to be perfectly honest, actors are only worth what the people will put in their cap. If you sing for your supper, you'll get the money if you sing well.'

Harry was buried at Penhurst, a little local hamlet where sheep still grazed amongst the headstones in the ancient Norman churchyard. He had always admired it. The day of the funeral was the only time the locals had ever seen a police car in the village. When we got to the church, photographers were perched on ladders to get a good shot. Maureen shook the vicar's hand and told him that she didn't think she could do it. But she did, and she did it well. As the coffin was lowered, the neighbouring farmer's cattle over the wall started mooing – the front legs of the cow had come home. The funeral was just for close friends and family. After all, he'd always been a private man. Ray and Alan came; it was the first time either had ever set foot in one of Harry's houses. After all the guests had left and no photographers would be about, we returned to the grave to look at the flowers. Maureen gravitated to a beautiful wreath, smiling as she read the card; it was from 'Lovely' Avis.

One of Harry's favourite sayings, alongside 'Fuck a stoat!' – don't ask me why it was a stoat – was 'Every day must end'. There's no glorious Technicolor pull back in that. No sunset-tinged clouds found in 'After all, tomorrow is another day'. No, there is just the complete and realistic certainty that no matter how crappy a day can be, you are safe in the knowledge that it will end. That day ended.

Avis, along with many others from the business, including Wilfrid, came to the more public goodbye a few weeks later on 29 April. Harry's memorial took place at St Paul's, Covent Garden, the actor's church. A lone piper played *Flowers of the Forest*. Harry had heard it once at a friend's send off and wanted it at his own. Victor Spinetti gave the tribute. After the service he and many others were nabbed by the autograph hunters going to work on a congregation who, like Harry's family, were trying to sidestep the backwards scampering paparazzi.

There was a further send off by way of a memorial concert at the Adelphi in June. Harry had done so many of them for others, now it was his turn. Sitting in one of the theatre boxes we watched the curtain open on a huge photo of him suspended upstage. At the start of the show a spotlight swung onto our box and the MC pointed us out to the audience. We got a very nice round of applause; it remains one of the most depressing things I have ever heard. The moment was only lightened by then seeing Harry's photo ascending heavenwards into the flies. Oh well, at least he was going up and not down.

As the months passed, Maureen tried to find a fitting epitaph for his headstone; it would one day serve for her as well. When asked once by a paper what he wanted, an extremely popular question amongst showbiz journalists (even I've been asked. In keeping with

Harry's spirit, my answer was: 'This way up'), Harry had replied: 'Closed down for renovations, be back shortly.' Night after night Maureen went to a bed covered in books, searching during the long sleepless hours for words that would sum him up.

We all tried to come to terms with his passing, taking scant comfort in that he was dead and not incapacitated, condemned to a half-life, unable to work and miserable. His lust for new horizons was such that Maureen always used to say that had the aliens landed, he would have skipped up the gangplank without a backwards glance. Had he lived, we might not have seen him for the last fifteen years, unless we could have found a way to surgically disconnect him from the internet. For him to have survived but been left incapacitated would have been very cruel.

Those first few years after Harry's death were very hard. Witnessing the effects of grief on Maureen was not pleasant, though she made valiant efforts to hide it from us and the rest of the family, always encouraging Jon and myself to get on with our lives. She became involved with the British Heart Foundation, donating for auction the 'Harold' costume Harry had kept for his charity appearances. He would have approved. We struggled financially, as the will never seemed to reach probate and was under the direction of outside executors. In some ways it was a welcome distraction. In an effort to keep hold of the cottage, Maureen turned it into a B&B and raised and sold plants. Pat raided her savings to keep us at school until we had finished our O levels. In the winter we would camp downstairs by the open fire as heating oil was beyond us. Beans on toast can quickly lose its attraction, but we were together in the home we loved. In the mid-1980s the BBC repeated a *Steptoe* series. Pat was paid back, the heating was turned on and Maureen, Jon and I took it in turns to wield the sledgehammer against the hated concrete bunker until it was quite removed.

In January of 1985 Wilfrid died of cancer at the age of 72. On the day of the service the heavens opened, the torrential downpour causing a delay in Wilfrid's arrival at the crematorium – Maureen, Ray and Alan finding it fitting that he actually was late to his own funeral. Wilfrid's final house had been rather select. Alan remembers: 'We went to Wilfrid's funeral and there were only six people there. It was pissing with rain. There was Ray and myself, Duncan Wood's secretary, Wilfrid's brother and I think Duncan Wood was there, and Maureen is six.'

Wilfrid's ashes were scattered at the base of a tree in Streatham Park Cemetery.

Maureen eventually got back into her swing. She tried dating though with little success: 'When you've had steak …' as she used to say. She helped Jon and I through adolescence into adulthood and enjoyed life, though was often plagued by ill health. Various lumps were removed, all benign. In spring of 1998 she found one that wasn't, though unfortunately it was misdiagnosed until the following January. She rode the cancer rollercoaster with her usual immense charm and stoicism. She died in November 1999 at home in Ashburnham, surrounded by her family. She was 56. She remains the bravest person I have known.

Maureen was buried with Harry at Penhurst. Their headstone bears the inscription she had chosen for him from Shakespeare's sonnets. It reads.

The earth can have but earth, which is his due,
My spirit is thine, the better part of me.

Sonnet LXXIV

20

Blow the Man Down

The only morality I have finished up with, in this business, is the morality of keeping my word.

Harry H. Corbett

Harry always kept his word. He was an honourable man and true to himself. This was something that Joan Littlewood would have approved of. Her obituary of him had perhaps been scathing, but was her honest opinion. As she had known him, she had earned it. But it did set the tone within the business that he was a lesson in the perils of typecasting. No matter that he had enjoyed *Steptoe*, no matter that one episode of that programme touched the social consciousness of millions more in one night than Theatre Workshop had ever done. No matter that his youthful ideals had inevitably paled in the light of mature responsibility to a family, something that any parent comes to appreciate and something that, without family, Joan could never do.

Of course Harry would have been irritated by the lack of serious roles that his *Steptoe* success denied him. But he was never consumed by it – he just walked through a different open door – and the perception that he had cast the pearls of his talent before the swine of television would have been insulting to him. He had the utmost respect for the medium. He knew how lucky he had been: he had achieved a career, a reputation and a success that would have been the envy of most of the profession.

A week after Harry's death, Robert Cushman, then theatre critic for the *Observer* was looking back at those who had worked, and who had not worked, for the RSC over the last twenty-one years:

'We have lost two superb actors who never played with either major company, though doubtless they were asked,' he wrote. 'Alan Badel – who in his generation ranked with Burton and Scofield – and Harry H. Corbett. Both died prematurely; both, maybe, had the careers they wanted. But both leave in their wake a feeling of waste.'[1]

According to Lynda Baron, not appearing at the RSC wouldn't have concerned Harry too much:

> He didn't want to do the National or RSC – you've got to turn up every day. It was the same thing with Ronnie Barker. People used to say 'If only the National would ask him to play "King Lear"' – they've already asked him. He doesn't want to go.
>
> There is a British thing though, when someone becomes so successful. We can't actually let them go on being like that. We must have a dig at them somewhere along the line. It's a British disease, digging at people and trying to deflate the balloon of success and happiness they've had.

But you never know. He may well have been enticed, at some point, to work on the classical stage again. When Harry was working, audiences were seen as needing time to disassociate actors from one role before accepting them in a new. But Harry was not afforded such a luxury. The BBC were repeating *Steptoe* in prime time as late as 1980, two years before his death. It is hard to find examples of actors with comparably successful careers. One is David Jason, with his work on the show that tips a nod to *Steptoe*, *Only Fools and Horses*. Had David Jason died after *Only Fools* but before his later work on *A Touch of Frost*, etc., he would have been known only for saying 'lovely jubbly' instead of being a comic institution. But Jason lacks the classical background. For someone who had a fine body of classical work one could look to John Thaw. Had he gone after *Sweeny* and before *Morse* he would have remained a hard man and not be remembered as an intellectual curmudgeon. Popular characters stay with all actors. Jason is seen as humorously bumptious, Thaw as curmudgeonly, Harry as disappointed and trapped. Whether they all were, only their family and friends know. But time, and a change in the perception of what an audience will accept, is lengthening actors' careers and diversifying their CVs. These days actors may battle with science fiction baddies, drip with sequins for panto and still be accepted when donning the tights for Shakespeare.

Had Harry lived, I'm sure he would have been allowed a renaissance as so many others have. I'm presuming he never would have retired, though he may have taken time out to direct and possibly teach – he would have been good at it.

There is one huge benefit of having done *Steptoe*. It remains. All great theatrical performances are gone the same night the show closes, as Alan Simpson remarked:

> Harry's left a body of work behind him. One thing these days, people like Harry and Hancock, they do at least leave a body of work behind them. Some of the old time comedians and actors – who knows? They didn't make recordings. Who knows anything about Dan Leno now, or Marie Lloyd? She was the highest-paid entertainer in the world for a long time.

Sadly, very little remains of the vast contribution made to the arts by Theatre Workshop and Joan Littlewood. I had the very good fortune of meeting her once, towards the end of her life. The Baron Philippe de Rothschild had died in 1988 and she had moved to Paris. She was still somewhat reclusive but regularly came to stay in the London flat of her old friend Peter Rankin. After her autobiography was published she recorded an audio version for radio. Her producer, Enyd Williams, persuaded her in front of the mic once more, this time as an actor in a dramatisation of Agatha Christie's *Evil Under the Sun*, in which I was also cast. After the end of production drinkies, I shook her hand as she was leaving and told her I was Harry's daughter. Her eyebrows rose. 'He never should have done that shit!' she barked. 'And he should have stayed with Avis, and never married your mother!' Ah, my own Joan moment – how I treasure it. I shook her hand again, said it had been a pleasure and wished her and Peter a safe journey home. How could I have taken her to task on her opinions? She was entitled to the first and had obviously confused the second as there had been one marriage and many dalliances for Harry between Avis and Maureen. Besides, during the preceding week, I had not been observing the Joan Littlewood of reputation, the magnificent bitch of British theatre, but a frail little old lady, deserving of respect and compassion. A few days later Enyd called to say that Joan had commented to her how good I had been and that Harry would have been so proud. What an awful woman and what a superb lady she was.

Joan died in 2002, at Peter's home. When asked, once, about what she would like as her epitaph (see, we all get asked that question) she had replied: 'Oh, I don't believe in any of that. I want to be chucked in the water with Gerry. Dust to dust, or rather water to water.'[2] Murray Melvin, still devoted, is raising funds to have a statue of her placed in the little square outside Theatre Royal, Stratford East. The square is named after Gerry Raffles. It would be a fitting tribute: something that Joan would have equally loved and loathed. One can imagine her ghost at the unveiling, courting the press while denigrating the sculptor's efforts, secretly revelling in the attention.

Almost nineteen years to the day after he died, on 25 March 2001, Harry had his own unveiling ceremony. The Heritage Foundation marked Harry's contribution to entertainment with a Blue Plaque at BBC Television Centre. There were some red faces when Ray and Alan unveiled the plaque alongside to Wilfred Brambell. That spelling caused confusion right to the end ... and beyond.

The following year, Channel 4 broadcast a documentary on Harry and Wilfrid entitled *When Steptoe met Son*. I had been contacted by the makers of the programme for a contribution but from the tone of the conversation, was able to guess what it would be like. I declined to comment. In all the years she had survived Harry, Maureen had never given an interview to the press about him, despite many enquiries. One time, a reporter would not accept a polite 'no' for an answer and turned up at the cottage hoping his persistence would pay off – it didn't. The one time she broke her silence was for a home video made by the Steptoe and Son Appreciation Society for their members. Maureen always said that Harry's work should speak for itself. Now that she was gone, I saw no reason to disagree with her.

The resulting programme concentrated on the pair's mutual hatred for one another, Harry's typecasting, Wilfrid's drinking and his sexuality. The last and the second of these have already been covered earlier. When it comes to Wilfrid's drinking the programme interviewed *Steptoe* production assistant, Mike Crisp, who stated:

> One of my jobs as a junior on the production was to attempt to keep Wilfrid sober before a recording by going to the bar with him and monitoring his consumption ... It was a fool's errand because you couldn't do it.
>
> All through the week, Wilfrid would never seem to know his words. Harry would be off the book by day two of rehearsal.

Wilfrid would be on the book sometimes almost up until the dress run.... Which we do on a Sunday before the audience came in ... Wilfrid would be all over the place.

Mike's boss at the time, series producer Douglas Argent, disagreed: 'What I don't understand was that my old assistant was very nasty about things and I can't see why because we had no problems whatsoever. All that business about how he used to go to the bar. Rubbish, absolute rubbish.'

From this distance it's hard to know whose account is more accurate, but Ray and Alan have never intimated that Wilfrid's drinking had become so completely out of control. As to the hatred between Harry and Wilfrid, during the documentary Kevin O'Neill, the promoter of the Australian *Steptoe* tour, recounted: 'Harry hated him from when he got off the plane on the first day. Harry Corbett pulled me to one side and said he didn't want to travel with Wilfrid under any conditions, he would not share a car with him, he didn't want to share the dressing rooms with him. Wilfrid hated Harry on the first day.'

I cannot comment on Kevin's opinion of either Harry's or Wilfrid's regard for one another, that is his prerogative. I would like to mention that Harry would have only wanted to cover the long distances by road with Maureen and, when we were with them, Jon and myself. To have also had Wilfrid in the car would have been a bit of a squeeze. Similarly, Harry and Wilfrid, as stars of their stature, would have been perfectly entitled to separate dressing rooms. Harry's pre-performance ritual of shoving a towel over his eyes while lying on a camp bed would have been far too irritating to share.

Kevin also stated that Harry refused to travel back home with Wilfrid on the same plane, such was his animosity. Again I cannot comment, I wasn't there and the subject never came up and by the time the programme was broadcast Maureen had been dead three years, and there was no one else left to ask.

As the programme drew to an end, the voice-over read:

In 1985, aged only 57, Harry H. Corbett died of a heart attack. His memorial service was attended by the leading lights of the British theatre. His partner of twenty years paid him a reluctant half-hearted tribute.

[We cut to footage of Wilfrid, who says:]

A nice guy and we did work well together despite the fact that we only met when we were working, cause we lived different lives and miles apart. I as you know have a two-room flat; he had a large farm with a wife, two kids, dogs, cats and a mother-in-law.

Other than the fact that Harry's year of death was incorrect, it is notable that the footage chosen of Wilfrid's reluctant tribute was not the one immediately after Harry's death, when he had broken down in tears. The programme wrapped up with the voice-over stating, 'They died hating the sight of each other', which poses the question why at the time of Harry's death, in 1982, the pair would have been signing on for another tour of Australia together; a burden not to be undertaken with someone you loathed. I don't know Wilfrid's inner feelings but for their part, Maureen and Harry were looking forward to the trip. The thought of them hating each other was something that Maureen would have taken exception to. Not once, in all the years we were together – and we had a very close relationship – did she ever mention that Harry disliked him. In her one interview for the Appreciation Society she was asked if they got on well. 'Oh yes, very well, very well,' she answered:

> I mean, I don't know if you're asking this because you have read somewhere that they didn't, perhaps?
> Well, because for some reason the press, well of course, you know, no one's interested in good news are they – like 'Harry and Wilfrid get on very well' [*yawns*]. It's much more interesting to say that they don't. But, in fact, that wasn't true, because they did get on terribly well.

Maureen was right; no one was interested in good news. From now on, as one comic quipped on television, 'The 'H' in Harry H. Corbett stood for Hatred' an undeserved epitaph for such an affable and well-liked man.

A few years later, I was again contacted about a programme on Harry and Wilf. This time it was the BBC, who had also seen *When Steptoe met Son* and wanted to 'redress the balance' with a docudrama. Maureen's policy of letting the work speak for itself weighed heavily, but this was the respectable Auntie Beeb. I relented and spoke to the writer of the proposed drama, Brian Fillis.

Later, it was announced the docudrama would be billed as *The Curse of Steptoe*, a title that did not bode well. Nor did Brian's offer to come to my home and watch it with me and explain what they had done – oh dear. The day before the programme was broadcast, Brian wrote on his MySpace webpage that there were 'no blow jobs, alas' in his drama … Oh fuck a stoat, as they say.

The Curse of Steptoe plot opens with Harry being the toast of Theatre Workshop, juggling his marriage to Sheila Steafel and his womanising. He enjoys the early fame with *Steptoe*, while a cowering Wilfrid, haunted by his homosexuality, abhors it.

Harry starts to resent his wife for her success with *The Frost Report*, Wilfrid for coming back to *Steptoe* after *Kelly* (he is seen throwing a chair across the room) and then the series for the limitations it had placed on his career.

An affair with a brunette helps the demise of his marriage to Sheila. This brunette later turns up on his doorstep heavily pregnant, informing him that the baby is his. He settles for the relationship with the brunette, Maureen, and after the birth of the child has an epiphany and decides to quit the series.

He is last seen talking to his agent who can only offer a panto or the prospect of a *Steptoe* tour to Australia.

If this were the BBC's attempt to 'redress the balance' one would have hated to see an attempt to malign.

Obviously, I was not best pleased. Harry would have found it hard to resent Sheila's success with *The Frost Report*, as she had landed the job two years after her divorce from Harry on the grounds of her adultery. Harry was not distraught at the thought of Wilfrid returning to the series after *Kelly*, as he was the one who wrote to Head of Light Entertainment, Tom Sloan, encouraging that the door be kept open. As to the affair between Harry and Maureen causing the breakdown in Harry's marriage – they met after his relationship with Sheila had broken down. Harry loved Maureen and loved having a family. Lastly, his son's birth did not cause him to quit *Steptoe*, as Jon was born in 1966 and the series came to a natural end in 1974.

Of course the programme could say anything it wanted – you cannot libel the dead. But even with the allowances of dramatic licence, the makers seemed to have ignored what I had told them of Harry, and I was not alone in that feeling. Alan Simpson recalled that: 'The implication of *The Curse of Steptoe* was that they didn't like each other from the word go.'

'Which was absolute rubbish,' interjects Ray Galton.

'They spent the day here,' continues Alan. 'Interviewed us about the whole background and tried to get us to say they didn't like each other and we said "No, they got on fine." What we were saying they weren't really interested in, cause it wasn't drama. There was no story … And as the years go by the myth becomes the truth, doesn't it.'

Murray Melvin had a similar experience:

> Normally I turn down all those interview requests because I don't have the time. But, because they were doing it on Harry, I said 'Of course, cause it's Harry.' I sat there for two hours and went through what we went through as a company and everybody and they said, 'Oh Murray, thank you so much.' I think they must have got out the front door and just wiped the tape – because there was certainly none of that in that programme.

For those who were not interviewed, but knew Harry, his portrayal came as something of a shock. Lynda Baron commented:

> One of the things I really hated about *The Curse* was as though his life was totally consumed by the fact that he wasn't at The National. We all get miffed about saying 'Shall we do this job as we've got to live or shall we not?' and you think, I really wish I hadn't. But at the time you know that's what you've got to do. It's one of the things about the business – you've got to do it, you've got families. I really don't think it consumed his every waking moment, that's ridiculous.
>
> He was lovely, that's all I can say about him, certainly not angst ridden. The last day I saw him, he was madly in love with the business and madly in love with his family and what he was going to do with the house. He was a lovely bloke – end of conversation.

But there he was, angst ridden on the screen. It was a vision endorsed by the actors who had portrayed Harry and Wilfrid. Harry was played by Jason Isaacs, Wilfrid by Phil Davis. Both very fine artists, employed to breathe life into a script – which they did admirably. Sitting on various chat show sofas, admittedly never a comfortable experience for most, Jason Isaacs set about plugging the show, 'To gradually unpick somebody's public life and find out what made their emotional heart beat was interesting …' he said. 'You get to watch the layers of a human life peel back.'³ 'If you want to see the story behind *Steptoe and Son*, watch ours.'⁴

Leaving no one in any doubt that their story was accurate, although its accuracy might be called into question by Jason also complaining, on one sofa, that the brown contact lenses he had had to wear in order to become Harry had killed him. It's a shame not one of the many crew listed in the credits of *The Curse of Steptoe* thought to pass around a colour photo of Harry while they were peeling back his layers. If they had, Mr Isaacs would not have needed to bother with the contacts, as Harry's eyes had been just as blue as his own.

Jason Isaacs finished up one interview by commenting: 'I watched it with my wife and she said, "That's the saddest thing you've ever done, I feel really bleak."' I have to say, I agreed with her.

Malcolm was feeling similarly bleak and disenchanted with the portrayal of Maureen, Harry and Wilfrid. Luckily, Pat, who had dearly loved both her daughter and son-in-law, never saw the programme. She died in 2009, her family were all there. She was 94 and had survived Maureen by ten years. Her ashes we buried at Penhurst.

After *The Curse* was broadcast on 19 March 2008 on BBC4, Malcolm, along with his son Simon, was at the start of a long complaint with the BBC, while the programme picked up awards and nominations. *The Curse of Steptoe* won the Royal Television Society's Award for single drama and, though deservedly nominated, Jason Isaacs unfortunately missed out on winning the Best Actor BAFTA for playing Harry H. Corbett – it would have tied in nicely with Harry's BAFTA for being Harry H. Corbett.

Two separate pieces of correspondence Malcolm received during the complaint process were from Ben Bickerton and Ben Evans, producer and executive producer of the drama (amazingly both wrote word-for-word the same letter). Within the standard, stock diatribe came the response: 'a drama of this nature includes an element of interpretation and it is regrettable that this interpretation is at odds with your own'. For someone who had been extremely close with Harry and Maureen, and gone through life and death with both (literally), this implication hit very hard, and made him ever more determined to salvage their reputations.

Unfortunately, Malcolm's complaint to the BBC would be hampered by the fact that the BBC had no specific guidelines on the portrayal of recently deceased people in drama (presumably when they were written no one thought there would be an incentive to write an inaccurate drama), and as a result complaints would only be considered if inaccuracies could be documented, and if inaccuracies were considered unfair to those portrayed. It is interesting to note that no such documentary evidence is required for a writer – word-of-mouth interviews are considered quite acceptable. Ultimately, it would be impossible to disprove the hatred between Harry and Wilf, or Harry's portrayed depression at being typecast, so Malcolm concentrated on the portrayal of Maureen and Harry's relationship and Jon's birth.

In their report published in November 2008, the BBC Editorial Complaints Unit upheld Malcolm's complaint that:

> The drama gave the impression that Maureen's relationship with Corbett preceded, and might have contributed to, the breakdown of his marriage with Sheila Steafel, whereas the chronology established by the ECU did not support this. The drama also gave the impression that the end of *Steptoe and Son* was immediately preceded, if not precipitated, by the birth of Corbett's first child. This was a dramatic device which had the legitimate intention of illustrating the change in Corbett's attitudes and priorities brought about by family life. However, the two events were separated by eight years, so the device tended to mislead viewers significantly on an aspect of the narrative central to their interest in the drama. The complaint was upheld on these two points.

It further stated that 'The BBC will not re-broadcast the programme without appropriate editing and content information.'

Malcolm had also complained about remarks made by Phil Davis during an item that advertised the show on the *Breakfast* sofa on BBC1 on 19 March 2008. The Editorial Complaints Unit found that:

> The item did not give an unambiguous impression that *The Curse of Steptoe* was entirely factual; while the actor playing Bramble [sic, yes they were still spelling his name wrong] described it at one point as 'all fact', he added that some of it was speculation. However, the suggestion that Bramble [sic] and Corbett loathed each other was presented as established fact, whereas the balance of first-hand evidence is that this was by no means the case.

On 28 and 29 December 2008, the BBC broadcast a revised version of *The Curse*, with the disclaimer that 'The following drama is inspired by the lives of real people. For the purpose of the narrative some events have been invented or conflated.'

This version wasn't good enough for Malcolm, who complained once more. This time the BBC Trust Editorial Standards Committee said that: 'The essential elements of unfairness to Maureen Corbett were still present in the revised version of the programme and that this constituted a breach of the Fairness and Accuracy guidelines.' Once more 'the timeline of the drama with regard to the relationship between Maureen and Harry, and Harry's separation from his first wife, did not correlate with the facts ... the implication in the drama that the child of Maureen and Harry had been conceived as a result of a casual relationship between the two was inaccurate and unfair.' The Trust went so far as to say that 'while it was the right of dramatists to change events for dramatic purposes, the basic facts should remain as a framework on which to build the drama'. The Trust also commented on the new version's disclaimer, stating that 'the use of captions such as this should not be regarded as a "blank cheque" for the indiscriminate and excessive use of dramatic licence'.[5] It also stated: 'The Committee will write to the BBC Executive requesting that the revised BBC editorial guidelines address dramatised biopics with regard to the presentation of fact and the use of dramatic licence.'

We didn't have to wait long to see if another version would be shown. On 2 December 2009 the drama was broadcast again, this time on BBC HD, but it only contained a few minor edits since the previous version. This still wasn't good enough for Malcolm who again complained to the BBC Trust.

Despite the ongoing complaint, it was announced that the drama would be released on a DVD entitled *Legends of Comedy*, together with other episodes in the 'Curse of Comedy' season. Cue another blizzard of letters, this time with the publishing company 2 | Entertain. In the full knowledge that the complaint was ongoing with the BBC Trust, and that it would be unlikely to be resolved until the autumn, the DVD was released anyway in June 2010.

That autumn the BBC published their long-awaited revised editorial guidelines and, true to their word, 'biopics' were now covered. Section 6.4.29 states:

Whenever appropriate, and where their role is significant, real people portrayed in a drama or their surviving near relatives should be notified in advance and, where possible, their co-operation secured. There is less requirement to secure co-operation when dealing with people in the public eye, particularly if the portrayal is primarily of public aspects of their life.

Any proposal to go ahead against the wishes of the individual portrayed or their surviving near relatives must be referred to Director Editorial Policy and Standards for approval before a commitment is made to the production.

Unless dealing with people in the public eye and the public aspects of their lives, approval will only be given when it can be shown that the following three criteria are met:

The portrayal is fair.

The portrayal is based on a substantial and well-sourced body of evidence whenever practicable.

There is a clear public interest.

There would be further success when the BBC Trust published its ruling in December. The Trust stated that the committee:

> wished to reiterate its earlier concern that whilst it did not want to inhibit writers and producers from using creative licence with a drama of this kind, it was important when dealing with facts not to unfairly distort the truth. The Committee agreed that the overall impression of a casual relationship between Maureen and Harry remained.
>
> The Committee therefore concluded that despite the edits made, further action was required by the BBC to remove this impression of the relationship between Maureen and Harry.[6]

But what about the DVDs that had been on sale since June? On 15 December 2010, The BBC Trust 'agreed that, in addition to not rebroadcasting the programme in its current form, the BBC should request that all existing copies of the programme available as part of the Legends of Comedy DVD box-set be withdrawn from sale with immediate effect.'[7]

However, the BBC Shop was still offering the DVD for sale up until 3 January, an apparent oversight by its publishers, 2 | Entertain. They had not informed the BBC Shop that it had been withdrawn.

Informed and 'following removal of the DVD from the BBC Shop, 2 | Entertain had instructed its lawyers to perform a worldwide trawl to ensure that no other retailers were still selling the DVD. As a result of this action the DVD was removed from sale from two small overseas retailers which were still selling it.'[8]

On 5 January 2011 *The Stage* newspaper announced that the BBC executive producer of *The Curse of Steptoe*, Ben Evans, had been made redundant. 'Evans confirmed to *The Stage* that he was leaving the BBC, but refused to comment on whether his redundancy was compulsory or voluntary.'

At the start of his campaign, Malcolm had requested an apology from the BBC. He finally got one in 2011:

> The Committee noted that an apology should have been pro-vided to the complainant with the original finding of a breach of the guidelines. It accepted that this was an oversight, and it wished to apologise on behalf of the BBC for the original edito-rial breaches in *The Curse of Steptoe* and the fact that subsequent remedial action had been ineffective in removing the unfairness.[9]

There had been three years' worth of days between broadcast and apology. But as a good man once said: 'Every day must end.'

Notes

1 *Observer*, 28/3/82.
2 *Independent Magazine*, 26/4/94.
3 *This Morning*.
4 *The One Show*.
5 BBC Trust 'Editorial Standards Findings: Appeals and other editorial issues to the Trust considered by the Editorial Standards Committee, May 2009', 30/6/09.
6 Editorial Standards Findings, Appeals to the Trust and other editorial issues considered by the Editorial Standards Committee. November 2010 issued December 2010.
7 *Ibid.*, February 2011 issued March 2011.
8 *Ibid.*
9 *Ibid.*

Epilogue

Harry never started an autobiography. Not only was he a modest and private man, traits that tend to handicap a memoir, but he was too damn busy living his life to write about it. Even if he had enjoyed an expected dotage in which to reflect, I doubt he would have. It would have been an act of finality completely at odds with a lifetime spent scanning the next horizon. I wish he had been here to tell his story himself, I wish Maureen had…

It is a curious thing to tell the story of a parent while walking the tightrope between sentiment and impartiality. Knowing that for some, you will always be too sentimental, for others, not enough. I have just tried to tell his story, and the story of those he knew, fairly, while keeping in mind the one question I have been asked most in my life: 'What was he like?'

He was a fine actor and a finer man. Generous to a fault. Shy, gregarious and bloody funny. He could be nervous around those whose intellectual veneer intimidated him, usually without cause, for he was an intelligent and perceptive man with an unending thirst for knowledge. He had surprisingly old-fashioned morals and loathed being embarrassed in public. He was over-trusting of those he thought needed his friendship and help. He was easy to be friends with but hard to know well, and when he was gone he was missed. When I first started in the business there were still old crew members who had worked with him; I lost count of the amount of times gnarly old buggers would sidle up to me and, with a lopsided smile, murmur, 'He was a diamond, your old man.' Yeah, he was.

As I look through the photos of his life, real and remembered, from Harry Boy to Harry C., H. and even Harold, and reflect on his talent, his generosity, his ethics and his work, I realise that this is for none of those people, and for none of those reasons. In the end it is for a golden moment, frozen in time, walking hand in hand along the soft, still-warm beach of Surfers Paradise, picking out the stars as they peeped from behind the glow of the neon strip, shy diamonds over the Southern Hemisphere. It's for knowing what spit and polish means and how to dine at the Ritz; it's for climbing St Paul's and diving for thrown pennies. It's for running the lines and catching the juggling clubs; it's for the thousand little times in the wings, seeing him silhouetted as the dust mites sparkled in the spotlights. It's for the stories and the kisses goodnight. It's for the warmth, strength, and laughter and for knowing just how much he loved us. It is for my Dad.

As such, I'll leave the last word to him. He was once asked for a formula to keep young: 'Oh, who cares about being young, who cares about being old?' he said. 'The thing is to *be*, to enjoy, to live life fully. That's all that really counts.'

Harry H. Corbett OBE

Actor

1925–82

Index

Susannah Corbett is an actress and author. She has worked on radio, the West End stage, television and film, and has had leading ongoing television roles in *Dalziel and Pascoe* and *Peak Practice*. As a children's author, she has written *Dragon's Dinner* (Hodder, 2009) and *One Cool Cat* (Egmont, 2012).